Baptist Church Perpetuity

W. A. JARREL
1849-1927

Baptist Church Perpetuity,

OR

THE CONTINUOUS EXISTENCE OF BAPTIST CHURCHES FROM THE
APOSTOLIC TO THE PRESENT DAY DEMONSTRATED
BY THE BIBLE AND BY HISTORY.

By W. A. JARREL, D. D.,

Author of "Liberty of Conscience and the Baptists;" "Old
Testament Ethics Vindicated;" "Gospel in Water or
Campbellism;" "The Origin, the Nature, the
Kingdom, the Works and the Destiny
of the Devil," etc., etc., etc.

INTRODUCTION

—BY—

REV. W. W. EVERTS, JR.,

Formerly in the Chair of Ecclesiastical History in the
Chicago Baptist Theological Seminary.

"Upon this rock I will build my Church and the gates of hell
shall not prevail against it." —JESUS CHRIST.

1894:
PUBLISHED BY THE AUTHOR,
Dallas, Texas.

he Baptist Standard Bearer, Inc.

NUMBER ONE IRON OAKS DRIVE • PARIS, ARKANSAS 72855

Thou hast given a *standard* to them that fear thee;
that it may be displayed because of the truth.
-- Psalm 60:4

*Reprinted
by*

THE BAPTIST STANDARD BEARER, INC.
No. 1 Iron Oaks Drive
Paris, Arkansas 72855
(501) 963-3831

THE WALDENSIAN EMBLEM
lux lucet in tenebris
"The Light Shineth in the Darkness"

ISBN #1-57978-906-4

DEDICATION.

TO THE MEMORY OF THE LAMENTED

PROF. R. J. W. BUCKLAND, D.D.,

AT THE TIME OF HIS DEATH PROFESSOR OF ECCLESIASTICAL HISTORY IN ROCHESTER THEOLOGICAL SEMINARY, WHO, NOT LONG BEFORE HIS DECEASE, WROTE ME HE WAS WORKING TO PROVE THE PERPETUITY OF BAPTIST CHURCHES FROM THE APOSTOLIC AGE TO THE PRESENT;

TO THE MEMORY OF THE LAMENTED

J. R. GRAVES, LL.D.,

TO WHOM, MORE THAN TO ANY OTHER MAN OF THIS AGE, THE BAPTISTS ARE INDEBTED FOR FAITHFULNESS TO DENOMINATIONAL TRUTH AND FOR DENOMINATIONAL CONSISTENCY; AND

TO MY DEAR WIFE,

WHO HAS, IN THE MASTER'S SPIRIT, SO HEROICALLY HELPED ME BEAR THE LABORS AND THE SACRIFICES, IN GETTING THIS BOOK OUT, I AFFECTIONATELY DEDICATE IT.

W. A. J.

Sicut lilium inter spinas sic amica mea inter filias

On The Cover: We use the symbol of the "lily among the thorns" from Song of Solomon 2:2 to represent the Baptist History Series. The Latin, *Sicut lilium inter spinas sic amica mea inter filias*, translates, "As the lily among thorns, so is my love among the daughters."

PREFACE.

Notwithstanding that many of the ablest Biblical expositors and theologians rightly regard the Romish church as the apocalyptic, "Babylon the great, the mother of harlots and abominations of the earth . . . the woman drunken with the blood of the saints, and the blood of the martyrs of Jesus," some church historians and some professors in Theological Seminaries, treat her as the "Christian church," and the true witnessing church as "heretics" and "heresies." Surely, it is high time this was reversed.

Baptist churches being regarded as but one among the Reformation sects, no wonder there is so little interest in Baptist history that several of the best publications on Baptist history, by the American Baptist Publication Society, have hardly returned the financial outlay in publishing them. Regarding Baptists but one of modern sects, thinking and conscientious people naturally reject their exclusive claims and practices. Seeing this, Baptist opponents leave "unturned no stone" to teach the people that Baptist churches are in origin "but of yesterday." In this, Baptist opponents are wiser than Baptists who are content that Baptist Church Perpetuity be presented as a trifle.

Seeing that one man has as much right to originate a church as has another, ambitious and

PREFACE.

designing men, by originating new sects, are continuously adding to the babel of sectarianism. Thus the answer to Christ's prayer—"that they may all be one . . . *that* the world may believe that thou hast sent me"—is hindered and infidelity is perpetuated.

Calling on God to witness his sincerity, the author of this book gladly expresses his Christian affection for every blood-washed soul—*whatever may be his or her creed*. He begs that this book be taken not as an assault on any dear child of God, but as a Biblical and historical exposition and demonstration of very important practical truth — truth sorely needed for this *falsely* liberal and sectarian age.

The book has been *worded* and the proof read by time snatched in revival meetings from needed rest. For any little oversights which possibly may appear in it, let this be the explanation. Nearly all quotations within this volume having been made in person by its author—excepting a *very few*, and they from reliable sources—the reader can use them with the greatest assurance.

The author thanking the public for the generous reception given his other books, which has encouraged him to send this one out, with profound gratitude to God for the opportunity and the grace to publish this one, signs himself,

A SINNER SAVED BY GRACE,
DALLAS, TEXAS.
May, 1894.

INTRODUCTION.

The Baptist movement in history has always been back to the New Testament. This people has always refused to follow others away from the teaching and practice of that book. In the New Testament are plainly stated certain great principles which lie as foundation stones in the base of the Church of Christ. These principles are the regeneration of the believer by the Holy Spirit and the word of God, the baptism of the believer in water, the equality of believers in the church, the separation of church and State, and in the church the sole authority of the Bible. But these distinctive principles of Christianity were soon set aside and Jewish or pagan notions were put in their places. The doctrine of regeneration by the Spirit, and the word was the first to be abandoned and in its place was introduced the notion of regeneration by water. To water, a material element, was ascribed the virtue which the New Testament gives to the word as the seed of life. With the attention directed to the performance of a sacrament instead of to hearing and believing the word, it was not long before the churches were filled with members who were Christians by sacrament, who had the form of godliness, who had a name to live, but were dead.

Then it was about 150, A. D. that the first Baptist protest was raised by the Montanists. The Montanists with all their faults, stand in the line of the Apostles. They raised their voices against the increasing formalism and worldliness of the churches and proclaimed an ever present Holy Spirit in the hearts of believers. They were wrong in magnifying fasting and forbidding second marriage, but were right in looking for the Holy Spirit not without in forms, but within in the heart. This is the chief mark of the Baptist movement in history, the demand for evidence of regeneration, for a personal experience of the grace of God, for the witness of the Holy Spirit with the human spirit. In a Baptist church this is an unalterable condition of membership. The intimacy with God observed by Max Goebel in the prayers and hymns of the Anabaptists, and which he contrasts with the formal devotion of others, is traceable to the universal and deep-seated conviction of the Anabaptists, that union with Christ is essential to salvation and that a new life is the only evidence of that union.

The second fundamental principle of the New Testament, to wit, the baptism of believers only, was displaced with the first, for as soon as baptism became a synonym for regeneration and water was supposed to wash away sin, it was natural that dying or sickly, and then all infants should be brought to the priest to have their sins washed away. It is the protest which Baptists have raised against this innovation and revolution in gospel order that has attracted the attention of the world and occasioned most of the wickedness that have been invented to describe them. The refusal to have their own infants baptized and the denial of the validity of baptism received in infancy, placed them in conflict with the authorities of church and State and made an impression upon multitudes who inquired no further and cared nothing about their doctrine of the secret operation of the Holy Spirit in the heart of the believer. To this day, most people when they think of Baptists, think of baptism and not of what goes before baptism—the new creation of the soul.

The third fundamental principle of the New Testament, namely the equality of believers in the church, was discarded with the other two, for when regeneration was reduced to the sacrament of baptism, the servant of the church who administered the saving rite, was a servant no longer, but a priest, a magician, a little god. In this way the clergy were exalted above the laity and became a separate class. This official distinction of the ministers did not improve their character. It was not a question of character any longer, but of ordination. Those who were properly ordained had the power to wash away sins whatever their character might be. The office hallowed the man and not the man the office.

The next two protests in church history were raised by the Novatians in the third century and by the Donatists in the fourth, against the false view of the priesthood. The persecutions of Decius and of Diocletian had exposed many hypocrites who were said to have "lapsed." After peace was restored, the question arose as to the proper treatment of these lapse christians who sought restoration to church fellowship and office. The majority, led on by Cyprian and Augustine, took a lenient view of their apostacy, but the Novatians and Donatists declared that the rights of apostles were forfeited. Hence they were called "Puritans" and "Anabaptists" because they demanded a pure and loyal record for the ministry, and because they rebaptized those who had been baptized by the disloyal ministers of the Roman Catholic church. Baptists have always insisted not only on a holy ministry and on the equality of ministers, but also on the ministry of all believers. Lay preaching has been favored by Baptists from the beginning. No bishop is allowed to lord it over the pastor, and the pastor is not allowed to lord it over the humblest member. The highest place a minister can occupy, is to be the servant of all.

The fourth fundamental principle of the New Testament, that is to say, the separation of church and State, was necessarily maintained for three centuries, because the Roman State persecuted the church during that period, but when the Emperor Constantine made the offer of an alliance between church and State, the offer was accepted, and the union then formed remained in force everywhere until a Baptist obtained his charter for Rhode Island. Except in the United States, Australia and Ireland, the old order still prevails. Thus the Lord's decree, "Render unto Cæsar the things that are Cæsar's, and unto God the things that are God's"—the most momentous utterance, Von Ranke says, that ever fell from his lips, is disregarded by the rules of church and State. The interesting historical fact is that a Baptist in Rhode Island was the first to try the application to civil affairs of our Lord's decree, and that Baptists were the first to move to secure the adoption by Congress, before its adoption by the States, of this Baptist principle. It may be called a Baptist principle because before Rhode Island was formed, only Baptist voices were heard in the advocacy of the separation of church and State. Total separation is the logical outcome of the Baptist principles already stated. Beginning with a regenerated soul and the baptism of believers only, and holding firmly to the equality of all believers, there is no place for the State in the church and there is no need of the State by the church. As a Baptist church is founded upon voluntary faith, persecution is prevented from the start. Is it not time that Baptists, the first and foremost friends of liberty, should be cleared of the charge of bigotry?

INTRODUCTION. xi

The last fundamental New Testament principle, namely, the Bible, the sole authority in the church, was discarded soon after the union of church and State under Constantine. Some other authority was needed to justify that union and many other departures from New Testament precept that had already taken place. That authority was found in the church itself and in tradition. "I would not believe the New Testament if the church did not command me to," said Augustine. "I esteem the four general councils," said Pope Gregory, "as highly as I do the four gospels." Throughout the middle ages tradition held full sway. When the Waldensians translated the New Testament into the vernacular, Pope Innocent III compared the Bible to Mt. Sinai, which the people were forbidden to touch. The fourth Lateran council, held in 1215, forbade laymen to read the Bible, and the Bishop of Tarragona, in 1242, forbade even the priests to do so. Baptists have always done their share in translating the Bible into the languages of earth. Carey, Marshman, Ward, Judson and many others have let the light of life shine in heathen lands. Joseph Hughes was the Baptist founder of the British and Foreign Bible Society. Baptists were the leaders in the movement to revise the English Bible, and furnished Conant, Hackett and Kendrick to represent them in the enterprise.

While they hold fast to these fundamental principles of the New Testament, Baptists have a bright future before them. By insisting, on evidence of regeneration in every candidate for baptism, this will prevent the spirit of worldliness, which weakens other churches, from entering the assembly of the saints. By maintaining the equality of believers, the temptation of ambition, so strong in all human organizations, will find nothing in them. By guarding the independence of the church, they will preserve the independence of the State, and by upholding the Bible as the sole authority and as interpreter of its own decrees, they will be safe from the attack of rationalism on the one hand or superstition on the other.

W. W. EVERTS.

HAVERHILL, Mass., May, 1894.

INDEX AND CONTENTS.

CHAPTER I.
DEFINITION AND EXPLANATION OF CHURCH PERPETUITY -- PAGES 1-3

CHAPTER II.
CHURCH PERPETUITY A FUNDAMENTAL TRUTH OF THE BIBLE -- PAGE 4

Literally, the word church always means local organization.—pp. 5, 6, 11-14. Figuratively, the term church means the church institution and the totality of New Testament churches.—p. 5. Relation of the kingdom and the churches to each other.—pp. 6-9. "Branches of the church" anti-New Testament.—pp. 15-16. An "invisible" kingdom, or an invisible church, an absurdity and not taught in the New Testament.—pp. 5, 10-13. The notion of an "invisible" kingdom, or of an "invisible" church the basis of ecclesiastical anarchy and ecclesiastical nihilism.—p. 27. Only an organized local church during centuries one and two.—p. 27. Church Perpetuity necessitated from Bible promises and the churches' mission.—pp. 14-31. The perpetuity of the kingdom involves the perpetuity of the church.—p. 14. Attempts to evade the proofs of Church Perpetuity.—pp. 24-27. Church apostasy an infidel doctrine.—pp. 32-33. Church apostasy the origin, the basis and the perpetuity of new sects and sectarianism.—pp. 33-37.

CHAPTER III.
CHURCH PERPETUITY A BAPTIST POSITION -------------- PAGES 38-41

CHAPTER IV.
CHURCH PERPETUITY ADMITS OF VARIATIONS AND IRREGULARITIES IN BAPTIST FAITH AND PRACTICE ------ PAGES 42-48

Statement of Professor O. B. True, D. D.—pp. 42-43. Statement of Dr. Armitage.—pp. 42-43. Dr. Armitage silent before the challenge.—p. 44. Statement of a prominent Campbellite Professor of History.—p. 46. Answers to why own Baptist churches which are in error as in the Perpetuity Line, and deny the same to Pedobaptist churches.—p. 47. The only true test.—p. 48.

CHAPTER V.

THE BURDEN OF PROOF ON OPPONENTS TO BAPTIST CHURCH PERPETUITY. THE MATERIAL ON WHICH THE HISTORIAN MUST DEPEND. THE DEGREE OF PROOF NECESSARY------PAGES 49-55

Testimony of Greenleaf and Whately on the burden of proof.—p. 49. Statement of J. Wheaton Smith, D. D., on history unnecessary to prove Baptist Church Perpetuity.—p. 50. The material for proving Baptist Church Perpetuity.—p. 50. Romish forgeries and perversions.—pp. 51-52. Baptist history destroyed.—p. 53. Modern illustration of slanders on ancient Baptists.—p. 54.

CHAPTER VI.

THE NEGATIVE PROOF. BAPTIST CHURCH PERPETUITY EVIDENT FROM BAPTIST OPPONENTS BEING UNABLE TO ASSIGN OR AGREE ON ANY HUMAN FOUNDER AND POST-APOSTOLIC ORIGIN OF BAPTIST CHURCHES------PAGES 56-64

Statements of Roman Catholic scholars.—pp. 56-57. Statements of Protestant Pedobaptist scholars.—pp. 58-59, 61. Statements of Campbellite scholars.—p. 59-60. Why these scholars are puzzled and confounded.—p. 61. Origin of the Romish church.—p. 62. Only believer's baptism administered by the apostolic churches.—pp. 62-63. Origin of the leading modern churches.—pp. 63-64. Why modern sects are so anxious to prove Church apostacy.—p. 64.

CHAPTER VII.

IN THE PERPETUITY OF BAPTIST PRINCIPLES FROM THE APOSTOLIC AGE TO THE PRESENT, IS NECESSARILY THE PERPETUITY OF BAPTIST CHURCHES------PAGES 65-68

CHAPTER VIII.

THE MONTANISTS------PAGES 69-76

Origin of the Montanists.—p. 69. Great numbers of Montanists.—pp. 69-70. Montanists rejected baptismal regen-

eration.—p. 69. Purity of Montanist churches.—p. 70.
Montanists believed in a visible church.—p. 70. Montanists democratic in church government.—pp. 70, 73-76.
Montanists did not reject marriage of ministers.—p. 71.
Montanists and female teachers.—p. 71. Montanists and
time immersion.—p. 71. Montanists and "visions" and
"inspirations."—pp. 71-74. Montanists characterized by
purity of church membership, and reliance on the Holy
Spirit.—pp. 73-76.

CHAPTER IX.

THE NOVATIANS------PAGES 77-88
Origin of the Novatians.—pp. 77-80, 86. Great number of
Novatians.—p. 77. Believed in a spiritual church and in
strict church discipline.—pp. 77, 79, 83, 85-88. Novatian not
prompted by vain ambition and jealousy.—pp. 78-80.
Slanders on Novatian.—pp. 78, 80-81. Novatian's pouring
intended for immersion.—pp. 80-81. Novatians rejected
baptismal regeneration.—p. 81. Novatian church government Baptist.—p. 82. Novatians did not deny there was
forgiveness with God for fallen church members.—pp.
83-87. Novatian did not believe church membership a
condition of salvation.—p. 84. Novatian a prudent man.—
p. 85. Novatian churches Baptist churches.—p. 88.

CHAPTER X.

THE DONATISTS------PAGES 89-106
Origin of the Donatists.—pp. 89, 90-93. Their great numbers.—
p. 89. Adherents of church purity and church spirituality.—pp. 90, 91, 92-95. Donatists exonerated from the
violence of the Circumcelliones.—pp. 91-92. Strictness of
Donatist church discipline.—pp. 90-94. Donatists rejected
infant baptism.—pp. 95-97. In church government Baptists.
—pp. 98-100. Rejected baptismal regeneration.—p. 100.
Opposed union of church and State.—pp. 100-103. Opposed
persecution.—pp. 103-104. Were immersionists.—pp. 104-
105. The slander that Donatists believed in suicide.—
p. 105.

CHAPTER XI.

THE PAULICIANS------PAGES 107-122
Origin of the Paulicians.—pp. 107-108. Were not Manichæans.—
pp. 107-111. They did not reject parts of the Bible.—pp.

111-115. Did not reject marriage.—pp. 115-116. Did not reject baptism and the Lord's supper.—pp. 115-119. Rejected infant baptism.—pp. 116, 118-119. Rejected baptismal regeneration.—pp. 116, 117-118. How the charge that they rejected baptism and the Lord's Supper originated.—pp. 115-117. Administered single immersion.—p. 118. In church government were Baptists.—pp.119-121. Were Baptists.—p. 122.

CHAPTER XII.

THE ALBIGENSES----------------------------------PAGES 123-128
Origin of the Albigenses.—pp. 123-125. Were not Manichæans.—pp. 125-126. Did not reject marriage.—p. 126. Origin of the charge that they rejected marriage.—p. 126. Rejected infant baptism.—pp. 126-127. Did not reject baptism and the Lord's Supper.—pp. 126-127. Rejected baptismal regeneration.—p. 127. Consideration of the charge that they refused to take oaths.—p. 127. Were Baptists in church government.—pp. 127-128. Pure in their lives.—p. 128. Their influence on Europe.—p. 128.

CHAPTER XIII.

THE PATERINES------ ----------------------------PAGES 129-139
Origin of Paterines.—pp. 129-130. Their great numbers.—p. 130. Did not oppose marriage.—pp. 130-131. Were law abiding.—p. 131. Examination of the Manichæan and Dualistic charges against them.—pp. 132, 133-139. In church government Baptists.—pp. 134-138. Modern researches exposing the slanders on them.—pp. 134-136. No infant Baptism or seventh dayism among them.—p. 135. Followed only the Bible.—p. 138. Believed in election and the Spirit's power in conversion.—p. 139. Believed that demons dwell in sinner's hearts.—p. 139. Pure in their morals.—pp. 133, 137-139. Did not attend saloons and theatres.—p. 137. Strict in church discipline.—p. 138. Did not reject the Old Testament.—p. 138. Continued to the Reformation.—p. 139. Diligent employment of "spare hours."—p. 138.

CHAPTER XIV.

THE PETROBRUSSIANS AND HENRICIANS ---------------PAGES 140-148
Their first appearance.—p. 140. Their great numbers.—p. 140.

Their faith.—p. 141. Rejected infant baptism.—pp. 141, 142, 143, 144, 146. Believed in the Trinity.—p. 143. Had a confession of faith.—p. 143. Received the whole Bible.—p. 143. Rejected baptismal regeneration.—pp. 143-145. Baptism and the Lord's Supper only symbols.—p. 143. Believed in marriage.—p. 147. Meaning of their opposition to church buildings.—p. 148. Believed in regeneration by the Holy Spirit.—p. 143. Believed in only a regenerated church.—pp. 146-147. Henricians were but the Petrobrussians perpetuated.—pp. 145-147. Immersionists.—p. 146. Strict Bible followers.—p. 147. Were Baptists.—pp. 145, 146, 147, 148.

CHAPTER XV.

THE ARNOLDISTS ---------- PAGES 149-158

Opposed the securalization of the church and union of church and State.—pp. 149-158. Rejected infant baptism—pp. 150, 155, 157. Rejected transubstantiation.—p. 150. Inspiring idea of Arnold's work was a spiritual church.—p. 157. Arnold opposed to riotous conduct.—pp. 151-153. Arnold's reforms all of a practical character.—p. 153. Arnold's character.—pp. 149, 151, 153, 156. Modern estimate of Arnold.—pp. 154-156. Arnold a Petrobrussian.—p. 158. Arnoldists were Baptists.—pp. 155-158.

CHAPTER XVI.

THE WALDENSES ---------- PAGES 159-181

Multitudes of Waldenses.—p. 159. Different periods of Waldensian history.—p. 159. Different kinds of Waldenses.—pp. 159, 161, 181. Connected with Hussites.—p. 160. A spiritual people.—p. 161. Believed in only a professedly regenerate church membership.—p. 161. Were immersionists.—p. 162. Rejected baptismal regeneration and believed in the symbolism of baptism.—p. 163. Baptists as to confessions of faith.—p. 164. Believed in the operation of the Spirit.—p. 165. Believed in total depravity.—p. 165. Did not believe in the necessity of weekly communion.—p. 165. Believed in salvation by grace and justification by faith.—p. 165. Believed in election.—p. 166. Rejected infant baptism.—pp. 166-176. Were immersionists.-pp. 175, 169. Restricted communionists.—p. 168. Lollards were Waldenses.—p. 166. Origin

xviii   INDEX AND CONTENTS.

of infant baptism among modern Waldenses.—p. 176. Were Baptists in church government.—pp. 177-181. Were Baptists.—pp. 175-181.

CHAPTER XVII.

THE ANABAPTISTS ——————————————————PAGES 182-215
Anabaptist faith.—pp. 182, 184, 194, Believed in following the Bible.—pp. 182-194. Believed in only a professedly regenerate church.—pp. 182-194. Believed in spirituality of life.—p. 182. Believed in salvation by faith.—pp. 182, 184, 185, 189. Believed in church sovereignty.—p. 182. Rejected union of church and State.—pp. 182-194. Rejected baptismal salvation.—pp. 183, 190-193. Rejected communism.—p. 184. Believed in financially supporting ministers.—p. 184. True believers will not reject baptism.—p. 185. No baptism, no church or ministry.—pp. 185-194. Believed in the symbolism of baptism.—pp. 185-192. Believed in liberty of conscience.—pp. 186, 188, 189, 194. Believed the doctrine of inherited depravity.—p. 187. Believed in the miraculous origin of faith.—pp. 187-188. Rejected the word alone theory of conversion.—pp. 188, 189. Believed in election.—p. 189. Purity of morals.—pp. 189-194. Strictness of church discipline.—pp. 189-194. Baptists in church government.—p. 189. Were missionary Baptists.—pp. 189-190. Were restricted communionists.—p. 193. Rejected infant damnation.—p. 193. The only denomination believing in baptism which never was stained with belief in infant damnation.—p. 193. They immersed.—pp. 192, 195, 215. Affusion among Anabaptists.—pp. 205-206. Were sound in doctrine.—p. 194. Believed in repentance preceding faith.—pp. 190, 192, 194. Experience given before the church in order to baptism.—p. 191. Contrast between the positions of the Anabaptists and of the Reformers.—pp. 194-226. Not chargable with the Munster disorders.—p. 194. Baptist principles revolutionizing the world for liberty.—p. 195.

CHAPTER XVIII.

THE ANABAPTISTS AND THE MUNSTER DISORDERS ————PAGES 216-233
Different classes of "Anabaptists."—pp. 216, 220, 230. Munzer a believer in infant baptism and Baptist opponent.—pp. 219, 220, 231. Munsterites not Baptists, but Pedobaptists.—

pp. 219-220, comp. with p. 221. Munsterites to a great extent, also, Campbellites—Arminians in principle.—p. 222. The noble Baptist struggle against the Munster disorders.— p. 226. Contrast between the Anabaptists and the Reformers.—p. 226. Real origin of the Munster disorders.— pp. 227-230. The Anabaptists opposed and slandered by Romanists and Protestants.—p. 232. Anabaptists, by the losses of property, good name, liberty and life, have bequeathed the world its civil and religious liberty.—p. 233.

CHAPTER XIX.

BAPTIST CHURCH PERPETUITY LINE OR LINES—"SUCCESSION"—FROM THE APOSTOLIC AGE TO THE PAULICIANS, AND INCLUDING THEM .... PAGES 234-244
Connecting relation of Montanists, Novatians and Donatists.— pp. 235-238. Novatian not the founder of Novatians.—p. 235. Montanists, Novatians and Donatists, perpetuated under the name Paulicians.—pp. 238-244.

CHAPTER XX.

BAPTIST CHURCH PERPETUITY THROUGH THE PAULICIANS TO THE ANABAPTISTS .... PAGES 245-257
Cathari, Puritans, Patereni, Paulicians, Publicans, Gazari, Bulgari, Bugari, Albigenses, Waldenses, Henricians, Petrobrussians, Arnoldists, Bogomiles, etc., essentially one.— pp. 245-257. Examples of the Campbellite folly of identifying a church by its name or names.—pp. 244, 245, 246, 247, 248, 249, 253, 255, 257.

CHAPTER XXI.

THE WALDENSES OF APOSTOLIC ORIGIN .... PAGES 258-292
The date of the Noble Lesson.—pp. 258, 259, 264, 266, 271, 272-274. Bible preserved outside of the Romish church.—p. 261. Date of Waldensian MSS. - p. 259. Refutation of Herzog and Dieckhoff.—pp. 263-266, 270, 273-277. Dieckhoff and Herzog borrow the infidel, so-called, "higher criticism" on the Bible with which to assault Waldensian antiquity.—pp. 263-264. Disagreements of Herzog, Dieckhoff, Gieseler, Neander, etc., date of a Waldensian MSS. pp. 264, 265, 272, 273-276. Dieckhoff's charges characterized by Montgomery as "sustained" "by proofs ridicu-

lously slender."—p. 275. Examples of Dieckhoff's reckless criticism.—pp. 276, 278. Dr. A. H. Newman on Dieckhoff's criticism.—p. 274. Romish writers: Dieckhoff's main witnesses.—p. 264. Dieckhoff concedes his main witnesses "liable to suspicion." — p. 265. Romish testimony to Waldensian antiquity.—pp. 262, 266 - 270. Testimony of the Vaudois dialect to Waldensian antiquity.—pp. 270-271. Testimony of the *innere Kritik* to Waldensian antiquity.— pp. 271-272. M. Schmidt's fatal concession in favor of Waldensian antiquity.—pp. 277, 278. Testimony of tradition.—p. 277. Waldenses remained in the valleys from Apostolic to Reformation times.—pp. 278 - 284, 289, 290. Claude of Turin and the Waldenses.—pp. 279-284. Waldo found the Waldenses already existing.—pp. 280, 284-290. How modern Waldenses became Pedobaptists.—p. 263. Conclusion.—pp. 290-292.

CHAPTER XXII.

THE WALDENSES PERPETUATED IN THE ANABAPTISTS
    AND BAPTISTS------------------------------PAGES 293-316
Connection of Waldenses and Hussites.—pp. 293-295. The Romanic and German Waldenses "identical."—p. 295. Vedder concedes the Anabaptists and the Waldenses historically united.—p. 298. Latimer concedes the Donatists perpetuated in the Anabaptists.—p. 300. Anabaptists, at the Reformation, appeared wherever there were previously existing Waldenses.—p. 301. Armitage concedes that the Anabaptists "evidently sprang from the Waldenses."—p. 301. Keller says the Baptists existed "centuries" before the Reformation.—p. 305. Van Oesterzee says Baptists are "older than the Reformation."—p. 306. Luther said the same.—p. 303.

CHAPTER XXIII.

BAPTIST CHURCHES IN ENGLAND LONG BEFORE AND
    UP TO THE TIME OF JOHN SMYTH-----------PAGES 317-346
First English Churches Baptist.—pp. 317, 318. No record of Baptists having ceased to exist in England.— p. 318. Waldenses "abounded" in England.— pp. 318, 328. Lollards and Wickliffites identical.—p. 320. Wickliff's followers Baptists.— pp. 320-323, 331. "More than half

the people of England" Baptists long before the Reformation.— pp. 322, 323. Early English Baptist martyrs.— pp. 323-324. "Thieves and vagabonds" preferred to Baptists.—p. 325. The last martyr burnt in England a Baptist.— p. 328. Oldest Baptist churches in England of which we have record.— pp. 324, 328-329, 337-340. Spurgeon's testimony.—p. 330. Were organized into churches. —pp. 325, 336, 341-346. Persecution never rid England of Baptist churches.—pp. 345-346. Why Baptist churches of those times are so difficult to trace.—pp. 345, 357. Helwise's not the first Calvanistic Baptist Church of England after the Reformation.—pp. 345, 357.

CHAPTER XXIV.

JOHN SMYTH'S BAPTISM AND THE ORIGIN OF ENGLISH
    BAPTISTS------------------------------------PAGES 347-359
Smyth's alleged self-baptism not even done in England.—p. 347. Smyth never connected with the Particular Baptists.—p. 347. The story of Smyth's self-baptism not unlikely a slander.—pp. 348-351. The fact as to Smyth's baptism as revealed by the Church Record.— pp. 351-353. Where *some* English Baptists got their baptism.—pp. 354-355, 358. The Smyth story a slander on Baptists.—p. 359.

CHAPTER XXV.

BAPTIST CHURCH PERPETUITY THROUGH THE WELSH
    BAPTISTS------------------------------------PAGES 360-371
Attempted evasions of facts. — pp. 360, 361. Welsh Baptist Churches never ceased to exist.—pp. 361, 365-371.

CHAPTER XXVI.

AMERICAN BAPTIST CHURCHES DID NOT ORIGINATE
    WITH ROGER WILLIAMS--------------------PAGES 372-405
During the first one hundred and twenty years of the Providence Church it had no "regular records."— pp. 372, 374-375. The confusion attending the Williams claim.—pp. 372-375, 402. The Williams claim is of "modern" origin.—pp. 376, 384. The Williams Church dissolved soon after its origin.—pp. 380-383. Williams never a Baptist —pp. 377, 401. Baptist churches in America before Williams originated his church.—pp. 377-379, 400. Examination of Dr.

Whitsitt's attempt to "resurrect" the Williams claim.—pp. 382, 383. When the existing first church in Providence was founded.—p. 384. No Baptist church originated from the Williams Church.—pp. 383-385, 387, 400-402. How Benedict makes the Williams Church the mother of Baptist churches.—p. 387. Even thus Benedict ridicules the Williams Church being the mother of American Baptist Churches.—p. 402. Date of the origin of the First Newport Baptist Church. —pp. 390-392. Reply to Prof. Whitsitt on the origin of the First Newport Baptist Church. —p. 404. The First Newport Baptist Church the prolific mother of Baptist Churches. — pp. 397-398. Baptist opponents ignoring the First Newport Baptist Church as a Baptist mother, while they parade the Williams Church as a Baptist mother, though it was utterly barren.—p. 398. Origin of American Baptist Churches independently of the Williams affair.—pp. 377-379, 400, 392-405. Concessions of Baptist opponents.—pp. 402-405.

CHAPTER XXVII.

THE "MISSIONARY BAPTISTS" ARE THE "REGULAR,"
THE 'OLD," THE "PRIMITIVE" BAPTISTS—THE
ONLY TRUE BAPTISTS_____PAGES 406-436

Claims of "Missionary Baptists" and claims of Anti-missionary Baptists.—pp. 406-431. The Bible requires that preachers be liberally supported.— pp. 406-409. "Salaried" preachers authorized by the Bible.— p. 408. The statement that Rev. John Ryland said: "Young man, sit down; when God wishes to convert the heathen He will do it without your help or mine," is utterly *false*.—p. 417. Origin of Free Will and other so-called Baptists. — pp. 432-436. Open Communion modern.— pp. 432-434.

CHAPTER XXVIII.

BAPTIST CHURCH PERPETUITY MANIFEST IN THE
FRUITS OF BAPTIST CHURCHES_____PAGES 437-470

Indebtedness of the world and of Christendom to Baptist principles for spiritual — for genuine Chrisitanty.—pp. 437-441. Baptist preservation of sound doctrine.—pp. 441-445. The secret of Baptists remaining true to sound doctrine.—pp. 441-443. Wherever Protestant Pedobaptists have had the

INDEX AND CONTENTS. xxiii

opportunity they have been as persecuting as Romish Pedobaptists.—p. 466. Baptists have never persecuted, but have given the world its religious and civil liberty.—pp. 445-449. Despotic European thrones shaken by Baptist principles.—pp. 448, 449. Attempt to present the Romish Church on the side of freedom of conscience.—pp. 446, 447. No controversy on baptizo among scholars.—pp. 450-452, 454, 455, 459. Only Baptists have dared organize to render the *whole* Bible into other tongues.—p. 469. Sectarian treatment of Baptists by the American Bible Society.—pp. 453-460. Roman Catholic and Protestant Pedobaptist leaders *purposely* keep the people from reading the *whole* of God's will as the Greek reader reads it.—pp. 453-460. Baptist increase.—pp. 460-463. God's blessing on Baptist labors much greater than on labors of others.—pp. 461-463. Baptist statistics.—pp. 460-464. Bird's-eye view of Baptists throughout the world. p. 464. Summary of Baptist fruits.—pp. 465-469. "Baptists have solved the great problem."—p. 469. Dr. Philip Schaff's praise of Baptists.—p. 469. Baptists *better* than others.—p. 470. The non-propagation of Baptist principles would be disastrous to the world and to Christians of other denominations.—p. 470. Baptist opportunity and Baptist responsibility.—p. 470.

CHAPTER XXIX.

St. Patrick a Baptist----------------------------Pages 472-479
St Patrick's birth and early history.—p. 472. He taught the distinguishing Baptist principles and practices.—pp. 473-479. To call him a Roman Catholic a disgrace to his memory.—p. 479.

AUTHORS QUOTED OR REFERRED TO.*

S. H. Ford.	Beza.	Winebrenner.
J. R. Graves.	Raphaelius.	Armitage.
Hiscox.	Liddell & Scott.	Geo. B. Taylor.
J. M. Pendleton.	Trench.	Pengilly.
E. Adkins.	Bengel.	Peck.
H. Harvey.	Stier.	Orchard.
H. M. Dexter.	Adam Clarke.	John A. Broadus.
W. W. Gardner.	Scott.	Benedict.
Crowell.	Horsley.	Belcher.
E. J. Fish.	Vatringa.	William Williams.
Wardlaw.	Olshausen.	Lorimer.
A. Campbell.	Lange.	R. J. W. Buckland.
Lard.	Fanning.	Dayton.
W. M. F. Warren.	Lipscomb.	T. T. Eaton.
Barnes.	Mtth. Henry.	Cramp.
Andrew Fuller.	Edward Robinson.	J. Newton Brown.
G. W. Clarke.	J. M. Mathes.	William R. Williams.
A. Hovey.	Leslie.	J. Wheaton Smith.
Tholuck	Bannerman.	Ray.
Varden.	Owen.	Catchcart.
Rosenmuller.	Isaac Newton.	Everts, Sr.
Bretschneider.	Kelley.	Everts, Jr.
Alford.	Swedenborg.	Swindall.
Thayer.	Buckle.	T. G. Jones.
Godet.	Voltaire.	T. J. Morgan.
Bloomfield.	Bangs.	True.
Paulus.	Porter.	Greenleaf.
Fleck.	Cowherd.	Whately.
Borneman.	Fahnestock.	Lecky.
DeWette.	A. D. Williams.	William Jones.
Doddridge.	Burbank.	Davis.

* In this list I have not given full names, except where perhaps necessary to distinguish from others who have the same names.

AUTHORS QUOTED OR REFERRED TO.

Lyon.
Haeckel.
Gentille.
G. H. Elder.
John S. Murphy.
C. F Thomas.
H. C. Sheldon.
H. M. Scott.
A. C. Lewis.
L. L. Paine.
Ridpath.
Cobb.
B. D. Dean.
Wilston Walker.
Bergier.
Dollinger.
Alzog.
Darra.
Davidson.
Wadington.
McKnight.
Coleman.
Conybeare & Howson.
Kitto.
Philip Schaff.
Neander.
Jacobson.
Hackett.
Dowling.
Meyer.
Duncan.
Gesenius.
A. H. Newman.
J. L. M. Curry.
Kurtz.
Dorner.
Guericke.
Mosheim.
Hase.
Möller.

Tertullian.
Vales.
Cornelius.
Harnack.
Socrates.
Robert Robinson.
Dupin.
Bohringer.
Walch.
Long.
Guy de Bres.
Augustine.
Osiander.
Thos. Fuller.
Twisk.
Gotfried Arnold.
Iverney.
Merivale.
Gibbon.
Child.
Gass.
Brockett.
Jortin.
Lardner.
Petrus Siculus.
Photius.
Monachus.
Mathew Paris.
Alanus.
Hoveden.
Gevase.
Jirecek.
Geo. P. Fisher.
Massons.
Hallam.
Semler.
Rule.
Carl Schmidt.
Macaulay.
Limborch.

Allix.
Wall.
Vedder.
G. Schmidt.
Brewster.
Whitsitt.
Rainer Saccho.
Erasmus.
Mezeray.
Herzog.
A. A. Hodge.
Petrus Cluniacenis.
Montanus.
Hossius.
Bellarmine.
Perrin.
T. Sims.
Richard Baxter.
Thomas Waldensis
Ludwig Keller.
Grimmel.
Vecembecius.
Ermengard.
Stephen.
Moneta.
Hahn.
David.
Ypeij.
Dermout.
Baird.
Burrage.
Fusslin.
Schmucker.
Vives.
Lord
Muston.
Preger.
Hubmeyer.
J. A. Smith.
Denck.

AUTHORS QUOTED OR REFERRED TO.

John Muller.	Bayle.	Danvers.
Osgood.	Motley.	Heman Lincoln.
Grebel.	Daubigne.	J. C. L. Gieseler.
Overton.	Fessenden.	Eusebius.
J. B. Thomas.	Michelet.	Gretzer.
Featley.	Gerard.	Baltes.
Sears.	Brandt.	Wm. Hall.
Luther.	Palfry.	Purcell.
Menno.	Bancroft.	Sepp.
Zwingli.	May.	Van Der Kemp.
Kessler.	Moreland.	Vand Der Palm.
Wagenseil.	Leger.	Bennett.
Stumpf.	Jonas.	Ridley.
Simler.	Siessel.	Marsden.
Sicher.	Dieckhoff.	Evans.
Arents.	Montgomery.	Some.
Millard.	Pilchendorf.	Usher.
Schyn.	Charvaz.	Francis Thackeray.
Maatscheon.	Bernard.	Bede.
Trecksel.	Bernard de Fontcaud.	Knighton.
Turretine.	Gilly.	Rastell.
Winkler.	Metivier.	Collier.
Knight.	Todd.	Short.
Poole.	M. Schmidt.	Cardwell.
Bourasse.	Claude, of Turin.	Clifford.
Floyer.	Bert.	C. H. Spurgeon.
Crosby.	Merriam.	Bishop Burnett.
Spellman.	Morel.	Bonner.
Linwood.	M. Gieseler.	Joseph Cook.
Cutting.	Wattenbach.	Froude.
Christian.	Matthias Flacius Illy-	Withrow.
Conant.	ricus.	Henry Ward Beecher.
Mason.	H. Haupt.	Douglas Campbell.
Wilson.	Lémme.	Judge Story.
Neal.	Herberle.	Skeats.
Uhlborn.	Latimer.	President Elliot.
Frank.	Goebel.	Gervinus.
Wetzel.	Bullinger.	Ivimey.

CHAPTER I.

WHAT IS CHURCH PERPETUITY?

As the New Testament church is defined in Chapter II, of this book, I refer the reader to that instead of here defining it.

Webster defines perpetuity: "The state or quality of being perpetual . . . Continued existence or duration."

The late and lamented scholar, J. R. Graves, LL. D., wrote: "Wherever there are three or more baptized members of a regular Baptist church or churches covenanted together to hold and teach, and are governed by the New Testament," etc., "there is a Church of Christ, even though there was not a presbytery of ministers in a thousand miles of them to organize them into a church. There is not the slightest need of a council of presbyters to organize a Baptist church."

And the scholarly S. H. Ford, LL. D., says: "Succession among Baptists is not a *linked chain* of churches or ministers, uninterrupted and traceable at this distant day. . . The true and defensible doctrine is, that baptized believers have existed in every age since John baptized in Jordan, and have met as a baptized congregation in covenant and fellowship where an opportunity permitted." To this explanation of Church Succession by Drs. Graves and Ford, all believers in Baptist "Church Succession" fully agree.

As the term "Succession," from its being used by Romanists, may mislead the uninformed into the belief that Baptists believe the Apostles have been succeeded by apostles and hierarchal bishops — bishops who have received the Spirit from the laying on of the hands of the Apostles, and, then, episcopal grace, the phrase "Church Perpetuity" is preferrable to the phrase "Church Succession." The apostolic office terminated with the death of the last of the Apostles. It was intended only for the closing of the New Testament canon and the organization of the first churches. The New Testament, and other church history, certainly teach there were no other bishops in apostolic churches than pastors of one congregation—the diocese and the diocesan bishop having been born in the third century.

Every Baptist church being, in organization, a church complete in itself, and, in no way organically connected with any other church, such a thing as one church succeeding another, as the second link of a chain is added to and succeeds the first, or, as one Romish or Episcopal church succeeds another, is utterly foreign to and incompatible with Baptist church polity. Therefore, the talk about every link "jingling in the succession chain from the banks of the Jordan to the present," is ignorance or dust-throwing.

The only senses in which one Baptist church can succeed another are that the church leads men and women to Christ, then through its missionaries or ministers baptizes them, after which the baptized organize themselves into a Baptist church; or, in lettering off some of its members to organize a new church; or, in case the old church has fallen to pieces, for its members to reorganize themselves into a church.

All that Baptists mean by church "Succession," or Church Perpetuity, is: There has never been a day since the organization of the first New Testament church in which there was no genuine church of the New Testament existing on earth.

CHAPTER II.

Church Perpetuity a Fundamental Truth of the Bible.

1. Inasmuch as many deny the Bible teaches that the Church of Christ should never totally apostatize, I will here prove that it teaches its preservation until the Second Coming of Christ. Let us first settle what is the church.

The M. E. Discipline defines the church: "The visible Church of Christ is a congregation of faithful men in which the pure Word of God is preached, and the *sacraments* duly administered *according to Christ's ordinance* in *all* things that are of necessity requisite to the same."[1] Substituting ordinances for "sacraments" and adding Scriptural Church Government, this definition is good.

Dr. Hiscox: "A Christian Church is *a congregation of baptized believers in Christ*, worshipping together, associated in *the* faith and fellowship of the gospel; *practicing its precepts;* observing its *ordinances;* recognizing and receiving Christ as their Supreme lawgiver and ruler; and taking His Word as their sufficient and exclusive rule of faith and practice in all matters of religion."[2] This expresses what the Methodist Discipline seems to mean, but with much more clearness. With equal clearness J. M. Pendleton, D.D.,[3] E. Adkins, D.D.,[4] H.

---

[1] Art. 13.
[2] Baptist Church Directory, p. 13.
[3] Pendleton's Church Manual, p. 7.
[4] Adkins' The Church; its Polity and Fellowship, p. 18.

Harvey, D.D.,[1] Henry M. Dexter, D.D.,[2] W. W. Gardner, D.D.,[3] William Crowell, D.D.,[4] say the same thing. The New Hampshire Confession says: " We believe that a visible church of Christ is a congregation of *baptized* believers, associated by covenant in *the faith* and fellowship of the gospel; observing the *ordinances* of Christ; governed by His laws; and exercising the gifts, rights and privileges invested *in* them by His Word,"[5] etc.

Ekklesia — the word for church — ($εκκλησία$) occurs 114 times in the New Testament. In all but three it is rendered church. It refers to the Christian Church once typically, (Acts 7:38) the remaining 110 occurrences antitypically. In 99 instances, by counting, I find it denotes *local organizations;* in 12, by synecdoche, it means all the *local organizations.* It is used by synecdoche in Matt. 16:18; Eph. 3:10, 21; 5:23, 24, 25, 27, 29, 32; Heb. 12:23, and, possibly, one or two other occurrences.

Says E. J. Fish, D.D.: " All investigation concurs with 'unequivocal uses of the term in pronouncing the actual church to be *a local society and never anything but a local society.*'"[6] " The real Church of Christ is a *local body*, of a definite, doctrinal constitution such as is indispensable to the unity of the Spirit."[7] Alluding to its application to all professors, of all creeds, scattered everywhere, as an "invisible," "universal church," Dr. Fish well says: "*Not a single case* can be adduced where the loose and extended use of the collective can be

[1] The Church, p. 26.
[2] Congregationalism, p. 1.
[3] Missiles of Truth, pp. 189, 190.
[4] Church Members' Manual, p. 35.
[5] Art. 13.
[6] Ecclesiology, p. 114.
[7] Idem, p. 116.

adopted without a forced and unnatural interpretation. The New Testament is *utterly* innocent of the inward conflict of those theories which adopt both the invisible, or universal, as it is now more commonly called, and the local ideas."[1]

H. M. Dexter, a Congregationalist, was forced to say: "The weight of New Testament authority, then, seems *clearly* to decide that the ordinary and natural meaning of εκκλησία (ekklesia, rendered church,) is that of a *local* body of believers."[2]

Says Ralph Wardlaw, D.D., a Congregationalist: "Unauthorized uses of the word church. Under this head, I have first to notice the designations, of which the use is so common, but so vague—of the *church visible* and the *church mystical,* or *invisible.* Were these designations to be found in the New Testament, we should feel ourselves under obligation to examine and ascertain the sense in which the inspired writers use them. This, however, *not being the case,* we are under no such obligation."[3]

A. Campbell: "The communities collected and set in order by the Apostles were called the congregation of Christ, and all these taken together are sometimes called the kingdom of God."[4]

Moses E. Lard, of the difference between the kingdom and the church: "My brethern make none."[5] On the same page: "God has not one thing on this earth called his kingdom and another called his church." That church refers to a local body, any one can see by such as Matt. 18:17; Acts, 8:1; 9:31; 11:26, 32; 13:1; 14:23,

[1] Idem, p. 102.
[2] Congregationalism, p. 33.
[3] Wardlaw's Cong. Indep., p. 54.
[4] Christian System, p. 172.
[5] What Baptism is For, No. 3, p. 5.

27; 15:3, 4, 22, 41; 16:5; 18:22; Rom. 16:1, 5; I. Cor. 1:2; 4:17; 7:17; 11:16; II. Cor. 8:1, 18, 19, 23, 24; 11:8, 28; 12:13; Gal. 1:2, 22; Rev. 1:4; 2:1, 7, 8, 11, 12, 17, 18, 23, 29; 3:1, 6, 7, 13, 14, 22; 22:16. A careful comparison of these references will prove that the church is a local body, administering the ordinances, discipline, etc., known as church when but one in any locality, and churches when several of them are spoken of. Kingdom, in the New Testament, means the *aggregate* of the churches, just as any kingdom means the aggregate of † its provinces—or countries of which it is composed. A kingdom includes the unorganized part of its geographical territory. In the New Testament, likewise, the term kingdom may include regenerate persons who have been misled so as to have never united with any of the churches or organized parts of the kingdom. Such an instance is Rev. 18:4, where Christians are exorted to come out of the Romish church. But, in no instance, either politically or ecclesiastically, can the application of the term kingdom to the organized localities, or parts, exclude the organized as necessary to the kingdom.

W. M. F. Warren, D.D., President of Boston University, Methodist: "The Christian Church is the kingdom of God, viewed in its objective or institutional form."¹ "In an earlier period this kingdom was identified with the church. . . . The Protestants regarded it . . . as the Christian institution of salvation."²

Barnes: The kingdom means "the state of things which the Messiah was to set up—his spiritual reign began in the *church* on earth, and completed in heaven."³

† Except that there is no general organization of the churches but each church is, in organization, independent of every other church, save as Christ is King over them all.
1 Essay before the Proph. Conf., held in N. Y., in 1873.
2 Schaff-Herzog Ency., vol. 2, p. 1246.
3 Com. on Matt. 3:2.

Neander, while stating that the kingdom is used in other sense,—which, by the way, can easily be included in the one he mentions—says: "The idea of the Church of Christ is closely *connected* in the views of Paul with that of the kingdom of God."[1] "At the time of which we are speaking, the *church* comprised the whole visible form of the kingdom of God."[2]

Andrew Fuller regards the kingdom and the church *indissoluble* when he says: "If the nature of Christ's kingdom were placed in those things in which the Apostles placed it, the government and discipline of the church would be considered as *means* not as ends."[3]

G. W. Clarke: "This kingdom, reign, or administration of the Messiah is spiritual in its nature (John 18:36; Rom. 14:17) and is exercised over and has its seat in the hearts of believers.—Luke 17:21. It exists on earth (Matt. 13: 18, 19, 41, 47) extends to another state of existence (Matt. 13: 43, 26, 29; Phil. 2: 10, 11) and will be fully consummated in a state of glory (I. Cor. 15:24; Matt. 8:11; II. Pet. 1:11). It thus embraces the whole mediatorial reign or government of Christ on earth and in heaven, and includes in its subjects all the redeemed, or, as Paul expresses it, (Eph. 3:15) 'the whole family in heaven and earth.' Kingdom of heaven and church are not identical, though *inseparately* and *closely* connected. The churches of Christ are the *external* manifestations of this kingdom in the world."[4]

In an excellent article in Smith's Bible Dictionary.[5] A. Hovey, D.D., President Newton Theological Seminary, says: "This kingdom, though in its nature spiritual, was to

---

[1] Plant. and Tr. of the Chr. Ch., p. 455.
[2] Idem. p. 458.
[3] Fuller's Works, vol. 2, p. 639.
[4] Com. on Matt. 3:2.
[5] Vol. 2, pp. 1541, 1543.

have, while on earth, the *visible form in Christian Churches*, and the simple rites belonging to church life were to be observed by every loyal subject (Matt. 28:18; John 3:5; Acts 2:38: Luke 21:17: I. Cor. 11:24.) It cannot, however, be said that the New Testament makes the spiritual kingdom of Christ exactly co-extensive with the visible church. There are many in the latter who do not belong to the former, (I. John 2:9,) and some, doubtless, in the former, who do not take their place in the latter."

Tholuck: "A kingdom of God—that is an *organic* commonwealth." "The New Testament kingdom of God, is both from within and from without, in the individual as in the whole *community*." "The idea of the kingdom of God . . . is an *organized community*, which has its principle of life in the will of the personal God."[1]

In the invisible church and kingdom theory are all disorganizers who reject baptism and church organization. Under the pretense of great zeal and spirituality they make the invisible everything and the organization nothing. This is illustrated by the following from *The Watchman*, of Boston:

"But, of late, there has been a marked disposition among certain thinkers to contrast the 'kingdom' with the 'church,' to the disadvantage of the latter. What we need to-day, they say, is not to strengthen the church, but to extend the kingdom of God; to work for the reorganization of society and the influence of Christian principles and motives in every department of life, and not for the salvation of individual men and women, which is the peculiar work of the church. Some of these writers have gone so far as to imply that the church is the greatest obstacle in the way of the advance of the kingdom of God."

[1] Sermon on the Mount, by Tholuck, pp. 71, 74.

As Luke 17:21 is the main passage for an invisible kingdom, I submit the following from that critical scholar, Dr. Geo. Varden:

".The *weight of critical authority* inclines mightily to 'in your midst.' Lexicon Pasoris (1735) so renders. Raphel (*Notæ Philologicæ* 1749) similarly. Rosenmuller (*Scholia*, 1803) seeks to show at some length that, though *entos* may in general mean *within*, the character of the persons addressed forces the other meaning. Bretschneider (*Lexicon*, 1829) translates, 'The founder of the divine kingdom is already in your midst.' Alford (Critical Greek Testament) 'The misunderstanding which rendered these words *within you*, should have been prevented by reflecting that they are *addressed to the Pharisees, in whose hearts it certainly was not.*' Then, 'among you' is the marginal reading of the authorized version: and it has justly been said that, as a rule, these readings are preferable to the text. Moreover, the latest revision of the A. B. Union reads, 'The kingdom of God is in the midst of you.' Writes Thayer in his Greek Lexicon of the New Testament (the latest and by many regarded the best) 'In the midst of you, others within you (*id est*, in your souls) a meaning which the use of the word permits, but *not the context.*' And Godet, in his recent critical Commentary on Luke, writes, 'These words are explained by almost all modern interpreters in the sense of *in the midst of you.*'"

To this I add the words of Dr. Bloomfield, on this passage: "Is among you . . . On this interpretation the best commentators are agreed and adduce examples of this use of ἐντὸς . . . The kingdom of God has even commenced among you, *i. e.*, in your own country and among your own people." So Paulus, Fleck, Bornemann, DeWette, Doddridge, Beza, Raphaelius, *et al.*

Inasmuch as Acts 19:32, where *ecclesia* is rendered "assembly," is presumed to prove it means, also, a "mob," I submit the following conclusive critical refutation, from the late and lamented J. R. Graves, LL. D.: "Let us, without prejudice, look into this question. (1.) Ecclesia is nowhere in the whole range of classical Greek usage used to denote a 'mob' or an unorganized or riotous crowd. (2.) It is nowhere so used in Septuagint Greek. (3.) It is nowhere else in the 111 instances of its occurrence in the New Testament used to denote a mob or riotous crowd. This should arouse suspicion that it may not have this unwonted meaning here. Certainly if it *can* mean a lawful and organized assembly here, we should give it that signification. It certainly can, and I believe should be, given the sense of a lawful assembly—even a political body possessed of civil functions.

"Ephesus was a free city of Greece. Every free city was governed by (1) jury courts—*Diakastres*—that had jurisdiction over all criminal cases. (2.) The ecclesia, which was an organized body composed of all free citizens entitled to vote, and presided over by a recorder. The meeting place of the ecclesia at Ephesus, as at Athens, was in the theater—as the capital at Frankfort is for the sessions of the Kentucky Legislature. (3) The council of five hundred corresponded to our Senate or the House of Lords. Ephesus, then, had an ecclesia, and its meeting place the great theater of the city, and its duty to look after the general peace and welfare of the city—not to sit as a criminal court to try personal offenses.

"Let us now examine Luke's account of what took place, remembering that the ecclesia may have been in session before the uproar commenced, or that it, as it was its duty to do, came immediately together as soon as cognizant of it. Demetrius and his workmen and the mob, having seized Gaius and Aristarchus, rushed with them into the assembly, 'and some [of the mob] cried one thing and some another, and the ecclesia was confused' by these varied cries, while no definite charge was brought to its notice of which it could take cognizance. Now mark it was not the ecclesia that was riotous, but '*oklos*'—crowd that had rushed into the theater where the ecclesia assembly of Ephesus was in orderly session, or had gathered to hold one; for it was the '*oklos*,' not the ecclesia, that the presiding officer of the ecclesia quieted. (See Acts 19:35.) He informed this riotous, '*oklos*' crowd, 'if Demetrius and the workmen with him had a charge against any man, there were the courts and the proconsuls; but if it was about other things the ecclesia would settle it.' The ecclesia was responsible for public tumults, insurrections, etc., and the officer appealed to the crowd to be quiet and disperse, 'for,' said he, speaking for the ecclesia, 'we are even in danger of being accused about the tumult of to-day, there being no cause by which we [the ecclesia] can excuse this concourse' —*sustrophes*—not ecclesia. And having said this, he adjourned, dissolved, the assembly—ecclesia—not the *sustrophes*—mob—which he could not dismiss. Now, in this account, we have, in Greek, four terms used: '*deemos*,' people; '*oklos*,' crowd; '*sustrophes*,' mob; '*ecclesia*,' assembly—a body having civil jurisdiction. Ecclesia and *sustrophes* are never used interchangeably, never mean the same body."

Were we to admit that ecclesia' here meant a "mob," since the church in no way involves a mob, this passage has no bearing on what is the church. Liddell and Scott, in their Greek Lexicon, define the word, "*ekklesia*, an assembly of citizens summoned by the crier, the legislative assembly."

Dean Trench says: "*Ekklesia*, as all know, was the lawful assembly in a free Greek city of all those possessed of the rights of citizenship, for the transaction of public affairs. That they were *summoned* is expressed in the latter part of the word; that they were summoned *out* of the whole population, a select portion of it, including neither the populace, not yet strangers, nor those who had forfeited their civic rights—this is expressed in the first. Both the *calling* and the calling *out*, are moments to be remembered, when the word is assumed into a higher Christian sense, for in them the chief part of its peculiar adaptation to its auguster uses lie."

If the kingdom and the church mean "the reign of grace in the heart without a visible organization," as grace had reigned in the heart, at least, from the time of Abel, Dan. 2:44 and Matt. 16.18, could not have spoken of the kingdom and the church as not built before the New Testament age.

A kingdom without *organization*—definite, *ascertainable* laws, is but the creature of the babel of sectarianism. It never did exist, in nature, in politics or in grace; and never can exist. It is twin brother to the notion that there is an "invisible church"—as if there were invisible men and women! The only part of the church which is invisible is the internal part and that part which has "crossed over the river."

That the term church in the New Testament, always means, literally, in the language of the New Hampshire Confession, "a congregation of *baptized* believers, associated by covenant in the *faith* and *fellowship* of the gospel, observing the *ordinances* of Christ," and, in its few figurative uses, the aggregate of the local churches, and that the church and the kingdom are so related that neither can exist without the other, I have now clearly demonstrated.

THIS BEING THE CASE, EVERY PROMISE OF PRESERVATION AND PERPETUITY, MADE TO THE KINGDOM, IS A PROMISE TO THE CHURCHES OF WHICH IT IS COMPOSED, AND *vice versa*.

I will now proceed to prove the Bible promises that the church should never so far apostatize as to lose its existence as a true church.

I. "*I will make an everlasting covenant with them, that I will not turn away from them to do them good, but I will put my fear in their hearts, that they shall not depart from me.*"—Jer. 32: 40. (1.) That this refers to the New Testament none will deny. (2.) That the church and the "covenant" are indissoluble, will not be denied. (3.) That this covenant and its subjects are in contrast with the old covenant and its subjects, is equally evident. From this it follows, that, inasmuch, as the people of the old covenant apostatized, and that they were repudiated of God, the new covenant and its people are everlastingly united to Him. This is positively affirmed: (*a*) an "everlasting covenant;" (*b*) "fear in their HEARTS;" (*c*) "that they SHALL NOT DEPART from me"—no departing from God, as under the old covenant, no apostate Israel, hence Church Perpetuity. The only possible way to deny that this is a positive promise of Church Perpetuity is to affirm that God departs from His people, who do not depart from Him, which is affirming that He is unfaithful.

II. "*In the days of these kings shall the God of heaven set up a kingdom which shall never be destroyed;* and the kingdom shall not be left to other people, but it shall break in pieces and consume all these kingdoms, and it shall stand forever."—Dan. 2:44. (1.) Here God affirms He will set up a kingdom—but one kingdom. (2.) This kingdom includes the church or churches, as the United States government includes the State or the States. (3.) That this kingdom and church or churches are indivisible, is certain. (4.) He affirms this kingdom, including His church, shall not be left to other people; *i. e.*, under the law of the old covenant, the kingdom, because of apostasy, was given to the Gentiles—"other people," but under the law of the new covenant there shall be no apostasy of the church, so as to cause it to be given to "other people"—to Wesley, Calvin, etc., and their followers. No room here for men to set up churches of their own on the ground of the original churches having all apostatized. (5.) This kingdom "shall NEVER be destroyed." (6.) This kingdom "shall stand FOREVER." (7.) This kingdom, instead of becoming apostate, shall be aggressive—"shall break in pieces and consume all 'other kingdoms.'" (8.) The days of these kings refer to the days of the Cæsars. The only possible way of avoiding this promise of Church Succession is to deny that this kingdom and church are indissoluble. That this denial is vain is evident, from the fact, that, in the New Testament, the two are *never separate*, and the promises of preservation therein to the one are equally to the other. So writers of all denominations hold them one. Here, then, in the Old Testament are the most unequivocal promises of Church Perpetuity.

III. *" Upon this rock I will build my church, and the gates of hell shall not prevail against it."*—Matt. 16:18. (1.) This is church, but one kind of church—a kingdom—not "branches." The New Testament says that, as individuals, Christ's disciples are "branches" of Him. But it nowhere so much as intimates there are "branches of the church." If there are "branches of the church" where is their trunk?? (2.) Christ built *His church*. Wesley, Calvin, Campbell, etc., built theirs. He built it on a *sure* foundation. — Isa. 28:16; Ps. 118:22; Eph. 2:20; II. Tim. 2:19. (4.) The church and its foundation are indissolubly joined together by undying love. (5.) "The gates of hell shall not prevail against it,"—it "shall *never* be destroyed," but "*shall stand forever.*" Bengel well says: "The Christian Church is like a city without walls, and yet the gates of hell, which assail it, shall never prevail." "A most magnificent promise."[1] So say Stier, Adam Clarke, Scott, Barnes, G. W. Clarke, Bloomfield, Horsley, Vitringa, Olshausen, Doddridge and Lange, *et mul al*. Has Christ's promise failed?

The following are Campbellite concessions:

"The rock is not that against which the unseen is not to prevail; neither has the church ever become extinct. These we deem gross errors."[2] Mr. Fanning: "The church was built upon the rock laid in Zion; that she has withstood the rough waves of eighteen centuries, and that she will finally triumph over all the principalities and powers of earth."[3] David Lipscomb: "God founded a church that 'will stand forever;' that the gates of hell shall not prevail against."[4] "True witnesses of Christ never failed from the earth."[5]†

† That these Campbellites and Pedo-baptists, when they come to justify the origin of their churches, say the gates of hell did prevail against the church, is true. But, then they speak from their churches; here they speak from the Bible.

[1] Com. in loco.
[2] Lard's Quarterly Review for 1886, p. 309.
[3] Living Pulpit, p. 520.
[4] Gospel Advocate for 1867, p. 770.
[5] Isaac Errett's Walks about Jerusalem, p. 142.

IV. "*Jesus came and spake unto them, saying, all power is given unto me in heaven and in earth.* Go ye, *therefore*, and teach all nations, baptizing them in the name of the Father, and of the Son, and of the Holy Ghost; teaching them to observe all things whatsoever I have commanded you, and lo, I am with you always, even unto the end of the world."—Matt. 28: 18-20. (1.) Christ here promises His presence. (2.) His presence is here implied to be the only guarantee of the fulfillment of the mission, but the sure one. (3) This promise is to His *church*. That this is true is evident from the Great Commission having been committed to only the church. This will hardly be questioned. (4.) Christ's promise is to insure that the nations will be discipled, *baptized*, etc. That He has promised to be with His church to guarantee the preservation of *baptism*—*all* things included in the commission—is, therefore, clear. (5.) Christ promises His presence always, all the days—*pasas tas heemeras*—not leaving a single day for apostasy. (6.) If this church has gone into Babylon He is gone there too, and all are lost—"Lo I am *with* you *alway* even unto the end of the world. Amen." Bengel says on this: "A continual presence, and one most actually present." "This promise also belongs to the whole church."[1] Inasmuch as Methodism, Presbyterianism, Campbellism, etc., are "but of yesterday," this promise cannot apply to them. On this Stier says: "He is present with his mighty *defense and aid* against the gates of hell, which would oppose and hinder His church in the execution of His commands."[1] So, G. W. Clark, Scott, Matthew Henry, Barnes, Doddridge, Olshausen, and Adam Clark, *et. mul. al.*

[1] Com. in loco.

V. "*For the husband is the head of the wife, even as Christ is the head of the church: and he is the Savior of the body* . . . Christ also loved the church, and gave *Himself* for it . . . that He might present it to Himself, a *glorious* church, not having *spot or wrinkle* or any such thing, but that it should be holy and without *blemish*."— Eph. 5:23, 29. (1.) This is taken from the relation of husband and wife. (2.) The husband that does not use his utmost power to save his wife is an unfaithful husband. (3.) Only his lack of power prevents him from saving his wife. (4.) For Christ to not use His utmost power to save His church would be for Him to be unfaithful to her. (5.) Only by His lack of power can the church apostatize. (6.) But, "all power in heaven and in earth" belongs to Him; therefore the church is insured forever against apostasy. He "gave *Himself* for it" and He is its "*Savior*." (7.) An apostate church is not a "glorious" church, has *spots, wrinkles*, serious *blemishes*. (8.) But, inasmuch as Christ's church has "*no such thing*," His church shall never apostatize. On this Adam Clark says: "Christ exercises His authority over the church so as to *save* and protect it."[1] Verses 26 and 27, Bengel, Matthew Henry and Adam Clark say allude to "the different ordinances which He has appointed;" hence they agree that the passages speak of the Church *organization*.

VI. *Having been "built upon the foundation of the Apostles and prophets, Jesus Christ himself* being the chief corner stone; in whom all the building fitly *framed together, groweth* unto a holy temple in the Lord."—Eph. 2:20, 21. (1.) This building—the church—is "fitly *framed together*." (2.) It is framed—JOINED to its foundation—"*in whom*." (3.) *A church being framed*

[1] Com. in loco.

to the foundation so as to be removed from the foundation is not "*fitly framed*," the only "fitly" framing, according to the spirit and the design of Christianity, is that which so frames the church into its foundation, that it can never be razed by the devil; and, thus, Wesleys, Campbells, Calvins left to rebuild it. (4.) As it is "fitly framed" into its foundation, if the devil has forced it into Babylon, the foundation, too, is gone; for they are "fitly framed together."

VII. "*Wherefore we receiving a kingdom which cannot be moved.*" — Heb. 12:28. Greenfield, Liddell, Scott and Thayer define the Greek, here rendered "moved," "shaken," and the Bible Union and the New Revision render it "shaken" instead of "moved." (1.) If this kingdom cannot be "shaken," surely the church cannot be forced from its foundation into Babylon. (2.) The church, therefore, must ever be faithful to its husband—Church Perpetuity.

VIII. *Christ is the King of His church.*—Matt. 21:5. (1.) To destroy the kingdom is to destroy the king as king. (2.) If Christ's church has been destroyed, *as king*, Christ is destroyed.† (3.) But as His kingship in His church is essential to save a lost world, if for no other reason, He would preserve His church from apostacy. (4.) In no instance has a king ever lost his kingship, except by being too weak to save it. (5.) But Christ has "all power;" therefore, He will save His kingship by saving His church from apostasy.

IX. *Christ is "High Priest" of His church.*— Compare Heb. 10:21 with I. Tim. 3:15. (1.) Christ's priesthood is essentially related to His church. (2.) Therefore to destroy His church is to destroy His priest-

---

† To the attempt to evade the force of this argument, by the fact that Saul became King, and thence infering God then was no longer King (1 Sam. 15:23) is a sufficient reply.

hood. (3.) Inasmuch as He can never permit His priesthood to be destroyed, He can never permit apostasy to destroy His church.

X. *Church Perpetuity grows out of the nature of the truth as the instrument of the Spirit.* The spirit through the truth preserved the apostolic church. Unless the Spirit and the truth lose their power, they must thence preserve the church from apostasy until Christ comes. The same cause, under like conditions, will always produce the same effect. The truth is conditioned for all time only by sinful nature and the unchangeable Spirit; therefore Church Perpetuity.

XI. *Church Perpetuity grows out of the mission of the Church..* Her mission is to preach the gospel to the world, preserve the truth and the ordinances. The Scriptures make the churches the custodians of the ordinances and of all affairs of the kingdom of Christ, on earth. The Commisson says, disciple, baptize and teach them to *observe* all the institutions of Christ —Matt. 28: 19, 20. (*a*) Those who make disciples are, naturally, the judges of the progress and the rights of the disciple. (*b*) Peter, on Pentecost, in that he commanded certain persons to be baptized, judged of their fitness for baptism.—Acts 2:38. (*c*) In asking "can any man *forbid* water," Peter implied that water can be scripturally forbidden for persons who are unfit for baptism. — Acts 10:47, 48. (*d*) In Philip saying to the eunuch, "if thou believest with all thy heart thou *mayest*," he implied his *right* to refuse to baptize him, if he regarded him as not born again. Compare Acts 8:37, with I. John 5:1.

Through the Apostles the *churches* were given the ordinances. (1.) Compare Acts 16:4:—I. Cor. 11:2. (2.) The Church is "the *pillar* and the *ground* of the truth."—I. Tim. 3:15. (3.) In caring for the things of the kingdom, the churches baptize into their membership —through their officers—those whom they think are *believers*. "Him that is weak in the faith receive."—Rom. 14:1. (*a*) How receive if no authority to receive or reject? (*b*) Again, if the Church is not the judge, how can it know whether the candidate is "weak" or strong in the faith—or whether he has any faith at all? (*c*) *Proslambanesthe* — προσλαμβανεσθέ — means, "to admit to one's society and fellowship."—*Thayer's, Robinson's and the other Lexicons.* Adam Clarke: "Receive him into your fellowship;" [1] so *Comp. Com., Doddridge, etc.* See I. Cor. 5:4-5, where the church excluded a member and II. Cor. 2:6-10, where she receives him back into her membership. (4.) In caring for the interests of the kingdom the churches exclude members.— I. Cor. 5:4-9; II. Thess. 3:6; Rev. 2:14, 15, 20; 3:10; Matt. 18:17-19. (5.) The church is to *watch, guard* the interest of the kingdom as a soldier, on guard, guards what is under his care. *Teereo* — τηρέω — rendered "observe" in the Commission — Matt. 28:20 — means to "watch, to observe attentively, to keep the eyes fixed upon, to keep, to guard, *e. g.*, a prisoner, a person arrested. . . . to keep back, to keep in store, to reserve." [2] In the following passages it, and its family, are rendered, "watched," "keepers," "keep," "kept."— Matt. 27:36; 28:4; Mark 7:9; John 2:10; 12:7; 17: 12, 15; Acts 12:5, 6; 16:23 : 24:23; 25:4, 21; II. Tim. 4:7; James 1:27. Thus the "*keepers* did shake;" "they *watched* him;" "Peter was *kept* in prison;" "the keepers before the door *kept* the prison;" "charging the jailer to *keep* them safely;" "commanded a centurion to *keep* Paul;" "that Paul should be *kept* in Cæsarea;" "I commanded him to be

[1] In loco.
[2] Thayer's, Robinson's and other Lexicons.

kept;" "*keep* yourselves in the love of God." Thus the church, at Philadelphia, is commended concerning the interests of the kingdom, in that "thou didst *keep* my word."—Rev. 3:8.

In I. Cor. 11:2, *katekete* —κατέχετε— "to hold down, to detain, to restrain, to retain, hold firm in grasp, to maintain "— see the Lexs. — is used — "*keep* the ordinances"— Revised Version, "*hold fast.*" Thus we see, as plainly as that Jesus Christ is the Son of God, that as the Jews, under the Old Dispensation, had the exclusive care of the word, the ceremonies, etc., so has the church under the new; that the church, as a soldier, with its eyes *fixed* on the interests of the kingdom, is to propagate, practice and guard them — as the Commission reads, " teach them to *guard* all things whatsoever I have commanded you." As the Church, according to *the* word and the Spirit, obeys the Great Commission, Jesus is with it.—Matt. 28:20.† If the church were necessary in apostolic times it is necessary " alway, even unto the end of the world."—Matt. 28:20. Did not Christ provide for this necessity by providing for Church Preservation ? Or, was there, here, a little omission which Wesley, Calvin, Campbell and other church builders provided for ?

No doctrine of the Bible is more clearly revealed than is the doctrine of Church Perpetuity. As easily can one deny the atonement. Convince me there is no church to-day that has continued from the time of Christ, and you convince me the Bible is false. " Pedo-baptists" and Campbellites have admitted that Church Perpetuity is a

---

† Inasmuch as the objection against Restricted Commission is based on the presumption that the church is not the custodian of New Testament institutions, the reader now has, in a nut shell, the key to the whole subject of "Close Communion." No church which believes itself a New Testament church can extend its privileges to those outside its membership—those who differ from it.

Bible doctrine, so clearly is it taught in the Bible. Prof. Bannerman, a Presbyterian, says: "There are statements in Scripture that seem distinctly to intimate that the Christian Church shall *always* continue to exist in the world, notwithstanding that all is earthly and hostile around her. He has founded it upon a rock; and the gates of hell shall not prevail against it.' . . . That Christ will be with His church 'alway, even unto the end of the world,' ministering the needful support and grace for its permanent existence on earth, we cannot doubt."[1] "He has left us a promise that the powers of evil shall never finally prevail against or sweep it entirely away; and as belonging essentially to the due administration of that kingdom, and forming a part of it, the outward dispensation of the ordinances and worship in the church shall never fail."[2] "The ministry, embracing an order of men to discharge its duties, is a standing institution in the Christian Church since its first establishment until now, and Leslie, in his *Short Method with the Deists*, has fairly and justly appealed to the uninterrupted existence of the office as the standing and permanent monument of the great primary facts of Christianity, and, therefore, as demonstrative evidence of its truth."[3]

Eld. J. M. Mathes, a leading Campbellite, adduces the recent origin of the Methodist church as one evidence that it is not the church of Christ. He says: "The M. E. church, as an organism is not old enough to be the church of God."[4]

"In the darkest ages of Popery, God never 'left Himself without a witness.' It is true that from the rise

[1] The Church of Christ, by Bannerman, vol. I, p. 51.
[2] Idem., p. 333.
[3] Idem., p. 439.
[4] Letters to Bishop Morris, p. 140.

of that anti-christian power till the dawn of the Reformation, the people of Christ may be emphatically denominated a 'little flock,' yet small as their number may appear to have been to the eye of man, and unable as historians may be, to trace with accuracy the saints of the Most High, amidst 'a world lying in wickedness,' it cannot be doubted that even then, there was a remnant, which kept the commandments of God, and the testimony of Jesus Christ. *If God reserved to Himself ' seven thousand in Israel who had not bowed the knee to Baal,' in the reign of idolatrous Ahab, can we suppose, that during any preceding period, His Church has ceased to exist*, or that His cause has utterly perished?"[1]

The attempt is made, in two ways, to weaken the force of these Scriptures for the Perpetuity of Churches. **(1.)** By resorting to the loose, assumed meaning, of the word church, as not including organization. But in reply (*a*) I have shown that *ekklesia* (εκκλησία) always indicates organization. (See the first part of this chapter.) (*b*) No man can show where it ever excludes organization.[2] (*c*) There can be no reason why God—if there is such a church—should care so much for a general, indefinable, intangible, "invisible" body of men and women who have no definite places of meeting, no gospel and gospel ordinances committed to it, no definite and tangible objects before it, as to promise to preserve it, while He cared so little for a special, definable, tangible, visible body of men and women, with definite places of meeting, tangible objects before it, and gospel and gospel ordinances committed to it, as to give it no promise of preservation! (*d*) The preaching, the ordinances, the administration of discipline—all the work of the gospel—having been com-

---

[1] History Waldenses, Published by American Sunday School Union.
[2] Ecclesiology, p. 102.

mitted, not to a general, indefinable, intangible, invisible, body of men and women, with no places of meeting, no objects before it, but to organization, it is clear that, whatever may be promised to a non-organization, the very mission and the very design of the church lead us to expect its preservation. When Paul directed Timothy "how men ought to behave themselves in the house of God, which is the church of the living God, the *pillar* and *ground* of the truth,"— I. Tim. 3:15 — he spoke of *organization* with officers — "bishops" and "deacons" — see the context, in verses 1-13. The election of officers, the receiving, the discipline and exclusion of members, the keeping of the ordinances,— everything necessary for the work of the gospel and the salvation of a lost world was committed to "organized churches." Compare Matt. 28:19, 20; Acts 1:26; 6:2, 3, 5; 10:47; 15:22; 16:4; Rom. 14:1; I. Cor. 5:4, 5; II. Cor. 2:6; I. Cor. 11:2; II. Thess. 3:6; Rev. 2:14; 3:10, in which it will be seen that the churches elected their officers, received, excluded members, preached the gospel, *kept* everything in order. In preaching, baptizing, receiving, excluding, the churches are the powers through which the king of Zion governs, extends His empire. A. Campbell, of the churches, says: "But as these communities *possess the oracles of God*. . . . they are in the records of the *kingdom* regarded as the only *constitutional citizens of the kingdom*." [1] Few deny this necessity for the churches, until they come to meet the impregnable stronghold of Bible promises of Church Perpetuity, when they disparage the churches for their own general, intangible, invisible — I must say it — *nothing;* and then they have Church Perpetuity promised to their pet — nothing. Some of them will say: "Yes, we admit, that

[1] Christian System, p. 172.

through all ages there were men and women who held Bible principles, Bible doctrines, Bible ordinances, etc." Yet, in the next breath, they deny that these were churches ! Just as if the life, evinced by the maintenance of these "principles," these "ordinances" and the "doctrine" would not maintain the scriptural church organization ! Where, to-day, find we men and women who maintain Bible principles, Bible ordinances, Bible doctrine, etc., without scriptural organization? *Indeed, what is such a life in manifestation but organization and the work of organization?* The Scriptures represent the organization as *indispensable* to the purity, the preservation of the doctrine, the gospel and the ordinances. But, to rob the church of the promise of preservation, it is denied that the church is necessary to such purposes. *What these deniers of Church Perpetuity think the church was instituted for, would require more than the wisdom of Solomon to tell.* (2.) It is claimed that the apostasy of some churches proves the apostasy of all. Excuse me for reducing the objection to a logical absurdity, in stating it. As well prove that a whole army deserts from some having deserted. The Scriptures speak of some churches being spewed out, their candlesticks being removed. The Romish church is only apostasy. But the promises to the church and to the kingdom, as institutions, are, that "it shall stand forever," that "the gates of Hades shall not prevail against it."

The attempt is, also, made to weaken the statements of commentators, etc., that the Scriptures promise Church Perpetuity. This is done in the same way by which the attempt is made to weaken the direct statements of the Scriptures, viz., by saying that these commentators mean the general, indefinable, intangible, "invisible" body of men and women—church means men and women—with no place of meeting, no objects before it—the "invisible church." To this I reply: Some of these writers have fallen into the error of speaking of an "invisible church," but (1.) I have shown that they speak of the "visible" church as being preserved. For example, Adam Clark says, that the church, of Eph. 5:23-29, is a church with *ordinances*.† (2.) But, if every one of these writers understood these promises as applicable to only an "invisible church" it does not, in the least, weaken their testimony to these promises guaranteeing Church Perpetuity. The promises of perpetuity to a church are one thing; to what kind of a church is given these promises is quite another. I have not quoted any of these writers as defining the church to which the promises were given; but I have quoted them all to prove that the promises clearly leave no ground to doubt that perpetuity of some kind of a church if promised. Having proved that the churches‡ of the New Testament are *organizations*, to which are committed the gospel, the doctrine, the ordinances, the discipline — that they are *thus* "the house of God, which is the church of the living God, the PILLAR and GROUND of the *Truth*," (I. Tim. 3:15.) whoever denies that these are the church to which the promises of preservation are given has his controversy not with me so much as with the King of Zion. § So far as the use of the

---

† An invisible church — if there is such a thing — has neither ordinances nor anything else. If any passage, in the Bible, seems to mean an "invisible" church, this passage is that one. The bad results of the "invisible" notion is seen in Cowboy-Deanism, now in Texas, and elsewhere. On the plea that the church is made up of all believers, wherever they are and to whatever they are connected, it is calling our churches "Babylon," those who maintain them, "church idolators," etc., and is endeavoring to destroy them. This is but the Pedobaptist notion of an "invisible church" "gone to seed." The "invisible" notion is the seed of ecclesiastical nihilism and anarchy.

‡ "The learned Dr. Owen fully maintains, that in no approved writer, for two hundred years after Christ, is mention made of any organized, visibly professing church, except a local congregation of Christians."— *Church Members' Manual*, p. 36, by William Crowell.

§ That the reader may neither be confused nor think that I am confused I will again state that I use "church," in the singular, to denote the aggregate of churches. Just as it is used in Matt. 16:18; Eph. 1:22; 5:24; Col. 1:18. It is

testimony of these writers is concerned, it matters not, if these writers believed the churches of the New Testament are Romish or Mormon churches. They agree that *whatever* the churches of the New Testament are, they are promised Church Perpetuity. And I have proved them all organizations.

I will close this argument with the testimony of one Methodist and two Presbyterian scholars.

Adam Clarke: "The church of the living God. The assembly in which God lives and works, each number of which is a living stone, all of whom, properly *united* among themselves,"—this is organization,—"grow up into a holy temple in the Lord."[1]

Barnes, Presbyterian: "Thus it is with the church. It is intrusted with the business of *maintaining* the truth, of *defending* it from the assaults of error, and of *transmitting* it to future times. The truth is, in fact, upheld in the world *by the church*. The people of the world feel no interest in defending it, and it is to the *Church* of Christ that it is owing that it is preserved and transmitted from age to age . . . *The stability of the truth on earth is dependent on the church* . . . Other systems of religion are swept away; other opinions change; other forms of doctrine vanish; but the knowledge of the great system of redemption is preserved on earth unshaken, because the church is *preserved* and its foundations can not be moved. As certainly as the church continues to live, so certain will it be that the truth of God will be perpetuated in the world."[2]

---

thus used by *synecdoche*, and I use "churches" for the independent organizations—the literal churches, as in Acts 9:31; 15:41; 16:5; 19:37; Rom. 16:4, 16; I. Cor. 7:17; 11:16; 14:33, 34; 16:1, 19. To say "Baptist church" for all Baptist churches is, therefore, correct, so is it to say Baptist churches.

[1] Com. on I. Timothy, 3:15.
[2] On I. Timothy 3:15, in "Old Landmarkism," p. 44.

Again, says Bannerman: "The visible church is Christ's kingdom; and the administration of government, ordinance, and discipline within it, is but a part of that administration by which He rules over His people. That kingdom may at different times be more or less manifest to the outward eye and more or less conspicuous in the view of men. But He has left us a promise that the powers of evil shall never finally prevail against it or sweep it entirely away; and, as belonging *essentially to a due administration* of that kingdom, and forming a *part of it*, the *outward dispensation of ordinances and worship in the Church shall never fail.* * * * There are *express* announcements in Scripture, warranting us to assert that the various *institutions and rites that make up the outward provision of government, worship, ordinance, and discipline in the Church of Christ, should be continued to the end of the world.*"[1]

"The ministry, embracing an order of men to discharge its duties, is a standing institution in the Christian church, since its first establishment until now; and Leslie, in his *Short Method with the Deists*, has fairly and justly appealed to the uninterrupted existence of the office as a standing and permanent monument of the great primary facts of Christianity, and as therefore demonstrative evidence of its truth. . . . There are a number of Scripture declarations of the promises, of the permanence and perpetuity of a ministry in the church, which have been appropriated and perverted by the advocates of apostolic succession into arguments in favor of the doctrine. . . . In short, most of those Scripture statements, which afford us warrant to say that there shall be a church always on this earth, and that the office of minister and pastor is a standing appoint-

[1] Bannerman's Church of Christ, vol. 1, pp. 332, 333.

ment in the church, have been pressed into the service of the theory that an apostolical succession in the line of *each individual minister* is essential to the validity of the ministerial title,† and, as most, if not all, the advocates hold essential also the existence of a church at all. Now, with regard to such statements of Scripture, it may readily be admitted—nay, it is to be *strenuously affirmed*—that they demonstrate this much, that a Church of Christ, *more or less visible, is always to exist* on the earth; but this conclusion has nothing to do with apostolic succession in the church. Further still, *many* of these texts may be held as *demonstrating* that the office of the *ministry* is a *standing and permanent one in the church*. . . . There are not a few statements in Scripture that justify us in believing that the *office of the ministry* in the church can *never*, as an office, *become extinct;* that an order of men *set apart* to its public duties can *never*, as an order, be *interrupted* and come *to an end*, so long as the church itself endures."[1]

Prof. Bannerman, feeling the force of this, against the Presbyterian church, tries to evade it by a resort to the *notion* of a "universal Christian society, and in all the branches of the Christian church." But this does not weaken the force of the quoted statements. How significantly, then, is every honest scholar bound to voice the Lord's statement: "Upon this rock I will build my church and the gates of Hades shall not prevail against it."—Matt. 16:18.

XII. "Unto Him be glory in the *church*, by Jesus Christ, throughout *all ages*, world without end."—Eph.

---

† Advocates for receiving persons into our churches, on alien immersions, have fallen into the Romanist and Episcopal error; for they claim that we can have no proof of a regularly constituted ministry until we can trace "every minister's pedigree back to apostolic times!" Just as if a *Scriptural Church* is not the authority to baptize!

[1] Idem, pp. 439, 442.

3:21. By her fulfilling the great commission—her godly life—the church perpetuates and extends Christ's glory. Many, in our age, rather reverse this by having this glory *out of* the church. But this makes His glory dependent on the church. As this glory is "in the *church* throughout all ages, world without end," the perpetuity of the church is assured.

The Scriptures more than justify the lines of Newton:

> "Glorious things of thee are spoken,
>   Zion, city of our God;
> He whose word cannot be broken,
>   Formed thee for His own abode.
>
> Lord, thy Church is *still* thy dwelling,
>   *Still* is precious in thy sight,
> Judah's temple for excelling,
>   Beaming with the gospel's light.
>
> On the Rock of Ages founded,
>   What can shake her sure repose?
> With salvation's walls surrounded,
>   She can smile at all her foes."

Or of Kelley:

> "Zion stands with hills surrounded,
>   Zion kept by power divine;
> All her foes shall be confounded,
>   Though the world in arms combine:
>   Happy Zion,
>   What a favored lot is thine.
>
> In the furnace God may prove thee,
>   Thence to bring thee forth more bright,
> But can never cease to love thee;
>   Thou art precious in His sight;
>   God is with thee;
>   God, thine everlasting life."

Thus poets join scriptural expositors in declaring church preservation a fundamental Bible doctrine.

Having proved that the church should never apostatize is a fundamental Bible doctrine, I pass

To notice that it is a fundamental infidel doctrine that it should apostatize.

A few years ago I met in debate a Spiritist, who affirmed, as a proposition, that the church has apostatized. So Mormonism teaches. Swedenborg says of the church: "Its condition may be compared with a ship, laden with merchandise, of the greatest value, which, as soon as it got out of the harbor, was immediately tossed about with a tempest, and presently being wrecked in the sea, sinks to the bottom."[1]

Says Buckle: "The new religion was corrupted by old follies, . . . until after a lapse of a few generations, Christianity exhibited so grotesque and hideous a form that its best features were lost, and the lineaments of its earlier loveliness were altogether destroyed."[2]

Infidels, of the present, seeing that the church yet stands, are preaching its apostasy. Voltaire said the church would be extinct before A. D. 1800. Robert Ingersoll, and every infidel lecturer and writer, proclaim the doctrine of the apostasy. The Devil has believed in and worked for church apostasy ever since its birth. Christ said: "The gates of Hades shall not prevail against" the church; the combined powers of hell have ever said "they shall" and "that they have prevailed against it." With which of these parties do you, my dear reader, agree? Remember, you cannot evade the question, by resorting to the assumption of an "invisible" church; for we have seen (*a*) that the only church which the New Testament speaks of is a local organization, and

[1] True Christian Religion, p. 269.
[2] Buckle's History of Civilization, vol. 1, p. 183.

(*b*) if there were "invisible" churches, the promise of preservation is given to the "visible."

Modern churches are essentially based on the infidel assumption, viz., the apostasy, harlotry of the blessed Bride or Church of Christ.

A wife is "off on a visit." To steal the wife's place, a woman circulates the report that the wife has been lost at sea. The woman knows this report is necessary to make room for her. So, every new sect builder and new sect—and sects now number hundreds—knowing there is no room for another Bride of Christ, while the first is alive or true to Him, proclaim the death or the unfaithfulness of His first Bride. Bangs, one of the earliest Methodist writers, said: "That the state of society was such in Great Britain at the time Wesley arose as to call, in most imperious language, for a Reformation, no one, at all acquainted with those times, I presume, will pretend to question."[1] Again: "Methodism arose from the necessity of the times."[2] Mr. Bangs omitted telling his readers that the very church—the Episcopal—that then ruled Britain, was a church which originated with the bold assumptions of the apostasy or harlotry of the Bride of Christ, and of the necessity of a "reformation."

Porter, another standard Methodist writer: "More than a thousand years the church was sunk in the deepest ignorance and corruption, so that it is exceedingly doubtful whether there was a valid bishop on earth."[3] "The church was dead."[4] A sect, calling themselves "Bible Christians"—wonder if the Campbellites cannot get a suggestion from this name, as to what to call their church?—says: "In subsequent times, when reformation

[1] Bangs' Original Church, p. 103.
[2] Idem, p. 302.
[3] Compendium of Methodism, p. 329.
[4] Idem, p. 337.

was needed, a Luther, a Calvin, a Melancthon and others have been raised up, etc. . . . Under Providence"—by the way, these sect builders *all* talk of a Providential call, but no one of them recognizes the others' call as sufficiently doing the work for which they were called, and *none* of them shows us what wonderful Providence called them!—"the body, known by the appellation of Bible Christians, began to assume an external, visible existence as a church, about the year 1800, principally through the labors of Rev. William Cowherd."[1] Of the German Seventh Day Baptists (?), William M. Fahnestock, M. D., of that sect, says: "About the year 1694 a controversy arose in the Protestant churches of Germany and Holland in which vigorous attempts were made to reform some of the errors of the church . . . In the year 1708, Alexander Mack . . . and seven others, in Schwartzenau, Germany, began to examine carefully and impartially the doctrines of the New Testament, and to ascertain what are the obligations imposed on Christians; determined to lay aside all preconceived"—the special plea of Campbellism—"opinions and traditional observances. The result of their inquiries terminated in the formation of the society, now called the Dunkers, or First Day German Baptists."[2] Of a sect called "The Free Communion Baptists" (?), Rev. A. D. Williams, one of its ministers, writes: "At the close of the seventeenth century two pernicious errors had crept into ecclesiastical matters in some parts of New England." As a result: "During the first-half of the eighteenth century a number of these societies were formed in Rhode Island and Connecticut."[3]

[1] Religious Denominations, p. 123.
[2] Religious Denominations, p. 109.
[3] Idem, p. 82.

Rev. Porter S. Burbank, of the "Free Will Baptists" (?), writes: "Generally there was but one Baptist denomination in America till the origin of the Free Will Baptists, a little more than *sixty years* ago. . . . The Free Will Baptist connection in North America commenced A. D. 1780, in which year its first church was organized." Then he proceeds to justify its organization, by such statements as: "Churches were in a lax state of discipline, and much of the preaching was little else than dull, moral essays, or prosy disquisitions on abstract doctrines."[1] John Winebrenner, the founder of the Winebrenarians, who call themselves "The Church of God"—a suggestion for the Campbellites as that name is as near as any name, which the Bible calls the church, nearer than most of the names they have given their church—says: "We shall accordingly notice . . . that religious community, or body of believers, who profess to have come out from all human and unscriptural organizations"—just what the Campbellite church professes—"who have fallen back upon original grounds, and who wish, therefore, to be called by no other distinctive name, collectively taken, than the Church of God." So he says: "In October, 1830," some persons "met together" and organized the "Church of God."[2] Of course, though Mr. Winebrenner founded his church, like A. Campbell, he says it was originated in the first century! In a tract, published by the "Seventh Day Adventists," at Battle Creek, Mich.,—a sect which is doing far more than Ingersoll to introduce Sabbath desecration and materialism—entitled "The Seventh Day Adventist: a brief sketch of their origin, progress and principles," we read: "Our field of inquiry leads us back

---

[1] Idem, pp. 74, 75.
[2] Idem, p. 172.

only to the great advent movement of 1840–'44. Respecting that movement, it is presumed that the public are more or less informed; but they may not be so well aware of the causes which have led since that time to *the rise of a class* of people calling themselves Seventh Day Adventists."[1] Then, on the assumption of all things needing reforming, it says: "A Seventh Day Baptist sister, Mrs. Rachel D. Preston, from the State of New York, moved to Washington, N. H., where there was a church of Adventists. From them she received the doctrine of the soon-coming of Christ, and in return instructed them in reference to the claims of the fourth commandment in the decalogue. This was in 1844. Nearly that whole church immediately commenced the observance of the seventh day, and thus have the honor of being the *first Seventh Day Adventist Church in America.*"[2]

Thus, we see how sects arise, how Christians are divided, how the world is led into infidelity by sectarianism. THE INFIDEL DOCTRINE, THAT THE BLESSED BRIDE OF CHRIST IS DEAD, OR HAS BEEN UNFAITHFUL TO HIM, IS THE BASIS, THE LICENSE OF THE WHOLE OF THE SECTARIAN TROUBLE. Once it is admitted, every one, good or bad, who becomes offended, and who can get a few followers, can get up a "new church," so on *ad infinitum.*†

Thus, here comes Alexander Campbell, like all the other sect founders, claiming to reform the church, to "get back to the Bible," etc. A. Campbell says that he originated the Campbellite church from "a deep and an abiding impression that the *power,* the *consolations* and *joys*—the *holiness* and *happiness* of Christ's religion were

---

† These sects, in the same breath, profess that "to have existed from the apostolic age is not necessary," then exhaust their ingenuity in "refuting Baptists," by attempting to prove them of modern origin!! Why this, if age is not necessary to a church???

[1] Page 1.
[2] Idem, p. 5.

lost in the forms and ceremonies, in the speculations and conjectures, in the feuds and bickerings of sects and schisms."[1] †

† See "Gospel in Water or Campbellism," p. 620; cloth bound, price, $2.00. by the author of this book. It is the most thorough refutation of Campbellism ever published and is recommended by Dr. John A. Broadus, Dr. Angus, of London, and many of our ablest scholars.

[1] Christian System, p. 6.

CHAPTER III.

Church Perpetuity a Baptist Position.

1. That Church Perpetuity is a Baptist position is inevitable from its being a Bible position. (See Chapter II. of this book.)

2. Notwithstanding that Dr. Armitage has denounced Church Perpetuity, in a letter to the author of this book, dated January 31, 1886, after his "History of the Baptists" was published, he virtually destroys his denunciation when, he says: "For nearly fifty years I have been feeling after that land with perpetual disappointment so far as the trend of ecclesiastical history is concerned. As is natural with every honest Baptist, there is a good instinct in his loving soul which feels after the links of a holy chain, which binds him to the apostolic age. . . . No person living would be more thankful than myself, if you will show by unquestionable facts that since the Holy Spirit established the church at Jerusalem there never has been a time when the church did not repeat itself in living and organic bodies of Christians." If Church Perpetuity is "a bulwark of error" and "is the very life of Catholicism," why did Dr. Armitage so long after proof for it, and why did he say that the belief in it "is natural with every honest Baptist?"

Geo. B. Taylor, D. D., a late writer, says: " Baptist principles and Baptist practices have existed in all ages from the Reformation back to apostolic times." "I humbly claim that we originated not at the Reformation, nor in the dark ages, nor in any century after the Apostles, but our marching orders are the commission, and that the first Baptist church was the church at Jerusalem."[1]

Pengilly: "Our principles are as old as Christianity. We acknowledge no founder but Christ."[2]

Dr. Peck: "Baptists in every age from the Apostles remained true to the kingdom which Christ came to establish."[3]

Dr. Howell: "I assert that from the days of John the Baptist to the present time the true Baptist church has ever been a missionary body."[4]

Mr. Orchard: "I have demonstrated so far as human testimony is allowed to prove any fact that the Baptist church, as the Church of Christ, has existed from the day of Pentecost to this privileged period."[5]

John A. Broadus, D.D., LL. D.: "And it would seem to be entirely possible and very probable that the patient research of generations to come may gather material for a much nearer approach to a continuous history of Baptists than is now practicable."

Many years ago Dr. Benedict, a Baptist historian, wrote: "The more I study the subject the stronger are my convictions that if all the facts in the case could be disclosed a very good Succession could be made out."[6]

Dr. Joseph Belcher: "It will be seen that Baptists claim the high antiquity of the Christian church. They can trace a succession of those who believe the same doctrine and administer the same ordinances directly up to the apostolic age."[7]

---

[1] The Baptists, pp. 5, 8, 35-published by the American Baptist Publication Society.
[2] Baptist Manual, p. 82.
[3] Religious Denom., p. 197.
[4] Letters to Watson.
[5] Orchards' Baptist History, vol. 2, p. 11.
[6] Benedict's Hist. of Baptists, p. 51.
[7] Religious Denom., p. 53.

The late William Williams, D. D., when Professor of Church History in the Southern Baptist Theological Seminary, refuting a statement that he taught that Baptists originated with the Reformation, wrote September 5, 1876: "I now hasten to reply that it is not the teaching of the Southern Baptist Theological Seminary, through its Professor of History, that the origin of Baptists is to be traced to the Church of Rome in the sixteenth century. . . . The Baptist churches, in my opinion, are of divine origin, and originated in the first century under the preaching and founding of the Apostles of our Lord."

The lamented Charles H. Spurgeon wrote: "We care very little for the 'historical argument,' but if there be anything in it all, the plea ought not to be filched by the clients of Rome, but should be left to that community which all along has held 'by one Lord, one faith and one baptism.' . . . It would not be impossible to show that the first Christians who dwelt in the land were of the same faith and order as the church now called Baptist. . . . The time will arrive when history will be rewritten."

Geo. C. Lorimer, D. D.: "There are reasons for believing that the Baptists are the oldest body of Christians who dissent from the assumption of the Romish church. Historically they are not Protestants, for while they sympathize with the protest offered by the reformers at the Diet of Spire, 1529, in which this now famous name originated, their existence antedates it by many centuries."

There has probably never been a superior in Baptist history to the late, lamented Dr. Buckland, Professor of Church History in Rochester Theological Seminary. Just before his death he wrote me that he was a strong believer in Baptist Church Perpetuity and that he was, at that time, preparing to prove it from history. In his Madison Avenue lectures Dr. Buckland says: "Have Baptists a history? Prejudice and passion have always answered, no."[1]

On the next page he says: "From the time when Christ walked the earth down to the present there has not been a period in which they have not suffered persecution. From the age of John the Baptist to the massacre in Jamaica, bigoted religionists have not ceased first to slaughter and then to slander them." On page 314 he says: "We cannot accept a place in the catalogue of sects or broken schismatical fragments of God's church."

To this could be added like statements from Drs. A. C. Dayton, T. T. Eaton, J. M. Cramp, J. Newton Brown, J. Wheaton Smith, J. R. Graves, D. B. Ray, William R. Williams, T. J. Morgan, S. H. Ford, both W. W. Everts, William Cathcart, T. G. Jones, D. D. Swindall, etc., etc., etc. Indeed, Armitage, indirectly conceded his position not in harmony with Baptists, when he says, at the conclusion of an assault on Church Perpetuity: "The principles above set forth are not generally adopted in Baptist history."[2]

[1] Madison Ave. Lect., p. 311.
[2] Armitage's Bap. Hist., p. 8.

CHAPTER IV.

Church Perpetuity Admits of Variations and Irregularities in Baptist Faith and Practice.

Thomas Armitage, D. D., in a letter to the author, wrote December 31, 1886: "No person living would be more thankful to you than myself if you will show by unquestionable facts that since the Holy Spirit established the church at Jerusalem, there has never been a time when that church did not repeat itself in living and organic bodies of Christians who followed all its principles and practices without addition or diminution. From early in the third century to about the twelfth, there was scarcely a denomination of Christians in any land, so far as we can now trace them by actual faith and practice, in all points great and small, who would be held in full fellowship with the regular Baptist churches of to-day, if they were living to-day."

Prof. B. O. True, D. D., who occupies the chair of Church History in a leading Theological Seminary, recently wrote the author: "Do we mean, then, by Baptist churches merely those which hold scriptural views on the subjects and acts of baptism or those who conform in all essential matters of conduct, doctrine and polity to the will of Jesus Christ? I certainly do not say that these were not Baptists (speaking of those claimed for Baptists in past ages) and possibly Baptist churches."

These statements, made by Dr. Armitage, contain the explanation for some Baptists arraying themselves among the opponents of Church Perpetuity.

If Prof. True's testing the churches, claimed in the succession line, by their agreement "in all essential matters of conduct, doctrine and polity," be the true test, Baptists may agree that there is the Church Perpetuity.

Hence Prof. True's statement of those claimed in the Perpetuity line: "*I certainly do not say that these were not Baptists and possibly Baptist churches.*" (My italics.) But, by Dr. Armitage's test, that those bodies claimed as Baptists, were "In all points, great and small," "without addition or diminution," exactly what Baptist churches now are and what they now hold "in full fellowship," many Baptist churches of the present as well as the past could not be fellowshipped as Baptists by our best churches. For many of them, to some extent, are Arminian; or feet washers; or have scarcely any church discipline; or disregard the Lord's day and command by meeting for worship "only once a month;" or contribute nothing or near nothing to their pastors, and nothing or near nothing to missions and education; and, in many cases, rarely look into their Bibles. The truth is, the good brethren who doubt historical and Bible Church Perpetuity because those churches of the past may not have been or were not "in all points, great and small, without addition or diminution," what the best Baptist churches now are, would most vehemently oppose applying the same test to English and to a large part of American Baptists of to-day. By their test, from the standpoint of Baptists in the Southern States, Baptists in the Northern are not genuine Baptist churches, because Baptists North, excepting that of the Campbellites, recognize alien immersion as valid, *vice versa*. Since man, "in all points, great and small, without addition or diminution," is not "in doctrine or practice what he ought to be," the test, by which these good brethren hesitate to acknowledge their Baptist brethren of the past ages as Baptist churches, would deny that we are men and women.

In case that history related that in case the Montanist, the Donatist, the Novatian, the Paulician, and other churches in the perpetuity line not only retained in their membership one who had his "father's wife," but that they " were puffed up and had not rather mourned " at such a state of things; that they had teachers among them who taught that "except ye be circumcised, ye cannot be saved," that we "are justified by the law," that held "the doctrine of the Nicolaitanes," "the doctrine of Balaam," and were taught and led by "that woman Jezebel," without rebuke of the church, with what a great noise would they be disowned as Baptists. Yet, such were several apostolic churches.—Acts 15:1; I. Cor. 5:1,2; Gal. 5:4; Rev. 2:14-15-22.

In reply to Dr. Armitage I proposed to find an error in apostolic and Baptist churches of our own day equal to any one he could find in those claimed to be in the Baptist line of Church Perpetuity. Of course, the good brother did not accept the challenge. That challenge I make to any one. Yet weakhearted Baptist brethren, as to Church Perpetuity, are hesitating to own our own Baptist ancestors because they may not have been or were not "in all points, great and small, without addition or diminution," "in doctrine and practice," just what the best Baptist churches now are! A very large part of the saints of the Old Testament, tested by the lives of the best saints of to-day, were not God's people; and were they now living and living as they then lived, they could retain membership in no orderly Baptist church.

Admitting that many of those in the line of Church Perpetuity could not be held in "full fellowship" with

ADMITS OF VARIATIONS. 45

our best churches now does not in the least militate against their being regarded as real Baptist churches, since, as I have just shown, the test of Dr. Armitage would cut off, as saints, the claim of the saints of the Old Testament, of English and of many American Baptist churches of to-day, as Baptist, and that its principle would cut off man's claim to be man. They were Baptist churches; but, like Old Testament saints, the churches of the first centuries, and those of the present, they were colored by their times.

By the test of Dr. Armitage and of all other weak-kneed brethren on Church Perpetuity, Baptist churches have no continuity from Christ to the present time, and, but few now known as Baptist churches are really Baptist churches. But dropping their test and applying the test by which we recognize, though not what they ought to have been or what they ought to be, all churches of the first century and the English and the American Baptist churches as genuine Baptist churches, Baptist churches have a continuous existence from the first century to the present.

That all true Baptists, when the true test is applied, with scarcely a dissenting voice among them, agree that Baptist churches have never ceased to exist since the first century, I believe true. Thus, Dr. Armitage, in the sentence I quoted from his letter to me, as much as says he believes in Church Perpetuity: "From early in the third century to about the twelfth, there was scarcely a denomination of Christians in any land, in all points, great and small, who would be held in full fellowship with the regular Baptist churches of to-day." "Scarcely," as in the sentence: "If the righteous scarcely be saved"—I. Pet. 4:18—implies that those churches, notwithstanding their incidental errors, were essentially Baptist churches.

At the expiration of from one to five centuries from now — saying nothing of from ten to fifteen — to prove from a historical contrast of the life and the practices of the churches of this century with those of that time that, in "doctrine, practice and polity" they were not, "in all points, great and small," such as could be fellowshipped by each other, were they contemporaneous, would be an easy thing to do. In other words, by Dr. Armitage's test, by which he denies Baptist Church Perpetuity, the superior life of the Baptist churches of a future age proves the same churches of the past age were not Baptist churches.

I thank God that the history of the church shows such growth in the divine knowledge and such improvement towards the high standard of perfect New Testament life that future churches hesitate to own their own denomination of the past. For the same cause, in the future world, to own we are the same children of God that we were here will be yet more difficult.—See Eph. 5:27.

Only by a man's habits or regular course of life are we to know he is not a child of God. Likewise, isolated, occasional and brief aberrations, even in essential matters, can not alter the nature of a church or prove it not a Baptist church. In the preceding remarks and Scripture references, in this chapter, this is demonstrated. The Professor of History in the Campbellite College, at Irvington, Indiana, in a letter to me, Oct. 9, 1893, says: "Nor is it true that a church may not depart, in some measure, from the perfect ideal church of the New Testament and still be styled a church. The Seven Churches of Asia, held pernicious doctrines and yet were called by an Apostle, churches." In the fellowship of Baptist churches of our own day this is recognized. An isolated and occasional error or temporary variation as to what is Christian baptism, as to church polity, as to whether certain books of the Bible are canonical, as to the exact relation of grace and works to salvation, or as to being slightly dyed with an essentially modified form of Manichæism, is not a more radical departure from the New Testament than is incest, following the error of Balaam, of Jezebel, substituting works for grace, or for the doctrine of Christ substituting the doctrine of the Nicolaitanes. In other words, as these errors of the churches of the first century invalidated them only when they became their permanent character, so errors, even when fundamental, in succeeding churches, cannot be allowed to invalidate their claim to a place in the perpetuity line, save when they become permanently characteristic.[1] Much less can we, for a moment, consider incidental errors in the history of our churches as entitled to any bearing on the succession question.

To the question, then: "Why recognize, as Baptist churches, sects in past ages which were guilty of errors equal to affusion, infant baptism, other Pedobaptist errors and errors of certain non-Pedobaptist bodies while you deny that Pedobaptist churches are New Testament churches?" the answer is: For the same reason that we recognize the churches of the first century, with all their errors — referred to in the foregoing — as Baptist churches, while we deny the recognition to all present contemporaneous non-Baptist churches. Pedobaptist and other non-Baptist churches by faith, constitution and practice, are essentially and permanently anti-New Testament. But, were we to admit much that is falsely laid to the charge of those sects which are usually

[1] See Rev. 2:5; 3:3, 16, 19.

counted in the succession line, it would be true of them only as greater errors were true of the churches of the first century, referred to in the preceding part of this chapter. Like it was with the church at Laodicea, Christ does not deny a church because of even a great temporary error, but He spews it out only because it becomes characteristically and permanently wrong.[1]

I, therefore, conclude this chapter with this rule: Only by becoming characteristically, fundamentally and permanently unscriptural, as to either or both faith and practice, has a church ever thrown itself out of the Church Perpetuity line, or can it ever do so.

[1] Compare Rev., 3:16; 2:5.

CHAPTER V.

The Burden of Proof on Opponents to Baptist Church Perpetuity. The Material on Which the Historian Must Depend. The Degree of Proof Necessary.

1. The burden of proof is on opponents of Baptist Church Perpetuity.

Says Greenleaf, the standard authority on Evidence in all our courts of law: "Presumptions are founded on the experience or permanency, of longer or shorter duration in human affairs. When, therefore, the existence of a person, a personal relation, or a state of things, is once established by proof, the law presumes that the person, relation, or state of things continues to exist as before, until the contrary is shown, or until a different presumption is raised, from the nature of the subject in question. Thus, when the issue is upon the life or death of a person, once shown to have been living, the burden of proof lies upon him who asserts the death."[1]

Whatley, an eminent authority on logic, in other words, makes the statement just quoted from Greenleaf: "There is a presumption in favor of every existing institution. No one is called on (though he may find it advisable) to defend an existing institution, till some argument is adduced against it."[2]

Applying this law against infidelity, Whatley says: "Christianity exists, and those who deny the divine

[1] Greenleaf on Evidence, vol. 1, p. 46, 47.
[2] Whatley's Rhetoric, p. 138.

origin attributed to it, are bound to show some reasons for assigning to it a human origin."[1]

With the law, announced by Greenleaf and Whatley, to govern this investigation, those who claim the post-apostolic origin of Baptist churches are bound to show "some reasons for assigning them a human origin."

Since all modern institutions, whether secular or religious, have a historical and well-known origin, whoever affirms the modern origin of Baptist churches must show where, when and by whom they were originated. Since "the law presumes that the person, relation, or state of things continues to exist as before, until the contrary is shown, or until a different presumption is raised, from the nature of the subject in question," with a Baptist church existing in the first and the present centuries, in the language of Whatley, "we are not called upon to defend an existing institution"—Baptist churches —"until some argument is adduced against it"—against their succession from apostolic churches. Reader and author may, therefore, join J. Wheaton Smith, D. D., of Philadelphia, in saying: "Why, sir, if between us and the apostolic age there yawned a fathomless abyss, into whose silent darkness intervening history had fallen, with a Baptist church on this side, and a New Testament on the other, we should boldly bridge the gulf and look for the record of our birth among the hills of Galilee."[2]

This book shoulders the burden of proof because Baptist Church Perpetuity can be sustained without the help of this law of investigation.

2. The material for proving Baptist Church Perpetuity:

[1] Idem, p. 143.
[2] Letters to Albert Barnes.

A well-known historian says: "But the pagan priests wrought so effectually on the fears of Diocletian, as to obtain from him in 303, an edict to pull down the sanctuaries of Christians and to burn their books and writings."

Lecky, an infidel historian, says: "No impartial reader can, I think, investigate the innumerable grotesque and lying legends that were deliberately palmed upon mankind as undoubted facts, during the whole course of the middle ages; or can observe the complete and absolute incapacity the polemical historians of Catholicism so frequently display, of conceiving anything good in their opponents' ranks, and their systematic suppression of whatever can tell against their cause, without acknowledging how serious and inveterate has been the evil. Yet it is, I believe, difficult to exaggerate the extent to which this moral defect exists in most of the ancient and very much of the modern literature of Catholicism."[1]

Buckle, another infidel historian, observes of these times: "There was, properly speaking, no history—men not satisfied with the absence of truth supplied its place with falsehood."[2]

As an illustration, infidel writers and lecturers quote from an anonymous writing, called "Synodycon," to prove the silly—unsupported by a shadow of history as well as contradicted by it—falsehood, that the New Testament canon was settled by the Council of Nice, and that, too, by putting all the books for which inspiration was claimed under the communion table, promiscuously, and asking the Lord that the inspired records should get upon the table, while the uninspired should remain beneath; and, that their prayer was thus answered. A

[1] History European Morals, vol. 2, p. 225.
[2] History Civilization, vol. 1, p. 222.

document made probably by some lying monk, no one knows by whom or when. Its internal marks clearly prove that it could not have been written earlier than the latter half of the ninth century.

The False Decretals are another illustration of the unscrupulous forgeries of Roman Catholic writers: "About the middle of the ninth century a collection of canons and decretals appeared in the Frankish Empire, which bore the venerable name of Isidore, and embodied the so-called Isidoriana, but contained besides, also, a large number of spurious decretals. This was composed of the Fifty Canones Apostt., which was followed by fifty-nine forged decretal letters, professedly written by the first thirty popes from Clemens Romanus to Melchiades."[1]

These forgeries were laws in the Romish church, not called in question, until the Magdeburg Centuriones exposed them, at the time of the Reformation. Turrianus, a Jesuit, in 1572, entered the list as their defender, only to be routed.

Take the history of the Paulicians, who figure so prominently in the Baptist perpetuity line, as another illustration. Until recent discoveries—and they are very limited—"The only authorities whence we derive any knowledge of their sentiments are Photius and Peter Siculus, who wrote against them with great bitterness, and on that account cannot be considered as worthy of entire credence. Photius was archbishop of Constantinople, and died A. D. 890, and Peter Siculus, a learned nobleman, died a few years later."[2]

Of the Paulicians, Jones, quoting Peter Siculus, says: "To their excellent deeds the divine and orthodox emperors added this virtue, that they ordered the

[1] Kurtz's Church History, vol. 1, p. 340, old edition.
[2] Baptist History by Cramp, p. 71-72.

Montanists and Manichæans (by which epithets they chose to stigmatize the Paulicians) to be capitally punished; and their books wherever found to be committed to the flames also; that if any person was found to have secreted them he was to be put to death and his goods confiscated."[1]

Of another important section of the Baptist perpetuity line says Dr. Armitage: "Early Bohemian books were burnt on suspicion or brand of heresy, and some individuals boasted that they had burnt 60,000 copies of their sacred literature."*

Of the German Baptists, another important link in the chain, Armitage says: "The Jesuits attempted to blot this book ('Reckoning of Their Faith') out of existence and nearly succeeded. No copy is known to remain of the first edition, and but two of the second, one of which is in the Baptist Seminary at Morgan Park, Illinois."[2] "Their enemies distributed forged articles of faith, called 'Nicholasburg articles.' "[2]

Of the early records of the Welsh Baptists—they are in the perpetuity line—Davis says: "Many of the Welsh writings, which were far more important than gold, were destroyed about the year 285."[3] "Diocletian's strict orders were to burn up every Christian, every meeting house and every scrap of written paper belonging to the Christians, or anything that gave any account of their rise and progress."[4]

Modern misrepresentations and slanders of Baptists illustrate the sifting necessary in taking the accounts of ancient Baptists as given by their enemies. Thus, in a letter from Leipsig, Germany, January 4, 1881, Prof. D.

*History of the Baptists, p. 32.
[1] Jones' Church History, p. 244.
[2] Idem, p. 384.
[3] Davis' History of the Welsh Baptists, p. 18.
[4] Idem, p. 9.

G. Lyon, of Harvard University, wrote: "Closely akin, indeed, another form of persecution, is the social ostracism which Baptists here must endure. They are regarded as the lineal descendants of the Anabaptists of Luther's time, and the word '*Wiedertaufer*'† is the German synonym for all that is low and evil. Persons who have social standing would lose it by visiting Baptist churches. A lady who attended a Baptist Sunday-school festival in Hanover, two weeks ago, was not willing for her name to be known. She had heard that it was there customary to turn the gas off and indulge in general kissing. In another place a lady whose husband intended visiting a Baptist meeting was fearful lest he should be won to Baptist views. When he persisted she warned him not to drink any of the coffee—which is sometimes served—evidently supposing that the coffee contained some secret winning power."

If in scholarly Germany such slanders are now made and credited against the Baptists, what of the ages of darkness preceding!

If the reader asks: "Why the diffiulty of tracing a succession of Baptist churches from apostolic time to our own?" in the destruction of records, the forgeries and the slanders of Baptist enemies he has the answer to his question.

3. The degree of proof necessary to historically prove a continuity of Baptist churches from the apostolic age to the present.

Prof. Haeckel, an infidel and an eminent scientist, says: "What do we know of the essential nature of electricity, or the imponderables generally, whose brief existence is not proved? What of ether, upon which our science of light and optics is founded; and what of the

---

†From *wieder*, meaning again, anew, and *taufer*, meaning baptizers—Rebaptizers.

atomic theory on which our chemistry is built? We do not certainly know these things." Yet what scientific man would question these sciences? Who can prove the present animal and vegetable world, by every link, to have descended from the creation? Who can prove the facts, link by link, in the doctrine of the correlation of forces and the conservation of energy? Who can prove his descent from Adam? More: Who can prove his genealogy ten generations back—even five? Yet who would deny these things until historically proven, *year by year?* Yet, strange to say, the demand upon Baptists is not simply to show that there were Baptist churches in the first century, and that we have glimpses of them as they occasionally appear in the past centuries, but that unless we can clearly see them in continuous line for the past eighteen centuries, they did not exist unceasingly during that time!

What reasonable man questions the Biblical canon because of the scarcity of the records for its history? Who denies the discovery of America because the time and the name of its discoverer are unsettled?

Greenleaf says: "In all human transactions, the highest degree of assurance to which we can arrive, short of the evidences of our own senses, is that of probability."[1]

I, therefore, close this chapter with the remark. Strict conformity to this rule, laid down by Greenleaf, which governs our courts of law, is all that the Christian apologist asks of the infidel and all that this book asks of the opponents of Baptist Church Perpetuity—not whether there is any room for doubting Baptist Church Perpetuity, but whether there is a historical "probability" of its being true.

[1] Test. of the Evangelist, p. 45.

CHAPTER VI.

THE NEGATIVE PROOF. BAPTIST CHURCH PERPETUITY, FROM THE APOSTOLIC AGE TO THE PRESENT, EVIDENT FROM BAPTIST OPPONENTS BEING UNABLE TO ASSIGN AND AGREE ON ANY HUMAN FOUNDER AND POST-APOSTOLIC ORIGIN FOR BAPTIST CHURCHES.

Answering my questions: When, where and by whom was the first Baptist church originated? I have the following from Roman Catholic bishops, priests and Protestant scholars, given me A. D. 1893:

The priest of Shreveport got out of the difficulty by writing: "You have in Dallas two or three priests with valuable libraries. Interview them."—J. Gentille, Shreveport, La. The Archbishop of Cincinnati wrote me: "I cannot get time to answer all my letters. These questions *cannot* be answered without explanations, which I have not time to make. And there is no reason why you come to me for them. You have men near you—priests and others—who can do it better than I.—G. H. Elder." (My italics.)

With more judgment, many other Romanists dropped my letters aside without so much as acknowledging their being received. With less judgment than any of the others, the following Romanists attempted to answer:

The bishop of New Orleans, answered: "In Germany, called Anabaptists, by Nich. Stork, 1522."

Priest Jno. S. Murphy, of St. Patrick's Church, Houston, Texas, answered: "Stork, a short time after Luther proclaimed his heresies."

It seems that the bishop of New Orleans, the Houston priest, and one or two Protestant writers, when they answered, must have had the same Romish, slanderous authority before them. But the Cincinnati archbishop, the Shreveport priest, and other scholars, either knew nothing of that authority, did not remember it, or did not think it reliable. Here comes the spokesman for Cardinal Gibbons, who contradicts the New Orleans bishop and the Houston priest, and, by his attempt to answer, without intending to do so, concedes the impossibility of assigning the origin of Baptist churches to any man or age since the first century. He writes: "Cardinal's residence, Baltimore, Md., Sept. 4, 1893. Your questions are *not possibly* capable of *exact* and *very positive* answers. The Baptist church of the present time *seems* to be the lineal descendant of the old Anabaptists of Reformation times. They have their most *probable* origin in the Mennonites or Dutch Baptists. These arose, as you know, after Martin Luther. The forefathers emigrated into England in the time of Henry the VIII, and of Queen Elizabeth. *However*, the first church known as the Baptist church *seems* to have been built in London in 1606. The year 1547 is *about* the earliest date set by *reliable* historians for the existence of a Baptist denomination. As a sect they can not go back to a more remote date than that. It is not sound history or good reasoning to try to connect them with an earlier sect or heresy; though you may find some *similarity* between their teachings and the teachings of the ancient Waldenses, or sects and controversies *even earlier*."—C. F. Thomas, Chancellor. (My italics.) The reader will notice how Cardinal Gibbons, by using the word "seems" and such phrases as "not possibly capable of an exact and very positive answer," concedes that no man can confidently fix a modern origin and on a modern originator for the Baptist church.

Turning to Protestant scholars, we find the same hesitancy and confusion. Prof. H. C. Sheldon, Methodist, Professor of History in Boston University, evasively wrote me: "A portion of the so-called Anabaptists who *appeared* in Germany in the third and the following decades of the sixteenth century, *might be* called Baptists." (My italics.)

The Professor of Church History in the Gettysburg Lutheran Theological Seminary, wrote me: The "Baptists were originated by '*some* Swiss, about 1523.'" (My italics.)

H. M. Scott, Professor of Church History in the Congregational Theological Seminary, in Chicago, wrote: "It arose in Zwickau, Saxony, A. D. 1520, under the Zwickau prophets, Storch and others."

A. C. Lewis, Professor of Church History in the Presbyterian Theological Seminary, in Chicago, wrote me: "I regret *not being able* to give you the *categorical* answers you seem to anticipate . . . The questions as put *do not admit of short and categorical* answers . . . The first Baptist church was *not formed* or *organized*, but *evolved* out of Anabaptist *antecedents.*" (My italics.)

Professor L. L. Paine, of the Congregational Theological Seminary, of Bangor, Maine, wrote me: "When Luther begun his reformation 'there were so-called Anabaptists. But the Baptist denomination is later. The origin of the English Baptists is very *obscure*. They *appear* in the reign of Elizabeth, persecuted.'" (My italics.)

Professor John Clarke Ridpath, Methodist, of Du Paw University, evasively answered: "The answers of your questions turns upon the definition of the word Baptist . . . There is, therefore, a sense in which we should say that there was a Baptist church in the age of Luther. There is another sense in which we should have to deny the proposition . . . I should not readily admit that there was a Baptist *church* as far back as A. D. 100, though without doubt there were Baptists then, as all Christians were then Baptists."

The President of the Campbellite College, at Bethany, Va., wrote me: "The Baptists *appeared* first in Switzerland." Who founded the first Baptist church that ever existed, *"cannot be determined.* There were no Baptist churches before the beginning of the sixteenth century though immersion was practiced from the beginning." (My italics.)

A. P. Cobb, Pastor of the First Campbellite Church, in Springfield, Ill., wrote me: "Was there a Baptist Church when Luther began his Reformation? *Yes.* In Switzerland, 1523. Large churches fully organized in 1525-30 in South Germany. Who originated the first Baptist church? *I cannot tell."* (My italics.)

The Pastor of the First Campbellite Church, Ann Arbor, Mich., wrote me: "Was there a Baptist Church when Luther began his Reformation? The Baptists *had* large churches fully organized between 1520-30 in Switzerland. They were persecuted by both Zwingli and the Romanists. Who originated the first Baptist Church that ever existed? *I do not know."* (My italics.)

The Professor of Church History in the Campbellite College, at Irvington, Ind., indorsed the following quotation—which he inclosed with his letter—from the *Journal and Messenger*, of Cincinnati: "Baptists believe that the churches founded by the Apostles were essentially Baptist. That they believed and practiced what Baptist churches believe and practice to-day. They also believe that persons holding these essential doctrines were found all along down through the centuries, from the days of the apostles until now. But they do not fix upon any particular time when the first Baptist church of modern times came into existence. They find that such churches existed in Switzerland in the early part of the sixteenth century—the days of Zwingli and Luther. They find that about the same time such churches were to be found in Holland and the Low Countries; and that soon after they were to be found in England. They find that as early as 1640-44 they were existing in various parts of our own country, and that their founders for the most part came from England or Wales. Not to speak of Roger Williams, it is found that Hanserd Knollys founded a little Baptist church in New Hampshire; that a similar church was founded in New Jersey, another in Pennsylvania and others in the Southern States, in the seventeenth century. No one church in this country can be called the mother church of Baptists."

His words are: "As it did not seem possible to answer in the brief space of your card, the reply has been delayed. In the meanwhile the enclosed extract from the *Journal and Messenger* . . . sets forth all the facts in the case, as given in church history."

B. D. Dean, Professor of Church History in Hiram College, wrote me: "Was there a Baptist church when Luther began his Reformation? No, *not under that name*. Baptist churches sprang up *simultaneously in different countries* as the result of the Reformation. I know of no *Baptist* churches calling themselves Baptist churches prior to 1600." (My italics.) Professor Dean, in his letter, indorses the following statement: "In Switzerland, in Germany, in Holland, it has been found *impossible to decide when Baptists first appeared*, or which were the *first* churches of Baptists in those lands . . . and it is *quite* as *diffcult* to decide the question about Baptists in *England*." (My italics.)

Had I asked any of the foregoing scholars: Who was the first President of the United States? When and by whom was the Methodist Church originated? The Presbyterian? The Lutheran? The Campbellite? The Episcopal? In a half dozen words they could have answered. Yet, in answer to when and by whom Baptist churches originated, we see they spend more time refusing to attempt an answer, than would be necessary to tell the name and the date of the origin of Baptist churches if they were of modern and of human origin; or, they evade the question; or, they annihilate each other's answers by their contradictions of each other; or, they admit the impossibility of answering my questions; or, they indirectly, without intending it, concede Baptist churches are neither of human nor of modern origin.

Closing these answers is the following, which I received when I received the others just quoted, from Prof. Walker, Professor of Church History in Harvard University: "As you are probably aware, your questions relate to one of the most disputed points in church history. Whether the Baptist movement can be traced back of the Lutheran Reformation or not, is a question which has been much debated of late . . . Some men of weight in church history, and notably the German scholar, Ludwig Keller, of Munster, would find a continuous relation between the Anabaptists of the Reformation period and individual sects like the Waldenses, and through them a line of free and possibly evangelical churches, back to the early days of the church."

In view of these statements of representative scholars—to which an almost unlimited number can be added—that HISTORY DOES NOT ASSIGN TO BAPTIST CHURCHES A HUMAN FOUNDER AND A POST-APOSTOLIC DATE OF ORIGIN IS SETTLED BEYOND DOUBT.

Turning to other denominations, we see there was nothing with the distinctive marks of the Romish church until many centuries after the first. The blasphemous title of "Universal Bishop" was conferred on Boniface the III, A. D. 606. This was the origin of the Pope and of the Romish church—originated by the Emperor Phocas. In A. D. 756 the Pope became temporal sovereign.[1]

See Smith's Dictionary of Christian Antiquities, vol. 2, p. 1651-1675, for a most scholarly and conclusive demonstration of the post-apostolic origin of Popery; and with it, vol. 1, p. 209, demonstrating the non-apostolic origin of the hierarchy.†

By consulting Bergier's Dogmatics, vol. 1, p. 488; Dollinger's First Age of the Church, pp. 318, 319; Darra's History of the Christian Church, p. 350; Alzog's Universal History, p. 105, it will be seen that Baptists are Scriptural as to baptism while Romanism is an apostacy. Thus, Darra concedes that in the first age of the church, "baptism was conferred by immersion." Dollinger concedes: "Like that of St. John, by immersion

---

† That there was no heirarchy, of any kind, in the apostolic churches, the reader may see by consulting Doddridge, Bloomfield, McKnight, the Bible Commentary, Olshausen, Barnes on I Cor 5:4; II. Cor. 2:6; or Jacobson on Acts 20:17, 18; Tit. 1:5; or Meyer Baumgarten, Olshausen, Doddridge, Hackett on Acts 6:2-5; or Schaff-Herzog Encyclopedia, vol. 1, p. 29٤; Coleman's Apostolic and Primitive Church, Davidson's Ecclessiastical Polity, p. 157; Kurtz's Church History, vol. 1, p. 67; Mosheim's, vol. 1, chap, 2, sec. 8; Schaff's, vol. 1, p. 134; Wadington's, p. 41; Neander's Plant., tr. p. 149; Fisher's, p. 37; Smith's Bible Dictionary, vol. 1, p. 310; Conybeare's and Howson's Life and Epistles of Paul, vol. 1, p. 465; Kitto's Cyclopedia, article Bishop; Ulman's Reformers before the Reformation, vol. 1, p. 124; Thayer's N. T. Lex., p. 536. Nothing is more certain from exegesis, lexicography and history than that the apostolic church was, in its government, Baptist.

[1] Dowling's History of Romanism, p. 55.

of the whole person, which is the only meaning of the New Testament word. A mere pouring or sprinkling was not thought of. St. Paul made this immersion a symbol of burial with Christ, and the emerging a sign of resurrection with Him to a new life."

Dollinger further concedes: "There is no proof or hint in the New Testament that the Apostles baptized infants or ordered them to be baptized. When the baptism of households is spoken of it is left doubtful whether they contained children and whether, if so, they were baptized."[1]

The same thing is true of transubstantiation, confession to priests, of giving only the bread to the laity, of purgatory, of penance, of image worship, of burning candles before the altar, of every distinctive feature of the Romish church. Thus, nothing is more certain than that, instead of the Romish church having the Christian Succession, it has the succession of being spewed out of Christ's mouth.[2] But Dr. Duncan says: "That when Gesenius, the great German Hebraist and Biblical critic, first learned what Baptist churches were, he exclaimed: 'How exactly like the primitive churches.'"[3]

The Lutheran church was originated by Martin Luther, A. D. 1525, in Germany.

The Episcopal, from a Romish church, became the "Episcopal church," A. D. 1534, by Henry the VIII forcing the Romish clergy to proclaim him the "supreme head of the Church of England."

The Presbyterian church was founded especially by Zwingli and John Calvin, A. D. 1516-1530, in Switzerland.

---

[1] First Age of the Church, pp. 318, 319. These are Romish historians.
[2] Rev. 3:15-18.
[3] Hist. Bap., p. 71.

The Methodist church was originated by John Wesley, A. D. 1729, in England.

The Campbellite church was brought into complete existence by Alexander Campbell, A. D. 1829, in the United States of America.

These are but illustrations of the recent and human origin of all non-Catholic churches, except the Baptist.

Except the Episcopal—and that, we have just seen, has not so much as a shadow of claim to be in the Apostolic Church Perpetuity line—only the Baptist church even pretends to be as old as Christianity. We have just demonstrated that *history points to no human or post-apostolic date of origin for Baptist churches.*

In a case a millionaire dies and leaves his estate to a man whom the will mentions as John Wilson, and, as having been born A.D. 1849, and there are, and have been, but four of that name in all the world, three of whom were born after 1849, that only the one born at that date can receive the estate is beyond question. As history agrees that all churches, excepting the Baptist, came into existence after the apostolic church was founded; and, as the apostolic church, by its very purpose of organization, mission and direct promise of the Scriptures, is assured of preservation until the second coming of Christ, that the Baptist is the only one that has the Church Perpetuity is certainly true.

CHAPTER VII.

IN THE PERPETUITY OF BAPTIST PRINCIPLES FROM THE APOSTOLIC AGE TO THE PRESENT IS NECESSARILY THE SAME PERPETUITY OF BAPTIST CHURCHES.

Prof. Albert H. Newman, D. D., December 13, 1893, wrote me: "The probability is that there never was a time when Christians of a decidedly evangelical type, possessing many of the features of the Baptists, and with organizations closely resembling Baptist churches, did not exist. There are times, however, when we can find no record of such churches. We can, I think, say with all confidence that there has been an unbroken succession of evangelical life. Beyond this I do not care to go." And, alluding to my question: "Has there ever been a time since the first century when there was no genuine Baptist church on earth?" Dr. Newman closes this statement in the next sentence: "But I should be very far from making the strong assertion which you suggest."

The *Journal and Messenger*, a leading Baptist paper, of Baptists and their doctrines, says: "They believe that persons holding these essential doctrines are found all along down through the centuries, from the days of the apostles until now."

Dr. Armitage's title page to his history reads: "A history of the *Baptists* traced by *Their Vital Principles* and *Practices* from the time of our Lord and Savior Jesus Christ to the year 1886." (My italics.) This concedes a perpetuity of "*Baptists*" who practiced "Baptist Principles from the time of our Lord and Savior Jesus Christ to the year 1886"—unless language is meaningless. But what are "Baptist Principles" and "Practices," as practiced by "Baptists," but church organization and church work—preaching, observing "the ordinances," administering discipline—church life? What more does this book affirm? To whose book does Dr. Armitage's title page better belong—to his, that denies the truth of his title page, or to mine, which avows it?

J. L. M. Curry, LL. D., in his Introduction to Dr. Armitage's History, well says: "Believers . . . came together into the primitive churches by an elective affinity, an inwrought spiritual aptitude and capacity; and constituted a brotherhood of the baptized, a holy fellowship of the redeemed, a community of regenerated men and women, united to one another by the same animating spirit. A New Testament church, the apostolic model, was a *result*, a *product*, an evolution from antecedent *facts* and *principles*."[1] Dr. Curry says: "Things *will follow tendencies*."[2] (My italics.)

If believers thus came together in apostolic times, into New Testament churches, and "things follow their tendencies," as reasonably affirm that while the "tendency" of the gospel in apostolic times was to make churches, yet, in the dark ages, it was the reverse. Only by imagining ourselves in "Hafed's chance world" can we imagine that the "principles and practices" and their Christ, which produced gospel churches in the first century, have not produced them ever since.

The Campbellite boasts of great faith in the power of the gospel. Yet, to make room for Mr. Campbell's church, he denies that the gospel produced New Testament churches during the dark ages. Who really believes in the power of the gospel—the Baptist who boldly affirms

[1] p. 8.
[2] Idem, p. 11.

that so great is the power of the gospel that from the first to the present century it has perpetuated gospel churches, or the Campbellite who denies this? Talk about Perpetuity of Baptist "principles and practices" or of Baptists without Perpetuity of Baptist churches—without Baptists to observe and propagate them! As well talk about Christian principles and practices perpetuated by Jews, Masonic principles and practices by non-Masons, or life without corresponding form or appearance, as to talk about the Perpetuity of "Baptist principles and practices" without Baptist churches to observe these "practices and principles." Or, as well speak of Masons, Oddfellows, Republicans, Democrats or Romanists continuing without organization, as to speak of Baptists continuing during the dark ages without churches. Or, as the principles and the practices of physicians inevitably imply physicians; of lawyers, lawyers; of engineers, engineers; of Buddhists, Buddhists; of Mohammedans, Mohammedans; of Mormons, Mormons; of Lutherans, Lutherans; of Episcopalians, Episcopalians; of Methodists, Methodists; of Campbellites, Campbellites; of Presbyterians, Presbyterians; so, "the principles and the practices of Baptists from the time of our Lord and Savior Jesus Christ to the year 1886," inevitably demand the existence of Baptist churches during the same period. Consequently, in response to a complimentary copy of Bro. Armitage's Baptist History which the publishers presented me as soon as it was published, soliciting a recommendation, I gave it a recommendation, commending it for "much valuable material and as also a refutation of the erroneous theory of its author," viz.: that there has not been a Perpetuity of Baptist churches with a perpetuity of their "principles and practices."

In the name of all reason and experience, what are people thinking about when they say: "I believe in the Perpetuity of Baptist principles and practices from the apostolic age to the present, but I am not so certain as to the same Perpetuity of Baptist churches!" Pray, do stop and answer the question: Whom do we now find believing and practicing the Baptist principles but Baptists?— Baptist churches? "Baptist principles and practices" being preaching, baptizing, observing the Lord's Supper and administering church discipline, they cannot be observed save in Baptist church *organization*. The moment they are done by individuals who are not in scriptural churches, by thus denying the necessity of Baptist churches, they cease to be "*Baptist*," thereby becoming subversive of New Testament church order. I therefore conclude this chapter by saying: "The principles and the practices of Baptists" being conceded to have existed—a belief of all true Baptists who are scholars—during the past 1800 years, all the demands of the bottomless pit cannot shake my faith in the truth that there has been the same Perpetuity of Baptist churches.

CHAPTER VIII.

The Montanists.

In historic times Phrygia comprised the greater part of Asia Minor. "Montanism" appeared there about the middle of the second century.

Montanism enrolled its hosts and was one of the greatest Christian influences throughout the early Christian centuries. As there was at the time, when Montanism arose, no essential departure from the faith in the action, the subjects of Baptism, church government or doctrine, the Montanists, on these points, were Baptists.

Of the Montanists, Armitage says: "Tertullian and the Montanists denied that baptism was the *channel* of grace." [1]

Kurtz says: "Its leading characteristics were a new order of ecstatic prophets, with somnambulistic visions and new relations; a grossly literal interpretation of scriptural predictions; a fanatical millenarianism; a self-confident ascetecism; an excessive rigor in ecclesiastical discipline. Thus, without dissenting from the doctrinal statements of the church, Montanism sought to reform its practice. In opposition to the false universalism of the Gnostics, the Montanists insisted that Christianity alone, and not heathenism, contained the truth." [2]

Schaff says: "Montanism was not originally a departure from the faith, but a morbid overestimating of the practical morality of the early church." [3]

---

[1] Armitage's Hist. of the Bap., p. 177.
[2] Kurtz's Ch. Hist., vol. 1, p. 131.
[3] Schaff's Hist. Chr. Ch., vol. 1, p. 302.

Kurtz further says: "Still their moral earnestness and zeal against wordliness and heirarchism and false spiritualism rendered important service to the church, both in the way of admonition and warning." [1]

Wadington concedes: "Another cause of the temporary fame of the Montanists was the severity of the *morality* inculcated by them." [2]

Dorner says of the Montanists: "This is a form of vigor and *widely* influential significance. In it the *original* Christian feeling, the Christian people, the *democratic* basis of the church predominated against the gnostic and against the hierarchal element." Against "Gnostocism, Montanism was the *shyest* and *most self-sufficient*." [3] Gnostocism was, at that time, the great and dangerous enemy of true Christianity.

Another well-known historian says: "Among those hostile to the Alexandrian school, is to be numbered Montanus. His aim evidently was to maintain or to restore the scriptural simplicity, nature and character of the religion of the New Testament with a constant reliance on the promise of the Holy Spirit." Guericke's crediting the statement, that the Montanists did not believe in any visible church, is refuted by Tertullian's statements on baptism and by their well-known character. It is discredited by Schaff and other historians. [4] Thus Schaff says of the Montanists: "Infant baptism only it seems to have rejected."†

---

† Let this refute the statement of Augustine and Palagius, so often quoted, that infant baptism was universal in the early churches.
[1] Idem, p. 131.
[2] Wadington's Ch. Hist., p. 78.
[3] Dorner's Person of Christ, vol. 1, p. 256.
[4] See Schaff's Hist. Chr. Ch. vol. 1, pp. 364, 365; Armitage's Bap. Hist. p. 176.

THE MONTANISTS. 71

Guericke concedes that "they received the general truths of Christianity, as understood by the universal church." [1]

Admit that the Montanists did have women teachers among them, and that some of them practiced trine immersion, since the position of women in the New Testament Church is a disputed point, and since both it and trine immersion are only an irregularity, neither of which is as bad as open communion, feet washing and non-cooperation in missions, they cannot invalidate those churches as New Testament churches. [Here read in Chapter IV of this book.] Their millenarian views, while they may have been extravagant, could but class them with the church of Thessalonica. [2]

Schaff charges the Montanists with believing in the celibacy of the clergy. But he admits they had no law or rule that forbade the marriage of ministers; and then concedes there are two sides to even the charge of discouraging their marriage. The explanation probably is: as owing to the persecutions of the Christians, Paul, in his letter to the Corinthians, rather favored celibacy as a temporary thing, so did the Montanists as to their ministers.

The charge of believing in the continuance of inspiration, of ecstacies, inward experiences and that their leader claimed to be the Holy Spirit, are much what Campbellites charge against the Baptists of our age.

Mosheim took up these charges and credited Montanus, their great leader, with calling himself the Comforter. But his translator, in a foot note, corrects him and says: "Those are *undoubtedly mistaken* who have asserted that Montanus gave himself out that he was

[1] Guericke's Ch. Hist., vol. 1, pp. 191-93.
[2] See II. Thess. 2:2, 3.

the Holy Ghost."[1] Hase says of Tertullian, one of the great Montanist leaders: "He placed a high estimate upon that consciousness of God, which he contended might be found in the depths of every soul, but he was fond of contrasting with proud irony the foolishness of the gospel with the wordly wisdom of his contemporaries, and the incredibility of the divine miracles with ordinary understanding of the world. His writings are partly controversial . . . and partly devotional. They are, however, so written that the devotional element constantly appears in the former, and the polemic in the latter, in behalf of strict morality and discipline."[2] Hase says of Tertullian's writings: "The Montanistic spirit is perceptible in them all, but in the earliest of them it holds up the simple, noble nature of Christian morality in opposition merely to an effeminate form of civilization, gradually it proceeds to severer demands, and shows an increasing consciousness of its pneumatic nature in opposition to those who were merely physical Christians; and, finally it was especially hostile to the Romish Church, in proportion as the latter ceased to favor Montanism. For it was not so much Tertullian as the Roman bishop who changed his views with reference to that system . . . Tertullian, to whom the Paraclete was rather a restorer of apostolic order than an innovator, and religious ecstacy was rather a theory than a principle, became so prominent that he was looked upon as the model for Latin theology. This theology was rather disinclined to philosophical theories respecting divine things; it spoke of Athens and the Academy as irreconcilable with Jerusalem and the church and turned its

---

[1] McLean's Note, p. 188, vol. 1, of Mosheim's Ch. Hist.
[2] Hase's Hist. Chr. Ch., p. 88.

whole attention to questions respecting the condition of the church, and things essential to salvation."¹

Of Tertullian, Möller says: "To him the very substance of the church was the Holy Spirit and by no means the Episcopacy whose right to wield the power of the keys he rejected." ² Thus, in Church Government they were Baptists. In the following, we have this yet more explained: Says Neander: "Montanism set up a church of the Spirit, consisting of *spirateles homines* in opposition to the prevailing outward view of that institution. Tertullian says: 'The church, in the proper and prominent sense, is the Holy Spirit in which the Three are One,— and next, the whole community of those who are agreed in this faith (that God, the Father, the Son, and the Holy Ghost are One,) is called after its founder and consecrator, (the Holy Spirit,) the church.† The Catholic point of view, expresses itself in this—viz., that the idea of the church is put first, and by this very position of it, made outward; next, the agency of the Holy Spirit is represented as conditioned by it, and hence derived through this mediation. Montanism, on the other hand, like Protestantism, places the Holy Spirit first, and considers the Holy Spirit first, and considers the church as that which is only derived* . . . The gifts of the Spirit were to be dispensed to Christians of every condition and sex, without distinction . . . They were thus led to give prominence once more to the idea of the dignity of the universal Christian calling, of the priestly

---

* Christian reader; decide which of these, in the light of the Bible, is the true church!

† Nam et ecclesia proprie et principaliter ipse est Spiritis, in quo est trinitas unius divinitatis. Illam ecclesiam congregat, quam Dominus in tribus posuit, (where two or three are gathered together in his name) atque ita exinde etiam numerus, qui in hanc fidem conspiraverint ecclisæ ab auctore et conscratore consetur. L. c.

1 P. 701.
2 Schaff-Herzog Ency., vol. 2, p. 1562.

dignity of all Christians, which had been in a measure suppressed."¹

Tertullian defines the ecstatic condition thus: "In spiritu homo constitutus, praesertim cum gloriam Dei conspicit, vel cum per ipsum Deus loquitor, necesse est excidat sensu, obumbratus scilicet virtute divina"— probably meaning only what David meant, when he said: "my cup runneth over;" or, as the poet, in describing the ecstacy of the young convert—"on the wings of a dove I was carried above."

Admiting the Montanists did run to the extreme as to visions and prophecies does not affect the validity of their churches, for Neander, describing the visions of one of their prophets, says: "The matter of her visions *corresponded* to what she had just heard read out of the Holy Scriptures, what was said in the Psalms that had been sung, the prayers that had been offered;" there are things, in our best churches, more harmful than that extreme.††

Gieseler admits that "the Montanists had not an uninterrupted series of prophets."² Thus, whatever was this extreme, it was not permanent or continuous.

Armitage: "The one prime idea held by the Montanists in common with Baptists, and in distinction to the churches of the third century was, that the membership of the churches should be confined to purely regenerate persons; and that a spiritual life and discipline should be maintained without any affiliation with the authority of the State. Exterior church organization and the efficacy

---

†† Tertullian thus narrates this: "Jam vero prouet scripturæ leguntur, aut Psalmi canuntur, aut allocutiones proferuntur, aut petitiones delegantur, ita inde materiæ visionibus subministrantur." Translated: But truly according as the Scriptures are read, or Psalms are sung, or addresses are delivered, or prayers are offered, thence, from that medium are materials by which we are assisted by visions.

1 Neander's Hist. Chr. Ch., vol. 1, pp. 518, 519.
2 Gieseler's Eccl. Hist., vol. 1, p. 141.

of the ordinances did not meet their idea of Gospel church existence without the indwelling Spirit of Christ, not in the bishops alone, but in all Christians. For this reason Montanus was charged with assuming to be the Holy Spirit, which was simply a slander."[1] Yet, from superficial examination, Armitage gives too much importance to the charge of "visions" and "revelations" against them.

The sum of these answers I give in the words of one of the highest authorities in church history:

Says Wm. R. Williams, D. D.: "The Comte de Champagny, who has written, though an ultramontane Catholic, so eloquently and eruditely on the early history of Christianity and the collision of it with Judaism on the one side and Paganism on the other side, has said of the Montanists, that it was hard to find any doctrinal errors in their views; that they were rather like Jansenists or Methodists in their high views of religious *emotion and experience*. They were accused of claiming inspiration, when they intended, probably only, like the early followers of Cameron among the Covenanters, or Wesley among the English Methodists, the *true experience of* God's work in the individual soul."[2]

Again, says Dr. Williams, of the Montanists: "They insisted much upon the *power of the Spirit*, as the great conservator and guardian of the life of the Christian church. Now, as far back as the days of Montanism, this was offensive to Christian churches, which became, under the power of wealth and fashion, secularized and corrupted."[3]

[1] Hist. Bap., p. 175.
[2] Williams' Lect. Bap. Hist., p. 129.
[3] Idem, pp. 118, 129.

Says Dr. Dorner: "Montanism may be styled a democratic reaction on the part of the members of the church, asserting their universal prophetic and priestly rank against the concentration of ecclesiastical dignities and rights in the episcopate." "In this aspect, Montanism was a reaction of the substantial, real principle against the formal unity of the episcopate, which entrusted to the unworthy, and those who were destitute of the **Spirit**, power over those who were filled with the Spirit."[1]

Again, says Dorner: "If now Montanism implicitly reproached the church with hitherto possessing too little of the Holy Ghost, it is evident that, dogmatically viewed, the charge implies, that however much the church might have spoken concerning the Son, or the Logos, and the Father, the doctrine of the **Holy Spirit** had been hitherto kept in the back-ground."[2]

The central power of Montanism was "$\rho\tilde{\eta}\mu\alpha$ $\varepsilon\tilde{\iota}\mu\iota$ $\kappa\alpha\tilde{\iota}$ $\pi\nu\varepsilon\tilde{\upsilon}\mu\alpha$ $\kappa\alpha\iota$ $\delta\acute{\upsilon}\nu\alpha\mu\iota\varsigma$" — I am word and spirit and power, which it represented as its conception of the Holy Spirit in His relation to the church. The character of the Montanists and their being the original church is thus clear.

Möller says: "But Montanism was, nevertheless, *not a new form of Christianity;* nor were the Montanists a *new sect.* On the *contrary*, Montanism was simply a reaction of the *old*, the *primitive church*, against the obvious tendency of the day, to strike a bargain with the world and arrange herself comfortably in it."[3]

That the Montanist churches were Baptist churches is the only legitimate conclusion from their comparison with the facts in this chapter. (My italics in this chapter.)

---

[1] Dorner's Per. of Christ, vol. 1, p. 363.
[2] Idem, p. 398.
[3] Schaff Herzog Ency., vol. 2, p. 1562.

CHAPTER IX.

THE NOVATIANS.

Says W. W. Everts, Jr.: "A century later than Montanus, 250 A. D., there was converted at Rome, on what seemed his dying bed, and amid severe conflicts, a distinguished Pagan philosopher, named Novatian. The genuineness of this conversion was attested, not only by his learned treatises—which, in Neander's estimation, rank him as the most distinguished of the early theologians of Rome—but, by his life of stern self-denial and his death by martyrdom. He renewed the moral protest of Montanus."[1]

The Novatians extended throughout "the Roman Empire, from Armenia to Numedia, in Spain. They were especially strong in Phrygeia, where the Montanists fused with them, and in the great cities, Constantinople, Alexandria, Carthage and Rome."[2]

"The occasion of the schism was the election of Cornelius bishop of Rome. Novatian was elected by a minority who objected to the lax discipline favored by Cornelius."[2]

Scriptural church discipline, consecrated church membership and church purity, being the issues between Cornelius and Novatian, in their candidacy for the pastorate of the church of Rome, the election of Cornelius was equivalent to a repudiation, by the majority of that church, of these marks of a scriptural Church. There

[1] Baptist Layman's Book, p. 17.
[2] Idem, p. 17.

being no other course left, the scriptural minority of that church, led by Novatian, withdrew fellowship from the unscriptural majority. In Baptist church life this has often since been done. Baptist councils and civil courts, whenever they have been called upon to decide which is the original church, have invariably decided it is that party which stands upon the original platform.†

The charge that the division was caused by Novatian's ambition and jealousy is the attempt of Cornelius to shield himself and his apostate party. (1.) From the great issue which historians agree to have divided them, the charge is evidently false. (2.) Historians exonerate Novatian and his people from this charge. Instead of jealousy being the ground on which Novatian and his people withdrew fellowship from Cornelius and his party the biographer of Socrates, the church historian of the fourth century, who did not belong to the Novatians, says: "Socrates takes no notice whatever of the declaration of Cornelius, that Novatian separated from ecclesiastical communion through jealousy, because he had not been elected bishop; that he managed to get himself elected by three prelates. whose reason had been clouded by the fumes of wine, and that pardon granted to those who sacrificed to idols during the persecution excited by Decius against the church was but a pretext for his schism."[1]

Says Schaff: "Novatian against his will was chosen bishop by the opposition."[2]

Of Cornelius' letter, whence these charges against Novatian are mainly gathered, Neander says: "Not less wanting in *good sense than unworthy of a Christian.*"[3]

---

†The action of Baptist councils, in all cases, is but advisory. That of civil courts only to protect the original body in its property rights.
[1] p, 9, 10, of the Life of Socrates, in Socrates' Eccl. Hist.
[2] Schaff's Hist. Chr. Ch., vol. 1, p. 450.
[3] Neander's Hist. Chr. Ch., vol, 1, p. 238, 239.

Neander says: "According to the accusation of this passionate opponent we must, indeed, suppose at the outset he was striving, from motives of ambition, after the episcopal dignity, and was thence trying to throw himself at the head of a party. . . . We have the less reasons to doubt that it was his zeal for the more rigid principles which inspired Novatian from the first, because they accorded so perfectly with his character. The accusations of his opponents should not be suffered to embarrass us; for it is the usual way with the logical polemics to trace schisms and heresies to some untoward, unhallowed motive, even when there is no evidence at all that any such motive exists. Novatian had on some occasion solemnly declared, after the Roman bishopric was vacated by the death of Fabian, that he would not be a candidate for the Episcopal dignity—an office to which, perhaps, on account of the high respect entertained for him by a large portion of the community he might easily have attained. But he said he had no longing for that office. We have no reason, with Bishop Cornelius, to accuse Novatian in this case with falsehood. He could say this with perfect sincerity; he, the quiet, loving ascetic, the theologian, glad to be left undisturbed to his dogmatic speculations, surely had no wish to burden himself with an office so overwhelmed with cares as that of a Roman bishop had already become. . . . Novatian was only contending for what he conceived to be the purity of the church and against the decline of discipline, without wishing or seeking for anything beside. Settled in his own convictions, zealous in the defence of them, but averse, by natural disposition, to everything that savored of boisterous, outward activity, he was, *against his own will*, made the head of a party by those who agreed with him in *principles*, and compelled by them to assume the episcopal dignity. In this regard he could say with truth, in his letter to Dionysius, Bishop of Alexandria, *that he had been carried on against his will.**[1]*"

To the charge that Novatian never was immersed,† the reply is (1.) His pouring was intended to be so profuse as to cover him in his sick bed—to be an immersion. "Baptizo" signifies that its object shall be covered and has nothing to do with *how* that covering is effected. While there may be a debatable question as to whether they really got Novatian covered with water, the *intent* being immersion as near as possible is clear from the Greek record.‡ (2.) Considering that immersion was the universally recognized law and custom at that time, as he recovered, if they did not get him covered in baptism at first, there is reason to believe that on his recovery he was baptized. Vales states that clinics, when they recovered, were required to go to the bishop to supply what was wanting in that baptism.[2]

That Novatian did not so do may be only another slander against him. Considering the extent to which he was slandered, to believe that on his recovery he was baptized, is much easier than to believe that, against the ruie,

---

* His own words are: [Ότιάκωνηχθη]

† Eusebius thus quotes Cornelius' slanderous letter, in which Novatian's baptism is mentioned: "Who aided by the exorcists, when attacked with an obstinate disease, and being supposed at the point of death, was baptized by aspersion, in the bed in which he lay; if, indeed, it be proper to say that one like him did receive baptism."—Eusebius' Eccl. Hist., b. 6, chap. 43.

‡ περιχυθεις, by which Novatian's baptism is mentioned, is from περι which means "around, about," and from χεω, to "pour, flow, stream." *Perikutheis*, therefore, should be here rendered, "poured around," with the idea of *intended covering over*, as when, on a dam giving way, the waters overflow and bury all before them—baptizing by pouring. Thus Liddell and Scott define *perikrino*, "to plaster over;" *perikusos*, "covered with gold;" *perikusis*, "a pouring round, or over;" *perikuteerion*, "a vessel for pouring over;" *pericuteerios*, "pouring round about or over, bathing;" *perikonnumi*, "to heap around with earth." These uses of *peri* with *keo* and its family, clearly show that Novatian's pouring was intended to cover him, as near as could be done. Had it been the intention to only pour *on* him, as affusion for baptism does, Cornelius would certainly have used the word *epikutheis* instead of *perikutheis*. See Liddell and Scott's Lexicon on *epikeo, epikusis*, etc.

1 Neander's Hist. Chr. Ch., vol. 1, pp. 239, 241.
2 Armitage, p. 178.

the custom and the Scriptures, which were for only immersion, he was content with his clinic baptism and *that so many hundreds of ministers and churches followed his leadership when he was unbaptized*, and that, too, *without protesting against his imperfect baptism.* (3.) Admit all that Baptists opponents claim, viz.: that he never was, in any way, immersed, as the Novatians were not founded by him and did not get their baptism from him, all it proves is, that one Baptist minister, among hundreds, from a failure in the *attempt* to cover him with water, was never baptized. But, as Novatian baptized by the authority of immersionist churches, his baptisms were all valid, though the churches were censurable for allowing him to baptize while himself imperfectly baptized. Should it, then, be conceded to Baptist opponents that Novatian was imperfectedly baptized, it proves but a censurable irregularity, in but one case, in no way invalidating any church claim

As to Novatian and his people believing in baptismal regeneration, the charge rests on Cornelius' slanderous account of his baptism. In fact, Cornelius does not say Novatian was baptized to save his soul. He says he was baptized on what was, at the time of his baptism, thought to be his death bed. Death bed baptisms are as reliable as death bed conversions. The Novatian high conception of spiritual life and the consequent battle of the Novatians for a spiritual church are utterly incompatible with the charge that Novatian and his people believed in water salvation. No party has ever contended for a scripturally regenerate church while holding to baptismal regeneration.

Hippolytus has been quoted as a Novatian and as proving the Novatians believed in baptismal salvation.

But Armitage says [1]Hippolytus "is supposed to have suffered martyrdom by drowning in the Tiber, A. D. 235-239." Hase[2] says: "Hippolytus could hardly have lived to witness the Novatian schism."

The Novatian church government was substantially that of Baptists of our own time. Bishop—*episcopos*—then meant what it meant in the first churches and what it now means with Baptists—a pastor, superintending the church of which he was pastor. Prelatical bishops in the Novatian age were just sprouting—not sufficiently adopted to be a characteristic of any large body of Christians. That the bishop of Rome was not a prelatical bishop is evident from the fact that Novatian was a bishop by an ordination, which gave to him no prelatical charge. Says Cornelius: "When he was converted he was honored by the presbytery, and that by the power of the bishop [the pastor] placing his hand upon him [according him] to the order of bishops."[3] Having by this no charge he became a candidate for pastor of the church of Rome. Of this age, Mosheim says: "But it is to be carefully observed, that even those who, with Cyprian, attributed this pre-eminence to the Roman prelate, insisted at the same time, with the utmost warmth, upon the *equality*, in point of *dignity and authority*, that subsisted among *all* the members of the episcopal order. In consequence of this opinion of an equality among all Christian bishops, they rejected, with contempt, the judgment of the bishop of Rome, when they found it ill-founded or unjust, and followed their own sense of things with a perfect independence."[4]

---

[1] Armitage's Hist. Bap., p. 184.
[2] Hase's Hist. Chr. Ch., p. 700.
[3] Eusebius' Eccl. Hist., p. 5, ch. 43.
[4] Mosheim's Church History, cent. 3, part 2, sec. 2.

To the charge that the Novatians would never restore to church membership one who had been excluded for a gross offence, even on his repentance: Admitting this true, it only proves an error of discipline, not so bad as when easily proved guilty, to retain such—a thing often now done, and even done in Baptist churches.

To the charge that the Novatians held there was no forgiveness from God for such, the answer is, (*a*) They taught no such thing. (*b*) Even if they did teach it, it is no worse than, by retaining them in the church, to teach they are on the road to heaven.

Says Adolf Harnack, one of the most eminent and critical historians: "Down to 220, idolatry, adultery, fornication and murder, were punished in the Catholic church by formal excommunication. . . . This practice was first broken by the peculiar power which was ascribed to the confessors, in accordance with an archaic idea which lived in the end of the third century, and then by an edict of Pope Calixtus I., which spoke of re-admittance into the church as a possibility. The edict caused the schism of Hippolytus; but as the schism was healed towards the middle of the third century, it seems probable that the successors of Calixtus returned to the old, more rigorous practice. At all events, it must be observed that the new and milder views were applied only to the sins of the flesh. As none, who in the peaceful period, between 220 and 250, relapsed into Paganism, was likely to ask for re-admittance into the Christian church, idolatry was left entirely out of the consideration. But with the outbreak of the Decian persecution a great change took place. The number of the lapsed became so great that the very existence of the congregation was endangered. . . . Novatian was not from principle opposed to the re-admittance of the lapsed. . . . It is simply a stubbornly repeated calumny that Novatian or his party ever declared penitence to be of no use. . . . Cyprian's argument was, that since salvation could be obtained only through the church, every one who was definitely severed from her must forever perish. Consequently, to refuse communion of the church to one who had definitely separated himself from the church, would be an anticipation of the judgment of God; while the re-admittance of a lapsus could in no wise prevent God from refusing him salvation. On the other side, when Novatian considered it the right and duty of the church to exclude forever all heavy sinners, and denied her power to give absolution to the idolater, it is apparent that his idea of the church, of the right of the priest, in short, his idea of the power of the keys is another than that held by his adversaries. The church is to him not the 'conditio sine qua non,' for salvation is an institution educating mankind for salvation, but the congregation of saints, whose very existence is endangered if there is one single heavy sinner among its members. To him the constitution of the church, the distinction between laity and clergy, the connection with the clergy, are questions of secondary importance. The one question of primary importance is to be a saint in the communion of saints. It is unquestionable that the Novatians retained many most valuable remnants of old traditions, and their idea of the church as a communion of the saints corresponds exactly to the idea prevalent in the first days of christendom."[1]

Socrates says that Novatian exhorted those who were excluded from the church for the gross offence of being traitors to the faith, "to repentance, leaving the pardon-

[1] Schaff-Herzog Ency., vol 2, pp. 1670, 1671.

ing of their offence to God, who has the power to forgive all sin." [1]

Neander says: "Novatian, too, declared the fallen brethren must be cared for and exhorted to repentance. He, too, acknowledged God's mercy toward sinners, and allowed it right to recommend the fallen to that mercy; but that men could once more surely announce to them that forgiveness of sins they had trifled away, this he was unwilling to concede, because he could find no objective ground for such confidence." [2]

Of course, Baptists know how to regard Harnack's succeeding statement, that such discipline was "an open injustice," and that "the idea of the church as a community of saints could not fail to end in either miserable delusions, or in bursting asunder the whole existing Christendom."

Says Hase: "Novatian was a *prudent* advocate of the faith generally embraced in the church. . . . The Novatians excluded from the church all who had been guilty of deadly sins † and taught, that while such should be exhorted to repentance and hope of divine mercy, no prospect should be held out to them that they should ever be re-admitted to a church* which should consist of saints and purified persons (καθαροί)" [3]

Much of the trouble was to avoid persecution. Thousands of unregenerate church members in time of persecution denied Christ; then, when persecution was over, to get back into the church, would come up with a

---

† A duty that Paul, in I. Cor., 5:1-5, makes obligatory on churches in all ages.

* By II. Cor., 2:6-10, this an error. But not as disastrous to the life of the church as disregard to I Cor, 5:5,— a sin in our churches now. The extreme corruption and aggravation of offenders in Novatian's time may be some excuse for this severity.

[1] Socrates' Eccl. Hist., p. 248.
[2] Neander's Hist. Chr. Ch., vol. 1, p. 246.
[3] Hase's Hist. Chr. Ch., p. 67.

whining confession. Thus the church was greatly scandalized, as this led on to greater disregard of church obligations. Hence, says Socrates: "Those who took pleasure in sin, encouraged by the *license* thus granted them, took occasion from it to revel in *every species of criminality.*"[1]

Robinson says: "The case is briefly this: Novatian was an elder in the Church of Rome. He was a man of extensive learning, and held the same doctrine[†] as the church did, and published several treatise in defence of what he believed. His address was eloquent and insinuating, and his morals were irreproachable. He saw with extreme pain the intolerable depravity of the church, Christians within the space of a very few years were caressed by one emperor and persecuted by another. In seasons of prosperity many rushed into the church for base purposes. In times of adversity they denied the faith and ran back to idolatry again. When the squall was over, away they came again to the church, with all their vices, to deprave others by their example. The bishops, fond of proselytes, encouraged all this, and transferred the attention of Christians from the old confederacy for virtue, to vain shows at Easter, and a thousand other Jewish ceremonies, adulterated, too, with paganism. On the death of Bishop Fabian, Cornelius, a brother elder, and a vehement partisan for taking in the multitude, was put in nomination. Novatian opposed him; but as Cornelius carried his election and he saw no prospect of reformation, but, on the contrary, a tide of immorality

---

[†]The Scriptures include all the Christian belief and practice as doctrine. But, since the latter part of the eighteenth century, ' the history of dogmas and dogmatics has been raised, in Germany, to the rank of a distinctive branch of sacred science." Hence, in church history, the word doctrine often or generally means only dogmatics—having no allusion to church government, ceremonies or discipline.—See Schaff-Herzog Ency., vol. 1, p. 650; Aldens' Univ. K., vol. 5, p. 341. Thus the term is used in stating that the various names agreed in "doctrine" with the Romish church.

[1] Socrates' Eccl. Hist., b. 4, ch. 28, p. 248.

pouring into the church, he withdrew and a great many with him. . . . Great numbers followed his example, and *all over the empire* Puritan churches were constituted, and flourished through the succeeding two hundred years. Afterward, when penal laws obliged them to lurk in corners and in private, they were distinguished by a variety of names *and a succession of them continued until the Reformation.*"[1]

Neander says: "The controversy with the Novatians turned upon two general points; one relating to the principles of penitence, the other to the question, what constitutes the idea and essence of a true church? In respect to the first point of dispute, Novatian had been often unjustly accused of maintaining that no person, having once violated his baptismal vows, can ever obtain the forgiveness of sin. . . . But, first, Novatian by no means maintained that a Christian is a perfect saint. . . . Novatian, too, declared that the fallen brethren must be cared for and exhorted to repentance. He, too, acknowledged God's mercy toward sinners, and allowed it right to commend the fallen to that mercy; but that men could once more *surely* announce to them that forgiveness of sins which they had trifled away; this he was unwilling to concede because he could find no objective ground for such confidence. With regard to the second main point in the controversy, the idea of the church, Novatian maintained that one of the essential marks of a true church being purity and holiness, every church which neglected the right exercise of church discipline, tolerated in its bosom, or readmitted to its communion such persons as, by gross sins, have broken their baptismal vow, ceased by that very act to be a true Christian church, and forfeited all rights and

[1] Robinson's Eccl. Researches, p. 126.

privileges of such a church. . . . Novatian . . . laid at the basis of his theory the visible church as a pure and holy one, and this was, in his view, the condition of the truly catholic church."[1]

Without adding other testimonies, suffice it to conclude this chapter with J. M. Cramp, D. D., whom Dr. Armitage pronounces, "A sound theologian and thoroughly versed in ecclesiastical history."[2] "We may safely infer that they abstained from compliance with the innovation, and that the Novatian churches were what are now called *Baptist churches*, adhering to the apostolic and primitive practice."[3]

The biographer of Socrates says: "The Novatian church was not only sounder in doctrine, but at the same time abounded with the most eminent clergy."[4]

(All italics in this chapter mine.)

[1] Neander's Hist. Chr. Ch., vol. 1, pp. 243, 246, 247.
[2] Armitage's Hist. Bap., p. 926.
[3] Cramp's Hist. of Bap., p. 59.
[4] Intro. to Socrates' Eccl. Hist., p. 7.

CHAPTER X.

THE DONATISTS.

"The Donatists agitation arose in north Africa, A. D. 311, in what are now known as the Barbary States; but it centered in Carthage, Numidia, and the Mauritanias. Its field covered nearly seven degrees of north latitude, immense centers of commerce and influence, soils and climate, marking a stretch of land 2000 miles long by about 300 wide, reaching from Egypt to the Atlantic and fringing the Atlas mountains, the Mediterranean and the desert . . . Mensurius, Bishop of Carthage, manfully opposed the mania which led thousands to court martyrdom in order to take the martyr's crown; because he thought it savored more of suicide than of enforced sacrifice for Christ. But he died in 311, and Cæcilianus, who was of the same opinion, was ordained in his place, with which election a majority were dissatisfied. Others were displeased because he had been ordained by Felix, who was charged with giving up the Bible to be burnt, and a division took place in the church. The retiring party first elected Majorinus, their bishop, who soon died, and after him Donatus, of Casæ Nigræ. This party was greatly increased and was read out of the Catholic body, Constantine taking sides against them."[1] On this account it is well to remember that the giving up of the Bible to be "burnt," in connection with the well known fact, that many readily denied Christ otherwise, throws much light upon the story of the Donatist party courting martyrdom. It furnishes the strong pre-

[1] Armitage's Bap. Hist. pp. 200, 201.

sumption that these cowardly and wealthy Christ deniers branded the true soldiers of the cross as hunting for an opportunity to die for Christ's sake. But, admitting that the enemies of Donatists have not overdrawn the matter, instead of essentially affecting their character as churches, it only shows that they had been persecuted until they morbidly courted the privilege of testifying for Christ by their deaths—an error far less serious than the compromising spirit of our own times by which Christ is so often denied. To attribute the split between the Donatists and their enemies to election of Felix as pastor, or the Novatian split to the election of Cornelius, would be as ridiculous as to attribute the American Revolution of 1776, to a little tea. All the revolutions were only the outburst of a storm, originating from great and intolerable wrongs. It was a protest of the pious part of the church against the impious; the necessary result of loyalty to the doctrine of a regenerate church membership. Says Kurtz: "*Like* the Novatians, they insisted on absolute purity in the church, although they allowed that penitents might be readmitted into their communion. Their own churches they regarded pure while they denounced the Catholics as *schismatics*, who had no fellowship with Christ, and whose sacraments were therefore invalid. On this ground they rebaptized their proselytes." [1]

Mosheim: "The doctrine of the Donatists was comformable to that of the church, as even their adversaries confess, nor were their lives less exemplary than that of other Christian societies, if we accept the enormous conduct of the Circumcelliones which the greater part of the sect regarded with the utmost detestation and abhorrence. The crime, therefore, of the Donatists lay properly in the following things: In their declaring the church of Africa,

[1] Kurtz' Ch. Hist. vol. 1; p. 246.

which adhered to Cæcilianus fallen from the dignity and privileges of a true church and deprived of the gifts of the Holy Ghost, on account of the offenses with which the new bishop and Felix of Aptungus, who had consecrated him, were charged; in their pronouncing all the churches which held communion with that of Africa, corrupt and polluted; in maintaining that the sanctity of their bishops gave their community *alone* the full right to be considered as the true, and pure, the holy church; and in their avoiding *all communication* with other churches from an apprehension of contracting their impurity and corruption. This erroneous principle was the source of that most shocking uncharitableness and presumption that appeared in their conduct to other churches. Hence they pronounced the sacred rites and institutions void of all virtue and efficiency among those Christians who were not precisely of *their* sentiments and not only rebaptized those who came over to their party from other churches, but even with respect to those who had been ordained ministers of the gospel, observed the severe custom either of depriving them of their office, or obliging them to be ordained the *second* time." [1]

Who can not see in this the picture of the Baptists of our own times and see the denunciation of Mosheim the very words of present Baptist opponents?

With Kurtz, Mosheim thus exonerates the Donatists of the violence of the Circumcelliones: "It *cannot* be made to appear from any records of undoubted authority that the bishops of that faction, those at least who had any reputation for piety and virtue, either approved the proceedings, or stirred up the violence of this odious rabble." [2]

[1] Mosheim's Hist., part 2, ch. 5, sec. 8.
[2] Idem, part 2, ch. 5.

" 'You,' said the Donatists, 'do *not prove* your charges against us, relative to the Circumcelliones.' 'Neither,' said Augustine, 'do you prove your charge against the church' "—thus admitting the charge not proven. "Strange as it may appear, neither in Mosheim nor Milner, nor any other writer who has made some lame apologies for this reputed confederacy, do we find any mention of the important fact that the *whole body* of the Donatists, both their bishops and their laity, disclaimed any knowledge of such a race of men as the Circumcelliones, or any concern with them." [1]

• While this violence was, perhaps, unjustifiable, yet it is a question as to whether, had we as full a history of that event as of the peasants' war of Munster, it would not, as in their case, show that they were far more right than wrong—that like them, they were goaded to desperation by the combined wrongs of corrupt and oppressive politico-ecclesiastical governments. Be this, however, as it may, history clears the Donatists of the doings of the Circumcelliones.

Schaff concedes: "*Like* the Montanists and Novatianists they insisted on *rigorous church discipline* and demanded the excommunication of all unworthy members." [2]

Chambers' Universal Knowledge: "The Donatists, *like* the followers of Novatian, went upon the principle that the essence of the true church consisted in *purity* and *holiness* of all its members individually, and not merely in the apostolic foundation and doctrine."[3]

Neander says the Donatist principle was: "That every church which tolerated unworthy members in its

---

[1] Benedict's Hist. Donatists, p. 148, 149.
[2] Schaff's Hist. Ch., vol. 1, p. 366.
[3] Vol. 4, p. 367.

bosom was itself *polluted* by the communion with them. It thus ceased to deserve the predicates of *purity* and *holiness*, and consequently ceased to be a true Christian church, since a church could not subsist without these predicates." . . . "The Donatists maintained that the church should cast out from its body those who were *known by open and manifest sins* to be unworthy members."[1]

Neander farther says: "According to the Catholic point of view, to the essence of the genuine Catholic church belonged its general spread through the medium of *episcopal* succession down from the Apostles. From the conception of the Catholic church in this sense was first derived the predicates of purity and holiness. On the other hand, according to the Donatist point of view, the predicate of Catholic ought to be subordinate to those of *purity and holiness.*"[*]

Dupin, a Roman Catholic, says: "The Donatists maintained that the true church ought to consist of none but *holy* and *just* men. They confessed the bad might be mixed with the good in the church, but only as *secret* sinners, not as *open* offenders."[2]

Böhringer sums up the meaning of the Donatist movement: "The Donatists, Novatians and Montanists wanted a *pure* and *holy* church, because the purity of its members constitute the genuineness of the church."[3]

Walch: "The chief cause of their schism was their abhorrence of communion with traitors."[3]

Neander says the Donatists, claimed: "When the church, however widely extended, becomes corrupt by

---

[*] Idem, p. 208
[1] Neander's Ch. Hist., vol. 2, pp. 203, 205.
[2] Baptist Layman's Book, p. 19.
[3] Idem, p. 21.

intercourse with unworthy members, then that church, in whatever work and corner of the earth it might be which had no *manifestly* vicious members within its pale is the *genuine* Catholic church."[1]

Guericke says: "The after of the Christian church would have been very different . . . had it once more resorted to the *primitive* discipline and hedged up the way to the *multitudes* of unconverted persons who were *crowding* into it, and had it sought, not indeed by a more *artificial* organization, but in the exercise of a deeper and simpler faith in *God*, to render the church more self-consistent and less dependent upon the *State*."[2]

These historians make very clear that in the third and fourth centuries, Montanism, Novatianism and Donatism were the great witnesses for New Testament church membership. Between the Baptists and their opponents was the contest that has been the contest ever since and which to-day is the great contest between Baptist and others, viz.: a *regenerate or an unregenerate church*.

But, I will give the reader a sample of their debates over this question: To the argument of Augustine, that the parable of the wheat and tares growing together till the end of the age taught that *known* unworthy members ought to be retained in the churches, the Donatists replied: "The field, the Lord says, is the world, therefore not the church, but this world, in which the good and the bad dwell together till the harvest; that is, they are reserved till the judgment day." This interpretation, which is that given by our Lord, they asserted, could not be gainsaid, since, said they, if the Apostles, the companions of our Lord himself, should have learned from the tares, that is, the children of the devil, springing up in the

[1] Neander's Hist. Ch., vol. 2, p. 208.
[2] Guericke's Ch. Hist., vol. 1, p. 281.

church by the neglect of discipline, were to be left in the communion of the saints, they never would have expelled from the thresholds of their churches, Simon, Erastus, Philetus, Alexander, Demas, Hermogenes, and others like them. Yes, indeed, said the reforming Donatists, the mixed policy of the Catholics would make void the whole public instructions throughout the divine writings pertaining to the separation of the wounded from the sound, the polluted from the clean."[1]

Any one who is familiar with the present controversy between the Baptists and their opponents will readily recognize that both sides and arguments are represented in the Donatist controversy.

It has been charged that the Donatist held to infant baptism. In reply (1.) As no church that ever believed in infant baptism held so tenaciously to converted church membership and spirituality, as did the Donatists, and as infant baptism and such a church are irreconcilably antagonistic, that the Donatists opposed infant baptism is evident. "Their principles would undoubtedly lead them to the rejection of infant baptism."[2] (2.) History otherwise refutes the charge. Says Armitage, "Long says: 'They refused infant baptism.' "[3]

Long was an Episcopalian and wrote a history of the Donatists.

Guy de Bres said: "That they demanded that baptized infants ought to be baptized again as adults."

Augustine, replying to the Donatists: "Do you ask for divine authority in this matter? Though that which the whole church practices is very reasonably believed to be no other than a thing delivered by the Apostles, yet

[1] Benedict's History Donatists, pp. 85, 86.
[2] Cramp's Bap. Hist., p. 60.
[3] Armitage's Hist. Bap., p. 201.

we may take a true estimate, how much the sacrament of baptism does profit infants, beg the circumcision which God's former people received."¹

Osiander, says: "Our modern Anabaptists are the same as the Donatists of old."

Fuller, Episcopalian: "The Anabaptists are the Donatists new dipt."²

As the Anabaptists were especially noted for opposition to infant baptism, Fuller's statement is very clearly against the Donatists having baptized infants.

Bullinger is often quoted as saying: "The Donatists and the Anabaptists held the same opinion."

Twick, Chron. b. 6, p. 201, says: "The followers of Donatus were all one with the Anabaptists, denying baptism to children, admitting believers only thereto who desired the same, and maintaining that none ought to be forced to any belief."³

D'Anvers, in his Treatise on Baptism, says: "Austin's third and fourth books against the Donatists demonstrated that they denied infant baptism, wherein he maintains the argument of infant baptism against them with great zeal, enforcing it by several arguments." ³

Böhringer, a late biographer of Augustine, says: "Infant baptism is the only point of difference between Augustine and the Donatists, and this grew out of the Donatist notion of the church." ⁴

Alluding to and endorsing Bohringer's statement, W. W. Everts, Jr., than whom, perhaps, no one in America has a better knowledge of church history, says: " This is only a more confident statement of what Gotfried Arnold

---
1 Idem, p. 20.
2 Fuller's Ch. Hist. Britain, book 5, sec. 5:11.
3 In the Baptist, by T. G. Jones, D. D., p. 70.
4 Ch. in the Wilderness, p. 42.

and Ivirney had said before in identifying the Donatists and modern Baptists."[1]

Augustine presided over a council of 92 ministers, which aimed at the Donatists, Montanists and Novatians, declared: "We will that whoever denies that little children by baptism are freed from perdition and eternally saved, that they be accursed."

Armitage says: "It is commonly conceded that Augustine wrote a separate work against them on infant baptism which has not come down to us. If he did, the fair inference would be that they rejected that doctrine."[2]

Yes, and if Armitage had thoroughly investigated, he would have learned that Dr. Benedict has, in his History of the Donatists, produced sufficient amount of Augustine's writings to so clearly prove that the Donatists rejected infant baptism as to leave the fact beyond any reasonable doubt. Cramp regards it possible that some Donatists practiced infant baptism.

In his history of the Donatists, Benedict mentions four divisions called Donatists,[3] the last two did not go out from the original company. If any of the people who were called Donatists ever held to infant baptism, some of the last two divisions must have been the ones.

Merivale says of the Donatists: "They represented the broad principle of the Montanists and Novatians, that the true Church of Christ is an assembly of real pious persons only. . . . Jerome and Augustine and others class the Donatists with the Novatians as to general aim and purpose, and Augustine sneers at them as 'spotless saints'"[4]

[1] Church in the Wilderness, p. 42.
[2] Armitage's Bap. Hist., p. 201.
[3] p. 135.
[4] Armitage's Bap. Hist., pp. 200, 201.

The church government of the Donatists was substantially the same as that of the Baptists of our own time. W. W. Everts, Jr., says: "We clearly trace among them the polity of the apostolic and Baptist church. Independence of the hierarchy was universally maintained, and no higher authority than the local church was acknowledged. Insubordination to bishops and councils was their conspicuous and unpardonable offence. . . . They maintained, therefore, a position of irreconcilable order."[1] The hierarchy at the time the Donatists split occurred being but in its bud, even Donatist opponents then had not the full grown hierarchy of later times. Muston represents the voice of history when he says: "In the first centuries of the Christian era, each church founded by the disciples had a unity and an independence of its own." "The bishops being elected by the people of their diocese." [2]

Long, an Episcopalian: "The Donatists rejected the Catholic liturgy and set up for themselves in a more congregational way." [3]

Says Benedict: "In all their operations as a religious community I have discovered nothing peculiar to episcopacy, or the episcopal regimen, except the diocese, which in early times was deficient in what in later times becomes essential to diocesan episcopacy." [4]

As Whatley observes: "A church and a diocese seem to have been for a considerable time, co-extensive and identical; and each church a diocese, and consequently each superintendent, though connected with the rest by

---

[1] Church in the Wilderness, pp. 16, 18.
[2] Israel of the Alps, vol. 1, pp. 4, 7.
[3] Long's Hist. Don., p. 55.
[4] Benedict's Hist. Don., p. 138.

the ties of faith and charity, seems to have been perfectly independent, as far as regards any power and control." [1]

" In point of fact. . . . the word (diocese), which perhaps retained to a certain degree its general rather than its technical sense, is found applied in turn to every kind of ecclesiastical territorial division. . . . Suicer alleges other authorities to show that the word is sometimes employed in a sense closely resembling our word parish, viz: The district of a single church or parish. It has been observed that this was a Latin and especially an African use of the term." [2] This use of the word diocese in Africa, the land of the Donatists, not only removes all ground to suppose that it implied episcopacy, but in its being there used for a single congregation, it proves the Donatist bishop and his diocese only a pastor and a congregation, as with Baptists now.

Only a few hierarchal bishops are necessary to the largest country. But among Baptists a very large number is necessary. The fact, therefore, that 279 Donatist bishops were present at the council of Carthage explodes the possibility of reasonably believing the Donatists had Episcopal prelates. Another like proof is, there were "410 Donatist bishops assembled together." [3] Who ever heard or dreamed of 410 Romish, Episcopal, Greek or Methodist bishops in as limited a territory as was North Africa? As W. W. Everts, Jr., well observes: " The number of the Donatist bishops proves that every pastor received the title, a name which Donatists very much disliked." [4]

[1] Benedict's Hist. Don., p. 139.
[2] Smith's Dic. Chr. Antiq., vol. 1, pp. 558, 559.
[3] Bap. Layman's Book, pp. 19, 22.
[4] Idem, p. 22.

The Donatists were not Campbellites and Romanists, but were Baptists, in that they believed in the blood before the water, salvation by grace and not by the work of baptism.

Says Benedict: (Optatus was the Donatus adversary.) "Optatus was in union with the Donatists in requiring *faith before baptism.* The repetition of the rite was the principle matter of dispute between the parties, *except* that Optatus, with *his* party held to the *salutary* influence of baptism. Baptism, said *he, makes a man a Christian*, and how can he be made a Christian the second time? Baptism in the name of the Trinity *confers grace*, which is destroyed by the second baptism." [1]

To the charge that the Donatists held to the union of church and State, I reply: (1.) As no other people, holding to a regenerate church membership, the blood before the water, only believers' baptism, and to a congregational church government ever, at the same time held to this adulterous union, the charge is incredible. (2.) The only ground of this charge is, the Donatists appealed to the emperor to decide whether they were heretics. Dr. Armitage well says: "Nothing could have been more stupid and inconsistent" than this, as "they were struggling for a pure church against the laxness of the Catholic party." [2] This remark of Armitage is on the report that the appeal was made, to unite church and State, a report not supported by history. A. D. 312, on gaining control of the empire, Constantine proclaimed freedom of religious belief to all.[3] But, to deprive the Donatists of this liberality, it seems their enemies accused them of being traitors to the emperor. Based on the Romish report,

---

[1] Benedict's Hist. Don., p. 19.
[2] Armitage's Bap. Hist., p. 201.
[3] Benedict's Hist. Don., p. 11.

Gibbon says: "Both parties accused each other of being traitors . . . The cause of the Donatists was examined with attention, perhaps it was determined with justice, but perhaps their complaints were not without foundation, that the credulity of the emperor was abused by the insidious acts of his favorite Otius."[1] As the result of the emperor's decision, the Donatists "were treated as transgressors of the imperial laws."[2] "He certainly exiled some, and is said to have deprived them of their churches."[3] This persecution is said to have been the cause of the violence of the Circumcelliones who,[4] though not being Donatists, were excited to their deeds by these cruel persecutors. Thus, it is probable that the Donatists consented to the appeal, not to get up a union with the State, but to get the emperor to decide they were orthodox Christians. This decision they seemed to have desired only to save them from persecution. It was on the same principle on which Baptist now, in case of a split in any of their churches, on the ground that one party is heretical, appeal to Cæsar's court to decide which is the true Baptist church—not for State aid or any form of union of church and State, but for their property rights. The first Baptist confessions of faith were especially to show the authorities that their enemies slandered them—that they were good citizens. An enemy, with the scarcity of history that characterized the time of the Donatists, could as easily pervert these appeals of Baptists of modern times, as of the time of Constantine, into an appeal for union of church and State. About sixty-eight years after the Donatists

[1] Idem, p. 9.
[2] Idem, p. 12.
[3] Wadington's Ch. Hist., p. 151, note.
[4] Hase's Hist. Chr. Ch., p. 158.

appealed to Constantine, "on his accession to the throne, the Donatist bishops transmitted to" Julian, his nephew, "a petition in which they besought a ruler who required only justice, to rescind the unjust decrees that had been issued against them."[1] Here they are appealing to the emperor to remove the very decrees against the passage of which they aimed in their first appeal, nearly sixty-eight years before. In this appeal there is not so much as an intimation of desire for union of church and State. Why; then, in the name of fairness to a people, confessed on all sides to have been a truly Christian people, should they everlastingly be besmirched with the charge of believing in union of church and State?

Even were we to admit they did, in the moment of error, seek the union of church and State, since it was opposed to their principles and is opposed to their usual position, it in no way affects their claim to be in line of Church Perpetuity.

Armitage says: "It is but just to say that, so far as known, this is an isolated act in their history, and not one of a number in the same line." [*]

All it can possibly prove is a momentary missing the mark. History clearly shows the Donatists utterly opposed to persecution and the union of church and State. Petillian describes a true church as one which "does not persecute, nor inflame the minds of emperors against their subjects, nor seize on the property of others, nor kill men."[2] Benedict says the Donatists "uniformly represented their community" as the one "which suffers persecution, but does not persecute."[3] "A people who suffer persecution,

---

[*] Armitage's Hist. Bap., p. 202.
[1] Benedict's Hist. Don., p. 41.
[2] Idem, p. 53.
[3] Idem, p. 83.

but do not persecute was their stereotyped and cherished motto."[1] "Nowhere in all church history, can be found a more non-resisting people under the assaults of their enemies except by arguments."[1] "They were treated as rebels by Macaries, the Roman general, and his mission and policy were to hurry them into the Catholic church, peaceably if he could, forcibly if he must."[1] in their controversy with the Catholics "one often finds repetition of the following pertinent questions of the reformers: 'What has the emperor to do with the church? What have the bishops to do at the palace? What has Christianity to do with the kings of this world?'"[2] "At an early period this persecuted people entirely renounced the church and State policy, and, of course, 'What has the emperor to do with the church?' was their reply to the offers of royal bounty."[3]

Guericke says: "The emperor sent them money for distribution as a loan, but Donatus Magnus, sent it back with the obstinate protestation against the union of church and State."[4]

Neander: "Another more important point of dispute related to the employment of force in matters of religion. The Donatists bore their testimony on this point with emphasis in favor of the cause which the example of Christ and the Apostles, with the spirit of the gospel, and the sense of man's universal rights, called forth by the latter, required. The point of view first set forth in a clear light by Christianity, when it made religion its common good of all mankind and raised it above all narrow political restrictions, was by the Don-

[1] Idem, p. 35.
[2] Idem, p. 100.
[3] Idem, p. 32.
[4] Guericke's Ch. Hist., vol. 1, p. 281; also Neander's Ch. Hist., vol. 2, p. 195.

atists manfully asserted, in opposition to a theory of ecclesiastical rights at variance with the spirit of the gospel, and which had sprung out of a new mixture of ecclesiastical with political interests."[1] "Quid est emperatori cum ecclesia?"—What has the emperor to do with the church?—was fundamental with the Donatists.

T. J. Morgan, D. D., ex-Professor of Church History in the Chicago Baptist Theological Seminary: "The Donatists . . . resisted the interference of the State in ecclesiastical affairs."[2]

Child, an infidel, says: "The members of their party were forbidden to receive presents from the reigning powers. The corruptions resulting from the union of church and State became their favorite theme of eloquence. They traced all degeneracy to the splendor and luxury of the times, and railed at bishops whose avarice led them to flatter princes."[3]

The Donatists, like the Novatians and the Montanists, in the following, were Baptist. Petillian, one of their most eminent ministers, said: "I baptize their members, as having an imperfect baptism, and as in reality unbaptized. They will receive my members . . . as truly baptized, which they would not do if they could discover any fault in our baptism. See, therefore, that the baptism which I give you may hold so holy that not any sacriligious enemy will have destroyed."[4] So, Baptist baptism, only, has, in all ages and in all countries, been universally conceded to be gold.

As to the action of baptism, as Benedict remarks: "It may be proper to notify the readers that not only the

---

[1] Neander's Ch. Hist., vol. 2, p. 212.
[2] In The Standard, of Chicago, March 18, 1880.
[3] Child's Prog. Relig. Ideas, vol. 3, pp. 29, 30.
[4] Benedict's Hist. Don., p. 56.

Donatists, but all others then, whether Catholics or dissenters, practiced immersion; and the practice also was prevalent with all parties of requiring faith before baptism." [1]

To the slander, that the Donatists believed in suicide, I let Benedict reply: "In his correspondence with Dulcitius, he, Gaudentius, was requested to surrender his church to the Catholics. In his reply to this request the resolute bishop addressed the Tribune in these terms: 'In this church, in which the name of God and his Christ is always invoked in truth, as you have always admitted, we will permanently remain as long as it may please God for us to live.' This is the whole of the threatened suicide of Gaudentius. The whole story which has gone the rounds of church history originated in the perverted language of Augustine. 'You,' said he to Gaudentius, 'declared with other words I grant, that you would burn your church, with yourself and people in it.'" [2]

In this contemptible and malicious charge, coming from where all the slanders against that whole band of witnesses for Christ came, we see the necessity of examining the charges against the Donatists and other ancient Christians with great allowance and care.

Prof. Heman Lincoln, D. D., recently Professor of Church History in Newton Theological Seminary, wrote: "The Donatists held. . . . many of the principles which are regarded as axioms by modern Baptists. They maintained absolute freedom of conscience, the divorce of church and a regenerate church membership. These principles, coupled with their uniform practice of immersion, bring them into close affinity with Baptists."

---

[1] Idem 130; Robinson's Eccl. Researches, p. 150.
[2] Idem, p. 125.

We may, therefore, having examined the only charges on which the Donatists are called in question as Baptists, conclude the examination as proving, beyond any reasonable doubt, that, in all essential respects, the Donatists were genuine Baptist churches.

CHAPTER XI.

THE PAULICIANS.

The origin of the *name*, Paulicians, is: "Constantine, from the neighborhood of Samosata and connected with a gnostic generation. . . . found in the perusal of the New Testament a world unknown, and became animated with the hope (about 660) of bringing back a state of things which had existed in the apostolic church.

He assumed the name of Silvanus, and called those communities which acknowledged him as a reformer, Pauline congregations. By their opponents they were called Paulicians."[1] Instead of Constantine having originated the Paulicians, or of their beginning in his time, Mosheim says: "Constantine revived, under the reign of Constans, the drooping faction of the Paulicians, which was now ready to expire and propagated with great success its pestilential doctrines."* Thus, they were revived, just were Schaff and others leave them, in a weak condition under the name Donatists. But, as is seen in Chapter XIX of this book, this is not the origin of the people who were called Paulicians.

Manichaeism being the main charge against the Paulicians, is here noticed first.

"Photius possessed great ability. . . . Gass says another synod deposed Photius in 867 as a 'liar and adulterer, parricide and heretic.' This is the chief witness on whose evidence the Paulicians are condemned."[2]

---

* Mosheim's Eccl. Hist., cent. 7, part 2, sec. 1.
[1] Hase's Hist. Chr. Ch., p. 159.
[2] Armitage's Hist. Bap., pp. 234, 236, 237.

Mosheim says: "The Greeks treated the Paulicians . . . . as Manichæans; though, if we may credit the testimony of *Photius*, the Paulicians, expressed the *utmost abhorrence of Manes and his doctrine.*" Even Mosheim concedes: "Most evident it is that they were not *altogether* Manichæans, though they embraced some opinions that *resembled* certain tenets of that abominable sect." [1]

Kurtz: "The *Catholic controversial* writers of the ninth century traced the sect of the Paulicians and even their name to a Manichæan family of the fourth century . . . . But *later* investigations have failed to discover *any trace* of Manichæan tenets in their system." [2] Universal Knowledge: "The charge of Manichæism was *falsely* brought against them by their *persecutors.*" [3]

Cramp: "Manichæism was looked upon as a concentration of all that was outrageously bad in religious opinion and became the *fashion* to call *all* heretics Manichæans. Hence *many excellent* men have been so stigmatized whose views and practices accorded with the word of God." [4]

Armitage: "They have always been coupled with Manichæans and *nothing* has been too base to say of them. Bossuett and Bowers have distinguished themselves in this *calumny*, but Bowers has been *effectively* answered by the learned Lardner. . . . The Paulicians *themselves* certainly should have known what they were, and both these witnesses (Photius and Siculus) *explicitly* state that they *repelled* the charge with *great spirit*. But what differences did it make with these maligners? So

---

[1] Mosheim's Eccl. Hist., cent. 9, part 1, sec. 5.
[2] Kurtz's Ch. Hist., vol. 1, p. 207.
[3] Art. Paulicians.
[4] Cramp's Hist. Bap., p. 68.

long as they could befoul their fame by that odious brand, they pinned it to them *as if it were true*. *Gibbon* states that the Paulicians *disclaimed* the theology of Manes, and the *other kindred* heresies, and the trinity generations of eons which had been created by the fruitful fancy of Valentine. The Paulicians *sincerely* condemned the memory and the opinions of the Manichæan sect, and complained of the *injustice* which impressed the invidious name on the simple *votaries of St. Paul and of Christ*. Although these witnesses judged them by a false standard of their *own raising*, to which the Paulicians are allowed no counter evidence, nor cross examination, nothing but denial and protest, Photius pretended fair play when he took up his pen to write 'Contra Manichæas' in one book, without telling what they did believe; and then, on a *false* assumption, followed by three others to confute them as though they were disciples of Manes. . . . There were different classes of Manichæans as well as Paulicians, but Photius and Siculus lump them *en masse* and convict themselves again and again of misrepresentations in matters of public notoriety. . . . They *admit* that Constantine, the leader of the Paulicians, received the New Testament as his inspired guide, and cited it to prove his tenets, and then charged him with claiming to speak by the Holy Spirit. They failed to charge him with any new doctrine, but alleged that he pretended to speak by the Holy Spirit, and then charged him with borrowing his doctrines from the Scythian, Pythagorean, and other pagan teachers. They condemned him for professing to be the power of God, but failed to show that he ever *attempted* miracles! They ridicule the Paulicians as an aristocratic organization, then sneered at them because they gave the *Scriptures to everybody* because they had no *priests*, and because instead of listening to the ravings of their inspired leader, they read the *Scriptures* publicly! They charged them with dissolute lives, with gluttony and obscenity at their festivals; and, in the *same breath*, tell us that they studiously *married*, drank *no wine* and ate no flesh! They taught that they might eat fruit, herbs, bread, but neither eggs nor fish. In other things they discredit their whole testimony under ordinary rules which govern evidence."¹ "Arnold, of Germany, Beausobre and Lardner have honored themselves and the subject with sedate investigation and judicial candor, and have set right many of the inconsistencies and contradictions of Photius and Siculus."¹

Wm. R. Williams: "The Paulicians, a later body, were eminent especially for their *love of Paul's Epistles*, which they so admired, that their teachers, many of them, *changed their names* for those of some of Paul's helpers and converts. For centuries *defamed* and pursued, they held their course, *testifying and witnessing*. Hase, the modern church historian, himself a Rationalist, speaks of them as *continuing under various names down quite near to our own age*."²

Dr. Brockett, a special investigator of the Paulicians, says: "With the proofs now at our command of the *identity of the Catharists and the Waldenses with the Bogomiles*," (Paulicianists) "this admission proves fatal to the Manichæan doctrines of the *whole*." †³

Sir William Jones, one of the most learned investigators, says: "Their public appearance soon attracted the notice of the *Catholic* party who *immediately* branded them with the opprobrious name of Manichæans; but they

---

† That some of them held to a modified, and, almost harmless Manichæism, is not denied. Some of them, for a time, may have been seriously Manichæan. [Here see Chapter IV, of this book.]
¹ Armitage's Hist. Bap., pp. 234, 236, 237.
² William R. William's Lect. on Bap. Hist., pp. 129, 130.
³ The Bogomiles, by L. P. Brockett, p. 125.

sincerely (says Gibbon), condemned the memory and the opinions of the Manichæan sect and complained of the *injustice* which impressed that invidious name on them." [1]

Of their great leader, Benedict says: "From the time he got acquainted with these writings (the gospels and Paul's Epistles) it is said he would *touch no other book.* He *threw away his Manichæan library* and exploded and rejected many of the abused notions of his countrymen."[2] So Jones substantially says.[3] Benedict: "The religious practices of this people are *purposely* mangled and misrepresented."[2]

Says Neander of the Manichæan charge against the Paulicians: "The truth is that in their period there was a universal inclination to call everything of a dualistic tendency Manichæan; while no one seemed to correctly understand the distinctive marks which separated the gnostic from the Manichæan tenets. We find *nothing* at all, however, in the *doctrines* of the Paulicians which would lead us to presume that they were an offshoot from Manichæism; on the other hand we find much which *contradicts such a supposition.*"[†]

Jortin: "Though charged with the Manichæan errors they have been *honorably freed* from this reproach by *respectable* writers."[4]

Notice, secondly, the charge that the Paulicians rejected parts of the Bible. Cramp does not so much as regard the charge worthy of notice. He mentions their leader as having had given him by a deacon, "a copy of the gospels and of the Epistles of Paul." That he "read,

---

†Neander's Hist. Chr. Ch., vol. 3, p. 244.
[1] Jones' Ch. Hist., p. 244.
[2] Benedict's Hist. Baptist, p. 12.
[3] Jones' Ch. Hist., p. 243.
[4] Jortin's Rem. on Hist., vol. 3, p. 478; Lardner's Cred. G. Hist., vol. 3, pp. 422, 546; Cramp's Bap. Hist., pp. 71, 73, 77.

believed and obeyed." Manichæism, by which he had been deluded, was immediately renounced. His Manichæan books were thrown aside and the sacred writings exclusively studied.[1] This is pretty conclusive evidence that so far as the Paulicians had knowledge of the Bible they fully accepted it as inspired. Gibbon says of Constantine, the Paulician leader: "The four gospels and the epistles" (it is not certain they were able to possess the whole Bible) "became the measure of his studies and the rule of his faith; and the Catholics who dispute his interpretation acknowledge that his text was genuine and sincere. But he attached himself with peculiar devotion to the writings and character of St. Paul. The name of the Paulicians is derived by their enemies from some unknown teacher; but I am confident that they gloried in their affinity to the Apostles to the Gentiles. . . . In the gospels and the epistles of St. Paul his faithful follower investigated the creed of Christianity; and whatever may be the success a Protestant reader will applaud the spirit of the inquiry."[2] This does not harmonize with Gibbon's and some others' statement that they rejected the Old Testament and the Epistles of Peter. No man can be a consistent follower of the gospels and Paul's Epistles and at the same time reject the Old Testament—their very root, so much preached from in these books. As this charge is, therefore, self-evidently false as to the Old Testament, there is no reason for believing the rest of it, especially as the Epistles of Peter in no way are discordant with the gospels and Paul's Epistles.

Hase says: " Their principal attention was directed to a revival of apostolic and spiritual Christianity. On

[1] Jortin's Rem, on Hist., vol. 3, p. 478; Lardner's Cred, G. Hist., vol. 8, pp, 422, 546; Cramp's Bap. Hist,, pp, 71, 73, 67.
[2] Armitage's Bap. Hist., p. 237.

every subject they appealed to the New Testament as a sacred book for the people in the text used by the church, but with the exclusion of the Epistles of Peter."*

Mosheim: "They received all the books of the New Testament except the two Epistles of Peter, which they rejected for reasons unknown to us, and their copies were the *same* with those used by all the Christians, *without the least interpolation* of the sacred text; in *which* respect they *also differed* from the Manichæans."[1]

Says Dr. Brockett, perhaps the highest authority as to the Paulicians: "This assertion that they rejected the entire Old Testament . . . is reiterated by all the Greek and Roman Catholic writers, from Petrus Siculus, in the ninth century, Monachus and Alanus in the thirteenth, down to Mathew Paris, Roger de Hoveden, and Gevase of Canterbury: *yet we have the most conclusive evidence that it was not true.* Euthymius Zygabenus, the secretary of the Emperor Alexius Comnenus when Basil was examined by the emperor, and a most bitter enemy of the Bogomiles, states in his Panoplia (as stated by Evans' Historical Review, etc., p. 36) the Bogomiles accepted seven holy books, which he enumerates as follows: 1. The Psalms; 2. The Sixteen Prophets; 3, 4, 5 and 6. The Gospels; 7. The Acts of the Apostles, The Epistles and The Apocalypse. Some writers have charged them with rejecting the Epistles of Peter and the Apocalypse, but there *is no evidence of this.* The Bogomiles' New Testament was *word for word* that of the early Sclavic apostle, Methodius. Of this Jirecek furnishes, on page 177, the most conclusive proofs. If, then, this statement of their enemies, like so many others, is proved to be false, what

---

* Hase's Hist. Chr. Ch., p. 160.
[1] Mosheim's Eccl. Hist., part 2, chap. 5, sec. 5.

assurance is there that their alleged dualistic doctrines were anything more than an old falsehood revamped."[1]

Considering the slanderous character of the witnesses who make this charge, the inconsistency and contradictory nature of their testimony for it, and the positive testimony to the contrary, all fair minded men must agree on throwing it out of court. Even it were proven, since they had not the necessary opportunities to test the Biblical canon; since it is not infallibly certain we have all the canonical books; and since, therefore, to test their being Baptists by their infallibility as to the canon, would be an unreasonably severe and unfair test, we may dismiss the charge.

Martin Luther, at one time, rejected the book of James. Giving them no opportunity to look into a book for an answer when asked, what are the canonical books, not near half the churches of any denomination could mention them; yea, more, there are useful preachers whom this test would confuse. Here, read Chapter IV. of this book: Let us quit torturing these ancient witnesses for the truth on a rack that few churches of our own time could stand.

The origin of the charge is given by Sir Wm. Jones: "One of their imputed errors is that they rejected the whole of the Old Testament writings; a charge which was also brought by the writers of the Catholic school against the Waldenses and others with equal regard to truth and justice. But this *calumny* is easily accounted for. The advocates of popery, to support their innovations and usurpations in the kingdom of Christ, were driven to the Old Testament for authority, adducing the kingdom of David for example. And when their adversaries rebutted the argument, insisting that the parallel did not hold, for

[1] The Bogomiles, by L. P. Brockett, p. 126.

that the kingdom of Christ, which is not of this world, is a very different state of things from the kingdom of David, their opponents accused them of giving up the divine authority of the Old Testament. Upon similar principles it is *not difficult* to vindicate the Paulicians from other charges brought against them."[1]

Says Prof. Geo. P. Fisher, D. D.: The Paulicians "did not oppose marriage." †

To the charge that they denied baptism and the supper, I reply, (1) they were accused of this by enemies, who, like Campbellites, were unable to see the differences between denying the ordinances *as ordinances* and denying them as *saving* institutions. (2.) History contradicts the charge. Kurtz does not so much as notice this charge. Neither does Wadington. See their histories. Jones says: "In these churches of the Paulicians, the sacraments of baptism and the Lord's supper they held to be peculiar to the communion of the faithful; *i. e.* restricted *to believers.*"[2]

Gibbon is quoted: "In *practice*, or at *least* in theory, of the sacraments, the Paulicians were inclined to abolish all visible objects of *worship*, and the gospels were, in their judgments, the baptism and communion of the faithful."[2] The reader will observe (*a*) that Gibbon is very uncertain as to what was the position of the Paulicians. (*b*) His statement, that the "words of the gospel were baptism and communion of the faithful," taken in connection with the statement that they "were inclined to abolish" the "sacraments as visible objects of *worship*," implies that while they observed the ordinances they did not look to them for a *medium* of salvation, but looked to

† Fisher's Hist. Chr. Ch., p. 162.
[1] Jones' Ch. Hist., p. 245.
[2] Benedict's Hist. Bap., p. 12.

the words of the gospel. Being a poor infidel and thus blind to spiritual things, Gibbon understood this to mean rejecting the ordinances.

Mosheim: "They rejected baptism and in a *more especial* manner, the baptism of infants, as a ceremony that was in no respect *essential to salvation*. They rejected, for the *same reason*, the sacrament of the Lord's supper."[1]

Whatever Mosheim may mean to teach, this statement must be taken in the light of its phrase, "As a ceremony that was in no respect *essential to salvation.*" Just as in cent. 11, part 2, chap. 5, sec. 4, he says: "They considered marriage as a pernicious institution, and absurdly condemned without distinction all connubial bonds," which a foot note to the same page thus explains: "The eleventh article is scarcely credible, at least, as it is here expressed. It is more than reasonable to suppose these mystics did not absolutely condemn marriage, but only held celibacy in high esteem, as a mark of superior sanctity and virtue." The truth is, while this note hits the mark as to their not rejecting marriage, it misses it as to the explanation of the charge. The explanation in this and in the case of baptism and the supper is: The Romanists accused them of rejecting *both* marriage and the two ordinances because they denied them as *sacraments*—rejecting them only as *saving* institutions. Mosheim's explanation of their meaning, in cent. 9, part 2, chap. 5, sec. 6, yet more clearly shuts us up to this interpretation: "They refused to celebrate the holy institution of the Lord's supper; for as they looked upon many precepts and injunctions of the gospel to be of merely *figurative and parabolic nature*, so they understood by the bread and wine, which Christ is said to

[1] Mosheim's Eccl. Hist., cent. 9, part 2, chap. 5, sec. 6.

THE PAULICIANS. 117

have administered to his disciples at his last supper, the divine discourses of the Savior, which are a spiritual food and nourishment for the soul, and fill it with repose, satisfaction and delight." Taking baptism and the supper as "merely figurative and parabolic," symbolizing the great truths of the gospel, is the Baptist position of all ages, for which, by those who look to them as saviors, from Campbellism to its mother Rome, Baptists have been unceasingly misrepresented and reproached.

Mosheim makes the same blundering interpretation in cent. 12, part 2, chap. 5, sec. 4, where, treating them as Catharists—from not knowing they were Paulicians—he says, they held "that baptism and the Lord's supper were *useless* institutions, destitute of all *saving* power." Just as Campbellites and other Romanists, to-day, charge Baptists with making these two ordinances "useless," simply because they can see no use in obeying Jesus unless the obedience saves from hell. Benedict gives us an illustration of the same charge, made in a discussion, against the Baptists, at a time when no one doubts that they baptized and observed the supper. In this discussion, between a Baptist and a Romanist, the Romanist says: "You Anabaptists, tell us once, something about supper. I suppose you observe none, since you know nothing about a *sacrament* * * * Yes, you have always the scriptures at your finger ends, for you Anabaptists read nothing but the holy scripture, hence it is that you read nothing concerning the *sacrament* of the altar. * * * Therefore you are ignorant of the sacrament of the altar." [1]

Says Brockett: "Harmenopoulos, a Byzantine monk of the tenth century, more candid than most of his fellows, says, as quoted by Evans, that the Bogomiles

---
[1] Benedict's Hist. Bap., p. 101.

practiced the right of water baptism (and if they did they must have received it from the Paulicians) but did not attribute to it any perfecting virtue ($\tau\epsilon\lambda\epsilon\iota ovv$) virtue.[1] This last expression is significant in this connection as showing that this rite was administered to all believers (Credentes) in distinction from spiritual baptism, or consolamentum . . . It is, we believe, generally admitted that the early Armenian church, of which the Paulicians were an offshoot, did not practice trine immersion, though they immersed their converts once."[2]

Brockett proves they baptized, by "Their well-known and universally admitted repudiation of infant baptism. Harmenopoulos, a Greek priest of the twelfth century, expressly declares that they did practice single *immersion* but without unction, etc., and *only* upon *adults*, on the profession of their faith. He adds that they did *not attribute to it any saving* or perfecting virtues, which is in accordance with their *other* teaching." Reinero, the inquisitor, who had originally been one of them, says: "They say that a man is first baptized when he is received into their community and has been *baptized* by them, and then hold that baptism is of no advantage to *infants*, since they cannot actually believe. We find in the histories of Jirecek and Hilferding *numerous* incidental allusions to the baptism of persons of high rank, such as the ban Culin, Tvartko III, King Stephen Thomas, the Duke of St. Sava, etc. * * * who are said to have been *baptized* into the Bogomile faith. That during the period of the greatest persecutions, the *ordinances* were administered secretly, and perhaps at night is very probable, *but there is no evidence that it was ever omitted.* That would have been impossible in an oriental

[1] The Bogomiles, p 119.
[2] Idem, p. 119.

church.[1] To the authorities here named for the proposition that the *Credentes*, or believers were baptized must be added Alanus de Insulis, a French writer of about A. D. 1200, whose treatise against heretics was published by Massons of Lyons, in 1612. He is cited by Hallam, Middle Ages, vol. 3, pp. 359, 360, note Am."[2] Alanus speaking of Albigenses, who were fully identified with the Bogomiles, says: "They rejected infant baptism, but were divided as to the reason . . . It does not appear they rejected either of the sacraments."[3] "*Nothing* is said by Hoveden of their rejection of the sacraments of baptism and the eucharist, which would have *certainly* been mentioned by as *careful* a writer as Hoveden *if it had existed*."[3]

As to their having opposed marriage, though it has been disprovingly alluded to, in the foregoing, I will quote the statement of Prof. Geo. P. Fisher: The Paulicians "did not oppose marriage."[4]

While I have more testimony to prove the Paulicians were Baptists as to the ordinances, I conclude this point with these as amply sufficient: (1.) They did administer the ordinances. (2.) Only to believers. (3.) They recognized the scriptural truth, that only immersion is baptism. (4.) As they baptized only believers they believed in a regenerate church membership.

The Paulicians were Baptists in church government. Of them Benedict quotes Gibbon: "Churches were founded upon the plan and model of the churches. They were incapable of desiring the wealth and honors of the Catholic prelacy; such anti-christian pride they bitterly

---

[1] Idem, p. 41.
[2] Idem, pp. 121, 122.
[3] The Bogomiles, p. 122.
[4] Fisher's Hist. Chr. Ch., p. 162; also p. 126 of Church Perpetuity.

condemned."¹ Armitage: "Dr. Semler accords them more correct ideas of godliness, worship and church government than the Catholics of their time, and these virtues drew upon them more persecution from the hierarchy than their doctrinal views."² Robinson: They were called "Acephali, or headless."³ They were doubtless as Benedict explains, so called because they rejected Romish rules. Mosheim: "They had *not*, *like* the Manichæans, an ecclesiastical government administered by bishops, priests and deacons; they had no sacred *order* of men *distinguished* by their manner of life or any other circumstance from the *rest* of the assembly; nor had councils, synods or *such like* institutions any place in their religious polity."⁴ This language might be misunderstood to mean that they had no ministers at all. But it is the *contrast* between the simplicity of the ministry, as among Baptists now, and the prelacy, as in the Romish churches now. The next words of Mosheim clearly so explain: "They had certain doctors whom they called Sunecdemi, *i. e. companions* in the journey of life, and also notarii. Among these there reigned a *perfect equality*, and they had no *peculiar* rights, privileges nor external mark of dignity to distinguish them from the people. The *only* singularity that attended their promotion to the rank of doctors was, that they changed their lay names for scripture ones."⁴ Wadington quotes and adopts the statement of Mosheim as his own.* Kurtz: "Their form of worship was very simple and their church government modeled after that of

---

* Wadington's Ch. Hist., p. 478.
[1] Benedict's Hist. Bap., p. 13.
[2] Armitage's Hist. Bap., p. 239.
[3] Robinson's Eccl. Researches, p. 92.
[4] Mosheim's Eccl. Hist., cent. 9, part 2, chap. 5, sec. 5; Wadington's Ch. Hist., p. 478.

apostolic times."¹ Kurtz shows the apostolic church government to be what we regard Baptist.

Says Hase: "The community of Paulicians had a chief. . . . , but neither he nor any of his fellow pilgrims (συνέκημοι) and scribes (νοτάροι) exercised any hierarchal powers."*

Neander says: "They recognized it as belonging to the popular essence of christianity. That it aimed to establish a higher fellowship of life among all ranks and all classes, tolerating no such *distinctions* as the existing ones between clergy or priests and laity. They had among them, it is true, persons who administered ecclesiastical *offices*, but these, like the rest, were to be looked upon as members of the *communities*. They were distinguished from others neither by dress, nor by any outward mark. The names, also, of their church officers were so chosen, as to denote the peculiarity of their vocation, which was to administer the *office* of spiritual teaching, to the exclusion of all sacredotal prerogatives."**

Dr. Brockett says: "A *hierarchy of any sort was utterly abhorrent* to the spirit and temper of both the Bogomiles and their *affiliated sects* in the West."² Some have supposed they had an ecclesiastical chief dignitary. But as Brockett says, and the foregoing quotations prove: "The Bosnian djed, or elder, seems to have been at this time about A. D. 1220 the presiding officer of the affiliated sects or denominations, somewhat like the former presidents of our triennial conventions. He was *primus inter pares*, but possessed no judicial or ecclesiastical author-

* Hase's Hist. Chr. Ch., p. 160.
** Neander's Hist. Chr. Ch., vol. 3, p. 264.
1 Kurtz's Ch. Hist., vol. 1, p. 271.
2 The Bogomiles, p. 58, 60, 71.

ity."[1] [See Jirecek, Geschichte der Bulgaren, p. 180.]

Neander says of their doctrine and life: "Certain it is, that the Paulician doctrines as a whole, not only required, but were calculated to foster, a spirit of sober and strict morality." †

Sir William Jones, of the Paulicians, says: *"I see no reason to doubt* that we should see in them the *genuine successors* of the Christians of the first two centuries."[2] (In this chapter italics are all mine.)

I, therefore, conclude this examination of the Paulicians in the language of perhaps the highest authority on the subject—Brockett—"The Armenian Paulicianists were clearly Baptists."[3]

† Neander's Hist. Chr. Ch., vol. 3, p. 266.
[1] Idem, p. 127.
[2] Jones' Ch. Hist., p. 245.
[3] Bap. Rev., vol. 4, No. 10.

CHAPTER XII.

THE ALBIGENSES.

I will introduce the treatment of the sects, between century ten and century sixteen, in the following words of Mosheim: " We find from the time of Gregory the VII. several proofs of the zealous efforts of those who are generally called by the Protestants the witnesses of the truth; by whom are meant such pious and judicious Christians as adhered to the pure religion of the gospel, and remained uncorrupted amidst the greatest superstition; who deplored the miserable state to which Christianity was reduced, by the alteration of its divine doctrines, and and the vices of its profligate ministers; who opposed with vigor the tyrannic ambition both of the lordly pontiff and the aspiring bishops; and in some provinces privately, and others openly, attempted the reformation of a corrupt and idolatrous church, and of a barbarous and superstitious age. This was, indeed, bearing witness to the truth in the noblest manner, and it was principally in Italy and France that the marks of this heroic purity were exhibited."[1] From these reformers were derived great hosts of recruits to the Baptist churches. The influence of Baptist churches created a great desire among the members of the Romish church for reformation. Out of Baptist influence originated Martin Luther's Reformation.

The name Albigenses was one of the designations of the Paulicians from "the beginning of the eleventh century to the middle of the thirteenth century." Coming

[1] Mosheim's Eccl. Hist., cent. 11, part 2, chap. 3, sec. 2.

from Asia, where they were known as Paulicians, they crossed the Balkan Peninsula and reached the Western empire. In the tenth and the eleventh centuries, under the name Paulicians, but especially Albigenses, from the town of Albiga in Southern France, and Cathari— from their pure lives—they filled and moulded both France and Italy, affecting in a less degree, other parts of Europe.

The Albigenses—and others, too,—are, in this book, treated under distinctive heads; not because they were not identical with their predecessors and contemporaries, but for the sake of clearness, to conform to the usual classification—a classification that recent researches demand should be abandoned. Here I remind the reader of a necessary caution: "It ought always to be borne in mind, however, that for the larger part of our information regarding those stigmatized as heretics, we are indebted, not to their own writings, but to the works of their opponents. Only the titles remain of the bulk of heretical writings, and of the rest we have, for the most part, only such quotations as prejudiced opponents have chosen to make. That these quotations fairly represent the originals would be too much to assume."[1] Kurtz: "The little town of Albi in the district of Albigeois, was regarded as the great center of the party, whence the name of Albigenses."[2]

The Encyclopedia Britannica says of the Albigenses: "The descent may be traced with tolerable distinctness *from the Paulicians.*"† Dr. Carl Schmidt, an eminent German authority of Strasburg, speaking of their being called Albigenses, says: "*Before* that time the sect was spoken of as Publicants or Publicani, *probably* a corruption

---
†Ency. Brit., Art. Albigenses.
[1] Vedder's Bap. Hist., p. 50; Mosheim's Eccl. Hist., cent. 12, chap. 5, sec 1.
[2] Kurtz Ch. Hist., vol. 1, p. 462; Schaff-Herzog Ency., vol. 1, p. 46.

of the name *Paulicians*, which the Crusaders had brought back from Western Europe."[1]

To the charge that the Albigenses held to Manichæism, I reply: (1.) By reminding the reader of Vedder's words beginning this article. (2.) That, as they are identical with the Paulicians, the refutation of this charge, in Chapter XI., is the refutation of this charge against the Albigenses. (3.) To this I add the following: Robinson, one of the most careful and reliable historians, did not sufficiently credit the charge to affirm it. His cautious words are: "The Albigenses were Manichæans, or *nearly so*," "Nearly so" is not "so."[2] There are certain modified forms of Manichæism which, while erroneous, would not unchurch any party. Mosheim says that those who held to Manichæism held it "differently interpreted and modified by different doctors."[3] Prof. Carl Schmidt says: "The representations which Roman Catholic writers, their bitter enemies, have given them, are highly exaggerated."[*] Even admitting them slightly tainted with Manichæism, since they lived in an age of little thought and learning, it would no more affect their claims to be churches of Christ than slight errors of the head, especially of the unlearned, now unchurch. (See Chapter V. of this book.) (4.) But there is no proof conclusive that the Albigenses were so much as tainted with Manichæaism. Wadington, speaking of the great Romish controversialists attempt to blacken their characters, (Bishop Bossuett) observes: *"He has failed to prove their Manichæan origin—still more their Manichæan doctrine.*

---

[*]Schaff-Herzog Ency., vol. 1, p 47.
[1] Schaff-Herzog Ency., vol. 1, p. 46; The Bogomiles, pp. 122, 123, 128, 131; Cramp's Bap. Hist., p. 99.
[2] Robinson's Eccl. Researches, p. 463.
[3] Mosheim's Eccl. Hist., cent. 12, part 2, chap. 5, sec. 5; Wadington's Ch. Hist., p. 478.

. . . He calls them indeed 'new' Manichæans and *admits* that 'they had *softened* some of their errors.' But they had parted with the characteristic error, or in fact they *never held it.* '"[1] On p. 291 Wadington observes: "Manichæism was the frightful term employed to express their delinquency; but it is more probable that their real offence was the adoption of certain mystical notions, *proceeding*, indeed, from feelings of the *most earnest piety*, but *too spiritual to be tolerated in that age and in that church.*"[2]

Though the charge that the Albigenses rejected marriage, baptism and the supper, has been refuted in page 119, refuting the same charge against them under the name Paulicians, the reader will notice that these charges are, incidentally, farther refuted in the following. The Encyclopedia Britannica says of them: "The statement that they rejected marriage, often made by Roman Catholics, has probably no other foundation in fact than that they denied marriage *as a sacrament;* and many other statements of their doctrines must be received at least with *suspicion*, as coming from prejudiced and implacable opponents."[3]

Alanus, speaking of the Albigenses, says: "They rejected *infant* baptism . . . It does not appear that they rejected *either* of the sacraments."[4] Collier says: "They refused to own infant baptism."[4] Brockett says: "Nothing is said by Hoveden of their rejection of the sacraments of baptism and the eucharist, which would certainly have been mentioned by so careful a writer as Hoveden, had it existed. Indeed, his strongest objection to them was their refusal to take an oath."[4] Favin, a

[1] Wadington's Ch. Hist., p. 552—note.
[2] Idem, p. 291.
[3] Art. Albigenses.
[4] The Bogomiles, p. 122.

THE ALBIGENSES.

historian, is quoted as saying: "The Albigenses do esteem the baptizing of infants superstitious." Izam, the Troubadour, a Dominican persecutor of these heretics, says: "They admitted another baptism." [1] Chassanion is quoted as saying: "I cannot deny that the Albigenses, for the greater part, were opposed to infant baptism; the truth is, they did not reject the sacraments as useless, but only as unnecessary to infants."

They had no Campbellism in them. As Armitage observes: "They rejected the Romish church and esteemed the New Testament above all its traditions and ceremonies. They did not take oaths, nor believe in baptismal regeneration; but they were ascetic and pure in their lives; they also exalted celibacy." [2] Their encouraging celibacy, as they believed in marriage, was probably for the reason that Paul encouraged it temporarily, because of persecution being harder to endure in families than when single. [3]

As refusing to take oaths was a practice of many of these ancient Baptists, I here stop to say: While that matter with Baptists is a matter of little importance, yet I believe they were, probably, nearer right than we are; for, while by "swear not at all" our Savior alluded to only profanity, yet, as Archbishop Whately observes, I believe that men who will tell a lie will swear one as readily, once the penalty is out of the way; hence, instead of taking oath annex the penalty of swearing a lie to telling it in court.

In church government the Albigenses were Baptists. A historian says: "Their bards or pastors were every one of them heads of their churches, but they acted on nothing without the consent of the people and the clergy,"

---

[1] Robinson's Eccl. Resh., p. 463.
[2] Armitage's Bap. Hist., p. 278.
[3] I Cor., 7:27, 40.

i. e., the ministers who had charge of no church. "Deacons expounded the gospels, distributed the Lord's supper, baptized, and sometimes had the oversight of churches, visited the sick and took care of the temporalities of the church." Chr. Schmidt says: "Their ritual and ecclesiastical organization were *exceedingly* simple." [1]

This was so much the case that the Romish church, not seeing any church in so simple an organization, thought they had no churches, and Prof. Schmidt has, thereby, been mislead into the same conclusion. In Chap. XI—noticing them as Paulicians—they are clearly proved to have been, in church government, Baptist.

The Albigenses were pure in their lives and a zealous people in good works. Carl Schmidt says of them: "Their severe moral demands made impression because the example of their preachers corresponded with their words . . . In a short time the Albigenses had congregations with schools and charitable institutions of their own . . . The Roman Catholic church, so far as it still could be said to exist in the country, had become an object of contempt and derision. This state of affairs, of course, caused great alarm in Rome." [2]

Thus, "the Albigensian heresy," as Lord Macaulay observes, brought about the civilization, the literature, the national existence . . . of the most opulent and enlightened part of the great European family." [3]

[1] Schaff-Herzog Ency., p. 421.
[2] Schaff-Herzog Ency., vol. 1, p. 47.
[3] Macaulay's Works, vol. 6, p. 463.

CHAPTER XIII.

THE PATERINES.

Though names are not essential to Church Perpetuity in this chapter I will notice the Paterines. In church history the Paterines are called Cathari, from Catharoi, meaning pure ones. Gazari, perhaps from the inhabitants of Crimea, the Chazars. Bulgari, from the supposition of their having come from Bulgaria. Pataria, Patereni, *i. e.*, black-guards. Tisserands, from many of them being weavers. Bogomils, from the Bulgarian Bog z'milui, signifying "God have mercy," meaning a praying people. Massalians, said to be from Syriac, signifying those who pray. Euchites, meaning those who pray. Albigenses, from the little town of Albi in the district of the Albigeois, in the South of France, being regarded as the great center of various parties, called Cathari. Paulicians was converted into a well-known term of reproach and into too many other terms to notice.[1]

While, in church history, the Paterines are generally called Cathari, as they are better known among Baptist writers by the term Paterines, I will use that term. As Roman Catholics used any term with which they could best reproach their opponents there may have been churches or parties of shades of faith who were called Paterines;[2] and some of them grossly erroneous.

---

[1] Kurtz's Ch. Hist., vol. 1, pp. 410, 453; The Bogomilles, p. 29.

[2] Pretentions of Baptists to Antiquity, by Clements, p. 326; Wadington's Ch. Hist., p. 288; Limborch, Hist. Inquist., lib. 1 C. 15; Johnson's Ency., Art. Cathari; Mosheim's Ch. Hist., cent. 11, part 2, chap. 2, sec. 13—note; part 2, chap. 5, sec. 2; Jones' Ch. Hist., p. 287; Robinson's Eccl. Researches, pp. 456, 405 and 408.

The Paterines are on record at least from the eleventh to the thirteenth centuries.* They *numbered hundreds of thousands*. They flourished especially in Italy, France and more especially in the South of France. The better part of them were Paulicians. But as they figure in Baptist history under the names Paterines and Cathari I give them this separate notice. In the study of all these names we must, also, bear in mind the remarks of Robinson and Armitage.

Robinson: "The practice of confounding heretics of all kinds in one common herd, devoted to the shambles, hath been an ancient custom with ecclesiastical historians and it hath obscured history."[1]

Armitage: "The Cathari, the pure, have been the subjects of much confusion in ecclesiastical history, largely in consequence of classing widely different sects under that general name both amongst ancient and modern writers, whether Catholic or Protestant."

While it may be that some people who were called Paterines were fundamentally in error, that there were distinct churches covered by the name which were essentially Baptistic, we must conclude in spite of the whole catalogue of errors with which Satan has never hesitated to blacken their character.

Thus, the Paterines are charged with opposing marriage. But, this being a charge so generally made by the Romish church of those times against those who denied marriage a "*sacrament*," and now, Romish theologians, presuming Protestant marriage invalid, as the charge originated with Romanists, it is not probably true. In an age when it was popular to do so, Roman Catholics with great effectiveness blackened all who did not regard mar-

---

*Jones' Ch. Hist., p. 288; Robinson's Eccl. Resh, p. 409.
[1] Eccl. Resh., p. 463; Bap. Hist., p. 277.

riage a sacrament as rejecting marriage. On 100 and 101 of Benedict's History of the Baptists will be found an illustration of how the Mennonites were charged by Romanists of denying baptism and marriage, simply because they denied they are sacraments. Since no moral people can perpetuate itself without marriage, the Paterines being by historians pronounced a people of the the purest morals, should brand this charge an infamous slander. Robinson positively refutes this charge: "That they denied the seven sacraments of the church, of which matrimony is one, is admitted; but they denied these *only in the sense in which the Catholics affirmed them, as all Protestants do.* That they married and had families is beyond all doubt, for in an authentic trial of Arman Punzilupe of Ferrara, who had held office among them, his wife and the wives and children of many more are mentioned."[1]

The serious errors which Mosheim and others record against the Paterines, so far as true, necessarily applies to others called Peterines and not to the moral ones, since their acknowledged morality and life, being the result of belief, clearly necessitates freedom of a part of the Paterine churches from the charges. We have already, from historic facts, refuted most of these charges, when charged on the Paulicians. Yet, the better part of the Paterine churches, being Paulicians, were free from those errors charged.

As to the charge against them of opposition to ecclesiastical and civil law, Hase says: "The name Catharists, by which this sect was *usually* designated . . . The accounts we have respecting them are almost exclusively from their *enemies*, or from *apostates* from them, and are *consequently full of errors and calumnies.*

[1] Robinson's Eccl. Resh., p. 407; compare, also, pp. 119, 126 of Ch. **Perpetuity.**

All agree in describing them as absolutely opposed to the Catholic church and all its pomp, in consequence of what they professed to be, an *immediate* communication of the *Holy Ghost*, exalting them above all necessity of ecclesiastical or civil laws." [1] As we know they believed in New Testament laws, exalting themselves above all necessity of ecclesiastical or civil laws is, evidently, a Romish intentional perversion, or a misunderstanding of their opposition to Romish ecclesiastical law, which, in the union of church and State, was a part of civil law.

As to the common Romish charge of Manichæism or Dualism,. Hase considerately says: "Their dualistic tendency, however, may have gone no farther than the popular notion of a devil and his subordinate spirits, † and in a portion of the Catharist church it appears to have been *modified* in *various ways*, to have been full of *moral seriousness and religious sincerity*, and yet to have laid great stress upon fastings," etc. [1]

Dr. J. M. Cramp, says: "But if one accusation is manifestly outrageous and unfounded, may not the other be? Are we not entitled to the inference that there was, at least, gross exaggeration if not malicious libel. And finally is it credible that those who avowed and manifested *unlimited deference to the word of God* were led astray by the fantasies of the Manichæan theory." [2]

Library of Universal Knowledge, on this charge, says: "There is much reason to think that the errors of a few were indiscriminately charged upon all, and that such charges, indeed, sometimes rested upon ignorant or willful misconstruction." *

---

* Art. Cathari.
† Hase should have said: "The scriptural teaching of a devil and his subordinate spirits."
[1] Hase's Hist. Chr. Ch., p. 252.
[2] Cramp's Bap. Hist., p. 103.

THE PATERINES.

Neander concedes that the charge of Manichæism is not proved. "The marks of Manichæism are by no means indisputable." *

Of another similarly disreputable charge against them Neander farther concedes: "We will not deny that as this account proceeds from the fiercest enemies of the sect, we might be tempted to consider the whole report as a manufactured conclusion, or a pure invention of heresy hating spite." [1]

The following account of them, by Neander, is irreconcilable with the reports against their character and doctrine: "The feature that so much distinguished the first Christian communities, seemed to have revived again in this party, more closely bound together as they were by persecutions . . . Their adversaries expatiate on the ample support which every one who professed their peculiar principles found among them as a means by which attachment to those principles was especially promoted. As in the first ages of Christianity, every Christian who brought with him a letter of recommendation from his community was certain of meeting a hospitable reception from his brethren in the faith, so any one belonging to the sect of the Catharists, when recommended by one of their communities, might expect to meet with a kind reception everywhere among the Catharists. Let him travel in Italy, or in South France, he was sure of finding everywhere, whatever he needed in abundance . . . In particular, the perfects, when on their travels were received into the houses of all believers with great respect. The inmates thrice bowed the knee to receive their blessing. The members of the sect in the whole place speedily assembled at the house where they

---
* Neander's Hist. Chr. Ch., vol. 4, p. 566.
[1] Idem, p. 570.

were entertained, and perhaps others also, who were not liable to be suspected as informers, were invited to hear them preach and expound the scriptures . . . In South France, they took in the daughters of indigent noblemen and educated them." [1]

There is no more reason to believe that the reports of their holding absurd doctrines are reliable than there is that the slanders on their character are reliable; and Neander says: "The most absurd reports of unnatural excesses and other abominations, said to be committed in the secret assemblies of the sect, were spread among the multitude; accusations similar to those brought against the primitive Christians . . . and such as are wont to be repeated against all opponents of a dominant religion." [2]

As an illustration of how history has begun to do that noble people justice, I quote: "The liturgy *lately discovered* by Kunitz dates from the close of the thirteenth century and gives a *more favorable* opinion of them than has been formerly entertained." [3] This was since Mosheim and others who have given such credit to the Romish slanders on this people wrote. In their zeal against Church Perpetuity, Vedder and Armitage credit those foul aspersions without so much as intimating there is another side to the question.

In church government they were clearly Baptists, as appears from Hase: "In the midst of a people thus professing to be filled with the spirit, and whose pope was the Holy Ghost himself, none of the existing officers of the church could exercise any of their hierarchal

---

[1] Idem, p. 584.
[2] Idem, p. 586.
[3] Kurtz's Ch. Hist., vol. 1, p. 455.

prerogatives."[1] Schmidt says: "Their ritual and ecclesiastical organization were exceedingly simple."[2]

In the following accounts appear not only their Baptist church government but other Baptist marks.

Robinson, than whom there is no better authority, says of them: " It is remarkable that in the examination of these people, they are not taxed with any immoralities, but were condemned for speculations, or rather for *virtuous rules af action*, which all informers accounted heresies. They said: 'A Christian church ought to consist of *only good* people; a church has no power to *frame any constitution;* it was not right to take oaths; it was not lawful to kill mankind; a man ought not to be delivered up to officers of justice to be converted; the benefits of society belonged alike to *all* the members of it, faith alone could not save a man,' (faith which had not the spirit of obedience) 'the church ought not to *persecute any, even the wicked;* the church cannot excommunicate;' (that is in the Romish sense of cursing) ' the *law of Moses was no rule to Christians;*' (no infant baptism or seventh day observance) 'there was no need of *priests*, especially of wicked ones; the sacraments and orders and ceremonies of the church of Rome were *futile*, expensive, oppressive and wicked; with many more such positions, *all inimical to the hierarchy*. In these reasons and rules they *all agreed*, but in speculations they widely differed.' "[3]

Thus, as Baptists to-day do, this people rejected the whole heresy of there being *sacraments* (sacraments mean saving ceremonies), priesthood, church and State persecution, *legislating* for the church of Christ and of an *un-*

[1] Hase's Hist. Chr. Ch., p. 252.
[2] Schaff-Herzog Ency., vol. 1, p. 421.
[3] Robinson's Eccl. Resh., pp. 407, 408.

converted membership. Robinson continues: "As the Catholics of those times baptized by *immersion*, the Paterines by what name soever they were called . . . . made no complaint of the mode of baptizing; but when they were examined they objected vehemently against the *baptism of infants and condemned it* as an error. They said, among other things, that a child knew nothing of the matter, that it had no desire to be baptized, and was incapable of making any confession of faith, and that the willing and confessing of another could be of no service to him. 'Here then,' says Dr. Allix, very truly, 'we have found a body of men in Italy, before the year 1026, 500 years before the Reformation, 'who believed contrary to the opinions of the church of Rome, and who condemned their errors.' Atio, bishop of Vercelli, had complained of such people eighty years before, and so had others before him, and there is the highest reason to believe they *had always been in Italy.* . . . . . Errors most gross are laid to their charge, but they *scent strongly of fable.* . . . . The adjacency of France and Spain, too, contribute to their increase, for both abounded with Christians of *their sort.* Their churches were divided into sixteen compartments, such as the English Baptists would call associations. Each of these was subdivided into parts, which would here be called churches or congregations. In Milan there was a street called Pataria, where it is supposed they met for divine worship. At Modena they assembled at some water mills. They had houses at Ferrara, Brescia, Viterbo, Verona, Vicenza and several in Rimini, Romandolia, and other places. One of their principal churches was that of Concorezzo, in the Milanese, and the members of churches in these associations were more than fifteen hundred. Their houses where they met seem to have been hired by the people, and tenanted by one of the brethren. There were *several* in each city, and each was distinguished by a mark known only by themselves. They had three, some say four, suits or officers; the first were teachers, called bishops. John de Casaloto was the resident teacher at Mantua; Albert and Bonaventura Belasmagra, at Verona; Lorenzo or Lawrence at Sermione. The second are called quæstors, and by some, *elders* and younger sons; here they would be named teaching elders or deacons. The third were messengers, that is, men employed in *traveling* to administer to the relief and comfort of the poor and persecuted. In times of persecution they met *in small companies of eight*, *twenty, thirty*, or as it happened, but *never in larger* assemblies for fear of consequences.† The different associations held different doctrines but they were all *united* in opinion against the whole of popery, and in perfect agreement among themselves on the great *leading* points above mentioned. . . . . The Paterines were decent in their deportment, modest in their dress and discourse, and their *morals were irreproachable*. In their conversation there was no levity, no *scurrility*, *no detraction*, *no falsehood*, *no swearing*. Their dress was neither fine nor mean. They were chaste and temperate, never frequenting * *taverns* or places of public amusement. They were not given to anger and other violent passions. They were not eager to accumulate wealth, but were content with a plain plenty of the necessaries of life. They avoided commerce because they thought it would ex-

---

† The smallness of these meetings is partly what renders it as difficult for the historian to find them and trace their history as it was for their persecutors to find them.

* With them taverns were saloons. Let all our churches enforce the same rule. The man who thinks he can be a member of a saloon or a theater or horse racing, etc., and a true member of the church at the same time is a shame on Christianity.

pose them to the temptation of collusion, falsehood and oaths; and they chose to live by labor or handicraft. They were always employed in spare hours in giving as receiving *instructions*.† . . . About the year 1040 the Paterines had become *very numerous* and conspicuous in Milan, which was their principal residence, and here they flourished at least *two hundred years*. They had *no* connection with the church for they rejected not only Jerome of Syra, Augustine of Africa, and Gregory of Rome, but Ambrose of Milan, and they considered them as all other *pretended* fathers and *corrupters* of Christianity. They particularly condemned Pope Sylvester as the *anti-Christ*, the son of perdition." [1] To the report made by Bonacursi, a traitor from their ranks, that they said "the devil wrote the Old Testament," Robinson well retorts: " He should have said, *he expounded it*, for this was their *meaning* "— alluding to its use by the Romish church.[2]

Alluding to the Romish church, Robinson says: " The Paterines let the church alone, constantly affirming the *sufficiency of Scriptures*, the competency of each to reform himself, the right of *all*, even women, to teach; and openly disclaiming any manner of coercion."

These three kinds of offices, mentioned, by Robinson in the foregoing account, corresponded substantially to Baptist church offices, thus: their first, to *settled* pastors; their second, to *deacons;* their third, to various kinds of *traveling* ministers—different functions of two offices.

" They maintained church *discipline*, even on their ministers, as examples are recorded." [3]

† That Baptists do not now always thus improve their time is but to be deplored.
[1] Robinson's Eccl. Resh., pp. 408-411.
[2] Robinson's Eccl. Resh., p. 415.
[3] Benedict's Hist. Bap., p. 20.

THE PATERINES. 139

They were Baptists on the doctrine of election and "appealed to the texts in the ninth chapter of the Epistle to the Romans, employed by others also in proof of the doctrine of unconditional predestination." Like Baptists they said: "We perform a miracle when we convert a man to God; then we drive out from him the evil spirits."[2]

Kurtz says: "Even their opponents admitted their deep and *moral* earnestness."[3] "It was by means of the Paterines," says another historian, "that the truth was preserved in the dioceses of Milan and Turin. . . . . They are also freed from the baleful charge of Manichæism."

Nor can their differences of "speculations," in the least, make them different from Baptists, since Baptists, freely allow such differences in their churches. Leaving out little variations, consequent on individual peculiarities, and the times in which they, this people, were Baptists, Robinson says: "It appears highly credible that this kind of people, Paterines, continued there till the Reformation."[4] No historian being able to show that they ceased to exist, this completes the Baptist Perpetuity line, through the Anabaptists, to the present.

[1] Neanders' Hist. Chr. Ch., vol. 4, p. 568.
[2] Idem, p. 569.
[3] Kurtz's Ch. Hist., vol. 1, p. 454.
[4] Eccl. Resh, p. 417

CHAPTER XIV.

THE PETROBRUSSIANS AND HENRICIANS.

The Petrobrussians numbered their hundreds of thousands. In the Middle Ages they were a great and shining light. Historians agree that the Petrobrussians appeared in the South of France about 1104. Of their great leader—Peter de Bruys—Kurtz says: "He rejected the outward or visible church, and only acknowledged the true, invisible church in the *hearts* of believers. In his opinion all churches and sanctuaries should be destroyed, since God *might* be worshipped in a stable or tavern. He used crucifixes for cooking purposes; inveighed against celibacy, the mass and *infant baptism;* and after twenty years of continued disturbance ended his days at the stake by the hands of an infuriated mob, 1124. He was succeeded by one of his *associates*, Henry of Lausanne, formerly a monk of the order of Clugny. Under him the sect of the Petrobrussians *greatly increased in numbers.*"[1]

Farther on we will see that in stating the Petrobrussians rejected the visible church, Kurtz is as much in error as he is in stating that the only true church is not an outward organization, but only internal or invisible. Indeed, in that he says they rejected infant baptism, implying that they practiced adult baptism, Kurtz confutes his own statement; since water baptism implies a visible church.

Kurtz's Chr. Hist., vol. 1, p. 456.

THE PETROBRUSSIANS AND HENRICIANS.

Says Mosheim: "A much more *rational* sect was that which was founded about the year 1110 in Languedoc and Provence by Peter de Bruys, who made the *most laudable* attempts to reform the abuses and to remove the superstitions that disfigured the beautiful simplicity of the gospel, and after having engaged in the cause a *great number* of followers, during a ministry of twenty years continuance, was burnt at St. Giles, in the year 1130, by an enraged populace, set on by the clergy, whose traffic was in danger from the enterprising spirit of the reformer. The whole system of doctrine, which this unhappy martyr, whose zeal was not without a considerable mixture of fanaticism, taught to the Petrobrussians, his disciples, is not known. It is, however, certain that the five following tenets made a part of his system. (1.) That no persons whatever were to be baptised *before* they were come to the fullness of their reason. (2.) That it was an ideal superstition to build churches for the service of God, who will accept of sincere worship *wherever* it is offered, and that such churches as had already been erected should be pulled down and destroyed. (3.) That the crucifixes as instruments of superstition deserved the same fate. (4.) That the real body and blood of Christ were not exhibited in the eucharist, but were merely *represented* in the holy ordidance, by their figures and symbols. (5.) And, lastly, that the oblations, prayers, and the good works of the living, could be in no respect advantageous to the dead. This innovator was *succeeded* by another, who was of Italian birth, and whose name was Henry, the founder and parent of the sect of Henricians."[1]

In Mosheim stating that notwithstanding Henry took up the work where Peter de Bruys left it and that Henry

---

[1] Mosheim's Eccl. Hist., cent. 12, part 2, chap. 5, secs. 7, 8.

founded the Henricians, we see how historians attribute the origin of any *previous* party to its new leader, naming it a new name, for that leader. Mosheim continues: "We have no account of the doctrines of this reformer transmitted to our times. All we know of the matter is, that he rejected *infant baptism;* censured with severity the corrupt and licentious manners of the clergy; treated the festivals and ceremonies of the church with the utmost contempt; and held clandestine assemblies, in which he explained and inculcated the novelties he taught. *Several writers affirm that he was a disciple of Peter de Bruys.*"[1]

After giving substantially the same account of the Petrobrussians and Henricians, as the foregoing, Wadington says: "Henry is *generally* described as a *disciple and fellow laborer* of Pierre de Bruys. The objection to this opinion, urged by Mosheim, is, that Henry was preceded in his expeditions by the figure of the cross, whereas Pierre consigned all crucifixes to the flames. Without supposing that the objection of Pierre might be to the image of the Savior, not to the form of the cross, the *objection is far from conclusive.*"[2]

To Wadington's answer may be added: Protestant and Baptist churches, while joining Peter de Bruys in destroying crucifixes as he found them used, do not hesitate to use the representation of the cross in song, picture and even on churches. Hence, Henry could have used the cross in harmony with his teachers.

After giving substantially the foregoing account, another historian adds: "The Petrobrussians, to justify themselves from the calumnies of Peter of Clugny and others, sent forth a work in answer to the question,

---
[1] Idem, ibid.
[2] Wadington's Ch. Hist.—note to p. 287.

'What is anti-Christ?' It is generally supposed to have been the production of Peter de Bruys, and is said to have been written as early as 1120. . . . In reference to the ordinances, it declares, 'A third work of anti-Christ consists in this, that he attributes the *regeneration of the Holy Spirit* unto the mere *external* rite,' (as Campbellism), 'baptizing infants in that faith, teaching that thereby baptism and regeneration must be had; on which principle he bestows and confers orders, and, indeed, *grounds* all his Christianity, which is contrary to the mind of the Holy Spirit. This view was supported by a confession of their faith, in fourteen articles, published about the same time. In this confession they acknowledge the Apostles' creed; belief in the *Trinity;* own the Canonical books of the Old and New Testament; scriptural character of God, of Adam and his fall; work of Christ as mediator; abhorrence of *human* inventions in worship; that the sacraments were *signs* of holy things and that *believers* should use the *symbol* or forms when it can be done; though they *may be saved without those signs;* they own baptism and the Lord's supper; and express their obedience to secular powers.'" Thus, we see the Petrobrussian and Henrician churches were far from being either *Campbellites* or *Pedobaptists*, and that they believed in the visible church. Neander says: "Henry became the *leader* of the Petrobrussians."[1]

Dr. J. M. Cramp says of them: "Baptism and the church were contemplated by Peter in the pure light of the *Scripture*. The church should be composed, they constantly affirmed, of *true believers, good and just* persons; *no others* had *any* claim to membership. Baptism was a nullity unless connected with *personal faith*, but all who believed were under solemn *obligation* to be

[1] Neander's Hist. Chr. Ch., vol. 4, p. 602.

baptized, according to the Saviour's command. Peter was not *merely* what is now called 'a *Baptist in principle.*' When the truths he inculcated were received and men and women were received to 'newness of life' they were directed to the path of *duty*. Enemies said that was Anabaptism, but Peter and his friends indignantly repelled the imputation. The right performed in infancy, they maintained, was *no* baptism at all, since it wanted the *essential* ingredient, faith in Christ. There and then *only* when they *professed* were the converts really baptized. *Great success* attended Peter's labors . . . Henry repaired to the district *where* Peter de Bruys preached and *entered into his labors* . . . This is *certain* that he *fully agreed* with Peter on the subject of baptism and those who received the truth were formed into '*apostolical societies,*' or, as we should now say, into *Christian churches.*"[1] Even Dr. Wall concedes that the Petrobrussians and Henricians rejected infant baptism.[2] Of one of the slanderous reports against them, Dr. Wall says: "I hope that those reports are *not true.*" Wall further quotes them: "It is therefore an *idle* and *vain* thing for you to wash persons with water, at such a time when you may indeed cleanse their skin from dirt in a human manner, but not purge their souls from sins. But we do stay till the proper time of *faith*, and when a person is *capable to know his God*, and *believes* in him, then we do (not as you charge, rebaptize him) but *baptize* him." On which Wall remarks: "This is, as to the practice, *perfectly* in agreement with *modern antipedobaptists.*"[3] Dr. Wall here reports a slander, that they believed in infant damnation, a slander so threadbare and contra-

[1] Cramp's Bap. Hist., p. 129.
[2] Wall's Hist. Inf. Bap., vol. 3, p. 250.
[3] Idem, vol. 2, pp. 256, 259.

dictory to what we know of them, that it is unworthy of notice. Says Dr. S. H. Ford: "Henry was a *Baptist*."[1] Vedder shows they were not Campbellites. He says: "A third *capital* error," the Romanist charged on them was they "*denied sacramental grace*."[2] Though Vedder seems as much prejudiced against Church Perpetuity, and more ready to credit slanders against some of our Baptist ancestors than candid Pedobaptist writers are, the Petrobrussians were so clearly Baptists, that he says: "In the *main, the beliefs* attributed to them are such as are firmly held to-day by Baptists the world over. The question is already practically answered, were the Petrobrussians Baptists? *In their main principles they certainly were.* Those, therefore, who attempt to trace the descent of modern Baptists through the Petrobrussians have at least a plausible starting point. Anybody that holds to the supremacy of the Scriptures, a *spiritual* church, and *believers'* baptism, is *fundamentally one with the Baptist churches of to-day*, whatever else it may add to or omit from the statement of its belief. Contemporary records have been sought in *vain* to establish any *essential* doctrine taught by this condemned sect that is *inconsistent either with the teaching of the Scripture or with the belief* avowed in *recent times by Baptists*."[3]

Vedder, farther, says: "There were other preachers of a pure gospel, nearly contemporary with Peter de Bruys, and more or less *closely* connected with him. Henry of Lausanne (1116–1150) is described by some as a *disciple* of Peter, though others insist that he did not share Peter's heresies. *Certain* it is that at one time *they were close companions* and the balance of evidence

[1] Ford's Origin of Bap., p. 97.
[2] Vedder's Hist. Bap., p. 60.
[3] Idem, p. 62.

indicates that Henry of Lausanne was *powerfully influenced by his predecessor and co-laborer* . . . He is described as a man of great dignity of person, of fiery eye, a thundering voice, impetuous speech, mighty in the *Scriptures*. His preaching was largely *scriptural*, and an exhortation to shun the prevalent corruption of life and seek righteousness . . . The words quoted from Bernard seem to prove that he taught and practiced the baptism of *believers only*, while it is certain that he held to the supreme authority of the Scriptures and rejected the authoritative clauses of the tradition and the church."[1] Dr. Armitage who has denounced "Succession" as intemperately as any one can well do, says: " The term Cathari has been applied to another *thoroughly Baptist sect* . . . the Petrobrussians . . . In the Petrobrussians we find a sect of *Baptists* for which *no apology is needed*. Peter of Bruis seized the entire Biblical presentation of baptism and forced its teaching home upon the conscience and the life, by rejecting the immersion of babes and insisting on the *immersion* of all *believers* in Christ . . . He held the church to be made up of a *regenerated* people *only*, counted the bishops and priests, as he knew them, mere frauds; and set aside *all* the ceremonial mummeries of the Romish hierarchy. He would not adore images, offer prayers to or for the dead, nor do penance. He laughed at the stupidity which holds that a child is regenerated *when baptized*, that he can be a *member* of Christ's flock when he knows *nothing of Christ* as a Shepherd, and demanded that all who came to his churches should be *immersed* in water on their *own act of faith* . . . No one is to be called baptized who is not washed with the baptism wherewith sins are washed away . . . The Petro-

[1] Idem, p. 64.

brussians were a *thoroughly* anti-sacerdotal sect, whose hatred of tyranny threw off the Roman yoke of the twelfth century; a democratic body, in distinction from the aristocratic organization . . . They demanded the words of Christ in the New Testament for everything and not the traditions of an inner and favored few . . . The Petrobrussians were thoroughly and deeply anti-Catholic in all that conflicted with the gospel. While they *were Puritanical* they were not ascetic. They abolished all fasts and penance for sin because Christ only can forgive sin, and *this he does on a sinner's trust* in his merits. They held marriage as a high and honorable relation not only for Christians generally, but for priests . . . With them a church did not mean an architectural structure, but a *regenerated congregation*, nor had consecrated places any charm for them; for God could hear them as well in the market place as in the temple . . . The death of Peter was not the end of his cause. Labbe calls him 'the parent of heretics,' for almost all who were then branded after his day trod in his steps; and especially all Baptist heretics. . . . When, like Elijah, God took Peter to heaven in a fiery chariot, he had Elisha ready to catch his falling mantle, in the person of Henry of Lausanne, or as Cluniacensis much prefers to put it, he was followed by Henry '*the heir of Bruis*' wickedness.' This petulant author imagined that Peter's principles had died with him, and like a simpleton writes: 'I should have thought that it had been those craggy Alps, and rocks covered with continual snow, that had bred that savage temper in the inhabitants, and that your land being unlike to other lands, had yielded a sort of people unlike to all others . . . Such a bold soul had Christ been preparing in Henry, the next brave *Baptist* of the Swiss valleys. He had formerly been a monk at Clugny and had *joined himself to his master, Peter of Bruis,* in the midst of his toils; and thus had caught *his* spirit and been *numbered with his principles* . . . He then made *common cause* with Peter, as Melancthon did with Luther . . . The land *swarmed* with Henry's followers."[1]

The opposition to church buildings, mentioned in the foregoing, was probably to them only as almost deified by the Romish church. As the Petrobrussians had been accustomed to church buildings only as used by the Romish church they may have opposed them in toto. If they did indiscriminately condemn church houses that in no way rendered them unbaptistic, since church houses are not a Baptist article of faith or necessary to the existence of a Baptist church. That the extravagances of the times should drive the Baptists of those ages into extremes is not to be unexpected. Yet God preserved them from essential departures from the faith. (See Chapter V of this book.)

That the Petrobrussians and the Henricians were Baptists is so certain that I conclude this chapter in the language of that very high authority, Prof. Buckland, late Professor of Ecclesiastical History in Rochester Theological Seminary: "We do reach a distinctively Baptist line in the Petrobrussians, in 1104, and I believe that we may claim that our distinctive principles were perpetuated continuously from that date onward into the Reformation period, and so to our day." Or of Dr. A. H. Newman, of Peter de Bruys and of Henry of Lausanne: "The views of these teachers are well known to have been substantially Baptist."[2] (My italics in this chapter.)

---

[1] Armitage's Bap. Hist., pp. 283-290.
[2] Baptist Quart. Rev., July, 1885, p. 321.

CHAPTER XV.

The Arnoldists.

Says Mosheim: "In Italy, Arnold of Brescia, a disciple of Abelard, and a man of extensive erudition and remarkable austerity, but also a turbulent spirit, excited new troubles and commotions both in church and State. He was, indeed, condemned in the council of the Lateran, A. D. 1139, by Innocent II., and thereby obliged to retire to Switzerland; but upon the death of the pontiff he returned into Italy and raised at Rome, during the pontificate of Eugenie III., several tumults and seditions among the people, who changed by his instigation the government of the city and insulted the persons of the clergy in the most disorderly manner. He fell, however, at last, a victim to the vengeance of his enemies; for, after various turns of fortune, he was seized, in the year 1155, by a prefect of the city, by whom he was crucified and afterward burned to ashes. This unhappy man seems *not to have adopted any doctrine inconsistent with the spirit of true religion;* and the principles upon which he acted were chiefly reprehensible from their being carried too far, and executed with a degree of vehemence which was as criminal as it was imprudent. Having perceived the discords and animosities, the calamities and disorders, that sprang from the *overgrown opulence* of the pontiffs and bishops, he was persuaded that the interests of the church and the happiness of nations in general required that the clergy should be divested of all their *worldly* possessions, of all their *temporal* rights and prerogatives.

He therefore maintained publicly that the *treasures* and *revenues* of popes, bishops and monasteries ought to be solemnly resigned and transferred to the supreme rulers of each State, and that nothing was to be left to the ministers of the gospel but a *spiritual* authority and a subsistence drawn from the *tithes*, and from the *voluntary* oblations and contributions of the people. This violent reformer, in whose character and manner there were *several* things *worthy* of esteem, drew after him a *great number* of disciples who derived from him the name of Arnoldists, and in succeeding times discovered the spirit and intrepidity of their leader, as often as any favorable opportunities of reforming the church were offered to their zeal."[1]

Kurtz says of Arnold: "His fervent oratory was chiefly directed against the secular power of the church and its possession of *property*, views which were probably based on a *more spiritual conception* of what the church *really* was. Otherwise his doctrinal opinions seem to have been in accordance with those commonly entertained."[2]

Wadington gives substantially the above account, adding: "It is, besides, asserted that his orthodoxy was liable to suspicion respecting the *eucharist and infant baptism*. In consequence of these various charges he was condemned by a Lateran council in 1139 A. D."[3] Of Arnold Wadington further says: "To diminish the *privileges*, to reduce the *revenues* of the church, to deprive the pontiff of *temporal power* and all *civil* jurisdiction, and to degrade (should we not rather say exalt?) his stately splendor to the homeliness of his *primitive* prede-

---

[1] Mosheim's Eccl. Hist., cent. 12, part 2, chap. 5, sec. 10.
[2] Kurtz's Ch. Hist., vol. 1, p. 456.
[3] Wadington's Ch. Hist., p. 258.

cessors; *these* were the projects preparatory to the political regeneration of Rome."[1]

Says C. Schmidt, regarded as one of the main authorities on this subject: "But comparing the first Christian congregation, the church of the Apostles, with the church of his own time, he felt scandalized at the *difference.* The root of all evil he found in the *wealth* of the church. All the vices and all the *worldliness of the clergy* he ascribed to their *riches.* . , . He was a gifted man, upright and fervent. The *frightful corruption* of the church naturally struck him, and in the Bible itself he found the corrective."[2]

To the charge that Arnold was turbulent and a creator of mobs and other disorders, the reader must bear in mind that any one, on behalf of liberty and a pure church, could not *then* speak out against such evils as he protested without being so charged. *Church and State* then being *united*, the people, under the *pretence of taxation*, *were robbed to enrich a licentious clergy* and to build up vast houses of ecclesiastical prostitution and kindred abominations.* Why, no greater praise could be accorded any one than that he made troublesome times for *such* a church and such a clergy. Treason against such government can but be loyalty to God. If, as reported, there were disorders attending Arnold's agitation, what were they but such as attended all great movements, from wicked men taking advantage of the state of war; or, more likely, from an *outraged people* being no longer able to control themselves, a thing for which not Arnold was to blame but the corrupt clergy and the church, from which the cause of outrage

---

*During the middle ages the Romish church robbed the people until it got much or most of their wealth into its own hands. The age of freedom brought the recovery of much of this property. But in Mexico, and in some other countries, it yet retains the property it obtained by this robbery.

[1] Idem, ibid.
[2] Schaff-Herzog Ency., vol. 1, p. 149.

proceeded. Arnold "exhorted the people to organize a government similar to the ancient Roman republic, with its consuls, its tribunes and equestrian order. But they, provoked by the treachery and opposition of the papal party, and disunited among themselves, gave way to the grossest excesses."[1]

As Cramp observes: " Had it not been for the support derived from the imperial power, Italy would have been Protestant before the Reformation. The success of Arnold of Brescia was an impressive warning. In the year 1143 he established a new form of government in Rome, which wrested the civil power out of the hands of popes and compelled them to content themselves with the management of ecclesiastical affairs. That the attempt was ill-advised, because society was not sufficiently *prepared for it*, is evident; but the continuance of the new order of things for *eleven years* and the alacrity with which the people adopted an *anti-papal policy*, were remarkable signs of the times."[2] " Arnold was formally condemned by the second general Lateran council, 1139. But his appeals to the people had found an echo in many breasts."[3] Baird: " At his suggestion the form of the ancient Roman commonwealth was *restored* with its consuls, senate, equestrian order and the tribunes of the *people*. But it was all in vain. The Romans were *no longer fit for freedom*, but like the Cappadocians of old, when offered the *boon*, they preferred the chains which they had been so long accustomed to wear. . . . We know little of this Arnold from any contemporaneous source, except the pages of Roman Catholic writers, who were not likely to do him justice. But by their *own*

---

[1] Universal Knowledge, vol. 1, p. 671.
[2] Cramp's Bap. Hist., p. 98.
[3] Kurtz's Ch. Hist., vol. 1, p. 403.

showing, it is manifest that *he contended for truth and justice.*"[1] Says G. Schmidt, of Arnold: "His reforms were *all* of a *practical* character."[2] Of Arnold, Armitage says: "God had endowed him with *rare* gifts. He possessed great fervor, purity and serenity, with a remarkable flow of eloquence; these he united to most graceful and attractive manners and charming conversational powers. As a preacher he filled Lombardy with resistance to the *pride* and *pretensions of the priesthood*. He was the purest, most severe and bold personification of *republican democracy*, both laical and ecclesiastical, of the century. . . . Under the stirring appeals of his deep convictions and impassioned eloquence the popular cry was raised: 'The *people and liberty*,' and he became as much its incarnation as Mazzini and Garibaldi in modern times. As the *apostle of liberty* he contended for a *full dissolution of the union between church and State*, and fired the cities to seek perfect freedom from both pope and empire by establishing a *republic*. As a patriot he looked upon these civil enemies only with contempt, and summoned Italy to shake them off. As a Christian he was an anti-sacramentarian, desiring to bring the church back to the New Testament standard; or, as Gibbon expresses it, he boldly threw himself upon the declaration of Christ: 'My kingdom is not of this world.' He would not use the sword, but maintained his cause by moral sentiment; and yet formed the daring plan of planting the standard of civil and religious liberty in the City of Rome itself, for the purpose of restoring the old rights of the senate and the people. *His pure morals and childlike sense of justice* startled the whole land. . . . Rome was thrown into insurrection; all Europe felt his power, and

---

[1] Baird's Prot. in Italy, pp. 20, 22.
[2] Schaff-Herzog Ency., vol. 1, p. 149.

the eyes of Christendom were turned to the Eternal City. After a desperate contest against three several popes, which cost Lucian his life, a new constitution was framed and the sanction of Adrian IV. was demanded to its provisions. The pope fled for his life, his *temporal* power was abolished, and a new government was established in 1143, which maintained the struggle with varying fortunes for about ten years. The violence of the people, however, prevented final success. They rose in insurrection, demolished the houses and seized the property of the papal party, while *Arnold was conservative* and touched nothing. Nevertheless, his holy apostolate planted the *seeds of that republicanism which controls the Italy, Switzerland and France of to-day.*" Speaking of his martyrdom, "Thus perished this great patriot and martyr to the holy doctrine of soul-liberty. But Italy will ever hold his name in hallowed remembrance.

"Down to 1861 a simple slab commemorated his noble deeds; then a modest statue took its place. But in 1864-65 the Communal and Provincial councils of Brescia each voted a sum of 30,000 lire (Itali) for a splendid monument to his honor. The city of Zurich made a large contribution, and from other sources the sum amounted to 150,000 lire, about $30,000. The ablest artists of Northern Italy competed for the prize model, which was awarded M. Tabacchi. The base after the design of the great architect, Tagliaferri, who has succeeded admirably in reproducing the old Lombard style of architecture in Arnold's time, is of various colored marbles, hewn from the rocks of Brescia. The statue itself is of bronze and is four meters (13 feet 4 inches) high. Arnold is represented in a preaching attitude; his gigantic figure being that of a monk, in a long robe with graceful folds. His long nervous arms extend from the wide sleeves, his wonderful face is serene, but inspired for address; and the simplicity of the whole conception is worthy of the greatness of the man. The first alto-relievo represents him expounding his doctrine to the Brescians, holding in his hand the book of truth; in the second he is on trial, defending himself before his judges against the accusations of his foes; in the third he stands preaching in the Forum, surrounded by shields, broken columns and capitals, among which is the arch of Titus; the fourth presents him on the scaffold with his hands tied behind his back, the judge at his side about to read the sentence, and a funeral pile ready for lighting behind him. This beautiful work of art was dedicated to him as the *forerunner* of Italian liberty in the nineteenth century, and was officially unveiled in Brescia, Aug. 14, 1882. Most eloquent orations were delivered, while redeemed Italy looked on, by the patriot Zanardelli, 'Minister of Grace and Justice' for that year.

"Although the great distinctive feature in which Arnold most sympathized with *Baptists* relates to his unbending opposition to *any union whatever with church and State*, he appears to have sympathized with them in *other respects*. Dr. Wall says that the Lateran Council of A. D. 1139, condemned him for rejecting *infant baptism*, and he thinks that he was '*a follower of Peter de Bruis*' *in this respect*. If so, then the council which condemned the Petrobrussians, condemned him. Bernard accuses him and his followers of deriding *infant baptism*. Evervine not only complains of the same thing but says that they administered baptism *only to believers*. Gibbon also states that Arnold's 'ideas of baptism and the eucharist were loosely censured; but a political * heresy

---

* History demonstrates this "political heresy" the result of Baptist principles.

was the source of his fame and his misfortunes.' "[1]

Gibbon says: "The trumpet of liberty was first sounded by Arnold of Brescia.".[2]

Says Brewster: "It is impossible not to admire the genius and the perseverving intrepidity of Arnold. To distinguish truth from error in an age of darkness, and to detect the causes of spiritual corruption in the thickest atmosphere of ignorance and superstition, evinced a mind of more than ordinary stretch. To adopt a plan for recovering the lost glory of his country, and fixing the limits of spiritual usurpation, demanded a degree of resolution which no opposition could control. But to struggle against superstition entrenched in power, to plant the standard of rebellion in the very heart of her empire, and to keep posession of her capitol for a number of years, could scarcely have been expected from an individual who had no power but that of eloquence, and no assistance but what he derived from the justice of his cause. Yet such were the individual exertions of Arnold, which posterity will appreciate as one of the noblest legacies which former ages have bequeathed."[3]

Dr. Allix says: "We may truly say that *scarcely any man* was ever *so torn and defamed* on account of his doctrine as was Arnold of Brescia. Would we know the reason of this? It was because, with all his power, he opposed the *tyranny and usurpation* which the popes began to establish at Rome over the temporal jurisdiction of the emperors."[4]

Says Jones: "But there was a still more heinous thing laid to his charge, which was this: Praeter haec

---

[1] Armitage's Bap. Hist., pp. 291-293; Wall's Hist. Inf. Bap., vol. 2, p. 265.
[2] Gibbon's Hist. Rome, vol. 3, p. 366, etc.
[3] Brewster's Edinburgh Ency., Art. Arnold.
[4] Allix's Ch. Pied., p. 169.

de sacramento altaris et *baptismo parvulorum*, non sane dicitur senisse! That is, he was unsound in his judgment about the sacrament of the altar and *infant baptism*. In other words, he rejected the popish doctrine of transubstantiation and the baptism of infants."[1] Arnold had no Campbellism in him; for the Romish church said of him: "Arnoldistæ . . . asserunt, quod nunquam per baptismum aquæ homines Spiritum sanctum accipiunt"—the Arnoldists assert that men never receive the Holy Spirit through baptism in water. †

Neander: "The inspiring idea of his movements was that of a *holy and a pure* church, a renovation of the spiritual order, after the order of the *apostolic* church. His life corresponded with his doctrine. . . . The corrupt bishops and priests were no longer bishops and priests; the secularized church was no longer the house of God . . . We must allow that the way in which Arnold stood forth against the corruptions of the church, and especially his inclination to make the objective in the instituted order, and in the transactions of the church, to depend on the subjective character of the men, might easily lead to still *greater aberations*."[2]

Modern historians rightly conclude that Luther's Reformation was only the outburst of principles and doctrines agitated by the "heretics" long before and up to his time; to the *Baptist agitation which had prepared the people for the great uprising against the old " mother of harlots."* Without that preparation Luther's work would have been impossible. Only by keeping in mind the previous Baptist agitation, can we rightly appreciate the origin of Arnold's work. Their agitation of the great

† Quoted in Recent Researches Concerning Mediæval Sects, p. 192.
[1] Jones' Ch. Hist., p. 286.
[2] Neander's Ch. Hist., vol. 4, p. 149

principles on which Arnold did his work had made hundreds of thousands of converts and honey-combed the old Romish fortress with gospel shot. Hence the people so readily gathered around Arnold as their God-sent leader. Ivimey says: "Arnold of Brescia seems to have been a follower of Bruis."[1] Peter de Bruys having been, probably, a pupil of the famous Abelard of Paris, * of whom Arnold had been a pupil † the *latter would naturally fall into line with the Petrobrussians*, especially as their cause was *identical*, and as they both took only the Bible for their guide. No great movement, believing, as did Arnold's, in a spiritual church, in the baptism of only believers—regenerate persons—and the separation of church and State, has been other than Baptist. Hence, with Dr. Ford, we may safely say, the Arnoldists were "Baptists."[2] Or, in the language of Vedder, an opponent of Church Perpetuity: Arnold "may fairly be claimed by Baptists as belonging to them."[3] Or with the *Watchman*, a leading Baptist paper, of Boston: "As to Arnold, of Brescia, from what we read of him, we are not ashamed to call him brother, or to *join his goodly fellowship.*"

* Armitage's Bap. Hist., p. 284.
† Neander's Hist. Chr. Ch., vol. 4, p. 148.
1 Ivimey's Hist. Eng. Bap., p. 21.
2 Ford's Origin of Bap., p. 102.
3 Vedder's Bap. Hist., p. 65.

CHAPTER XVI.

THE WALDENSES.

Of the twelfth century, Mosheim says: "Of all the sects that arose in this century none were more distinguished by the reputation it acquired, by the multitude of its votaries, and the testimony which its bitterest enemies bore to the *probity and innocence* of its members, than that of the Waldenses. . . . This sect was known by different *denominations.*" [1]

Prof. William Whitsitt, D. D., of the Southern Baptist Theological Seminary, has said, the Waldenses joined the Catharists.[2] The Catharists, in previous articles, we have seen, were Paulicians, Albigenses, etc.

Prof. Whitsitt has conveniently divided the Waldensian history into two periods. The first from the origin of the term Waldenses to the Reformation; the second, during and since the Reformation. Prof. Whitsitt says that no doubt the Waldenses altered their opinions under Luther's influence. Until we come to Anabaptist history we are concerned only with the first period of Waldensian history.

To unravel much entanglement in their history and to prevent farther entanglement, it is probably well to here introduce Mosheim's statement: "It is, however, to be observed that the Waldenses were not without other intestine *divisions.* Such of them as lived in Italy *differed considerably* in their opinions from those who dwelt in France

---

[1] Mosheim's Eccl. Hist., cent. 12, part 2, ch. 5, sec. 11.
[2] MS. Lect.

and other European nations. The former considered the church of Rome as the church of Christ, though much corrupted and sadly disfigured. They acknowledged, moreover, the validity of the seven sacraments, and solemnly declared they would always continue in communion with it, provided they might be allowed to live as they thought proper, without molestation or constraint. The latter affirmed, on the contrary, that the church of Rome had apostatized from Christ, was deprived from the Holy Spirit, and was, in reality, the whore of Babylon mentioned in the Revelation of St. John."[1]

Prof. A. H. Newman makes about the same distinction.[2]

Another thing may be well remembered: The party of Waldenses which first, in a great measure, agreed with Rome, would gradually, by study of the Scriptures and the influence of more evangelical parties, become more Scriptural. Herein lies the explanation of Kurtz's statement, that "their dogmatic views underwent a complete change," and that the time when they received the "doctrine of justification by faith alone, commenced about the time of Huss."[3] Huss, in the main, in principle, was a Baptist.[4]

As Hase remarks: "The Waldensians. . . . were *connected* with the Hussites by fraternal ties."[5] The views of Wickliffe, who was in principle, at least, a Baptist, must have had a great influence, too, over the erroneous Waldensians.

Dorner says that in the Waldenses "the Christian *ground ideas*" were "*long propagated incorrupt.*"[6]

---

[1] Mosheim's Eccl. Hist., cent. 12, part 2, ch. 5, sec. 13.
[2] Bap. Quart. Rev. for July, 1885.
[3] Kurtz's Ch. Hist., vol. 1, p. 460.
[4] Hase's Hist. Chr. Ch., pp. 347, 348.
[5] Idem, p. 510.
[6] Dorner's Hist. Per. Christ., vol. 1, div. 1, p. 94.

A Dominican, named Rainer Saccho, of the Waldenses, acknowledged: "While other sects were profane and blasphemous, this retains the utmost show of piety; they live justly before men, and believe nothing respecting God which is not good; *only* they blaspheme against the Romish church and the clergy, and thus gain *many* followers."[1] To multiply like testimonies to the godly character and the right views of the Waldenses, to the weariness of my readers, is an easy thing. Hence, several Protestant bodies have tried to make out ecclesiastical kinship to the Waldenses; not by way of proving Succession from them, but identity of faith.

Whether or not we recognize Mosheim's Italian and French distinction between the different Waldenses, there is so much evidence that, in this period, there were parties of different characters, known as Waldenses, that we *must recognize different beliefs and practices among them*. This will readily harmonize the different documents, showing some Waldenses of this period remained in the church of Rome; some separated from it; some were *never* in it; some may have had infant baptism and other Romish trumpery, while most of them were Baptistic.

I now invite the reader to the proof that part of the Waldenses were Baptists.

(1.) They were Baptists in that they believed only in a *professedly regenerate* church membership. In article 12 of the Waldensian Confession, dated by Sir Samuel Morland, A. D. 1120 — an eminent authority on Waldensian history — we read, of the ordinances: "We regard it as proper and even necessary that *believers* use these *symbols* as visible forms when it can be done."[2] In their Confession of 1144 they thus reiterate this confession:

[1] Wadington's Ch. Hist., p. 290.
[2] Jones' Ch. Hist., p. 333.

"We believe there is *one* holy church, comprising the whole assembly of the *elect* and *faithful*. . . . In the church it behooves all *Christians* to have fellowship." Using the symbols for only believers, and stating the church is a "holy" church, "comprising the elect and faithful"— comprising "Christians"— clearly and inevitably imply the Waldenses were Baptists.[1] That the Waldenses believed in a professedly regenerate membership is also certain from their rejecting infant baptism. (See proof farther on of their rejecting infant baptism.)

(2.) The Waldenses were Baptists in that they practiced only immersion. To all who are familiar with church history it is well known there was no affusion till the middle of the third century, and that from that time to the Reformation immersion was the rule and affusion allowed only in cases of sickness—called "clinic baptism." Thus the Prayer Book of 1549 says: "If the child be weak it shall suffice to pour upon it." While "clinic baptism" was practiced by the Romish church it was never sanctioned by any council until sanctioned by the council of Ravenna, A. D. 1311. We have seen that that the Waldenses affiliated with the Hussites; and Erasmus wrote of them: "The Hussites renounced all rites and ceremonies of the *Catholic* church; they ridicule our doctrine and practices in both the sacraments; they deny *orders* (the hierarchy) and *elect* officers from among the laity; they receive no other rule than the Bible; they admit none into *their communion* until they are *dipped* in water, or baptized; and they reckon one another without *distinction or rank* to be called brothers and sisters."[2] Living in an age in which immersion was the universal law and the custom, and in which affusion was *only*

---

[1] Art. 4.
[2] Ivimey's Hist. Bap., vol. 1, p. 70.

allowed for sick infants, and in, possibly, a very few cases for sick adults, and then to save from hell, and practicing *only believer's baptism*, rejecting, as we will see, water salvation, that the Waldenses were Baptists as to the action of baptism is the inevitable conclusion. Hence, Armitage says: "They believed and practiced *immersion only*."[1] Mezeray says: "In the twelfth century they (Waldenses) plunged the candidate in the sacred font."[2]

(3.) The Waldenses were Baptists as to the design of baptism. In their Confession of A. D. 1120, just quoted, the Waldenses say: "We consider the sacraments as *signs* of holy things, or as the visible *emblems* of invisible blessings. We regard it as proper and ever necessary that *believers* use these *symbols* or visible *forms* when it can be done. Notwithstanding, we maintain that believers may be saved *without* these signs, when they have neither place nor opportunity of observing them."[3] In their Confession of 1544, they say: "We believe that in the ordinance of baptism the water is the visible and external *sign*, which *represents* to us that which by virtue of *God's* invisible operations is *within* us, namely, the *renovation of our minds* and the mortification of our members through the *faith* of Jesus Christ. And *by* this ordinance we are received into the congregation of *God's* people, *previously* professing and declaring our *faith and change of life*."[4] As Baptists do now, taking the ordinances for mere signs of grace which is *already in the heart* and for only believers or Christians, Armitage well says: "They rejected the error of regeneration *by baptism*."[5] Hence,

---

[1] Armitage's Bap. Hist., p. 305.
[2] Hist. France, cent. 12, p. 288—quoted.
[3] Art. 12, in Jones' Ch. Hist., p. 333.
[4] Art. 7, in Jones' Ch. Hist., p. 335.
[5] Armitage's Bap. Hist., p. 305.

in the Waldensian tract, describing anti-Christ, they say: "A third mark of anti-Christ consists in this, in that he attributes the regeneration of the Holy Spirit unto the mere *external rite*, baptizing infants in that faith, teaching that *thereby* baptism and regeneration must be had; on which *principle* he bestows orders, and, indeed, *grounds* all his Christianity, which is contrary to the mind of the Holy Spirit."† Leaving out infant baptism, this, condemned, is also a good picture of Campbellism.

(4.) The Waldenses agreed with Baptists in that while they said: "In *articles of faith* the authority of the Holy Scriptures is the *highest;* and for that reason is the *standard* of judging,"[1] they said we "agree with the general *Confession of Faith*,"[2] etc. *They believed in Confessions of Faith as useful in making known their faith.* Hence I have the opportunity of just quoting from two of their Confessions. In their trial before a court, they said: "But according to the decree of the court it is upon our *Confession of Faith* that we ought to be examined." As a result of this examination, showing the *utility* of Confessions of Faith, the examiner said: "I have not only found this paper conformable to the Holy Scripture, but, moreover, I have learned to understand them better during these two or three days, than during all the rest of my life." To this the Romish prelate, impliedly accusing the examiner of being led over to Waldensian belief, said: "You are under the influence of the devil." On which Muston remarks: "The councillor withdrew; and as we shall not meet with him again in the course of this history, it may here be added that this circumstance led him to search the Scriptures still more than he had

---

† Jones' Ch. Hist., p. 338.
[1] Jones' Ch. Hist., p. 333.
[2] Idem, p. 336.

yet done, and that a year after he went to Geneva, where he embraced Protestantism. *Had the Confession of Faith of the Vaudois churches produced only that result,* there is enough of good in the conversion and salvation of one immortal soul to make us regard it with feelings of satisfaction, whatever temporal misfortunes may have ensued from it."[1]

(5.) The Waldenses were Baptists as to the operation of the Holy Spirit. Article III. of their Confession of A. D. 1544 reads: "We believe that the Holy Spirit is the Comforter, proceeding from the Father and the Son, by whose inspiration we are *taught to pray;* being *by Him renewed in the spirit of our minds;* who *creates us anew** unto* good works, and from whom we recover the knowledge of the truth."[2]

(6.) From the foregoing they agreed with Baptists on depravity. The new creation inevitably implies "total depravity;" otherwise no need of the mighty power of the Spirit and the new creation in saving a soul. †

(7.) Instead of believing in weekly communion they held the Baptist position, that the New Testament does not set the observance of the supper for every Lord's day. Says Armitage: "Herzog" says "certain of the Waldensians' 'met every year for the observance.' "[3]

(8.) The Waldenses agreed with Baptists in the doctrines of salvation by grace and justification by *faith only*. In their belief in the new creation of the soul by

---

*People do not work to be created anew or saved; but they are saved in order to work, as this article declares.—See Eph, 2:10.

† By "total depravity" Baptists do not mean inability to pay honest debts, to tell the truth, to be kind and charitable, and other such acts. But all they mean by the phrase is: Until 'created anew in Christ Jesus," no sinner has any love to *God* in his heart or any *holiness*. Compare Job 11:12; 14:1-4; Psa. 51:5; 58:35; Isa. 48:8; 64:6; Jer. 17:9; Prov. 28:26; Gen. 6:5; 8:21; Matt. 15:19; John 3:6; Eph. 2:3; John 8:44; Matt. 23:27-28; Rom. 7:18; Isa. 1:6; Rom. 3:10-18.

1 Israel of the Alps, vol. 1, p. 61.
2 Jones' Ch. Hist., p. 335.
3 Armitage's Hist. Bap., p. 309.

the mighty power of the Holy Spirit, and their rejection of sacramental regeneration, as just proved, this is manifest.

(9.) The Waldenses were Baptists as to the doctrine of Election.

Prof. A. A. Hodge, D. D., of Princeton Theological Seminary, says: "The Martyrology of Calvinism is pre-eminent in the history of the entire church. We call to witness John Huss and Jerome, of Prague, who perished for their adherence to the faith over one hundred years before Luther." [1]

"The *Waldenses*, of whom were the slaughtered saints, whose 'bones lie scattered on the Alpine mountains cold'; the victims of the reign of 'Bloody Mary,' John Rogers and Hooper, Farras, Ridley. . . . were all Calvinists."[2]

"The Lollards, another name for the Waldenses, the followers of Wickliffe, in the fourteenth century, were all of the general school of St. Augustine."[3]

(10.) The Waldenses were Baptists in rejecting infant baptism.

From the extracts, under a previous head, given from their Confessions, that they rejected infant baptism is evident. Notice the words of Article XI, of their Confession of 1120: "We regard it as proper and even necessary that *believers* use these symbols."[*] Their Confession, of 1544, says in Article VII: "We believe, in the ordinance of baptism the water is the visible and external *sign* which *represents* to us that which by virtue of God's invisible operation, is within us. . . . and by this ordinance we are received into the holy congregation of God's people, previously *professing and declaring* our

[*] Jones' Ch. Hist., p. 333.
[1] Johnson's Ency., vol. 1, p. 733.
[2] Idem, ibid.
[3] Idem, p. 734.

faith and change of life."[1] These articles are almost verbatim the present articles of Baptist faith, and the present Baptist articles are as much in accord with infant baptism as they are.

In the Waldensian tract against anti-Christ, said to have been written about the middle of the twelfth century, the Waldenses say of "anti-Christ:" "He teaches to baptize *children* into the faith, and attributes to *this* the work of regeneration."[2]

Evervinus, of Stanfield, is said to have complained to Bernard, Abbot of Clairval, that Cologne was infested with Waldensian heretics who denied baptism to *infants*.[3]

Petrus Cluniacenis, or Peter the Abbot of Clugny, wrote against them; and among the errors he imputes to them are these: "That *infants* are not baptized, or saved by the faith of *another*, but ought to be baptized and saved by their *own* faith. . . . and that those that are baptized in *infancy*, when grown up, should be baptized again. . . . rather *rightly baptized*."[4]

Wall says: "They speak that baptism does no good to *infants*, and because they cannot profess faith."[5] "Ermengendus, a great man in the church, charges the Waldenses with denying infant baptism."[6] The Waldenses were condemned in conference at Albi, when the Bishop of Lyons, to convince them of their error, produced what were considered proofs of *infant* baptism, and tried to solve their objections from infants wanting faith, without which they said it was impossible to please God."[†]

[†] Allixs' Ch. Albig., ch. 15, p. 133, quoted.
[1] Jones' Ch. Hist., p. 335.
[2] Idem, p. 338.
[3] Allixs' Ch. Pied., ch. 16, p. 140.
[4] Ivimey's Hist. Eng. Bap., vol. 1, pp. 20, 21.
[5] Wall's Hist. Inf. Bap., vol. 2, p. 250, Oxford ed.
[6] Danvers on Bap., p. 298, quoted.

Alanus Magnus states that they denied baptism to children. He disputes their views and refutes their opinions.[1]

The Waldenses admitted the catechumeni after an exact instruction, a long fast in which the church united, to witness to them the concern they took in their conversion, and a confession of sins in token of contrition. The newly baptized were, the same day, admitted to the eucharist, with all the brethren and sisters present.[††] Thus they, like Baptists, first instructed; second, baptized; third, *being in the church, admitted them to the supper* [†] believers' baptism and "close communion."

The Ordibarians, or Waldenses, say that baptism does no good to *infants*, unless they are perfected, by instruction first, in that sect.[2]

"A catechism emanating from the Waldenses, during the thirteenth century, has no *allusion* to infant baptism. It says of the church catholic, that it is the *elect* of God, through the merits of Christ, gathered together by the *Holy Spirit*, and *foreordained* [*] to eternal life."[3]

Montanus is quoted as saying: "The Waldenses, in the public declaration of their faith to the French king, in the year 1521, assert in the strongest terms the baptizing of believers and denying that of infants."

Robinson says: "They hold on to the baptism of *only believers*, and the right of private judgment, in which they *all agreed*."[4] "There is no positive proof, *there can be none*, that they baptized their *babes*."[5] Speaking of a

---

[††] Allix's Ch. Pied., ch. 2, pp. 7-8 — quoted.
[†] This is Baptist "Close Communion."
[*] Election vs. Arminianism.
[1] Allixs' Ch. Pied., ch. 16, p. 145, quoted.
[2] Wall's Hist. Inf. Bap., vol. 2, p. 254, Oxford ed.
[3] Gilly's Nar. App., p. 12 — quoted.
[4] Robinson's Eccl. Resh., p. 446.
[5] Idem, p. 71.

liturgy of ,, certainly very high antiquity " among the Waldenses, Robinson says: "In this liturgy there is *no office* for the baptism of children, nor the *least hint of pouring and sprinkling;* on the contrary, there is a directory for making a *Christian of a pagan* before baptism† . . . preparatory to baptism." This creed runs thus: " You are about to hear the creed, therefore, to-day, for without that neither can Christ be announced, nor can you exercise faith, nor can baptism be administered"[1] "While baptism was left to the choice of the people it was not administered to babes."[2]

Cardinal Hossius, who presided at the council of Trent, and made a history of the heresies of his own times, says the Waldenses, "*rejected infant baptism* and rebaptized all who embraced their sentiments."[3]

Bellarmine, a Catholic writer of repute, is said to have "acknowledged the Waldenses to have held that *only* adults ought to be baptized."[4]

Article XXIX of the Waldensian Confession of 1635, says: "That God has ordained the sacrament of baptism to be a *testimonial* to our adoption, and of our *being cleansed* from our sins by the blood of Jesus Christ and *renewed* in holiness of life."[5]

The modern Waldenses are Pedobaptists. An eminent historian says: "This confession is altered by the Protestants of the valleys, which may be seen by a comparison of the above with a confession in Peyrins' Historical Defence, edited by Rev. T. Sims, 1826, sec.

---

†Had they been of Campbellite belief they would have tried to make Christians by baptism.
[1] Idem, pp. 473-474.
[2] Idem, p. 475.
[3] Hossius' Letters, Apud Opera, pp. 112, 213—quoted.
[4] Facts Op. to Fic., p. 42—quoted.
[5] Gilly's Nar.,-app., p. 12—quoted.

27, p. 463." Baxter did refer to a Waldensian Confession of 1176 for infant baptism, but Wall admits the Catholics *forced* that out of them under threats, and says: "It is a wonder Mr. Baxter would urge it."[1] Perrin endeavored to make infant baptism appear among the earlier Waldenses by quoting a catechism of early date. But Wall, virtually, gives that up when he says: "But what date that catechism is I know not."[2]

Says W. W. Everts, Jr., one of the highest authorities on the subject: "The creed of the Bohemian Waldenses, published in 1532, quoted by Starck, is equally explicit on this point of dispute, saying: "It is as clear as day that *infant baptism does no good*."[3] "The same is true of the English Waldenses . . . for according to the testimony of the chronicler, Thomas Waldensis, they acknowledged but two sacraments and administered baptism *only to adults*."[4] Rechinius affirms that "in their opinion baptism was neither necessary nor useful to *infants*."[4] "In the full statement of Waldensian doctrine and practice made to Ecolampadius, the reformer of Basle, by George Maurel, a delegate from the old reformers to the new . . . he says that *sometimes, to avoid detection*, Waldensian parents offered their children to the Catholic priest to be baptized. The most natural inference is, that though they did not *believe in infant baptism*, rather than suffer unnecessary persecution they *allowed* it."[5]

Ludwig Keller, a very late, careful and original investigator (Lutheran) of highest authority, says: "*Very*

[1] Wall's Hist. Inf. Bap., vol. 2, p. 288, Oxford ed.
[2] Idem, vol. 2, p. 403, Oxford ed.
[3] Church in the Wilderness, pp. 46, 47, a 10-cent pamphlet published by Am. Bap. Pub. Soc.; a work you should get and scatter everywhere.
[4] Idem, p. 46.
[5] Idem, pp. 46, 47.

many Waldenses considered, as we *know accurately*, the baptism on (*profession of*) faith to be that form which is conformable to the words and example of Christ. They held this to be the *sign* of a *good** conscience with God, and it was certain to them that it had no value only as *such*."[1] As Vedder properly observes: "This belief would logically exclude infant baptism."[1] Keller says: "Mostly they *let* their children be baptized, yet with the *reservation* that this ceremony was *null and void*."[1] Probably by Romish priests the baptism was done. Keller farther says: "The Waldensians *ever* held to the baptism upon *faith;* wherever they omitted it, it was owing to the stress of *painful* circumstances." "Throughout the fifteenth century, up to 1536, they observed the baptism of adults as a *sign and seal of covenant 'twixt *good* conscience* and God."[2] To this Dr. Grimmell on Keller's authority, adds: "At *different times*, in *different parts* of Europe, their trial reveals that they held to baptism in *adult* years and upon a profession of fellowship with Jesus."[2]

Peter Vecembecius, in an oration delivered in the academy of Jenna in 1585, on the Waldenses and Albigenses, said they caused their men to be baptized. Perrin, a Pedobaptist historian of the Waldenses, whom Todd and other Pedobaptist scholars have convicted of otherwise distorting Waldensian history, substituted for "*homines* baptızari*,*" "saisoyent baptizer leures *enfans*," thus making Vecembecius testify they practiced infant bap-

---

*As the Waldenses regarded baptism a "sign" of our salvation, to be obeyed only by those of a "good conscience"—compare I. Pet. 3-21, where baptism is seen to be for only those of a "good conscience," and Heb. 9:14; 10:22, by which you will see that only the blood washed have a good conscience—that they had no leading to the Romish-Campbellite baptismal salvation is certain.

[1] In Vedder's Bap. Hist., p. 71.
[2] Quoted by J. C. Grimmell, D. D., in Am. Bap.

tism! Because Jones, in his Church History, quotes this as it is, in the Campbell and Rice Debate, Rice tried to convict Jones of purposely perverting testimony! Pope, a Congregationalist, in his debate with McGuire, a Romish priest, correctly quoted it, sustaining Jones and convicting Perrin. But until Dr. S. H. Ford, a few years ago, from the British Museum, copied the original of this oration, there was some question as to who had falsified history.† But Perrin is now convicted as basely perverting history, to prove the Waldenses practiced baby baptism—a thing which would have been unnecessary had there been sufficient other evidence to prove it. Armitage: "*Almost all the Roman Catholic writers agree with Cardinal Hossius, who says the 'Waldenses rejected infant baptism.'*"[1] Addis and Arnold declare of them: "As to baptism they said that washing of infants was of no avail to them." Armitage adds: "This impression is deepened by the fact that Farrel, Ecolampadius and others at the time of

† The original is: "*Petri Wesenbecij Oratio de Waldensibus, et Albigensibus* 'Anno MDLXXXV. Excudebat Johannes Schleer. Anno MDCIII. In ea intermissione interg: inducias istas persecutionum universalium occidit, quod dignum commemoratio permittendum haud viedetur. Incandebant Regem Ludovicm quo dodecimus in Gallia regnavit, cardinales et episcopoi aliquot adversus Merindolanus et Cabrevienses, reliquias (vt dixi) Waldensium et Albigensium Christianorum, quippe veneficos incestos haereticos ae proiende esse. Merindolani et Cabravienses subordorati quæ cardinales et episcopos in se consilia coquerent et quam atrocibus delationabus aures animum; regis implerere niterenter, mitunt ad regem legatos et innocentiam suam tutantur. Eos legatos aditu regis cardinales prohibere conabantur regem, momentes ne illis prodescendi apud se protestatum facerat jurehibere ne quis cum heriticus communicis. Tum rex, 'etiam si,' inquit, 'mihi in Turcum aut diabolum bellum suscipiendum esset, eas tamen prius andire vellem.' Dignum prossus Rege responsum; quippe inauditum et indefensum quem quam damnate sceptro et iure abuti est. Ergo accitus Ludovicus introduci inbet. Ille reverantur exhonunt, Merindolanenses et Cabrisienses Evangelium Biblis symbolicum expostolicum Dii proecepta sacramenta agnoscere at que ampliciti: coeteriem nec Papæ, nec ipsius doctrinæ credere, se secus esse Rex deprehenderet se nullum supplicasius recusare. Ea itane haberent an secus esse, Rex scire voluit. Itaq ea de re Adamio Finnæo libellorum supplicum Magistro et M Parno Dominicano qui ille a confessionii erat questionem man—*Illi in loco profecti et questionibus perfectis reversi ad Regem referunt illis in locis homine* baptizari, articulos fidei et decalogum doceri, dominicos die religiose coli, *Dei verbum* exponi, veneficia et stupra apud los nulla esse. Coeterum re in ipsorum templis neque arnamenta missæ ulla reperisve. His auditis rex adit jurejurando addito, me inquit, et cetero popolo meo Catholico meliores illa viri sunt. Ad hunc modem prinipes non sunt et prudenter expenderere debent nullum neq indictis neq infactis innocentiam fore si accusare sufficiat.—P. 7, original, 1603.

[1] Armitage's Bap. Hist., pp. 302, 303.

the Reformation, made strenuous efforts to convince the Waldenses of Eastern Dauphine and Savoy of the righteousness of infant baptism."[1]

Ermengard, about A. D. 1192: "They pretend that this sacrament cannot be conferred except upon those who *demand it with their own lips*, hence they infer the other error, that baptism does not profit *infants* who receive it."[1]

Stephen of Barbone, A. D. 1225, says: "One argument of their error is, that baptism does not profit *little children* to their salvation, who have neither the *motive* nor the act of *faith*, as it is said in the latter part of Mark, he who will not believe will be condemned."[1]

Pseudo Reinerius, A. D. 1230–1250, concerning baptism they say "the catechism is of no value. Again, that the washing that is given to *infants* is of no value. Again, that the sponsors do not understand what they answer to the priest. They do not regard compaternity, *i. e.*, the *relation of sponsors*."[1]

Moneta, the Dominican, who wrote before A. D. 1240: "They maintain the nullity of the baptism of infants." Hahn, in quoting Moneta, makes him say: "These *heretics* charge that the Roman Catholic church baptizes first and teaches afterward, while the church of Christ *taught at first before baptizing;* also, that Christ and his Apostles *never* baptized any one without *faith and reason*."[1]

One of the Austrian inquisitors: "Concerning baptism some err in saying that little children are not saved by baptism, for the Lord says, he that *believeth* and is baptized shall be saved."[1]

[1] Armitage's Bap. Hist., pp. 302-303.

David of Augusburg, A. D. 1256-1272: "They say that a man is then truly for the first time baptized, when he is brought into their heresy." [1]

Drs. Ypeij and Dermont, two of the ablest and most eminent Pedobaptist scholars of Holland, who made this subject a matter of years' research in the archives of Europe, say: "The Baptists who were in former times called Anabaptists . . . *were the original Waldenses.*" [2]

Robert Baird, in his "The Waldenses," says: "But it is *due to candor* to say, that we deem it quite probable, if not *certain*, though we have never examined this point with much care, that there were *other* branches of the Waldenses, for they were numerous, which did *neither hold nor practice infant baptism.* It would be difficult upon any *other hypothesis to account for the opinion*, confidently maintained and, *without doubt*, most honestly too, by the *excellent* brethren who reject pedobaptism, that the Waldenses were *Baptists.*" [3]

Henry S. Burrage: "*Certain* it is that some of the Waldensians, how many we cannot say, but doubtless they were *not* few, adopted early in the thirteenth century the views of other separatists who were *antipedobaptists.*" [4]

Fusslin: "They not only *reject infant baptism*, but highly esteem baptism itself." [5]

"There were in Switzerland Waldensians who rejected *infant baptism.*" [6]

---

[1] Armitage's Bap. Hist., pp. 302-303.
[2] *Gercheid. d. Nederl. Hervormde Kerk*, t. i., 1819, p. 148 in William R. Williams' Lect. on Bap. Hist., p. 172.
[3] Note to p. 398, of his Waldenses.
[4] In Bap. Quart. Rev. vol. 9, No. 3, p. 356.
[5] *Kirch. u. Ketz. Hist.*, vol. 1, p. 462—in Bap. Quart. Rev. vol. 9, No. 3, p. 356.
[6] Idem, in Bap. Quart. Rev., vol. 9, No. 3, p. 357.

Fusslin: "The Anabaptists were not wrong, therefore, when they say that anabaptism was no new thing. The *Waldensians* had practiced it before them." [1]

Of Waldo and the Waldenses, Samuel M. Schmucker says: "One of the most prominent doctrines which he and his followers believed was the impropriety of the baptism of infants and the necessity of immersion to the validity of any baptism."[2]

Mosheim says of the Baptists: "It may be observed . . . . that they are not entirely mistaken when they boast of their descent from the Waldenses and the Petrobrussians."[3] But if the Waldenses were adherents of infant baptism the Baptists could not have descended from them.

The Baptists "appear supported by history in considering themselves the descendents of the Waldenses."[4]

Limborch: "To speak candidly what I think of all the modern sects of Christians, the Dutch Baptists mostly resemble the Albigenses and the Waldenses."[5]

Ludo Vives, who wrote in the sixteenth century, having observed that "formerly no person was brought to the holy baptistry till he was of adult age, and when he had both understood what the mystical water meant, and desired to be washed in it; yea, desired it more than once," alluding, presumably, to the Waldenses, adds: "I hear in some cities in Italy the old custom is still in a great* measure preserved."[6]

---

*Audio in quibusdam Italiae Urbibus morem veterem magna ex parte adhuc conservari. Comment, in Aug. de Civ. Dei., Lib. I., c. 27.

[1] Idem, in Bap. Quart. Rev., vol. 9, No. 3, p. 358.
[2] Schmucker's Hist. of All Religions, pp. 37, 38, 39.
[3] Mosheim's Eccl. Hist., cent. 16, sec. 3, chap. 3, 2.
[4] New Royal Encyclopedia.
[5] Limborch's Hist. Inquis.—in Jones' Ch. Hist., p. 358.
[6] Ivimey's Bap. Hist., vol. 1, p. 29.

In an old Waldensian tract we read: "Those that *believed* they *baptized* in the name of Jesus Christ."¹

Prof. George P. Fisher, D. D.: "There had been opposition to infant baptism in earlier days among the *Waldenses* and other sects."²

I have quoted this overwhelming amount of testimony because Pedobaptists, to prove the Waldenses did not hold to only believers' baptism, have made a desperate fight. Possibly some Waldenses who had just come out of the Romish church, or who were yet within it—who were never of the original Waldenses, which had continued from apostolic times—may have been adherents of infant baptism. Possibly, to avoid the fiery ordeal of persecution, having no faith in it and thinking it would be harmless to their children, some Waldensian parents consented to have their children baptized.† But that infant baptism was generally detested by the ancient Waldenses is certainly, in this chapter, demonstrated.

The Waldensians of the Reformation and the Post-Reformation period, by the reformers, were converted from only believers' baptism. Says Armitage: "A great council of the Waldensians was held at Angrogna, in Savoy, 1532, to which the Swiss Protestants sent Farel and Olivetan, and then a *new departure* was taken. Henceforth the Piedmontese Waldensians were joined to the Swiss Protestant Pedobaptists."³

Robert Baird says of modern Waldenses: "That there was a falling off in relation to sound doctrine towards the close of the last century, and in the beginning of the present, cannot be denied. This was brought about by

---

† Just as in our own age, to have peace at home, Baptist wives of Pedobaptists have carried their children to church to have them sprinkled.

1 Idem, page 26.
2 Fisher's Hist. Chr. Ch., p. 424.
3 Armitage's Bap. Hist., p. 304.

the influence of Geneva and Lausanne, especially the former, whither the Waldenses have been in the habit of sending their young men to pursue their studies for the ministry. When Calvin established the academy at Geneva provision was made for the education of two students from the valleys. At Lausanne provision was made for five in the academy or university of that city. In consequence of this there have always been seven Waldensian students of theology prosecuting their studies in those institutions during the last three hundred years."[1]

In church government the Waldenese were essentially Baptists. Gieseler speaks of "their anti-hierarchal system."[2] "The Catholic hierarchy and its pretensions to a mediatorial character, ordained of God, they rejected."[3] To reconcile Gieseler's statement, that they may have had some kind of bishops, with their being anti-hierarchal, it is only necessary to remember that they used the term bishop as Baptists use it—a term they, like the Baptists, rarely used—and that some Waldenses, who were just coming out of Rome, probably had bishops.*

Dr. Lord: "They have had a ministry of their own, consisting *only* of presbyters and deacons."[4] Lord farther says: "It has held, professed and vindicated the great doctrines of the Bible; (1.) That God has the *sole* right to legislate in respect to his worship. (2.) That the Scriptures are the *only* authoritative rule of faith. (3.) That Christ is the only redeemer. (4.) That yet it is by the RENEWING agency of the *Spirit alone* that men are led to repentance, faith and love. (5.) That neither

---

*Remember that the names of these dissenters were applied to persons coming out of the Romish church as well as to the churches, known by that name, which were older than it.

[1] Baird's Wald., pp. 396, 397; also Dr. Whitsitt's MS. Lect., *et mul. al.*
[2] Gieseler's Ch. Hist., vol. 2, p. 587.
[3] Idem, p. 589—note.
[4] Apoc., chap. 11.

rulers nor ecclesiastics have any right to oppress and persecute. . . . (6.) It has disowned alike the authority of the civil magistrate and the nationalized church to dictate its faith and worship. They obstinately maintained that nothing that is not *expressly* commanded by Christ or taught by the Apostles can ever be constituted alone by those of latter ages, though decreed even by synods, inasmuch as the latter church has no legislative authority."[1]

Muston says of the Waldenses: " ' In place of priests and cures,' says a Catholic of that country, 'they had ministers, who, under the names of Barbas, presided in their secret religious conventicles. However, as they were seen to be quiet and reserved, and as they faithfully paid their taxes, tithes and seigneural dues, and were, moreover, very industrious, they were not disturbed upon the subject of their practices and doctrines.' "[2] Of the Waldenses in the fifteenth century, Muston says: "The right was granted them of combining themselves into one or more independent communities, of naming their own rulers, both civil and ecclesiastical."[3] As proof that their ministers were controlled by no higher authority than the church, in one of their general meetings, in the sixteenth century, they say: "The ministry of the word of God ought not to wander about, nor to change their residences, unless it shall be for the good of the church."[4]

Says Robert Baird: "There is nothing in the organization or action of these churches that in the *slightest degree savors of prelacy*. And, in answer to our inquiries on this subject, the pastors have, without exception, stated that prelacy has *never* existed in these val-

---

[1] Idem.
[2] Israel of the Alps, vol. 1, p. 54.
[3] Idem, p. 74.
[4] Idem, p. 99.

leys; and that such has *ever been the uniform* opinion
of their ancestors, so far as it has been handed down
to them. As to their bishops, spoken of in some of
their early writings, they believe that they were *nothing
more than pastors*. They say what is *undeniable*, that
their histories speak continually of their barbes, as being
their religious teachers and guides, but that the word
bishop is hardly ever met with." [1]

Reinerius says of the sect in *general:* "They say
the bishops, clergy and other religious orders are no better
than the scribes and Pharisees." [2] As Armitage remarks:
"This relates to character, however, but they did not despise a *true* Christian ministry, for the same writer, who
was a resident of Lombardy, says there they had 'elders.'
Yet, there is nothing to show that they had any *order* of
ministers amongst them as a universal thing; or even
regularly located pastors, as we should deem them. They
had barbes, or preachers, but on the principle of the
seventy disciples which Jesus sent forth two by two.
These were not divided into *orders*, but into three moral
classes, from which the mistake has arisen concerning an
episcopal form of church government." [3]

Of them Preger, than whom there is no higher authority, says that *all* "ecclesiastical authority was vested in
the *congregation*, so that there was no *room for bishops*." [4]
"Reinerius represents them as holding that all men in
Christ's church stand on an *exact parity*." [3]

Armitage says: "In this fraternity of preachers, in
the absence of orders, distinction was made between them
as major and minor. This arose from the custom of

[1] The Waldenses, by Baird, pp. 389, 390, 346, 347.
[2] Armitage's Bap. Hist., p. 305.
[3] Idem, p. 304.
[4] Idem, p. 305.

180   CHURCH PERPETUITY.

sending them out in twos, a young man and an elder, that the younger might learn from the elder."[1] This may explain Mosheim's statement, that "The government of the church was committed by the Waldenses to bishops, presbyters and deacons," while a foot note says, "the bishops were also called majoralies or elders."[2]

Prof. Whitsitt, of the Southern Baptist Theological Seminary, says: "At *first there was no distinction between clergy and laity.*" That is, as we have seen, no kind of *prelatical* distinction was between their ministers and members.[3]

They had (as are the general secretaries or superintendents of missions among Baptists of to-day) general superintendents. But, as Dr. A. H. Newman observes: "The *early* Waldenses. . . . refused to employ the word bishop to designate their general superintendents. Speaking of the Humiliati, Dr. Newman says: "Like the Waldenses, they ascribed to the *local* body of believers, or to the general assembly of the *local* bodies, the *highest ecclesiastical powers.*"[4]

A well-known historian says: "Their barbas or pastors were every one of them heads of their churches, but they acted in nothing without the *consent* of the people and clergy," *i. e.*, the people and ministers in their churches who were not pastors.

Drs. Dermont and Ypeij: "The Baptists. . . . were originally Waldenses."[5] If "Baptists," of course, Baptist in church government, so Ypeij and Dermont say the "*Baptists.* . . . were the original Waldenses."[6]

---

[1] Idem, p. 305.
[2] Mosheim's Eccl. Hist., part 2, cent. 12, ch. 12, sec. 13.
[3] Lect. to his classes.
[4] Bap. Quar. Rev., July, 1885, p. 309—note.
[5] *Gercheid. d. Nederl. Hervormde Kerk*, t. i. 1819, p. 148, in William R. Williams' Lect. on Bap. Hist., p. 172.
[6] Idem, p. 172.

THE WALDENSES.

Says Rev. W. W. Everts, Jr.: "The Waldenses were excommunicated by Pope Lucius III, for rejecting the lordship of anti-Christ, all *clerical titles* and offices not contained in the *New Testament*, and insisting on their *independence* in worship and discipline." [1]

Speaking of the Waldenses, Reiner, the Romish inquisitor, says: "This is a true picture of the heretics of our age, particularly the *Anabaptists*." Reiner's words are: "Vera effigies hæreticorum nostræ ætatis (1013), præsertim anabaptistarum." [2]

Limborch: "To speak candidly what I think of all the modern sects of Christians, the Dutch *Baptists* most resemble both the Albigenses and Waldenses." [3]

Jones quotes from a translation of Mosheim: "Before the rise of Luther and Calvin, there lay concealed in almost all the countries of Europe persons who adhered tenaciously to the principles of the Dutch *Baptists*." [4]

As Dr. William R. Williams says: "It is not claimed that our denominational views were universal among the Waldenses." * But I am willing to close this chapter with the statement, that the Waldenses were, certainly, as a whole, Baptists.

---

* Lect. on Bap. Hist., p. 126.
[1] Ch. in Wild., p. 21.
[2] Robinson's Eccl. Resh., p. 315.
[3] Limborch's Hist. Inq., vol. 1, ch. 8, in Jones' Ch. Hist., p. 358.
[4] Mosheim's Eccl. Hist., cent. 16, part 2, ch. 3, sec. 2, in Jones', p. 358.

CHAPTER XVII.

THE ANABAPTISTS.

In the time of the Reformation, the genuine Anabaptists were the great and evangelical movement. Out of their principles and spirit grew all that was good in Luther's Reformation. Historians credit the Anabaptists with being the originators of the separation of church and State, of modern liberty and of the doctrine of a regenerate church membership.

In faith the Anabaptists of the Reformation were one with the Baptists of to-day.

In a paper read by Rev. Henry S. Burrage, D. D., one of the highest authorities on this subject, before the "American Society of Church History," in 1890, on "The Anabaptists of the Sixteenth Century," he says: "What were some of the ideas that characterized the Anabaptist movement of the sixteenth century? The following are especially worthy of attention: (1.) That the Scriptures are the only authority in matters of faith and practice. (2.) That personal *faith* in Jesus Christ only secures salvation; therefore infant baptism is to be rejected. (3.) That a church is composed of believers who have been baptized upon a *personal* confession of their faith in Jesus Christ. (4.) That each church has entire control of its affairs, without interference on the part of any external power. (5.) That the outward life must be in accordance with such a confession of faith, and to the end it is essential that *church discipline* should be maintained. (6.) That while the State may properly demand obedience in all things not contrary to the law of

God, it has no right to set aside the dictates of conscience, and compel the humblest individual to set aside his views, or to inflict punishment in case such surrender is refused. Every human soul is directly responsible to God. These ideas characterized the Anabaptist movement in Switzerland. They appeared in the public discussions held with Zwingli and his associates. The *supreme authority* of the Scripture was made *especially* prominent in these teachings. The great evangelical truth which the Swiss reformers preached, they held. They believed in *regeneration* by the *atoning blood** of Christ, but they demanded the *fruits* of regeneration. Their hymns, which happily have been preserved, show no trace of revolutionary or fanatical doctrines, but abound in devout sentiments pertaining to Christian experience and hope, and exhortation to fidelity and steadfastness in the faith, although persecution and death should be the result. These ideas the banished Swiss leaders made known in other lands. Prominent among these was Balthazar Hubmeyer. Indeed, no one influenced the Anabaptist movement from 1525 to 1528 more profoundly than he. . . . His numerous publications bear witness to his evangelical spirit and his devotion to Baptist principles. 'Baptism,' he says, 'is an ordinance of Jesus Christ. It is not enough that one believes in Jesus; he must confess him openly. He who confesses Christ before men, Christ will confess before his Father. The divine order is, first, the preaching of the word; second, faith: third, baptism.' When it was charged against the Anabaptists that they proposed to establish a church of sinless persons, Hubmeyer replied:

---

* This demonstrates they were not Universalists or Unitarians. Since there can be no human blood atonement for sin, they certainly were sound on the deity of Christ.

'You do us an *injustice*. If we say we have no sin, we deceive ourselves and the truth is not in us.' The charge of *communism he indignantly repels*. 'I have always said with reference to a community of goods,' is his testimony, 'that one should have regard to others, so that the hungry may be fed, the thirsty receive drink, and the naked be clothed; for we are not lords but stewards. There is certainly *no one* who says that all things should be common.' When it was said that those who were opposed to infant baptism hold that no one can be saved *without water* baptism, Hubmeyer replied: '*Salvation is conditioned neither on* † *baptism nor on works of mercy*. Condemnation is the result, *not of neglect of baptism*, but of *unbelief alone*.' And when it was added that the thief on the cross believed, and on the same day was with Christ in Paradise, yet he was not baptized with outward baptism, Hubmeyer replied: 'The man who has the excuse of the thief on the cross will have the favor of God, though unbaptized.' " † †

W. W. Everts, Jr., who is another of the highest authorities on the subject, says Hubmeyer says: "Nothing but Christ can draw the sinner. Nevertheless, as pictures are in the churches, let no violence be used, but of the preaching of the word let the people be instructed till they are in favor of their removal. . . . Among the reforms which he advocated are justification by faith only, the confession of sin, the marriage of priests, the proper *support of ministers* who preach the gospel, and the right of a congregation to dismiss a minister who does not preach the gospel. . . . He used to say: 'Baptism

---

† No Campbellism or water salvation among the Anabaptists.
† † Am. Soc. of Ch. Hist., pp. 157, 158.

stands for faith and the supper for love. If one knew no other word of Scripture, but understood the true *meaning* of baptism and the supper, he knows God and angels, faith and love, law and prophets.' '*Where there is no baptism there is neither church nor ministry*, neither brothers nor sisters, neither discipline, exclusion nor restoration. As faith is a thing of the *heart*, there must be an external confession by which brothers and sisters can mutually recognize each other.' Replying to Zwingli, Hubmeyer said: 'We must do as God pleases, consult the word, not the church; hear the Son, not Zwingli or Luther. . . . We are not condemned for not being *baptized* . . . but for *unbelief*. *He that believes will be baptized if he can get to water and a baptizer.*' To Oecolampadius he said: 'Baptism is a *mere sign*, but the meaning of the sign namely, the pledging of faith till death, is the essential part of the sign, and is wanting in pedobaptism.' . . . 'The visible church,' he said, 'is a general assembly of all living believers.' "

Of course, Hubmeyer, in his conceptions of the church, was not, in every respect, fully up to the understanding of the best expositors of Baptist church polity in our own time; but the above statements, as well as the preceding from Dr. Burrage, show Hubmeyer and his people essentially Baptist.[1]

In a tract,[2] Hubmeyer says: "A heretic is one who knowingly resists the Holy Scriptures; . . . likewise, one who falsely interprets the Scriptures, putting Rome for church and Lord for shepherd. Although we cannot look for much good from such men, still they should be instructed with all mildness, and if that accomplishes

[1] Bap. Rev., vol. 10, pp. 205, 217, 218.
[2] Quoted by Dr. W. W. Everts, Jr., in Tex. Hist. Mag, vol. 1, p. 135.

nothing dismiss them free. For Christ wished that the tares should grow up with the wheat. From this and many other passages of the Holy Scriptures, it appears that persecutors of heretics are themselves the greatest heretics. For Christ did not come to butcher, to kill and to burn, but to deliver and improve all. It is necessary, therefore, to pray for the improvement of the erring, and to look for it as long as a man lives. *The Turk, or the heretic, can be overcome, not by fire or sword, but only by patience and instruction.* Burning heretics is, therefore, nothing less than a sham confession and actual *denial of Christ.* . . . The chief art consists in testing errors, and in refuting them by the Holy Scriptures."

In a document which the Anabaptists presented to the authorities of the Gruningen district, we read: "Believers are those who walk in the will of the Spirit, and bring forth the fruits of the Spirit; they are the company of the body of Christ, the Christian church. To this, therefore, the Anabaptists belong."[1]

In A. D. 1527, Denck, a great Anabaptist leader, "in a letter frankly laid his views before Oecolampadius, and asked for himself what he was willing to accord all men, religious freedom."[2]

In a tract Denck said: "Those who walk in the footsteps of Christ I rejoice in and love, wherever I find them. But with those who will not keep silent, I cannot have much fellowship, for I do not discover in such the mind of Christ, but a perverted mind, which will force me to abandon my faith and compel me to adopt its own, whether it be right or not. And even if right, zeal may be very commendable but unwise. For it should be

---

[1] The Anabaptists of Switzerland, by H. S. Burrage, D. D., p. 180.
[2] Idem, p. 184.

known that in matters of faith everything should be *free, voluntary and without compulsion.*" [1]

The Anabaptists believed *children inherit the moral depravity of their parents.* Denck said: "There is something in me that strongly opposes my *inborn* inclination to evil." [2]

They believed faith the *miraculous gift of God:* "What our parents and teachers tell us, and what is written in books, we may regard as true and believe; I myself," says Dr. Denck, "have *'believed' in this sense:* but this faith has never helped the infirmities which were *born in me,* and has not released me from the conflict in my soul between good and evil inclinations. For me, therefore, it is incontestable that merely to hold as true that which has been handed down to me cannot lead me to the life for which a deep longing slumbers within. Since it is true we are *saved by faith,* the word must be understood in the right sense. 'Faith,' says Denck, 'is the accordance of our will with the will of the good, or with the divine will. . . . Faith, therefore, must be built upon other foundations; indeed upon the immediately given facts of experience.' As such a fact Denck designates the feeling within, which says to every one that he must do good, 'which impels me wholly without my will and assistance.' . . . The Scripture . . . teaches that the unfolding of the good seed is not possible through *our power alone.* . . . The inclination to evil has its seat *deep in the nature* of man; it is indeed possible for us to strive after the good; but we cannot accomplish it without the help of Almighty God. . . . But the more I am filled with the divine source of the

---

[1] Idem, pp. 185, 186.
[2] Preussische Jahrbucher, for Sep 1892—from an article by Ludwig Keller, translated in Bap. Rev., by Dr. H. S. Burrage.

doctrines of Christ, which are transmitted in the Holy Scriptures, the more is my conviction that he only can rightly understand them who has himself been illuminated by the light of the divine *Spirit*. . . . Yes, it is true, that the inclination to evil resides deep in human nature; *if, however, the Holy Scriptures were the only means of leading men to the good, there never would have been good men among those who are ignorant of the Scriptures*, and God would not have given to many millions of men even the possibility of attaining to the good and salvation." [1]

These Anabaptists believed in *election:* "Christ, the Lamb of God, has been from the beginning of the world a mediator between God and men, and will remain a mediator to the end. Of what men? Of you and me alone? Not so, but of all men whom *God has given to him for a possession*." [2]

John Muller, another Anabaptist leader, in 1525, wrote: "Since faith in the free *gift* of God and not in every man's possession, as the Scriptures show, do not burden my conscience. It is born not of the *will of the flesh*, but of the will of God. . . . No man cometh unto me except the Father draw him. The secret of God is like a treasure concealed in a field which no man can find unless the *Spirit* of the Lord reveal it to him."

In an article in the *Standard*, Prof. Howard Osgood, D. D., than whom there is no higher authority on this subject, says: "Like their brethren in southern Europe they sought only soul liberty, freedom to serve God according to their understanding of the Scriptures, while they acknowledged their full duty of obedience to the civil power in all matters not contrary to God's word.

[1] Idem, pp. 38, 43.
[2] Idem, p. 43.

Their church discipline was strict, almost to severity, and wherever they were allowed to remain in peace the desert smiled and bloomed around them. They sought to obtain no deserted Roman Catholic church buildings for themselves; they were renowned *for the purity of their domestic relations in life;* and in their confessions and practice they urged the duty of *complete religious liberty for all.* . . . They held that there could be no contradiction between God's doctrine of his church and of salvation, that *election* and justification by faith and regeneration by the *Spirit* result in a church of *believers.* To bring in those as children who give no evidence of having been *elected* of faith, or of regeneration, is to institute a practice at war with the doctrines and for which there is not the first evidence of Scripture. . . . The claims of Baptists were, freedom to preach the gospel, to form churches after the scriptural pattern which should be separated from the world and worldlings, to exercise church discipline over their members, and that each church should have entire control over its own ecclesiastical affairs without interference of the State. . . . They *choose their own pastors and supported* them and *sent forth a multitude of missionaries* so that Melancthon could say that they went where no evangelical, Lutheran and Zwinglian, had penetrated. . . . For a hundred years Switzerland was drained of her sturdy sons, who in great numbers braved the loss of their goods and *the long journey through hostile territory* and the price set upon their heads by the Bavarian dukes in order to reach Moravia, where they might enjoy some little freedom to worship God. From Moravia, they *sent out missionaries in scores to all parts* of Germany, Tyrol and Switzerland, to Hungary, Silesia and Poland, who took their lives in their hands that they might preach the word of their Redeemer and raise up churches to his praise. The Romish church historians say that these *missionaries* were very successful in their efforts to delude the people."

While speaking of these Baptists and missions I will here quote from a letter recently received from one of the highest authorities on this subject, Rev. W. W. Everts, Jr.: "I am much interested in your question about missions and the Anabaptists. They were the *most determined colporteurs and missionaries throughout Europe.* The only reference I have found to any heathen land I have given in Armitage, where the persecuted flock think of settling in America among 'the red Jews Columbus has just discovered.' This was in 1524, I believe."

Though I have already noticed that they agreed with present Baptists against Campbellite positions, I will give further proofs of this. As to believing repentance *precedes* faith, Hottinger, at his execution, exhorted the people to "Repent and believe on the Lord Jesus Christ." †

They utterly rejected "*sacramental salvation.*" Grebel, a great Anabaptist leader, said: "From the scriptures we learn that baptism *declares* that by *faith* and the *blood* of Christ our sins *have* been washed away, that we *have* died to sin and walked in newness of life; that assurance of salvation is through the inner baptism, faith, so that water does *not* confirm and increase faith as Wittenberg theologians say, *nor does it save.*" ††

Hubmeyer said: "In order to live a Christian life there must be a *change* in the natural man, who is by *nature*

---

† The Anabaptists in Switzerland, p. 72; Dr. Philip Schaff, in Bap. Quart. Rev., July 1889.
†† Idem, p. 124.

sinful and with no remedy in himself by which the wounds that sin has made can be healed. . . . When a man *has* received this new life he confesses it before the *church* of which he is made a member according to the rule of Christ; that is he shows to the church that, instructed in the Scriptures, he *has* given himself to Christ to live henceforth according to his will and teaching. He is *then* baptized, making in baptism a public confession of his faith. . . . In other words, in baptism he confesses that he is a sinner, but that Christ by his death *has* pardoned his sins, so that he *is* accounted righteous before the face of his God."[1]

Again, says Hubmeyer: "Condemnation is the result *not of a neglect of baptism* but of unbelief alone."[2] Again, "we ascribe *nothing* whatever to water baptism. It is an ordinance instituted by Christ and by the Apostles and received by believers."[3] Again, he says: "No element or *outward* thing can cleanse the soul, but *faith* purifies the hearts of men. It follows that baptism cannot wash away sin. If, therefore, it can not wash away sin, and yet is from God, it must be a public *testimony* of inward faith, and an outward *pledge* to live henceforth a new life as God gives grace."[4] Says Denck, another great Anabaptist leader: "In themselves ceremonies are not useful, and he who thinks thereby to *attain anything whether through baptism* or the breaking of bread is *superstitious*. . . . He who makes ceremonies burdensome is not much of a gainer thereby, for should one lose all ceremonies, he would not suffer any

---

[1] Idem, p. 88.
[2] Idem, p. 149.
[3] Idem. p. 151.
[4] Idem, p. 152.

injury, and indeed *it is better to want them than to misuse them.*" *

In an Anabaptist confession of faith, called the "Schleitheim Confession," made in 1527, we read: "Baptism should be given to all those who *have* learned repentance and change of life, and believe in truth that their sins *have* been taken away through Christ." †

Hans Overton, in 1520, said: "It is not enough that we have received baptism on the confession of our *faith* and *by that faith* have been engrafted into Christ." [1] In 1529, Anabaptist sufferers in prison said in their appeal to their persecutors: "Baptism is the registering of believers in the eternal church of God. *Faith* confessed is wine and baptism is the *sign* hung out to show that wine *is* within. What a thing is this to hang out a sign while the wine is *still in the grape* on the vine, when it may be dried up." [2]

"In 1532, a book appeared in Holland, without the name of the author. . . . It was soon translated into English, French and Italian, and so many editions were sold that it added largely in spreading Baptist views throughout Europe. . . . On baptism it says: 'So we are *dipped* under as a *sign* that we are as it were dead and buried as Paul writes in Rom. 6 and Col. 2. . . . The pledge is given when we are *plunged* under the water.'" [3] An Anabaptist woman, when "on the rack was asked whether she 'expected to be saved by *baptism?*' She answered: '*No, all the water in the sea cannot save me, nor anything else but that salvation which*

---

* Idem, pp. 186, 187.
† Armitage's Bap. Hist., p. 950.
[1] Idem, p. 412.
[2] Idem, p. 387.
[3] Idem, p. 409.

is in Christ.'"[1] That the Anabaptists did not believe in water salvation or Campbellism is certain from abundance of testimony, additional to this. But I will close the testimony on this point in the language of Dr. Philip Schaff, of the Anabaptists: "They denied that baptism is necessary for *salvation.*"[2] The Anabaptists in the Schleitheim Confession said that "he who serves the gospel should also *live from it* as the Lord has ordained."[3]

The Anabaptists were what are called "close communion" Baptists. On the terms of communion the Schleitheim Confession says: "We are one and are agreed concerning breaking of bread. . . . that all who would drink one draught as a memorial of the poured blood of Christ should *before hand* be united to one body of Christ, to-wit: *by baptism.* . . . Hence, also it should and must be whoso has not the call of one God to one faith, to *one baptism*, to one spirit, to one body, common to all the children of God, he cannot be made one bread with them, as must be if he would in truth break bread according to the command of Christ."[4]

The Anabaptists had no sympathy with the doctrine of infant damnation. "They denied that baptism is necessary for salvation and maintained that infants are saved *without baptism* and by the *blood of Christ.*† But baptism is necessary for church membership."[2] As infants thus appear to need the "blood of Christ" it thus appears that these Anabaptists believe that *infants are depraved*, a belief clearly demanded by the Scriptures and maintained by all well instructed Baptists.

† Dr. Schaff says: "The Baptists and Quakers were the first organized Christian communities which detached salvation from ecclesiastical ordinances and taught the salvation of unbaptized infants and unbaptized but believing adults."— Teaching of the Twelve Apostles, p. 56.
1 Idem, p. 412.
2 Dr. Schaff, in Bap. Quart. Rev., July 1889.
3 Armitage's Hist. Bap., p. 951.
4 Idem, p. 950.

I will close this by the testimony of Dr. Philip Schaff, as to various points of Anabaptist belief. "The reformers founded a popular State church; the Anabaptists organized on the *voluntary* principle, select congregations of baptized believers, separated from the world and from the State . . . . They were cruelly persecuted by imprisonment, exile, torture, fire and sword, and almost totally suppressed in Protestant as well as in Roman Catholic countries. The age *was not ripe for unlimited religious liberty and congregational self-government.* The Anabaptists perished bravely as martyrs of conscience. Luther calls them martyrs of the devil. . . . They preached repentance and faith, baptized converts, organized congregations, and exercised *rigid discipline.* . . . They accepted the New Testament as their *only* rule of faith and practice. . . . *They were generally orthodox.* . . . Their demand of rebaptism virtually unbaptized and unchurched the entire Christian world. . . . These two ideas of a pure church of believers and of baptism of believers only were the *fundamental* articles of the Anabaptist creed. . . . *It is unjust to charge the extravagant dreams and practices upon the whole body.* . . . The Anabaptist psalms and hymns resemble those of Schwenkfeld and his followers. They dwell on the *inner* life of the Christian, the *mysteries of regeneration,* sanctification d *personal union with Christ.* They breathe *throughout* a spirit of piety, devotion, cheerful resignation under suffering and readiness for martyrdom. They are hymns of the cross, to comfort and encourage the scattered sheep of Christ, ready for the slaughter in imitation of the divine Shepherd. . . . The blood of martyrs is never shed in vain. The Anabaptist movement was defeated by fire and sword, but not destroyed; it revived among the Mennonites, the *Baptists* in England and America, and more recently in isolated congregations on the continent. The question of the subjects and the mode of baptism still divides* Baptists from the Pedobaptist churches; but the principle of religious liberty and separation of church and State, for *which the Swiss and the German Anabaptists suffered and died, has left its imprint upon the course of history, has triumphed in America and is making steady progress in Europe.*" [1]

The genuine Anabaptists were exclusive immersionists. Of the Anabaptist age, says Dr. Philip Schaff: "The controversy between the reformers and the Anabaptists referred *only* to the subjects of baptism. . . . The mode of baptism was no topic of controversy, because *immersion was still extensively in use, and decidedly preferred by Luther and the other reformers* as the most expressive and primitive, though not the only mode." [2]

That the Anabaptists were exclusive immersionists is evident. (1.) From their making the Bible their *only* rule of faith and practice. (2.) From their having *inherited* immersion from their Baptist ancestry. (3.) From their having been persecuted AS DIPPERS. "That some of these preferred and practiced immersion we infer from the fact that their persecutors, who delighted in fitting the penalty, as they cruelly judged it, to the fault, put many of them to death by *full immersion*, swathing the sufferers to large sacks with their living contents into huge puncheons where the victims were drowned. So the Swiss, some of them, at least, immersed in rivers. This appears from the work Sabbata of Knertz, a concontemporary Lutheran." [3] The translator of Luther's

---

[1] In Bap. Quart. Rev., pp. 266, 268, 270, 272, 273, 276.
[2] The Bap. Quart. Rev., July 1889.
[3] William R. Williams' Lect. on Bap. Hist., pp. 246, 247; Cramp's Bap. Hist., pp. 18¹, 182.

Controversial Works, speaking of Luther's sermon on Baptism,[1] on p. 8, of his Introduction, says: "The sermon and letters are directed principally against the Anabaptists, a fanatical sect of reformers who contended that baptism should be administered to adults only, *not by sprinkling, but by dipping*." A writer who has given this special investigation, says: "And thus it is through the whole book of Luther on the sacraments. I have read it over and over again, years ago, and marked all the places in controversy concerning the Anabaptists, and in not one single instance is there the remotest hint that they practiced *sprinkling and pouring*. . . . When the Anabaptists spoke of the sprinkling of the Lutherans they called it '*a handful of water*,' doubtless in *derision;* and when they alluded to the dipping of Luther, without faith either on the part of the administrator or the subject, they called it 'a dog bath,' also in derision. Nothing satisfied them but the *immersion* of a professed believer."

Robinson says: "Luther bore the Zwinglians dogmatizing, but he could not brook a reformation in the hands of the dippers. . . . Notwithstanding all he had said in favor of dipping, he persecuted them under the names of *re-dippers*, ré-baptizers, or Anabaptists."[2]

Dr. J. B. Thomas, Professor of Church History in Newton Theological Seminary: "Usually they insisted upon immersion as the *only* baptism."[3]

Dr. Featley published a work against them as "*Dippers Dipped*," etc. Says Rev. W. W. Everts, Jr., "Dr. Sears' inference from their alleged failure to magnify the significance of immersion, and from their

---

[1] Vol. 10, pp. 2513, 2593.
[2] Robinson's Eccl. Resh., p. 542.
[3] Ms. Lect., p. 59.

apparent agreement with the reformers as to the mode, *falls to the ground* when we learn from an authority like Hofing, that at that time immersion was as common as sprinkling, that the Roman ritual, Luther's books on baptism, *and almost all the Lutheran rituals instruct the administrator to immerse the candidate and that the word sprinkle is hardly ever to be found in the earlier regulations.* It is well known that the church of England put immersion first, and allowed sprinkling only in case of the feeble. Logically, therefore, it might be admitted that the Anabaptists did not differ from the prevalent mode of baptism and *still the presumption would be that they immersed.* . . . Gastins was wont to say, with ghastly sarcasm, as he ordered the Anabaptists to be drowned: 'They *like immersion* so much let us immerse them,' and his words became a proverb. Zwingli used to call them '*bath* fellows.' Hubmeyer destroyed the font as well as the altar at Waldshut, denouncing them both as nests of evil. . . . He says, 'the soul must be sprinkled with the blood of Christ and the body be washed through pure water.' The subjoined tract of this scholar and martyr is unmistakable on this point. Bullinger admits all the spiritual significance of *immersion*, in his controversy with the Anabaptists. Finally, the English Baptists practiced immersion and the first of them came from the *continent*." From a form for baptizing in water, Niclolsburg, 1527, Dr. Everts, quotes: "Do you upon this faith and duty desire to be baptized *in* water."

Says Dr. J. A. Smith, formerly Lecturer on Church History to the Baptist Theological Seminary, in Chicago: "Whether Menno Simon was or was not strictly a Baptist, has been lately called in question. Pertinent to the matter is a quotation from his writings, Mennonis Simons Opera,

p. 24, by a writer in the *Nonconformist and Independent*. At the place noted, Simon Menno says: ' After we have searched ever so diligently, we shall find *no other baptism besides dipping that is acceptable to God and maintained in his word*.' We can from PERSONAL KNOWLEDGE testify to the accuracy of this quotation.'' The writer goes on to say: " It is true that the followers in Holland *departed* from the practice."¹

Of Menno's words — *Doopsel in den water* — Dr. Howard Osgood says: "The words, *indoopenege, onderdoopinege, onderdompelinge*, are employed in Dutch to express immersion. . . . *Doop and doopen* in Dutch *exactly* correspond to *taufe* and *taufen* in German. All these words come from the *same root* and etymologically signify *dipping and dip.*" Dr. Osgood gives the following proofs that the Anabaptists immersed: "Zwingli was all powerful in the council at Zurich and the council passed the following decree, '*Qui interum mergat, mergatur.*' Under the decree in 1527, the first Anabaptist martyr in Switzerland, Felix Mantz, one of the first scholars in his day, was drowned in the lake of Zurich, near Zwingli's church. . . . Within the canton of Zurich the *usual* punishment was *drowning*, as will be seen by instances related in the martyrology, published by the Hanserd-Knollys Society. John Stumpf, a contemporary of Zwingli in his history of Switzerland, p. 2444, says: 'What was worst of all, they, the Anabaptists, repeated the baptism . . . and were rebaptized *in the rivers and streams.*'

"Again, Kessler, in his Sabbata, vol. 1, p. 266, says that ' Wolfang Uliman, of St. Gall, went to Schaffhausen and met Conrad Grebel,' the most prominent leader,

¹ In *The Standard*, of Chicago.

preacher and scholar among the Anabaptists, 'who instructed him in the knowledge of Anabaptism that he would not be sprinkled out of a dish, but was drawn *under* and *covered over* with the water of the Rhine by Conrad Grebel.' On p. 268, Kessler adds that Grebel came to St. Gall, Kessler's home, where his preaching was attended by hundreds from the town and surrounding country and the longing desire many had nourished for a year, was accomplished by following Grebel to the Sitter river and being baptized by him there. When I was at St. Gall, in 1867, I made special investigation upon this point. A mountain stream, sufficient for all sprinkling purposes, flows through the city, but in no place is it deep enough for the immersion of a person, while the Sitter river is between two and three miles away, and is gained by a different road. *The only solution of this choice was that Grebel sought the river in order to immerse the candidates.* August Naef, secretary of the council at St. Gall, in a work published in 1850, on p. 1021, speaking of the practices of Anabaptists, in 1525, says: 'They baptized those who believed with them *in rivers and lakes*, and in a *great* wooden cask and the butchers' square before a great crowd.'

"These immersions were in Switzerland from 1524-30. An old historian of Augsburg, Sender, says: ' The hated sect in 1527 met in the gardens of houses, men and women, rich and poor, more than 1100 in all, who were rebaptized. They put on *peculiar clothes* in which to be baptized, for in the houses where their *bapisteries were*, there were a number of garments *always prepared*.'

"A later historian of Augsburg, Wagenseil, says: 'In 1527 the Anabaptists baptized none who did not believe with them; and the candidates were not merely sprinkled with water but were *wholly submerged.*' These are the testimonies of Pedobaptists.

"Zwingli entitles his great work against the Anabaptists, '*Elenchus contra Catabaptistas.*' *Catabaptistas*, a word of post-classical Greek, according to Passow and Liddell and Scott, means 'one who *dips or drowns*,' and that Zwingli uses the word in this signification, is *shown* by his repeated endeavor in this work to make all sorts of fun of the baptism of the Anabaptists, *immersion*, '*dying people*,' '*redying them*,' '*plunging them into the darkness of water* to unite them to a church of darkness,' '*they mersed*,' etc.

"The following I find from the Anabaptists on the mode of baptism. . . . Belthazar Hubmeyer, in his treatise on baptism, '*von dem Christenlichen Tauffder Glaubigen*,' A. D. 1525, page 5, says: '*Tauffen im wasser ist dem bekennenden verjeher seiner sunden auss dem Gotlichen beneleh mit eusserlichem wasser ubergiessen und den in die zal der sundern auss eygner erkantuss und bewilligung einschreiben.*' Translation: 'To baptize *in* water is to *cover* the confessor of his sins in external water, according to the divine command, and to inscribe him in the number of the separate upon his own confession and desire. I have translated *ubegiessen* to cover, we *cannot* translate here 'to pour the confessor' . . . with external water, for which signification see Sanders' Lexicon under, '*giessen*.' [1]

"The fact that a baptistry was built at St. Gall, and that John Stumpf, a Lutheran pastor, who lived in Zurich from 1522 to 1544, and who wrote of them from personal knowledge of their practices, says they 'rebap-

---

[1] In *The Religious Herald.*

tized in rivers and streams' is good evidence that they immersed."[1]

Then Sicher, a Roman Catholic, gives the account of their baptisms at St. Gall: "The number of the converted increased so that the baptistry could not hold the crowd and they were compelled to use the streams and the Sitter river."[2]

Simler says that: "Many came to St. Gall, inquired for the Tauffhaus (Baptistry) and were baptized."[2]

Dr. Rule, who speaks contemptuously of them, says that they took their converts "and plunged them in the nearest streams."[3]

Mosheim says the Socinians, in their Catechism of 1574, say: "Baptismus est hominis Evangelio credentis et penitentiam agentis in nomine Patris et Filii, et Spiritus Sancti, vel in nomine Jesu Christi in aquam immersio et emersio"[4]—Baptism is an immersion and the emmersion of a man who believes and is truly penitent, in the name of the Father and of the Son and of the Holy Spirit, or in the name of Jesus Christ, in water. The Socinians were surrounded and mingled with the Baptists. How absurd, then, even with only this to the contrary, to take the position that "exclusive immersion began among the Baptists in the seventeenth century," because, "until the seventeenth century—and that near its middle—exclusive immersion had been abandoned."

Replying to the statement that "the only instance in which immersion among the Anabaptists occurred during the sixteenth century, is the immersion of Wolfang Uliman, at Schaffhausen, in 1525," H. S. Burrage, D. D.,

[1] Armitage's Bap. Hist., p. 352.
[2] Idem, p. 353.
[3] Idem, p. 352.
[4] Mosheim's Eccl. Hist., cent. 16, sec. 3, chap. 4, sec. 10—note.

says: "Well, let us see. In the '*Bekenntniss von beiden Sacramenten*' which at Munster, Oct. 22, 1533, was subscribed by Rothman, Klopriss, Staprade, Vienne, and Stralen, and was made public on the eighth of November following, occurs this statement: 'Baptism is an *immersion* (eintauchung) in water, which the candidate requests and receives as a true *sign* that, dead to sin, buried with Christ, he rises to a new life, henceforth to walk not in the lusts of the flesh, but obedient to the will of God.' "[1]

Prof. Howard Osgood, D. D., says: "In 1666 and '68, Arents, a Mennonite[†] author, published a treatise in favor of immersion." "In 1740 an anonymous Mennonite author defends immersion. Schyn, the historian of the Mennonites, certainly leans in favor of immersion."

S. H. Ford, LL.D., who has made Baptist history rather a specialty, says: "In the Dutch Martyrology, translated by the eminent Dutch scholar, Rev. Benjamin Millard, of Wigan, the name given to the Anabaptists or Mennonites is that of Dippers. Thus, on page 34, are found these words: 'Some of the principal Dippers, that is, Baptist people, were seized (*De voornaemste Doopers: verstaet Doops Gesinde.*)' That Millard gave a false rendering of Doops is not to be supposed, and consulting seven Dutch Lexicons, they all agree with the one now before me. It is by Tauchnitz, Leipsic:

"*Dooping*—baptizing, christening, dipping, plunging.

"*Doopsel*—baptism, dipping.

"*Dooper*—dipper, plunger, Baptist.

"Now, *Dooper* was the term of reproach given to these Anabaptists by their foes in Holland, as its equivalent, *Dipper*, was in England.

[†] Some early Anabaptists were called Mennonites from Menno, one of their great leaders.

[1] In *Zion's Advocate*.

"We read in the Dutch Martyrology that one Herz Lowrys, in 1528, persecuting the Baptists, ' addressed the council in strong terms, inquiring what they intended to do with these *dipping* heretics' (Martyrology, vol. 1, p. 71), and again, in the next pages he is quoted as exclaiming: ' O, the dippers, the dippers!' Several such instances might be cited. But these are surely sufficient to show that the use of such expressions and epithets can be accounted for only on the ground that they immersed all candidates for baptism. . . . . We close this by affirming that every scholar knows, who has consulted the original, that the words of Menno, *Doopsel inden water*, are correctly translated—immersing, as dipping in water.

"But Menno adds to this its explanation: ' Yet, whoever will oppose, this is the *only* mode of baptism that Jesus Christ instituted, and His Apostles taught and practiced.' "[1]

As to the argument for affusion among the ancient Mennonites, derived from modern Mennonite authors, I will reply in the words of Mosheim: "Many circumstances persuade me that the declarations and representations of things given by the modern Mennonites are not always worthy of credit." †[2]

That some Mennonites practiced immersion is proved from the fact that, in 1620, there were Mennonite pastors who served two churches—a Mennonite and a Collegiant church—and the Collegiants always practiced immersion.

---

† Mosheim's Eccl. Hist., cent. 16, sec. 3, chap. 3—note to 1.
[1] Chr. Repository.
[2] As an illustration of Mosheim's statement I quote the following from Prof. Howard Osgood, D.D.: "Schyn, the historian of the Mennonites, certainly leans in favor of immersion, and is severely taxed for so doing by his late editor, Maatschoen, who, vol. 2, p. 72, note, says: ' No true Mennonite has ever practiced immersion or defended it in writing.'" Yet, Schyn is the old and main Mennonite historian!

Barnes Sears, D.D., thus quotes Trecksel, a recent writer of much weight: "The Anabaptists baptized in running streams and in† barns."[1]

Turretine, called the theological Blackstone: "The Anabaptists are so called from their repetition of baptism in the case of those who have been already baptized, whether in respect to infants †† or adults, who pass from one sect of this people to another, whom they again baptize—immerse—(*tingunt*) that they may receive them into their communion."[2]

Cramp quoting Bullinger, concerning the Anabaptists, brings out the fact, that both the people and himself regarded the Anabaptists as exclusive immersionists: "For *the people* said, 'Let others say what they will of the *dippers*, we see in them nothing but what is excellent.'"[3]

Samuel H. Schmuker says: "The Anabaptists held to the baptism of believers by immersion, denying the efficacy of infant baptism."[4]

Of Anabaptists Neal says: "They differed about the subject and *mode* of baptism, whether it should be administered to infants, or in any other manner than in dipping the whole body under water."[5] This shows there was a kind of Anabaptists who baptized infants and who were not exclusive immersionists; and, that there was a kind who were the reverse. From the former kind and from some who were just coming out of the Romish

---

† When they baptized in any kind of houses they used "pails" or tanks sufficiently large for immersion. See in another place, in this chapter.

†† In this appears the error, that they rebaptized only because the former baptism was in infancy. They were Anabaptists because they admitted no baptism scriptural except that of the *true church*.

[1] In *The Religious Herald*.
[2] Quoted by the eminent scholar, E T. Winkler, D.D.
[3] Cramps' Bap. Hist., p. 179.
[4] History all Relig., by Schmuker. pp. 37, 38, 39.
[5] Neal's Hist. Puritans, vol. 1, p. 137.

church—as is seen in another part of this chapter—comes "the testimony that the genuine Anabaptists did not exclusively immerse!"

Jacob Ditzler, a famous Methodist controversialist, conceded that the Anabaptists were immersionists: "The German Anabaptists restored baptism by coming out of the Romish church and *immersing* each other when they had been sprinkled."[1]

Regarding the examples, related in Armitage, and by others, of affusion among Anabaptists, I cannot better answer than in the language of that lamented and eminent historical and exegetical scholar, the Rev. E. T. Winkler, D.D.: † "Neither do the cases of pouring decide anything. For the administrators who acted on their own authority, were members of the Reformed Party and would still, if permitted, retain connection with it. The pourings were administered by those who were associates or disciples of Zwingli and Luther, . . . who began their public labors at Wittenberg and Zurich. Except that they insisted on a converted membership they agreed in doctrine and ordinances with the Reformers. Nay, some of them, as we are expressly told, held aloof from the general body of the Anabaptists; so it was with the Anabaptists of Munster, who were Separatists, and considered all others bearing the name as damned, (Luther's Ger. Works, vol. 2, quoted by Michelets' Luther, p. 54.) These cases of pouring were due to these advanced reformers . . . and that at the very chaos of the Reformation. The practice of these dissenters, under such circumstances, can afford no satisfactory evidence of the

† In a letter I received from the excellent Baptist historian of Rochester Theological Seminary, Prof. R. J. W. Buckland, D.D.,—just before his death —he confirms Dr. Winkler' statement.

[1] Graves-Ditzler Deb., p. 828. As I quote Mr. Ditzler, not because he is any authority with scholars, but only for those who blindly follow him, I beg the pardon of *scholars* for quoting him. When such a man is driven to make this concession the evidence ought to convince all *candid* persons.

customs which prevailed among the general body of the Anabaptists, as the opinion of Luther a year or two after he broke from Rome cannot be identified with the established creed of Lutherianism. The incohate Anabaptists advanced according to the light they had. Thus Grebel, who in 1525, baptized Wolfgang Uliman, afterwards immersed him in the Rhine."

Inasmuch as the Anabaptists, in the language of Mosheim: "Before the rise of Luther and Calvin . . . lay concealed in almost all the countries of Europe, particularly in Bohemia, Moravia and Switzerland and Germany,"—under other names—[1] Dr. Winklers' statement conclusively shows that those cases of affusion have no bearing whatever as to the immersion of the general body of Anabaptists. In but one month after Grebel poured Uliman he immersed him.

In the chapter, in this book, in which I show the connection and perpetuity of these various dissenters, appears how these Anabaptists received immersion in an orderly manner.

Inasmuch as the Anabaptists sometimes baptized in "tubs," "pails," houses and barns they have been presumed not exclusive immersionists. As Dr. Winkler has so conclusively met this I will give his answer: "We can prove from ecclesiology and from the testimony of Luther himself that the pail or tub, such as Hoffman used at Emden ('a large pail') was the baptismal font of the Western churches. There was even a certain sacredness connected with it. We find in Luther's Table Talk (*Bohns' Ed.*, *p. 165*) the following incident: 'Dr. Menius asked Dr. Luther in what manner a Jew should be baptized?' The Doctor replied: 'You must

---

[1] Mosheims' Eccl. Hist., cent. 16, sec. 3, chap. 3 and 1, 2.

fill a large tub with water, and having divested the Jew of his clothes, cover him with white garments. He must then sit down in the tub and you must then baptize him quite under the water. This garb,' added Luther, ' was rendered the more suitable from the circumstance that it was then, as now, the custom to bury people in a white shroud, and baptism, you know, is an emblem of our death.'

" Here Luther alludes to these immersions which are very familiar to ecclesiologists. . . . There is reason to believe that the baptismal fonts in early Europe were tubs. The ecclesiologist, Poole, says (*Structures, etc., of Churches, p. 45*): ' The first defined shape which the font assumed in England is that of a circular tub-shaped vessel, some probably of Saxon, many of them of Norman date, as the antique font of St. Martins' church, at Canterbury. Knight says (*Land we Live In, I., p. 261*): ' It is even supposed to have been built by Christians in the Roman army, A. D. 187. It was certainly one of the first ever made in England. It was about three feet high and capacious within. It has no stand; but rests upon the ground. The sculptures upon it are a sort of ornamental interlacings in low relief. It closely resembles the font delineated by the old illuminators in representing the baptism of King Ethelbert; and it is believed to be the very first font in which the first of our Christian kings were baptized.'

"Under this division, the tub fonts, Poole, an Episcopalian antiquarian, groups the font of Castle Frome, Herefordshire, that at Bride Kirk, in Cumberland, that at West Haddon, in Northamptonshire, and that at Thorpe Emald, in Leicestershire. And in regard to all the ancient fonts of England, he says: 'The rule of the church of England, however many the exceptions, and however accounted for, is to baptize by immersion; and for this all the ancient fonts are sufficiently capacious.' (*Structure, etc., p. 59, note.*)

"We learn from Bourrasse, a Catholic archæologist, that the leaden font in the cathedral of Strasbourg has a tub-shape, and so has the baptismal font at Espanburg, Diocese of Beauvais. Both of these baptismal tubs are represented on the plates of *Bourasses' Dictionaire D'Archaologic Sacree.* At Notre Dame, in Rouen, the font was made in the form of a coffin, six feet long, with a covering of black wood. This sepulchral figure was the symbolical translation of the words of Paul: 'We are buried with him by baptism into death.' *Bourasse, p. 493.*"[1]

In Smith's Dictionary of Christian Antiquities[2] the position of Dr. Winkler is confirmed.

The lamented Prof. Heman Lincoln, D.D.—Professor of Ecclesiastical History in Newton Theological Seminary—a little while before his death, wrote me of the Anabaptists: "My own impression is that the majority of them accepted both immersion and baptism upon a profession of faith."

Answering Dr. Sears, Prof. W. W. Everts, Jr., well said: "Dr. Sears would have been nearer right if he had made 'pouring the exception and immersion the rule among the Anabaptists." Just as with the Campbellites, who have poured and sprinkled, but are, as a people, exclusive immersionists.

Prof. W. W. Everts, Jr., wrote: "The English Anabaptists practiced immersion, and the most of them came from the Continent."

[1] In Alabama Baptist, of 1875?
[2] Arts. on Baptistry and Fonts.

Inasmuch as it has been denied that the English Baptists immersed—and even, therefore, that the first American Baptists did so—I close this chapter with proof that the English Anabaptists were exclusive immersionists. Only because of the effrontery with which this denial is made is it here noticed. Crosby quotes Sir John Floyer: "The practice of immersion, or dipping in baptism, continued in the church until the reign of James I., or about the year 1600. . . . Sir John Floyer says: 'My design being to recommend the use of cold bathing to this country, I thought it necessary for the assuring of all people of the innocency of that practice to represent to them the ancient custom of our church in the immersion of infants, as well as all other people at their baptism. And I do here appeal to you, as persons well versed in the ancient history and canons and ceremonies of the Church of England; and therefore are sufficient witnesses of the matter of fact which I desire to prove, viz.: *That immersion continued in the Church of England until about the year 1600.* And from thence I shall infer that if God and the church thought that practice innocent for sixteen hundred years, it must be accounted an unreasonable nicety in this present age to scruple either at immersion or cold bathing as dangerous practices.' . . . In the Synodus Wigorniensis, 'Trina semper fiat immersio baptizandi,' Anno 1240. And in the Synodus Exoniensis, 1287, 'Si puer rite baptizatus, non ipsa submersio, nec praecedentia, sed subsequentia persacerdotem suppleantur,' and the Synodus Wintoniensis, Anno 1306, mentions the immersion. I have quoted all the preceding passages, says Sir John Floyer, from Spellman, whose credit cannot be questioned, and I desire all thence to observe that the immersion was always used to children as well as adult persons. . . . Linwood, who began to write his

Constitutiones Angliae, about the year 1422, interprets a competent baptistry to be big enough for the immersion of the person to be baptised. . . . It is evident, by the rubrick in the days of King Edward VI., that the English church used that practice: ' Then shall the priest take the child into his hands, and ask the name, and naming the child, shall dip it in water thrice; first dipping the right side, secondly, the left side, and the third time, dipping the face downwards in the font, so it be discreetly and warily done.' In the Common Prayer Book, in Queen Elizabeth's days, the rubrick says, naming the child: ' You shall dip it in the water, so it be discreetly and warily done, but if the child be weak, or be baptized privately in a case of necessity, it was sufficient to pour water upon it.' King Edward's injunctions were published in 1547, by which all were forbidden the breaking obstinately the laudable ceremonies of the church. And in Sparrow's collection of articles, etc., in the articles of Queen Elizabeth, 1564, it is ordered, ' That the font be not removed, nor that the curate do baptize in any parish in a basin, nor in any other form than is already prescribed. . . . When Christianity was first planted, the bath structures were turned into temples, and the Piseinas' or cold baths were called Baptisteria by Pliny, Jr., and in them they baptized frequently. And the Saxons, who succeeded the Romans, brought in the German custom of washing in rivers for preserving of their healths; and that made them receive the baptismal immersion in rivers and fountains without any scruple. . . . That I may farther convince all my countrymen that immersion in baptism was very lately left off in England, I will affirm that there are yet persons living who were so immersed, for I was informed by Mr. Berisford that his parents immersed not only him, but the rest of his family at his baptism. He is now about 60 years old, which by the date of the letter must be about 1640.'"[1]

Dr. Cutting says: " No known service book of the English church gave authority to substitute something else for dipping, down to the period of the Reformation. . . . Simpson, in his excellent work on Baptismal fonts, says: 'Not one of the rituals which we have examined (he is alluding to those preceding the prayer book of Edward VI.) contains any permission to use pouring or sprinkling when the child is brought to the church.' . . . In the prayer book of Edward VI. the exceptional allusion was first put into the rubrick. . . . 'This,' says Simpson, 'was the first instance of pouring being allowed in public baptism.' "[2]

Dr. Wall says: "The offices of liturgies for public baptism in the Church of England, did *all along*, as far as I could learn, enjoin dipping *without any mention of pouring or sprinkling*. And John Frith, writing in the year 1533, a treatise on baptism, calls the outward part of it the plunging down into the water, which he often mentions without ever mentioning sprinkling and pouring."[3]

Says Dr. Schaff: " King Edward and Queen Elizabeth were immersed. The first prayer book of Edward the VI., 1594, directs the priest to dip the child in the water. . . . In the second prayer book, 1552, the priest is simply directed to dip the child discreetly and warily, and permission is given, *for the first time in Great Britain, to substitute pouring*, if the godfathers and godmothers certify that the child is weak. During the reign of Elizabeth, says Dr. Wall, ' Many fond ladies and gentlewomen first, and then by degrees the common people, would obtain the

---

[1] Crosby's Hist. of Bap., vol. 2, pp. 46-54.
[2] Cutting's History Vindications, pp. 78, 79.
[3] Wall's Hist. Inf. Bap., vol. 1, p. 350

favor of the priests to have their children pass for weak children, too tender to endure the dipping in the water.' The same writer traces the practice of sprinkling *to* the period of the Long Parliament and the Westminster Assembly. This *change* in England and other Protestant countries from immersion to pouring, and from pouring to sprinkling, was encouraged by the authority of Calvin, who declared the mode to be a matter of no importance, and by the Westminster Assembly of Divines, 1643-1652, which decided that pouring or sprinkling is 'not only lawful but also sufficient.' "[1]

Says Dr. Wall: "As for sprinkling, properly so called, it seems it was, in 1625, *just then beginning and used by very few*. It must have begun in the *disorderly* times after 1641, for Mr. Blake had never used it, nor *seen it used*."[2] Dr. Wall also says: "*France seems to have been the first country in the world in which baptism by affusion was used ordinarily to persons in health, and in the public way of administration.* . . . From France it spread, but not until a good while after, into Italy, Germany, Spain, etc., and last of all, into England."[3] As late as John Wesley's time, 1736, "He refused to baptize, otherwise than by *dipping*, the child of Henry Parker, unless the said Henry Parker and his wife could certify that the child was weak and *not able to bear dipping;* and added to his refusal that, unless the said parents would consent to have it dipped, it might die a heathen."[4]

To the universality of immersion in the Episcopal church, up to and at the Reformation, like testimonies can

---

[1] Teaching of the Twelve Apostles, pp. 51, 52.
[2] Wall's Hist. Inf. Bap., vol. 2, p. 311.
[3] Idem, vol. 1, pp. 576, 577.
[4] Life and Times of John Wesley, by Tyerman, vol. 1, pp. 156, 157.

be added almost *ad infinitum*. Surely, these, which no authority contradicts, must be superabundant. Any one desiring more testimonies is referred to Conant's Baptizein, Robinson's History of Baptism, Edinburgh Encyclopedia, J. T. Christian on Baptism, etc.

In view of the foregoing, to say the Baptists of England, before, up to and at the time of John Smyth, were not immersionists, involves the following incredible things: First, that, though claiming to follow only the Bible, they were not as obedient to it as the creed-ridden Episcopalians, who never permitted affusion for adults, but *only for sickly infants*. Second, that we have the strange somersaults of Baptists, who were then affusionists, becoming immersionists, while Episcopalians, who were then immersionists, have become affusionists! We, therefore, find the writers and others, who were contemporaneous with the Baptists of England, in the sixteenth century, universally, whenever they mention the matter, speaking of them as "Dippers." Dr. Featley, one of their bitterest enemies, who eagerly seized on anything he could to make them opprobrious, and who lived between 1582-1645, and who wrote the bitter work entitled, "*The Dippers Dipt; or*, the Anabaptists *Plunged Over Head and Ears*," at a disputation in Southwark, between 1641-1645—in the language of Dr, Armitage—"*Never* accuses the English Baptists of substituting dipping, or some other practice which they had previously followed. *He gives not one hint that in England they had ever been anything else but 'Dippers,*' an *unaccountable silence if they had practiced something else there within the previous fifty years*."[1] Fuller knew the English Baptists *only as*

---

[1] Armitage's Hist. Bap., p. 458.

immersionists. He says: "These Anabaptists, for the main, are but 'Donatists' *new dipped*."[1]

Of John Smyth's baptism, which bears on the point before us, Armitage says: "Those who wrote against the Baptists after 1640, make no distinction on the matter of *immersion between the Baptists of that period and those who had continued down from 1610, nor report any change among them, from affusion, or perfusion, to dipping*. On the contrary, they speak of them as *one stock*, from Smyth downward. . . . *Uniformly in contempt they call them 'Dippers*,' Barbone says in his Discourse: 'They want a '*Dipper*' that had authority from heaven.' Featley bitterly complains that they 'Flock in multitudes to their *Jordans*, and both sexes *enter the river* and are *dipped after their manner*.' . . . There is not a particle of evidence that Smyth affused himself, and it is a cheap caricature to imagine that he disrobed himself, walked into a stream, then lifted handfuls of water, pouring them liberally upon his own shoulders and chest. We have the same reason for believing *that he immersed Helwys, as much as that he dipped himself*."[2]

Mason writes: "Heluissies' folk differed from the Independents generally on the subject of infant baptism and dipping." He thinks that Busher was a member of that "congregation" in 1614, the man who described a baptized person as one "*dipped* for the dead in the water."[3]

Wilson's History of Dissenting Churches, (pages 29–30) says of Smyth: "He saw grounds to consider *immersion* as the true and only meaning of the word baptism."[3]

---

[1] Fuller's Ch. Hist. of Britain, cent. 16, sec. 5, 11.
[2] Armitage's Hist. Bap., pp. 457-459.
[3] Idem, p. 459.

Neal says that Smyth "*plunged* himself."[1]

That the English Baptists were closely related to the Dutch and German Baptists is well known to the historian. The Dutch and German Anabaptists being immersionists is assurance of the English Baptists practicing only immersion. Of Smyth's time Evans says: "There were Baptists in Holland, those who administered the ordinance of *immersion*."[2]

Evans thus quotes from the editor of John Robinson's works: "The Dutch Baptists, by whom they were surrounded, *uniformly* administered baptism by immersion," and Evans adds: "There was a portion of the Dutch Baptists who uniformly administered baptism by immersion."[3] Hence, Rev. W. W. Everts, Jr., says: "The English Baptists practiced immersion and the first of them came from the continent."

That any early English Baptist church ever changed from affusion to immersion there is not even a shadow of proof. In the name of all reason I ask: Who can believe that they could have made so great a change without leaving one mark of it on history's page?

That the genuine early English Baptists were exclusive immersionists is beyond all reasonable doubt.

(The italics of this chapter are mine.)

[1] Neal's History Puritans, vol. 1, p. 243.
[2] Idem, ibid.
[3] Evans' Early Eng. Bap., vol. 1, p. 203.

CHAPTER XVIII.

THE ANABAPTISTS AND THE MUNSTER DISORDERS.

In the consideration of the Anabaptists and the Munster disorders:

(1.) There were several kinds of Anabaptists at the time of the Munster troubles. Says Hase: "These Anabaptists. . . . were. . . . a class of enthusiasts resembling each other, but *very unlike* each other in moral and religious character. . . . Some of them were persons who renounced the world, and others were slaves of their own lusts; to some of them marriage was only an ideal religious communion of spirit; to others it resolved itself into a general community of wives; some did not differ from the reformers with respect to doctrine, but others rejected original sin and the natural bondage of the will, denied that we are to be justified by the merits of Christ alone, or that we can partake of his flesh and maintained that our Lord's body was from heaven, and not begotten of the virgin."[1]

Mosheim: "It is difficult to determine, with certainty, the particular spot which gave birth to that seditious and *pestilential sect* of Anabaptists. . . . It is most probable that several persons of this odious class made their appearance at the same time in different countries. . . . The first Anabaptist doctors of any eminence were, almost all, heads and leaders of particular sects. For it must be carefully observed, that though all

[1] Hase's Hist. Chr. Ch., p. 431.

these projectors of a new, unspotted and perfect church were comprehended under the general name of Anabaptists, on account of their opposing the baptism of infants, and their rebaptizing such as had received the sacrament in childhood in other churches, yet they were, from their very origin, *subdivided into various sects* which differed from each other in points of *no small moment.* The most pernicious faction of all those that composed this motley multitude, was that which pretended that the founders of the new and perfect church, already mentioned, were under the direction of a divine impulse, and were armed against all opposition, by the power of working miracles. It was this *detestable* faction which began its fanatical work in the year 1521, under the guidance of Munzer, Stubner, Storck and other leaders of the same furious complexion, and excited the most unhappy tumults and commotions in Saxony and other adjacent countries."[1]

They were called Anabaptists, not because they were the *same denomination*, but solely because they rejected all baptisms not administered by themselves. Just as all immersionists of the United States are often, in books and newspapers, classed as Baptists, though radically different. Some who believed in infant baptism were classed as Anabaptists.

Says Dr. Ludwig Keller, the Munster archivist, a Lutheran, than whom there is no higher authority on this subject: "The name Anabaptist, which is used to designate alike all the South German societies, generally awakens the conception of a party homogeneous and of like religious views. The conception, however, is *an entirely erroneous one.* It has been usual since the time

---

[1] Mosheim's Eccl. Hist., cent. 16, sec. 3, ch. 3, sec. 4.

of Luther to designate as Anabaptists, Catabaptists, or fanatics, all those who renounced the Catholic church, but would not become Lutherans. Indeed, Luther at the very outset designated *Zwingli and his followers* as the party associates of those who held views in reference to infant baptism that were different from his own. It is susceptible of *proof* that not even in reference to the *last* mentioned doctrine, which was the occasion of the designation of Anabaptist was there a perfect agreement among the so-called Baptists. Much less was this the case on other points which possessed a *greater* significance for a religious party than that special dogma. It were the more correct, therefore, when the reference is to the religious conflicts of the period of the reformation in general, to speak not of the spread of the Anabaptists, but of the anti-Lutheran parties in Germany. . . . Among the so-called Anabaptists, retaining here the usual designation, we must distinguish *three principal parties* which come upon the scene in three epochs, under the preponderating influence of different personalities. These three groups were *not the only ones into which the party were divided*—indeed, *not less than forty* are enumerated by their contemporaries—but there were three parties which in the number of their followers and in the importance of their leaders, were especially prominent in the whole movement. All other groups were only degenerate, independent interests of ephemeral and limited influence."[1]

From the statement, that there were different kinds of Anabaptists, no reliable historian or well read and honest person, upon this subject will dissent.

While the absurdity and the injustice, therefore, of branding Baptists with the disgrace of the Munster riots,

[1] *Preussische Jahrbucher*, Sept. 1892—translated by Rev. H. S. Burrage, D. D., in Bap. Quar. Rev., vol. 7, pp. 33, 34.

simply because they were then known under the word Anabaptists, is apparent, from the foregoing, yet, as so many Baptist opponents resort to this injustice, I will next notice the verdict of those who have carefully and honestly investigated the charge.

(2.) Historians and other writers exonerate Baptists from the disgrace of taking any part in the Munster riots.

Says Burrage, alluding to a conference between Thomas Munzer, Grebel and Mantz: "Nor do we find that the Swiss radicals had any subsequent dealings with him. As Grebel's letter shows, he and his associates were not in agreement with Munzer in reference to *baptism*. They did not believe in the use of the *sword* as he did. Doubtless, they now found that in purpose they and the Saxon reformer *differed widely*. Munzer's aims were social and political chiefly."[1]

Says Mosheim, whom, we have seen, clearly recognizes different sects of Anabaptists: "It would betray, however, a *strange ignorance*, as an *unjustifiable* partiality, to maintain, that even all that professed, in general, this absurd doctrine, were *chargeable* that with furious and brutal extravagance, which has been mentioned, as the character of too great a part of their sect. This was by no means the case; several of these enthusiasts discovered a milder and more pacific spirit, and were free from any other reproach than that which resulted from the errors they maintained, and their too ardent effort of spreading them among the multitude. It may still further be affirmed with truth, that MANY of those who followed the wiser class of Anabaptists, nay, some who adhered to the most extravagant factions of that sect, were men of *upright intentions and sincere piety*, who were seduced into this mys-

[1] The Anabaptists of Switzerland, p. 89.

tery of fanaticism and iniquity, by their ignorance and simplicity on the one hand, and by a laudable desire of reforming the *corrupt state of religion* on the other . . . *those who had no other marks of peculiarity than their administering baptism to adult persons only, and their excluding the unrighteous from the external communion of the church ought undoubtedly to have met with milder treatment* than what was given to those seditious incendiaries, who were for unhinging all government and destroying all civil authority. . . . . It is true, indeed, that MANY *Anabaptists* suffered death, not on account of their being considered rebellious subjects, but *merely because they were judged to be incurable* heretics, for in this century the error of limiting the administration of baptism to adult persons only, and the practice of rebaptizing such as had received that sacrament in a state of infancy, were looked upon as *most flagitous and intolerable heresies*. . . . A HANDFUL of madmen who got into their heads the visionary notion of a new and spiritual kingdom," were the madmen of Munster.[1]

Says Armitage: "Gieseler says that 'no traces of *Anabaptist* fanaticism were seen' in the Peasants' War."[2] "Some individual Anabaptists were drawn into the contest, as at Muhlhausen, under the lead of Munzer, who was not, in any *proper sense of the term*, an Anabaptist himself. On the *contrary*, Keller, in his late work on the Reformation, (p. 370), says that Cornelius has shown that in the *chief* points Munzer *was opposed to the Baptists.*'[3] "But differing from Baptists, he *practiced infant baptism* twice a year, christening all born in his congregation. In 1522, at Alstedt, he threw aside the

---

[1] Mosheim's Eccl. Hist., cent. 16, sec. 3, chap. 3, sec. 5, 6, 7.
[2] Armitage's Bap. Hist., p. 366.
[3] Idem, ibid.

Latin liturgy and prepared one in German, in which he retained the formula for infant baptism. . . . It is, therefore, a singular perversity that so many writers should have attempted to palm him off as a Baptist, and the father of them. Dr. Rule, in his 'Spirit of the Reformation,' says: ' He performed a ceremony on baptized persons which they mistook for baptism, and with his followers received the designation Anabaptist.' But Ulhorn says that he did not practice rebaptism, and did not form a congregation."[1] "Few writers have treated this subject with greater care and clearness than Ypeij and Dermout in their 'History of the Netherland Churches.' They say of the Munster men that while they are known in history as ' Anabaptists,' they ought by no means to be known as Baptists. ' Let the reader,' they request, ' keep this distinction in mind in the statement which we now make respecting them. Since the peculiar history of the Anabaptists and Baptists has exerted so powerful an influence on the reformation of the church in this country, the nature of our historical work requires that we present in its true light the whole matter from its origin. After speaking at length of the Munster men and their excesses, especially of their leaders, they say of Mathiesen: ' He laid as the foundation of his new system of doctrine, that teaching respecting the holy ordinance of baptism which, in part, had *long before been maintained* by the Baptists. He considered infant baptism not to be of the least advantage to the religious interests of the Christian. In his opinion baptism should be delayed to years of discretion, and after a profession of faith on the part of the baptized. Therefore every one who passed over to the community of which he was the head

[1] Idem, pp. 367, 368.

must first be baptized, even if he had been baptized into another society at an adult age. When he renounced his confession of faith he renounced also his baptism. . . . It can now be easily understood how the followers of the Munster leaders received the name of Anabaptists, or rebaptizers. So far as their views of baptism are concerned, these could be easily tolerated and they need not have been hated by reasonable persons on account of these. But besides these, they taught doctrines fraught with important errors, partly founded on Pelagianism,† partly Unitarianism, partly Mysticism, and partly impure principles. Yet, with all these opinions they could have been suffered to exist had they behaved themselves properly as members of society. . . . Since the enlisting of the rebel Anabaptists happened in this manner, it is sufficiently evident that the *great majority* cannot be supposed to have been Baptists in belief. They were people of every *variety* of religious beliefs, and many of them of *no religion* at all in heart, although they aided the Protestant cause. From the nature of the case *the majority of Romanists knew no difference between the various Protestant parties and sects, and would make no distinction*. Hence, the abhorrence only deserved by *some* of the Anabaptists was bestowed upon all Protestants. The honest Baptist suffered most severely from their prejudice, because they were considered by the people to be the same, and were called by the same name. . . . On this account the Baptists in Flanders and in Friesland suffered the most terrible persecutions. . . . . We have nowhere seen clearer evidence of the injurious influence of prejudice; nowhere have we met with more *ob-*

---

† "Pelagianism," "Unitarianism" are held by Campbellites in general, to a greater or less extent. Pelagianism is the boldest Arminianism. Hence, the Munster disorders are chargable to Campbellite *principles* and to Arminianism as otherwise held.

stinate unwillingness to be correctly informed, and a more evident disposition to silence those who better understood the truth of the matter. Prejudice, when once deeply imbibed, blinds the eye, perplexes the understanding, silences the instincts of the heart, and destroys the *love of truth and rectitude*. . . . Their religious teachings were pure and simple and were exemplified in their daily conduct.' "[1]

"Brandt attributes them to some 'enthusiastic Anabaptists,' but is careful to add: '*Not to the well meaning Baptists.*' '*Schaff pronounces it the greatest injustice to make the Anabaptists*, as such, responsible for the extravagances that led to the tragedy at Munster.' Uhlhorn says that 'sedition, or a call to sedition, is not chargeable against the Anabaptists of Southern Germany at this time; I have found no trace of any fellowship with the seditious peasants.' But their contemporaries who knew them well, bear the same testimony. Capito, their *stern opponent* at Strasburg, says that he must 'openly confess' that most of them manifest '*godly* fear and pure zeal. Before God I testify that I cannot say that their contempt for life springs from blindness rather than from a divine impulse.' Wetzel, the *Catholic*, declared that 'Whosoever speaks of God and a Christian life, or earnestly strives after personal improvement passes as an arch Anabaptist.' And Frank, who wrote in 1531, says of them: 'They teach love, faith and the cross. They are long suffering and heroic in affliction. . . . The world feared they would cause an uproar, but they have *proved innocent everywhere*. If I were emperor, pope or Turk, I would not fear revolt less from any people than this. . . . . . All the *Baptists* oppose those who fight for the gospel with the sword. Some object to war or any use of

[1] Idem, pp. 369, 370.

the sword, but *the most favor self-defense and justifiable war.*' Bayle tells us that Turenne remonstrated with Van Benning for tolerating them, when he replied: 'They are good people, and the most commodious to a State in the world, because they do not aspire to places of dignity. . . . They edify the people by the simplicity of their manners, and apply themselves to arts and business without dissipating their substance in luxury and bebauchery.' Nay, Bayle himself says that their great enemy, De Bres, says nothing to insinuate that the Anabaptist martyrs suffered death for taking up arms against the State, or for stirring up the subjects to rebel, but represents them as a *harmless* sort of people. . . . 'Tis *certain* many of them who suffered death for their opinions had no thought of making an insurrection. . . . Cornelius sums up the whole matter, covering the time from 1525 onward, when he says: 'Anabaptism and the Peasants' War had no conscious connection.' The two movements were generally distinct. The Baptists in the Schleitheim Articles, Article VI, said: 'Scandal has been brought in amongst us by certain false brethren, so that some have turned from the faith, imagining to use for themselves the freedom of the Spirit and of Christ. But such have erred from the truth and have given themselves (to their condemnation) to the wantonness and freedom of the flesh; and have thought faith and love may do and suffer all things, and nothing would injure or condemn them because they believed. They warn that 'faith' does not thus prove itself, does not bring forth and do such things as these false brethren and sisters do and teach. . . . Beware of such, as they serve not our father, but the flesh, with its lusts and longings.' "[1]

[1] Armitage's Bap. Hist., pp. 373, 374.

One of the Baptist martyrs, Dryzinger, in 1538, only three years after the craze, was examined as to whether he and his brethren approved of these vile proceedings. He answered: "They would not be Christians if they did." Hans of Overdam, another martyr, complained of these false accusations of violence. He said: "We are daily belied by those who say that we defend our faith with the sword, as they of Munster did. The Almighty defend us from such abominations." Young Dosie, a beautiful character, who was a prisoner to the Governor of Friesland, and endured cruel slaughter for his love to Christ, was asked by the governor's wife if he and his brethren were not of the disgraceful people who took up the sword against magistrates. With the sweet innocence of a child he replied: "No, madam; those persons greatly erred. We consider it a *devilish* doctrine to resist the magistrates by the outward sword and violence. We would much rather suffer persecution and death at their hands and whatever is appointed us to suffer.' All this is no more than Erasmus said of them in 1529: 'The Anabaptists have seized no churches, have not conspired against the authorities, nor deprived any man of his estate and goods.' They had no sturdier foe than Bullinger, yet he renders this verdict: 'Say what we will of the Baptists, I see nothing in them but earnestness, and I hear nothing of them except that they will not take an oath, will not do *any wrong*, and aim to treat *every man justly*. In this, it seems to me, there is nothing out of the way.' But Cornelius tells us plainly: '*All* these excesses were condemned and opposed *wherever* a large assembly of the brethren afforded an opportunity to give expression to the religious consciousness of the *Baptist* membership.' . . . No one outside of their number has better described their advanced position as a people in all respects than Fusslin, in his preface to volume II of Beitrage: 'The reformers rejected the superstitious abuses attached to the sacraments; the Anabaptists restored the sacraments themselves to *memorials for believers*. The reformers preached against unnecessary bloodshed; the Anabaptists denounced war of every kind. The reformers protested against Catholic tyranny; the Anabaptists denied to any civil power authority in matters of religion. The reformers decried public vices; the Anabaptists *excluded*† the immoral from their fellowship. The reformers sought to limit usury and covetousness; the Anabaptists made them impossible by their practice of communion. The reformers educated their preachers; the Anabaptists looked for the inner annointing. The reformers condemned the priests for simony; the Anabaptists made every preacher dependent on the labor of his own hands and the *free gifts of* the people*. . . . *There was a great difference between Anabaptists and Anabaptists*. There were those among them who held strange doctrines, but this cannot be said of the whole sect. If we should attribute to every sect whatever senseless doctrines two or three fanciful fellows have taught, there is no one in the world to whom we could not ascribe the most abominable errors.' Grebel tells us that two hundred moral and moderate Baptists in Munster heroically withstood the iniquity, and it was not established until forty-eight of that number had been put to a bloody slaughter for their resistance. *So that in the struggle nearly fifty* Baptists *fell martyrs to purity in the German Sodom;* and at last

---

† In this strict church discipline the German Baptists of to-day agree with these. Baptist churches of the United States surely need a revival of discipline.

* Thus, as Baptists of to-day—when people were able they supported their pastors; when they were unable their pastors supported themselves They had educated men among them who were educated before they left the Church of Rome, but their persecuted condition prevented them from educating those who were raised among them.

the ministers and most of the people yielded to the clamor for polygamy under this reign of terror. While this *handful* of madmen had not been educated in visions, violence and indecency by the Baptist leaders of Switzerland and Germany, *others* had impregnated them with these doctrines from the cradle. For *centuries* these teachings and practices had filled the air. The doctrine of wild visions, both of God and the devil, was taught in the monastic institutions, and wonders of this sort were blazoned abroad by bishops, cardinals and popes everywhere. The Catholic communion believed then and still believes in new revelations from God. Saints innumerable are mentioned who heard voices from heaven, had visits from the Virgin and Father, the Son and angels—as Ignatius Aquinas, Teresa, Felix and Anthony. Francis was not only inspired to read men's minds and consciences as well as their faces, but he received the rules of his new order of monks direct from God. Like John of Leydon, he appointed twelve apostles, and one of them hanged himself to boot. He also 'prophesied' that he should be a 'great prince,' and be adored over the whole earth. Bridget, Catharine and Rosa, with endless nuns, were prophetesses. Teresa took the crucified Christ by the hand, was espoused to him, and went up to heaven in the shape of a white dove. The Munster men never had such dreams, raptures, apparitions, phantasms and ecstacies as the canonized saints of Rome. Neither did Luther help the lunatics to sounder doctrine, when he saw the devil in the form of 'dog,' a 'whisp of straw,' a 'wild boar,' and a 'star;' nor when he threw the ink-stand at his head. As to violence, Catholics and Protestants taught them that tradition, reason and Scripture made it the pious duty of saints to torture and burn men as heretics out of pure love for their holiness and salvation.

. . . Who educated these fanatics in Christian love and gentleness? The law of their times was to repel force with force. When the Munster men came into power they applied the reasonings of their tutors in atrocity, saying: 'Our bounden duty is to rid the earth of Christ's enemies and ours, as they would rid it of us.' And who will say that all these murderers did not stand on the same plane of outrage and barbarity in this respect? As to immoralities—every pure mind shrinks from the indecencies of Munster. And who had set them this example? They practiced polygamy; but ten long years before this, 1524, Luther had written: 'The husband must be certified in his own conscience and by the word of God that polygamy is permitted to him. As for me, I avow that I cannot set myself in opposition to men marrying several wives, or assert that such a course is repugnant to Holy Scripture.' About the same time he preached his famous sermon on 'Marriage,' which chastity may well pass in silence, beyond this one expression: 'Provided one has faith, adultery is no sin.' . . . And what better example had the Catholics set the Munster men in that line of purity? From the ninth century down, as Bowden says in his 'Life of Hildebrand,' 'The infamies prevalent among the clergy are to be alluded to, not detailed.' The open licentiousness of the popes was appalling. The popes of the fifteenth century were profligate and debased beyond belief. Innocent III. publicly boasted of the number of his illegitimate children. Alexander was a monster of iniquity, who gave dispensations for crimes that cannot be written. Baronius says that the vilest harlots domineered in the papal see, at their pleasure changed sees, appointed bishops, and actually thrust into St. Peter's chair their own gallants, false popes. Take the simple case of John XII. Bowden wrote: 'The Lateran palace was disgraced by becoming a receptacle for courtesans; and decent females were terrified from the pilgrimages to the threshold of the Apostles by the reports which were spread abroad of the lawless impurity and violence of the representative and successor of two others equally vile.' But these were no worse than Sixtus, who entered a house of ill-fame in Rome, the inmates of which, according to Justin, paid his holiness a weekly tax, which amounted sometimes to twenty thousand ducats a year. The purest spirits in the hierarchy blush to tell the hard narrative of monastic life in the sixteenth century, although it made pretensions to spotless virtue. Archbishop Morton, 1490, accused the abbot of St. Albans with emptying the nunneries of Pray and Sapnell of modest women and filling them with vile females. The clergy kept concubines openly from the popes down. . . . For centuries the *fanaticism of Rome* had immersed all people in a state of nudity. . . . Rome practiced the same indecencies in flagellation, borrowed from the heathen feast of Lupercale, in which, according to Virgil and Plutarch, young noblemen walked through the streets naked, cutting themselves with whips and rods, in austerity, while sacrifices were burning to their gods. The same barbarity was practiced by Christian woman of France, Mezeray being authority. For two centuries this flagellation madness ran through Bavaria, Austria, the Upper Rhine and Italy, nay through Saxony itself. These morbid fanatics practiced all stages of undress, formed a brotherhood, swept in thousands through these lands, singing hymns, having revelations from angels and the Virgin, and with a letter from Christ himself, which they exhibited in their pilgrimages. Motley calls the Munster men 'Furious fanatics, who deserve the madhouse rather than the scaffold;' and how much better were Catholics and Protestants in practicing the same things?"[1]

Says Vedder, who is too ready to credit slanders on the ancient Baptists: "Fanatical outbreaks in South Germany had no connection with Hoffman. Their chief leader, if not instigator, was Thomas Muntzer. He is invariably called an Anabaptist, *but in reality he never belonged to that body*. It is true that he wrote and spoke against the baptism of infants, but he regularly *practiced it*, and was therefore a *Pedobaptist*. The disorders of his leadership. . . . cannot be laid to the charge of the Anabaptists."[2]

Says Prof. Geo. P. Fisher, D. D., of the Anabaptists: "The church they insisted must be composed exclusively of the regenerate, and they insisted, it is not a matter to be regulated and managed by civil rulers. Under the name of Anabaptists are included different types of doctrine and Christian life. It is a gross injustice to impute to all of them the wild destructive fanaticism with which a portion of them are chargeable. . . . This fanatical class are first heard of under Thomas Munzer, as a leader. . . . Grebel and other Anabaptists . . . were enthusiasts but not fanatics. They were peaceful in their spirit, and, as it would appear, sincerely devout."[3]

The new American Encyclopedia is quoted: "There was another class of Anabaptists, *widely* different from those who have been described" as the Munster men.

Fessendens' Encyclopedia—a work quoted with approbation by Daubigne, is quoted: "Anabaptists: The English and Dutch Baptists do not consider the word

[1] Armitage's Hist. Bap., pp. 366, 378.
[2] Vedder's Hist. Bap., p. 98.
[3] Fisher's Hist. Chr. Ch., p.

as applicable to *their* sect. It is but *justice* to add that the Baptists of Holland and England and the United States are to be regarded *essentially distinct* from those seditious and fanatical individuals."

The New American Encyclopedia is quoted: "It is *certain* that the disturbances in the city of Munster were begun by a Pedobaptist minister of the Lutheran persuasion, . . . that he was assisted in his endeavors by other ministers of the same persuasion."

Says Keller: "Nothing can be *more false* than the assertion that any casual connection existed between these revolutionary efforts and the teachings of Denck and the better part of the Anabaptists generally."[1]

In the *Examiner and Chronicle*, Dr. William Whitsitt, says: "I believe that we *cannot avoid accepting* the testimony of Sebastian Frank, to the effect that Munzer, though at one time he rejected infant baptism, like many other men of a 'like sentiment in that age, never went to the length of adopting Anabaptism.' Frank says: 'He himself never baptized any, as I am credibly informed. Erkbam, 495, note.'"

Daubigne is quoted concerning the Munster troubles, as saying they came out of the bosom of the *Reformation:* "Confusion and ruin had taken hold of the city. The Reformation had seen an enemy spring up from its *own* bosom more formidable than all the popes and emperors. It was on the very verge of the abyss."[2]

Luther himself distinguished between the Anabaptists and the Munsterites. He said: "I have got over three cruel storms—Munzer, the Sacramentarians and the Anabaptists."[3]

---

[1] Quoted from p. 200 Ein Apostel Der Weidertaufer, by Dr. Burrage.
[2] Hist. Ref., vol. 3, p. 53.
[3] Michelet's Life of Luther, p. 72—quoted by E. T. Winkler, D. D.

232   CHURCH PERPETUITY.

In *The Independent*, the lamented specialist in Baptist history, Dr. Buckland, of Rochester Theological Seminary, refuting the Munster slander, called attention to the fact that Hase, Gerard, Gieseler, Fusslin, Brandt, Dorner, and indeed, that the concensus of candid, critical historians clear the Anabaptists of the Munster slander.

He adds: "That kingdom has attracted the attention of writers in a remarkable degree because of its excesses; still it was a mere episode of the Reformation, lasting from February, or more strictly, from December, 1534, to the 22d of June, 1535, or about six months in its full organization. But the peaceable Anabaptists—who made it a religious principle to bear no weapons, use no force, love their enemies and suffer all things unresistingly — existed by many tens of thousands, during and after the time in Switzerland, Germany, Moravia, and the low countries. In these distinctive principles they were identical with the Waldenses before them and the noble Mennonites after them."

The late Dr. Philip Schaff, Presbyterian Professor in Union Theological Seminary, and the most prominent church historian of the United States: "The history of the Anabaptists of the Reformation period has *yet to be written from an impartial, unsectarian standpoint.*† The polemical attitude of the reformers against them has *warped the judgment of historians*. They were cruelly treated in their lifetime by Romanists and Protestants, and *misrepresented* after their death as a set of heretical and revolutionary fanatics who could not be tolerated in a Christian state. The excesses of a misguided faction have been charged upon the whole body. They were made responsible for the peasant's war and the Munster

---

† This shows that Baptists yet have no history worthy of the name history.

tragedy, although the *great majority of them were quiet, orderly and peaceful citizens,* and would rather suffer persecution than do an act of violence. The Mennonites and regular Baptists of America *are the true successors of the Anabaptists* of the sixteenth century, and help us to understand and appreciate the latter. The official reports of the proceedings against the Anabaptists are from their enemies, and are more or less colored. The works of Anabaptists are few and scarce." [1]

Of Roger Williams' departure to America and of the Baptists Palfry, one of the bitter enemies to Baptists, says: "The Baptists many years before his departure had stated and maintained the doctrine of religious liberty in the most unqualified terms." [2]

May says of the Baptists: "Renouncing all connection with the State. . . . separation and isolation were the very foundation of their creed." [3]

Froude says of them: "In their deaths they assisted to pay the purchase money of England's freedom." [4]

Bancroft says of them: "The plebeian sect of the Anabaptists, 'the scum of the Reformation,' with greater consistency than Luther applied the doctrine to the Reformation to the social relations of life and threatened an end to kingcraft spiritual dominion, tithes and vassalage. They were trodden under foot with foul reproaches and most arrogant scorn; and its history is written in the blood of myriads of the German peasantry; but its principles, safe in their immortality, escaped to Providence." [5]

[1] In The Bap. Quar. Rev., vol. 12, No. 43.
[2] Palfry's Hist. New Eng., vol. 1, p. 414.
[3] May's Const. Hist. Eng., vol. 2, p. 269.
[4] Froude's Hist. Eng., vol. 2, p. 358.
[5] Bancroft's Hist. U. S., vol. 2, p. 457—old ed.

CHAPTER XIX.

The Baptist Church Perpetuity Line, or Lines from the Apostolic Age to the Paulicians, and Including Them.

In the previous chapters of this book we have seen that there were Baptist churches in all the ages from the apostolic age to the seventeenth century. This we have seen demonstrated by the doctrine and the practice of the churches which we have examined. The doctrine and the practices of Baptists, from the seventeenth century to the present, being too well known to call for examination—save as to "who are the old Baptists"—as to the Perpetuity of Baptist churches, I now proceed to show the *historical* connection of the Baptist churches which the previous chapters have examined. †

Though the Perpetuity of Baptist churches is shown in the continuity of their doctrine and practice, and, thus, the purpose of this book accomplished, yet, to give the reader some conception of the abundance of proof sustaining the position, that Baptist churches have an existence from the time of Christ to the present, I will,

---

† Every Baptist church is a complete church. No Baptist church is united to any other Baptist church by church organization. From the point of *church organization* no Baptist church is connected with any other Baptist church. Just as each man is as completely a man as if there were no other man in existence, so each Baptist church is as completely a church as if no other church existed. The only connection, therefore, that Baptist churches have to each other is that of *likeness, spirit and mutual relation and obligation to their Lord and to His cause*. Much confusion in examining Baptist Church Perpetuity grows out of the mind being prepossessed by the Romish doctrine of the church being made of all the congregations and their hierarchy, all in one organization, and thus connected by outward organization. I mean only by historical connection of Baptist churches that they are connected by the bond of spiritual brotherhood and service to their Lord, by identity of doctrine and practice and by one being the production of another, as one college produces another, or as offspring is the production of parent.

also, demonstrate Baptist Church Perpetuity from the connection which history shows that these churches sustained to the first churches and to each other.

First. The historical relation of Montanists, Novatians and Donatists.

That Montanists, Novatians and Donatists, were in doctrine and practice, essentially identical, appears in the previous chapters.

Neander, says of Novatian: "His principles admit of so natural an explanation from the sternness of his Christian character, and he was acting in this case so entirely in the spirit of a *whole party of the church* in his time."[1]

Robinson says: "They tax Novatian with being the parent of an innumerable multitude of congregations of Puritans all over the empire; and yet he had no other influence over any than what his good example gave him. People saw *everywhere the same cause of complaint* and groaned for relief, and when one man made a stand for virtue *the crisis* had *arrived*, people saw the propriety of the cure and applied the same means to their own relief. They blame this man and all these churches for the severity of their discipline; yet, this severe moral discipline, was the only coercion of the primitive churches, and it was the exercise of this, that rendered civil coercion unnecessary."[2]

Moller: "Condemned in Rome, Montanism found a new home in North Africa and its most prominent representative Tertullian."[3] Naturally the Baptists, who were persecuted under the stigma of Montanists, found refuge in North Africa with their brethren who were

---
[1] Neander's Hist. Chr. Ch., vol. 1, p. 239.
[2] Robinson's Eccl. Resh., p. 127.
[3] Schaff Herzog Ency., vol. 2, p. 1562.

stigmatized Donatists. The Montanists were so strong that Tertullian tells us the corrupt party felt inclined to recognize their claims in order for peace."[1]

Says Adolph Harnack: " According to Philostorgius, Novatian was a native of Phrygia. Probably, however, this notion arose from the circumstance that he found many adherents in Phrygia; or, perhaps it was purposely manufactured in order to insinuate a connection between him and the Montanists."[2] Admit Novatian was a native of Phrygia, and we see in the admission his early Montanist education manifest after his conversion. Deny he was Phrygian, and we have in the denial the explanation of the cause of the extraordinary prosperity of Novatian on Phrygian soil, in that Montanism had educated the people there into Novatian belief and practice. Deny both, and we have the story as proving that Baptist enemies recognized Montanists and Novatians as really or essentially the same people. Harnack farther says of the Novatians: " The schism gradually assumed very dangerous proportions, in the *East*, the views of Novatian finding many adherents in Egypt, Armenia, Pontus, Bithynia, Cappadocia, Syria, and Mesopotamia."[3]

Hase says: Montanism was "an excitement which originated in Phrygia, and extended over *all* the churches of Asia Minor."[4]

Of the locality where the Donatists controversy originated, in giving account of its rise, Guericke says: " In Northern Africa the fanatical spirit of Montanism had propagated itself here and there."[5]

[1] Schaff-Herzog Ency., vol. 2, p. 1562.
[2] Idem, vol. 2, p. 1670.
[3] Idem, vol. 2, p. 1671.
[4] Hase's Hist. Chr. Ch., p. 66.
[5] Guericke's Ch. Hist., vol. 1, p. 278.

Prof. Geo. P. Fisher, says: "The controversy concerning church discipline, which had been maintained in the former period by the Novatians, was revived again by the Donatists."[1]

Hase says of the Novatians: "They *withdrew all fellowship* from the Catholic church and rebaptized all who came from it to them. . . . In *other* countries also a *similar* uncertainty with respect to the true idea of a church and strict discipline produced similar divisions."[2]

Of the Novatians, W. W. Everts, Jr., Says: "They extended throughout the *Roman Empire*, from Armenia to Numedia, in Spain. They were especially strong in Phrygia, where the Montanists *fused with them*, and in the great cities, Constantinople, Alexandria, Carthage, and Rome."[3]

Gieseler, says of the Novatians: "This party was *widley* extended and continued for a *long time*. In Phrygia they *united* with the remnant of the Montanists."[4]

Schaff, says of the Novatians: "In Phrygia it combined with the remnants of the Montanists."[5]

Harnack, says: "After the Decian persecution, the church of the Cathari." *i. e.* Novatians—and probably Donatists—"became *consolidated*. Many Montanist congregations joined it, especially in Phrygia."[6]

From the statements of the historians, we see that Montanists and Novatians were "united" together in church fellowship, that they excluded the so-called Catholics instead of first being excluded themselves; and that instead of Novatian being the founder of the Novatians,

[1] Fisher's Hist. Chr. Ch., p. 109.
[2] Hase's Hist. Chr. Ch. p. 67
[3] Baptist Layman's Book. p. 17.
[4] Gieseler's Ch. Hist., vol. 1, p. 255; see also Socrates' Eccl. Hist., Book 4, ch. 28.
[5] Schaff's Hist. Chr. Ch. vol. 1, p. 451.
[6] Schaff-Herzog Ency., vol. 2, p. 1672.

he was only the leader of multitudes of churches which withdrew fellowship from the disorderly ones. The Donatists holding the same doctrine and practice that the Montanists and the Novatians held, and withdrawing fellowship from the corrupt part of the churches, on the same complaint on which the Montanists and Novatians withdrew from it, and to a great extent, contemporaneous and occupying the same territory with them, could but have been in church fellowship with them. While, like American and foreign Baptists, they may have possibly differed in minor matters, they were evidently the same people.

Second. The Montanists, the Novatians and the Donatists perpetuated in the Paulicians.

Says Schaff: "A remnant of the Donatists, as we learn from the letters of Gregory II, perpetuated itself into the seventh century."[1]

Hase says: They "struggled and suffered on till some time in the seventh century, and had shown the *prodigious power* which even a mistaken faith may exert over sincere, vigorous and gloomy dispositions."[2]

Schaff-Herzog Encyclopedia: "They had not become extinct when in the seventh century the Saracens occupied the territory and destroyed the African church."[3]

Guericke: "Relics of this *great* party continued to exist until about the year 600, evincing even in their fragments the *power* of a mistaken belief, and the wrongs of ecclesiastical, civil persecution."[4]

Of Africa, A. D. 427, Wadington says: "When it was discovered by Belisarius, more than a hundred

---

[1] Schaff's Hist. Chr. Ch., vol. 2, p. 365.
[2] Hase's Hist. Chr. Ch., p. 158.
[3] Vol. 1, p. 660.
[4] Guericke's Ch. Hist., vol. 1, p. 283.

years afterwards, after 427, the sect of the Donatists was still found to exist there as a separate communion. . . . We are told that it dwindled into insignificance about the end of the sixth century, *but* it is not improbable that the Saracen invaders of Numidia found them some few years later, the remnant of a sect *not* ill disposed to favor any invader, nor unmindful of the sufferings of their ancestors."[1]

The Schaff-Herzog Encyclopedia says: "In the fifth century the Novatians had . . . *many* churches . . . the party lived on until the sixth or seventh century."[2]

Kurtz says: "Owing to the *moral earnestness* of their principles, even those bishops who took a different view from theirs were disposed to regard them more favorably; and almost *throughout the Roman Empire* Novatian communities sprang up, of which remnants existed as late as the sixth century."[3] Socrates, in his Ecclesiastical History tells us of *many* Novatian churches existing in Rome in the fifth century. Books V, section XIV; VII, sections IX and XIV. "Many of whose churches;" "their assemblies within the city" are some of the phrases which Socrates uses of the Donatists.

Wadington: "They subsisted until the fifth century *throughout Christendom.*"[4]

Schaff says: "In spite of strong opposition the Novatian sect, by virtue of its moral earnestness, *propagated* itself in various provinces of the West and East to the fifth century."[5]

[1] Wadington's Ch. Hist., p. 153.
[2] Vol. 2, p. 1672.
[3] Kurtz's Ch. Hist., vol. 1, pp. 134, 135.
[4] Wadington's Ch. Hist., p. 79.
[5] Schaff's Hist. Chr. Ch., vol. 1, p. 451.

Of the Montanists Kurtz says: "Still the sect of the Tertullianists continued in Africa for a *long time*."[1]

Guericke: "The Montanists maintained themselves as a distinct sect down to the sixth century, bearing beside their usual names the names of Cataphrygians (ὁι κατα Φύγας), Pepuzians and many other names of local or contemptuous signification."[2]

Gieseler says: "The Montanists in Asia continued down to the *tenth century*.[3]

Thus we see that the Montanists, the Novatians and the Donatists were not only identical in doctrine, practice and the complaint on which they excluded the so-called Catholics from their church fellowship, but that they were seen in church fellowship with each other, taking and being known by the same name or names.

To believe that a people of such "moral earnestness," of such unconquerable, unflagging and propagating zeal, of such vast numbers and occupying almost universal territory, and with God on their side against a false church, ceased to exist as the distinguishing names by which they were known in their early history drop from history—saying nothing of God's promises to his church—is certainly far more difficult than to believe that they were perpetuated under other names. In the case of the Anabaptists losing their name in the names Mennonite and Baptist and the various Baptist bodies, in the history of the Baptists of the United States, merging into but one body and afterwards known by but one name, we have illustrated the historical tendency which we should expect to often see operating in the Baptists of the remotely past ages. We have just seen, by the testimony of

---

[1] Kurtz's Chr. Hist., vol. 1, p. 133.
[2] Guericke's Ch. Hist., p. 192.
[3] Gieseler's Ch. Hist., vol. 1, pp. 143-144.

Guericke, that the Montanists, before the name Paulician appears, were given the names "Cataphrygians, Pepuzians and *many other* names of a local or contemptuous signification." Throughout the history of the various Baptist bodies which church historians in deference to the Romish church, call " sects " and " heretics " and which Revelation calls the " Mother of Harlots," we see them all given names, from their localities, their leaders and other things connected with their history. Thus, though as old as the Christian age, from Montanus, their first great leader, after the first century, called "Montanists;" from Tertullian, their next great leader, "Tertullianists;" from Novatian, another great leader, "Novatians;" from Donatus, another great leader, "Donatists;" from Waldo, another great leader, and the valleys, "Waldenses;" from Peter de Bruis, another great leader, "Petrobrussians;" from Henry, another great leader, "Henricians;" from Arnold, another great leader, "Arnoldists;" from Meno, another great leader, "Mennonites." In the seventh century, when the names Montanists, Novatians and Donatists are retiring from historical view appears the name Paulician. This name appears in its application to churches which in doctrine and practice—see previous chapters—were essentially identical with the Montanists, the Novatians and the Donatists, which *names* are here dropped out of history. It appears in application to churches which occupied the same territory which these occupied. The name Paulician appears when Montanists, Novatians and Donatists, instead of being extinct, must have numbered many hundred thousands of members. This, therefore, forms so strong a presumption that Paulicians were only Montanists, Novatians and Donatists, under another name, that, in the absence of any clear historical evidence to the contrary, we must conclude that Paulician is but a new label for the good old wine. The name is as strong contrary evidence as can be produced. But we have just seen that names originate from so many things which do not effect the identity of these churches that they are of no evidence as to their origin or identity.

(The reader here turn to and read the first part of Chapter XI of this book.)

The following, from Neander, illustrates the great and *significant* uncertainty and confusion in which all who claim the Paulicians were of post-apostolic origin are involved: "It is an hypothesis of both the authors to whom we are indebted for the most important information which we possess respecting this sect, though neglected by all succeeding writers, that this sect was an offshoot of Manichæism; and that it took its origin from a woman, Callinice by name, who lived in the district of Samosata, somewhere about the fourth century, and whose two sons, Paul and John, were considered as the founders of the sect. From the former of these, it is said, moreover, that the sect took its name; and it was the opinion of one party that the name Paulicians was derived from a combination of the names of both founders, in the form παυλοιωάνναι. But we have strong reason for doubting the whole account."[1] This Neander rejects, and Gieseler calls it a "later Catholic fiction . . . given to them on account of the high value they attached to Paul."[2] Rejecting this early Romish explanation of the origin of the Paulicians, Neander, Gieseler, Kurtz and others fall back on Constantine, of the neighborhood of Samosata, about A. D. 660, as the Paulician founder. But in view of what we have seen, as to the disappearance of the

[1] Neander's Hist. Chr. Ch., vol. 3, p. 244.
[2] Gieseler's Ch. Hist., vol. 2, p. 21.

names Montanists, Novatians and Donatists from view and the great power of the Paulicians *immediately* after this assumed origin, this explanation of the origin of the Paulicians must be rejected as being as utterly groundless as the Romish explanation, for which it is the substitute.

Others, seeing the groundlessness of either of the two just now mentioned explanations of the origin of the Paulicians, resort to the equally groundless hypothesis that they were originated by an "Armenian named Paul, who lived under Justinian II"—near a century before Constantine of Samosata.¹

But Wadington, having little or no confidence in any of these explanations of the origin of the Paulicians, and attempting to make none of his own, says: "The origin of these heretics have been the subject of much controversy; for while some *suppose* their errors to have been indigenous in Europe, there are some who derive them in a direct line from the heart of Asia."²

Rejecting as groundless and as destructive to each other all the explanations of the origin of the Paulicians which would make them of human and of post-apostolic origin, the laws of evidence demand that we see the Paulicians but the perpetuity of Montanists, Novatians and Donatists. *Only* this interpretation of the facts of the disappearance from history of the names Montanists, Novatians and Donatists, when in great numbers and in the same territory† where the name Paulicians came into use as designating, at first, a powerful body of Christians,

---

† Harnack says of the Novatians: "In the *East*, however, the party lived until the sixth or seventh century."—Schaff-Herzog Ency., vol. 2, p. 1672. And Wadington speaks of "Armenia the province of" the Paulician "birth."—Wadington's Ch. Hist., p. 478; Fisher's Hist. Chr. Ch., p. 162. We have seen that the Montanists, the Novatians and the Donatists numbered their converts "throughout the Roman Empire."

1 Universal Knowledge, vol. 11, p. 39.
2 Wadington's Ch. Hist., p. 289.

of like faith and practice to that of the Montanists, the Novatians and the Donatists, can be made to conform to the *facts of history*. With this explanation of the Paulician origin we readily account for the disappearance of the Montanists, the Novatians and the Donatists and the appearance of the Paulicians. Thus we have the true explanation of Guericke's statement, that this "remarkable sect" arose "out of old elements of a preceding time."¹ Instead of making Constantine the founder of the Paulicians, Guericke recognizes him as the great *leader:* "It is historically certain that some time after the middle of the seventh century the Paulicians had for an able *leader* a man named Constantine."²

The statement of Robinson—a historian of extensive and original research—covers the disappearance of the names Montanists, Novatians, Donatists, Paulicians and other names by which the same churches were known from the second century to the Reformation. Speaking of the Novatians, he says: "When penal laws obliged them to lurk in corners and worship God in private, they were distinguished by a *variety* of names, and a *succession of them continued until the Reformation*.' * ³

---

*The Campbellite, plea that names indicate Scriptural or un-scriptural character, and that perpetuity must be traced by names, has no basis in reason, history or Scripture.

1 Guericke's Ch. Hist., vol. 2, p. 76.
2 Idem, p. 78.
3 Robinson's Eccl. Resh., pp. 126, 127.

CHAPTER XX.

THE BAPTIST CHURCH PERPETUITY LINE, OR LINES, THROUGH THE PAULICIANS TO THE ANABAPTISTS.

Of the thirteenth century, Wadington says: "The heresy of the Paulicians and Cathari, another religious faction, had at that time considerable prevalence, *which under the various names* of Cathari, for Catharists, Puritans, Gazari, Patereni, Paulicians or Publicans, Bulgari or Bugari was more particularly charged with Manichæan opinions. The origin of these heretics has been the subject of much controversy, for while some suppose these errors to have been indigenous in Europe, there are others who derive them in a direct line from the very heart of Asia."[1] Hase says: "The Paulicians under the name of Euchites . . . had before" 1115 "become numerous among the Bulgarians . . . among which they were commonly called Bogomiles. . . . Small communities of Bogomiles were found among the Bulgarians through the *whole period of the middle ages*, and Paulicians have *continued* to exist under many changes in and around Philopopolis and in the valleys of the Hæmus until the present day."[2] Says Fisher: "Certain sects arose in the south of France which with a zeal for *purity of life* and in opposition to the claims of the priesthood, as well as to ecclesiastical abuses in general, combined peculiar doctrinal beliefs which were somewhat akin to the dualistic ideas prevalent in the East. They

[1] Wadington's Ch. Hist., p. 286.
[2] Hase's Hist. Chr. Ch. p. 262.

were called Catharists, and because they were numerous in and near the city of Albi were named Albigenses. Their tenets threatened the very foundation of the *hierarchical* system."[1] C. Schmidt: "A sect which from the beginning of the eleventh century spread rapidly and *widely* in Southern France and maintained itself until in the middle of the *thirteenth* century, received its name from the city of Albi, Latin, Albiga, the present capitol of the department Tarn, which was one of their seats. The name does not occur, however, until the time of the Albigensian crusade. *Before that time the sect was spoken of as the Publicants or Publicani, probably a corruption of the name Paulicians*, which the crusaders had brought back to Western Europe. . . . Of the Cathari, the Bogomiles, Patoreni, Albigenses, etc., were only individual developments. *In general they all held the same doctrines* . . . the same *organization*. . . . The severe moral demands made impression because the example of the preachers corresponded to their words."[2]

Again, says Schmidt: "They spread during the middle ages over *all* Europe, more especially in the Southern part. . . . Even as late as the *fourteenth century* the inquisition in Italy was busy persecuting the Cathari. . . . Their name in Italy was not Cathari, however, but Patereni, from Patari, an obscure street in Milan, the headquarters of the rag-pickers, where they held their secret assemblies. Their principle seat in Western Europe the Cathari had in Southern France, where they were known as Albigenses. Thence they penetrated into the northern provinces of *Spain* where they numbered *many* adherents in the thirteenth century. To *Germany* they came partly from

---

[1] Prof. Geo. P. Fisher's Hist. Chr. p. 194.
[2] Schaff-Herzog Ency., vol. 1, p. 47.

the East, from the Slav countries, partly from Flanders and Campagne. . . . The sect lived in the regions along the Rhine, especially in Cologne and Bonn. In England the Cathari found very little sympathy. They came over in 1159 from Holland, and in 1210 some are said to have been discovered in London. This system was based upon the *New Testament* of which they possessed a translation, probably derived from the Orient and deviating considerably from the Vulgate."[1]

Kurtz: "The principal centers of the Cathari were in Lombardy and in the South of France, but *numerous* communities also existed in Belgium, Germany and Spain. . . . The liturgy lately discovered by Kunitz dates from the thirteenth century, and gives a more favorable opinion of them *than had formerly been entertained.*"[2]

"The great stronghold of the numberless sects which were designated as Cathari, Bulgarians, Manichæans, etc., was in the South of France, where they had secured the protection of Raymond the VI, Count of Toulouse, and of other powerful vassals. . . . The little town of Albi, in the district of Albigeois, was regarded as the great center of the party; whence the name Albigenses, by which these sects were designated."[3] Says Hase: "Paterini, the name Catharists, by which this sect was generally designated, shows what were their ordinary pretentions. A *similar* opposition prepared the way for the influences exerted by the Paulicians who had been transferred into the western countries of Europe (hence called Publicani Bugari). The accounts we have of them are almost exclusively *from their enemies*. All agree,

[1] Idem, p. 420
[2] Kurtz's Ch. Hist., vol. 1, p. 455.
[3] Idem, pp. 461, 462

however, in describing them as universally and absolutely opposed to the Catholic church and all its pomp, in consequence of which they professed to be in *immediate communication of the Holy Ghost*, exalting them † above all conscious necessity of ecclesiastical or civil laws."[1]

That the reader may better understand how the Baptists of past ages have been known by so many names I will here give but few of the many examples of how liberal the Romish church was in naming its opponents: "Haeriticus est omnis non orthodoxus. . . . Manichæi ad imam usque scelerum necquitiam pervenerunt. . . . Manichæos seu, *vel* Donatistas meritissama severitate persequimur. Huic itaque homnium generi nihil ex moribus, nihil ex legibus commune sit cum caeteris. Ariani, Macedoniani, Pneumatomachi, Apolinariani, Novatiani, Eunomiani, Tetraditiæ, Valentiani, Pauliani, Papiansitæ, Montanistæ, seu Pricillianistæ, vel Phryges, vel Pepuzitæ, Marcionistæ, Borboritæ, Messiliani, Euchitæ, sive Enthousiastæ, Donatistæ, Audiani, Hydroparastatæ, Tascodrogitæ, Batrachitæ, Hermogeniani, Photaniani, Marcelliani, Ophitæ, Encratistæ, Carpocratitæ, Saccophori, Manichæ, Haeretici, Acephali, Sabelliani, Eutychiani."

These names, with the above denunciation of all to whom they were applied as immoral, as without any merit and as deserving persecution to death, Robinson has copied from an ancient law concerning heretics—"Cod. . . . De haereticus."[2]

Wadington copies from Limborchs' History of the Inquisition, another Romish list of names for the

---

† The "laws" which they ignored were evidently the laws of Romish ecclesiastical government. Nowhere did this people ever repudiate legitimate rule of any government.
[1] Hase's Hist. Chr. Ch., p. 252.
[2] Robinson's Eccl. Resh. p. 166.

"heretics," of the thirteenth century. Here they are, with the curses: "Catharos, Paterenos, Speromistas, Leonistas, Arnoldistas, Circumcisos, Passaginos, Josephinos, Garatenses, Albaneses, Franciscos, Beghardos, Commissos, Valdenses, Romanolos, Communellos, † Varinos, Ortulenos, cum illis de aqua nigra, et omnes hereticos . . . damnamus."[1]

Gieseler says: "The number of names of the heretics in this period is far greater than that of new parties."[2]

In this great avalanche of names, and probably, at most, not more than three or four kinds of dissenters from the Romish church, we see the folly of attempting to identify any of the "sects" or trace Baptists, in history, by any name or names. Yet, strange to say, church historians are greatly influenced—yea, *led* by the names of these dissenters!

Kurtz says that after the beginning of the twelfth century those who continued to entertain the Paulician "views probably joined the Euchites and the Bogomils."[3] But who were the Euchites and the Bogomils? Evidently, a people of the same belief and practice as the Paulicians with which they were consolidated; or, more correctly expressed, the Paulicians themselves under these names. In either case the Baptist line is unbroken. The very fact of "consolidation" is *prima facie* evidence of identity of faith and practice.

Mosheim says of Henry, the Henrician leader: "*Several* writers affirm that he was one of the disciples

---

† Would not the Campbellites who propose to find the true church by its name have a sweet time with these names.
[1] Wadington's Ch. Hist. p. 288.
[2] Gieseler's Ch. Hist., vol. 2, p. 574.
[3] Kurtz's Ch. Hist., vol. 1, p. 273.

of Peter de Bruys."[1] On page 287 of his church history, Wadington shows the groundlessness of Mosheim's *theoretical* objection to Henry having been a disciple of Peter de Bruys.

Wadington says: "It is certain that a very powerful sect named Paulicians . . . . spread very widely throughout the Greek provinces of Asia during the eighth century. It is equally true that after a merciless persecution of about one hundred and fifty years, their remnant, *still numerous*, was permitted to settle in Bulgari and Thrace. Thence, it is believed by Muratori, Mosheim and Gibbon, they gradually immigrated towards the West; at first as occasions of fear or commerce or mendacity (another name for the pilgrimage) might be presented; and latterly in the returning ranks of the crusaders. It is asserted that their first migration was into Italy; that so early as the middle of the eleventh century many of their colonies were established in Sicily, in Lombardy, Insubria and principally at Milan; that others led a wandering life in France, Germany and in other countries; and that they everywhere attracted by their pious books and austere demeanor, excited the admiration and the respect of the multitude."[2]

Kurtz: "At the commencement of the eleventh century the Euchites (Messelians, Enthusiasts,) attracted the attention of the government, their opinions having widely spread in Thracia. . . . The Emperor Tzimisces transported the Paulicians to that province." † Kurtz further says of the Catharists: "Probably, however, the movement issued again from the East, in all likelihood from Bulgaria, where since the time the Paul-

---
† Kurtz's Ch. Hist., vol. 1, p. 240.
[1] Mosheim's Eccl. Hist., cent. 12, part. 2, chap. 5, sec. 8.
[2] Wadington's Ch. Hist., p. 289.

icians had settled in that district Gnostic and Manichæan views had been zealously propagated. . . . The most general designation was that of Cathari (καθαροί) but they were also called Bulgari. . . . Several of the charges preferred against them may have arisen from *misunderstanding or calumny.* The Paulician or Bogomile opinions which they had embraced " were " of a practical rather than of a speculative character, and variously *modified or kept in check.*" [1]

Brockett, one of the best authorities on this subject, says: "The Perfecti and Credentes are mentioned by all writers on the Bogomils and the sects with which they were affiliated; and it was one of the many evidences of the *substantial identity* with the Albigenses, Paterenes, Vaudois, Catharists, Ketzers, Publicans, Waldenses, etc., etc., that the same classes under *equivalent* names existed in all these sects of alleged heretics." [2]

Armitage: "The Bogomiles were a branch of the Cathari. Herzog thinks . . . they were an *offshoot from the Paulicians.*" [3] Of the Paulicians, Armitage says: "The empress Theodora issued fresh edicts against them and between A. D. 832 and 846 one hundred thousand of them were put to death in the most barbarous manner. Infuriated with their persecutors, they took up arms in self defense, and the contest continued in one shape and another until in 973 large numbers of them were transported to Phillippopolis, south of the Balkan mountains, in what is now called Bulgaria. For more than a century the Paulicians stood with unbroken fortitude, which the sword was unable to suppress. Like men they defended their rights to home,

[1] Kurtz's Ch. Hist., vol. 1, p. 453.
[2] The Bogomilles, p. 121.
[3] Armitage's Hist. Bap., p. 278.

religion and liberty under the holy sanctions of rebellion against intolerable tyranny. And now they were accorded full religious liberty in their transportation, on condition that they would guard the borders against the pagans. But the conflict between them and the Greeks continued till the twelfth century. Alexius Comnenus put forth some kind efforts to reclaim them but failed, and they finally took refuge in Europe, where we shall meet them again amongst the Albigenses."[1]

The Encyclopedia Britannica says: "The Paulicians continued to exist in Thrace until at least in the beginning of the thirteenth century, as did also the Euchites, afterwards Bogomilles, who had been attracted to that locality by the toleration of Tzimisces. Meanwhile *branch societies of the Paulicians* established themselves in Italy, France, and appear under *different names*, such as Bulgaria, Patereni, Cathari and Albigenses."[2]

Hallam says, the Albigenses came from one of the *seats* of Paulician power: "The derivation of these sects from Bulgaria is *sufficiently proved*."[3]

Well, therefore, says the Revised Edition of the Encyclopedia Britannica: "The *sect of the Albigenses may be traced with tolerable distinctness from the Paulicians*."[4]

In the foregoing is demonstrated that the Cathari, under its various names, are the Paulicians. Of course, there may have been, under the various names, some who were not Baptists. But the facts demonstrate that, in the main, they were essentially Baptists.

Gieseler says: "The Cathari, or as they were now commonly called, the Albigenses or Bulgarians. . . .

[1] Armitage's Hist. Bap., p. 240.
[2] Vol. 18, p. 434—9th Ed.
[3] Hallam's Middle Ages, p. 505.
[4] Vol. 1, p. 164.

maintained in all lands a *very close connection* with each other." ¹ Again: " With few exceptions all Cathari stood in *close connection* with each other, as also in their *practical principles and customs they quite agreed.*" ²

Prof. William Whitsitt, D.D., says: " The Catharists were as thick as hops and they—the Waldenses—joined them . . . . Not much difference between Waldenses and Catharists." *

Therefore, when, as Kurtz says, the Roman Catholic " church made no distinction between different sectaries, and one and the same sentence was pronounced on Cathari and Waldenses, on Petrobrussians, Arnoldists," its judgment as to their identity was *mainly correct;* and, with all his prejudice, Kurtz concedes: " Indeed, so far as their opposition to the papacy and hierarchy was concerned, they were *all at one.*" ³

Says Prof. A. H. Newman, D.D., LL.D.: "Keller has been accused of utterly confounding the mediæval parties, with treating Waldenses, Cathari, evangelical Beghards, Brethren of the Common Life, Friends of God, Taborites, Bohemian Brethren, etc., as *essentially one party*. What are the facts? It must be borne in mind that Keller is far more intent on proving the prevalence of a type of life and doctrine than on establishing the organic connection of the various parties among themselves. *He lays little stress upon the special sect names*, maintaining that they were not, as a rule, used by the evangelical Christians with reference to themselves, but that they were commonly applied to them by their *opponents.*" ⁴ Remember that the very nature of Baptist

* Lect. to his classes.
1 Gieseler's Ch. Hist., vol. 2, pp. 576, 578.
2 Idem, pp. 582, 583.
3 Kurtz's Ch. Hist., vol. 1, p. 461.
4 Recent Resh. Concerning Mediæval Sects, p. 173.

church polity renders "organic connection" of Baptist churches an impossibility.

Again, says Prof. A. H. Newman, D.D., LL.D.: "It would not be difficult to suppose that evangelical dissent *persisted*, even though we had no record of the fact, during the thirty-two years that intervened between the death of Henry and the appearance of Peter Waldo. It is in itself *highly probable* that Peter Waldo himself was influenced to a greater or less extent by *antecedent* evangelical life. It is highly probable that the followers of Peter de Bruys and Henry of Lausanne were driven beyond the regions in which these teachers labored. Northern Italy was at that time in *close relation* with Southern France, and the Cathari of the two regions *sustained a lively intercourse*. It is probable that evangelical heresy was likewise freely *interchanged*. The Waldenses who began their work at Lyons soon crossed the mountains to Lombardy and established *relations*, as we shall see hereafter, with evangelical Christians of a more pronounced type than themselves.

"These were, *no doubt*, in part, the result of the labors of *Arnold* of Brescia; but it is not by any means unlikely that Arnold himself was *influenced* by the teachings of Peter de Bruys, and it is highly probable that these great teachers were subject to *substantially the same* evangelizing influences and reached substantially the *same views* as to the evils of the time and the *remedy* therefor. In Cologne we find, about 1446, before the death of Henry, *evangelical* Christians of the Petrobrussian type, side by side with Cathari and vigorously opposing them."[1]

Dollinger, the great Romish historian, argues the indentity of these "sects." First, because "the Cathari

[1] Idem, p. 188.

are known to have existed in considerable numbers in the territory in which Peter and Henry labored;" second, "these regions were soon overrun with Manichæan or Catharistic heretics;" third, "there is no evidence that the followers of Peter and Henry persisted as a party distinct from the Cathari during the succeeding century;" fourth, "that to suppose Peter and Henry to have been other than Catharistic would be to admit the existence of a party and a set of views, *for the origin and the subsequent disappearance of which we cannot account.*" [1]

Says Brockett, one of the highest authorities: "The *substantial identity* of these sects, which under so many different names were spread over all Western Europe and their *origin from the Protestants of Bulgaria and Bosnia* was strongly suspected by others than Regnier even in the *twelfth and thirteenth centuries*. Perhaps the earliest writer who gives *positive* testimony on this point is William Little, of Newbury, A. D. 1136-1220." [2]

Again: "Evans in his recent monograph on the history of Bosnia, has with great labor and research made an *exhaustive* study of the subject, and brought the *most conclusive* proofs of all those early Protestants from a *common source* and that source the Bogomiles of Bosnia and Bulgaria. Jirecek, a recent Bohemian writer on Bosnia and Bulgaria, and Hilferding, a Russian historian of Servia and Bulgaria, under which he includes Bosnia, both adduce *official* evidence of the *affiliation* of the Bogomiles with the Waldenses, the Bohemians, and the Moravians, as well as their identity with the ' Poor men of Lyons,' the Vaudois, the Henricians and the so-called heretics of Toulouse, the Patarines of Dalmatia and Italy, the Petrobrussians, the Bulgares or Bourgres and the

[1] Idem, p. 186.
[2] The Bogomiles, by Brockett, p. 127.

Catharists of Spain. Matthew Paris, Roger of Hoveden and Ralph, of Coggeshale, three of the most renowned of the early British chroniclers, testify to their presence in *large numbers* at this period in Toulouse, in Provence, in Flanders, and in England, and that they were called in the latter two countries Publicani or Poplicani, a corruption of *Paulicians. All these writers* trace them directly or indirectly to their origin in Bosnia."[1]

Again, says Brockett: "A careful and critical examination of the civil and ecclesiastical histories of this period in England, France and Germany affords *abundant* corroborative evidence of the origin of all these sects from the Bosnian churches, and of the *complete identity of the doctrines professed by them all*. Under the fierce persecutions instituted against the Waldenses, Catharists, etc., of Western Europe by the popes in the twelfth and the beginning of the thirteenth centuries, we have the testimony of the popes themselves that very many of the Waldenses, Paterines, Publicans, etc., took refuge with their brethren in Bosnia, which at that time was protected by the good Ban Culin."[2]

Of the Bogomiles, Gieseler says: "In their peculiar doctrines and customs, they *agree so marvelously* with the Cathari of the Western world, that the connection of the two parties, for which there is historical testimony, cannot fail to be recognized."[3]

Cramp says: "The fact is, that the numerous names and descriptions found in imperial edicts and decrees of councils refer to parties who held substantially the same views."[4]

---

[1] The Bogomiles, by Brockett, pp. 69-70.
[2] Idem, p. 71.
[3] Gieseler's Ch. Hist., vol. 2, pp. 614-615.
[4] Cramp's Hist. Bap., p. 99.

The foregoing statements show, first, that the best part of the mentioned sects were essentially identical in doctrine and practice; second, that they were of *Paulician origin:* in other words, that they were Paulicians under other names. That they were Baptists was demonstrated in preceding chapters.

Of the abundant and uncontradictory evidence of their perpetuity in the sixteenth century — to the times of the Anabaptists — the following is but an illustration. We have seen the Paulicians were the Novatians perpetuated under another name. Robinson says of the Novatians: "They were distinguished by a variety of names and a succession of them continued until the Reformation."[1]

Hase says: "Small communities of Bogomiles were found among the Bulgarians through the whole of the middle ages and Paulicians have continued to exist, under many changes. . . . until the present time."[2]

Wadington says: "It is equally certain that, from the time of Peter de Bruis to that of Luther, there have subsisted from some quarter or other of the Western community various bodies of sectaries, who were at open or secret variance with the church of Rome."[3] For more proof of the continuance of these "sects" to the Reformamation, see Chapter III.

[1] Robinson's Eccl. Resh., pp 126-127.
[2] Hase's Hist. Chr. Ch., p. 262.
[3] Wadington's Ch. Hist., p. 553.

CHAPTER XXI.

The Waldenses of Apostolic Origin..

For the conviction of those who are not satisfied of the identity of the Paulicians and the Waldenses, as to origin, this chapter is written.

The Penny Encyclopedia, at great expense, published by one of the most learned societies of Europe, called "The Society for the Diffusion of Useful Knowledge," says of the Waldenses: "This little community is remarkable for having from time immemorial kept itself separate from the church of Rome, in ages when that church is generally considered as having been the only existing church in the West. We have memorials of the doctrines of the Vaudois, written in the early part of the twelfth century. . . . The 'Nobla Leycon,' a poem written in the Vaudois dialect, records in the text its having been composed in the twelfth century, . . . the translation of which is: 'O, brethern, hear a noble lesson. We ought often to watch and pray, for we see this world approaching its end.' Eleven hundred years are fully completed since it was written: 'The end of all things is at hand.' . . . The last sentence . . . fixes the date of the Nobla Leycon to within the first half of the thirteenth century or thereabouts. The text goes on to say that it was easy to see the sign of the accomplishments of the prophecy of evil in its increase and in the decrease of good, the perils of which the evangelist and Paul have mentioned. The poem is a sort of an abridgment of the history and doctrines of the Old and New

Testaments. It speaks of the missions of the Apostles and of the primitive church and of certain practices that were introduced afterwards in its bosom, of simony, the institution of masses and prayers for the dead, of absolution and other tenets of the church of Rome which it rejects.

"In one place it speaks of censure of the practice of all the popes which have been from Sylvester to the present time, and in another says: 'Now after the Apostles, were certain teachers who went on teaching the way of Jesus Christ, our Savior, some of whom are found at the present day, but they are known to a very few,' and after describing the life and conversation of such teachers, the text proceeds: 'Such a one is called a Vaudois.' There is also a confession of faith of the Waldenses, bearing date A. D. 1120, acknowledging the Apostle's creed and the canonical books of the Old and New Testaments, recognizing no other mediator between God the Father and man but Jesus Christ; denying purgatory, administering only two sacraments, baptism and the Lord's supper, as *signs* or visible forms of the invisible grace; discarding the feasts and vigils of saints, the abstinence of flesh on certain days, the mass, etc.

"Another MS. dated 1100, speaks of the Waldenses as having continued the same doctrines from time immemorial, in continued descent from father to son, even from the times of the Apostles. Besides these there are two controversial treatises, one entitled 'Of Antichrist,' and the other upon 'The Intercession of the Saints,' which seem to bear this internal evidence of their antiquity, that in enumerating the various tenets of the Roman church, which the Waldenses reject, they *speak* of the doctrine of the real presence and of the adoration of the Virgin Mary and all the saints, but in so doing they do not use the words, 'transubstantiation,' and 'canonization.' Now the terms 'transubstantiation' and 'canonization,' were just introduced under Pope Innocent and confirmed in the council of Lateran, A. D. 1215, and the first Papal Bull in which the word 'canonization' occurs is dated 1165. Nor do these treatises speak of the devotional exercises of the Rosary, introduced by St. Dominic, nor of the Inquisition which began in the thirteenth century. *Had these institutions existed when the treatises were written, they could hardly have escaped the notice of the writer.* MS. copies of these and other ancient documents relative to the Vaudois, amounting to twenty-one volumes, were brought to England by Sir Samuel Moreland who was sent by the Protector Cromwell as envoy to the Duke of Savoy in 1655, and were by him presented in 1658 to the library of the University of Cambridge. Moreland wrote a history of the Evangelical churches of the valleys of Piedmont, London, 1658, giving a transcript and English translation of the Nobla Leycon. P. Allix, D. D., who published ' Remarks upon the Ecclesiastical history of the ancient churches of Piedmont,' in 1690, notices the MS. brought by Moreland. But now only 14 or 21 are existing in the University library and nobody can tell what has become of the rest. The Nobla Leycon is one among those which are missing.

In 1669, Jean Leger, a pastor of the Valences, published at Leyden, ' Historie Generale des Eglises Evangelisques des Valleys du Piedmont,' in two books, the first of which treats of the early date and continuity of their doctrine, and he gives transcripts of several of the manuscripts brought to England by Moreland. Speaking of the Nobla Leycon, the Vaudois confession, and other manuscripts of which he has just been speaking, he says: 'There is, however, farther evidence brought forth for the antiquity of the Vaudois doctrines. . . . We find allusions as early as the ninth century to the existence of nonconformist churches in the borders of Italy. Jonas bishop of Orleans, in his work, 'De Cultu Imaginum,' addressing Charles the Bald, A. D. 840, speaks of Italian churches which he accuses of heterodoxy because they refused to worship images, and he charges Claudius, bishop of Turin, with *encouraging* the people of his diocese in their separation from the Catholic unity. . . . About 1230 Reinerus, a Dominican, who states that he had been himself a heretic, wrote a treatise against heretics. . . . The Waldenses: Reinerus begins by saying that these were the most pernicious of all sects for the reason: (1.) because they were the *most ancient*, more ancient than the Manichæans or Arians, dating their origin according to some from the time of Pope Sylvester, 314 to 335 A. D. and according to others from the time of the apostles; (2.) because they are more universally spread; (3.) because they have the character of being pious and virtuous, as they believe in the Apostles' creed and are guilty of no other crime than that of blasphemy against the Roman church and clergy. He also states that they were in all the States of Lombardy and Provence.'" Here I have shown abounded Paulicians called Albigenses, etc.,—another proof of their identity with Waldenses. "The heretics have more schools † than the theologians and more auditors; they hold public disputations and convoke the people to solemn discussions. . . . They have translated the Old and New Testaments into other tongues.* I myself have seen and heard a clownish layman who could repeat the whole of the book of Job by heart and many who were perfectly acquainted

† They were not anti-mission Baptists.
* All along we find Bibles which were not in Romish hands and were not preserved by Rome.

262   CHURCH PERPETUITY.

with the whole of the New Testament. They reject whatever is not demonstrated by a text in the New Testament; and then he goes on enumerating places where the heretics have churches and schools; all of which shows that dissent was very *widely* spread in North Italy and the South of France in the thirteenth century, *and it corroborates the traditions of the Waldenses*, that their doctrines spread at one time over many districts on both sides of the Alps. The book of Reinerus is very important, but we must refer those who wish for further information to the 'Vaudois of Piedmont,' 1831, section 3, where the author has placed in parallel columns passages from Reinerus' text, the corresponding opinions of Italian writers previous to the thirteenth century and those of the ancient and modern Waldenses concerning the same topics. John Marcus Aurelius Rorenco, grand prior of Brorch, was sent by Duke Charles Emanuel, about the *middle of the thirteenth* century to make inquiries concerning the Vaudois. He reports that those apostolicals, as they call themselves, were of an origin of which *nothing certain can be said*, further than that bishop Claudius *might have* detached them from the church in the *eighth century* and that they were *not a new sect in the ninth and tenth centuries*. And the monk of Belvidere who went to the Cottian Alps on a similar inquiry reported that heretics had been found in the valley of Angrogna in *all periods of history*.

"Claudius Seissel, archbishop of Turin, A. D. 1200, spoke of them as the Vaudois sect which originated with Leon, a devout man in the time of Constantine the Great." [1]

The following, from the same page, shows, as I have done in Chapter XVI, on Waldensian faith and practice, how that, by association with the sixteenth century reformers many of the Waldenses departed from the faith:

[1] Penny Ency., vol. 25, pp. 163-164.

"But after the spreading of the reformation in the sixteenth century, they began to correspond with Geneva and other places and invited some Protestant divines to come among them."

The arsenal of Germany, which furnishes the source of the so-called "higher criticism" against the Bible, shows itself equally adapted to the work of furnishing weapons against Waldensian history. In Germany, in 1851, A. Wilh. Dieckhoff sends out his " Die Waldenser im Mittelalter; Zwei Historische Untersuchungen von A. Wilh. Dieckhoff Licentiaten und Privatdocenten der Theologie Zu Gottingen." While, like the works of the "higher critics" against the Bible, this work manifests valuable research and learning, yet, like them, it manifests equally intemperate, reckless and wild criticism, intemperately charging forgery and falsification upon the authors of much of Waldensian ancient documents, and attempting to refute the claim of Waldenses to apostolic historical descent.

In 1853 this was followed by another equally learned work, not so wild, but of the same nature, by Dr. Herzog, entitled: " Die Romanischen Waldenser, ihre vorreformatorischen Zustande und Lehren, ihre Reformation im 16. Jahshundert und die Ruckwirkungen derselben, Haupsachlich nach ihren eigenen schriften (108) dargestellt Halle." Five years previous, at Halle, Herzog had issued a similar, but not so thorough a work, entitled: "De Origene et Pristino Statu Waldensium Secundum Antiquissma eorum scripta cum libris Catholicorum ejusdem aevi collata." There is room for but a glimpse at these and other works. The learned Dr. Montgomery's characterization of Dieckhoff's criticism may well apply to much of the conclusions of both Herzog and Dieckhoff: "He applied to it the *innere Kritik*—

a powerful weapon, certainly, but one which requires cautious handling. . . . With like confidence, and on similar grounds, his countrymen fix dates to different portions of Isaiah's prophecies, assigning some of them, therefore, to one author, and some of them to another; although indeed, they differ a little in the opinions which they so confidently advance." Until some other method be adduced to bring down the date of the Noble Lesson to the thirteenth century, we may be content to learn a little from it as to the state of things before that period. In refusing to accept the date 1100, which so many have imagined that they found in the text of the ancient poem itself, Dieckhoff also proceeds upon what he deems the ascertained historic fact of the Vaudois from Valdo, concerning which he thinks himself bound to accept the testimony of the 'Catholic' witnesses. But he refuses to adopt the method adopted by Gieseler, Neánder and Herzog, of dealing with the date of the poem itself. He cannot believe that the eleven hundred years are to be reckoned from any other period than from the beginning of the Christian era; he rejects this as an unnatural interpretation of the line. 'Eimnal namlich wird die Rechnung auf weise viel zu kunstlich.' Moreover, he adopts, as of great weight upon this point the argument of Muston, from the descripton of the Vaudois given in the poem, that it *cannot have been composed within a few years of the origin of the sect* and agrees with him that if it could be proved to have been composed, as Gieseler, Neander and Herzog suppose, in the end of the twelfth century, it would evince the existence of the Vaudois long before the time of Valdo.[1]

"Romish writers are the main witnesses Dieckhoff arrays against Waldensian antiquity. To this Dr. Montgomery

[1] Israel of the Alps, by Muston, vol. 2, p. 530.

well replies: Herzog "*blames* Dieckhoff, however, for *accepting* so completely and unhesitatingly the accounts given of them by their *Catholic adversaries*. For although, as to the relation of the Vaudois to Valdo, Dr. Herzog still proceeds upon the testimony of these authors, as when he wrote the Academic Programma he does not think it right to receive as perfectly accurate all their statements concerning the doctrines and character of these heretics whom they so cordially hated . . . and contradicts the assertion of Bossuet, so often made by popish writers, that they had more in common with Catholicism than with Protestantism."[1] Again: " We have seen already by what a *fallacious* argument it is that Dr. Herzog persuades himself to receive the testimony of the popish authors, who assert Valdo to have been the founder of the Vaudois." Dieckhoff is also driven to concede that Romish writers are "liable to much suspicion."[2] Yet, in the face of this, on the uncertain theories of Dieckhoff and Herzog, together with that of Todd and like critics, some histories, encyclopedias, and certain professors of church history, having, in servility to the spirit by which some American scholars ape "higher critics" of Germany on their criticisms on the Bible, swallowed the statements, " feathers and all," that Valdo originated the Waldenses, we are asked to believe that "late researches" have demonstrated that the antiquity of the Waldenses is a "mere fable" and that Baptists are but of Rome—as other sects. Thus, dear reader, the chip is lifted off the "bug" which some highly reputed authorities (?) have made many think was death to Baptist Church Perpetuity; and that "bug" turns out to be a composition

---

[1] Israel of the Alps, vol. 2, pp. 534-535.
[2] Idem, p. 518.

of so-called "higher criticism" and Romish slanders—a humbug!

Let us farther examine the origin of the Waldenses:

(1.) These assailants of Waldensian history, like the witnesses against the resurrection of Christ, are not agreed among themselves. Dieckhoff made the line in the Noble Lesson, proving the antiquity of the Waldenses, an interpolation. But Herzog, "in his anxiety to maintain the descent of the Vaudois from Valdo, would evidently be glad to accept Dieckhoff's theory of an interpolation of the two troublesome lines. *But this he does not find himself warranted in doing*, as the lines are certainly present in *all* existing copies of the poem, in print and MS., and thus certainly appear not to have been interpolated since the Reformation. . . . He maintains, indeed, that the Noble Lesson is certainly of Vaudois origin, in *opposition to Dieckhoff*, who in a long note sets forth reasons for thinking that it may have been originally a production of the Bohemian brethren." Todd farther differs and concedes: "Since we admit (until duly advised to the contrary) that the verse is genuine, and acquit its author of any dishonesty."[1]

(2.) In relying on Romish testimony against Waldensian antiquity these assailants of Waldensian history have very unfairly rejected a greater number of Romish writers which, against their own side, testify in favor of the antiquity of the Waldenses. As witnesses when testifying against their own side are rightly regarded as much more worthy of belief than when testifying for it, the Romish writers in favor of Waldensian antiquity are entitled to much greater credit than are those against it.

Pilchendorf, a Romish author of the fourteenth century, in his "Contra Haeresin Waldensium" acknow-

[1] The Books of the Vaudois, pages 183, 126, 184.

ledges their origin may be traced back in the early part of the fourth century. He reproaches the Vaudois for concealing themselves, to which one of them replies: "Non possum esse talis Lucerna publica, propter instantes persecutiones, quia vacant me haereticum—I am not able to be the light of the world because of continuous persecution; because they call me a heretic."[1]

Polichdorf says, instead of the Waldenses acknowledging Waldo their founder, that " dicentes sectam eorum durasse a temporibus Sylvestri papæ "—they teach their sect continues to Pope Sylvester.[2]

Moneta, "a celebrated Romish professor of the University of Bologna, A. D. 1244," while opposing the claim of the Waldenses to antiquity, unwittingly gives up his case, in challenging them: "But if the Vaudois assert that their way existed before Waldo, let them prove it," which, he adds, "they can by no means do."[3] If they originated with Waldo, as Moneta lived near Waldo's time, their origin must have been *so clearly recent as to have excluded all controversy* as to its time.

Reynerus, who is called Reineri, Reinerius Saccho, Reiner Saccho, was a native of Plascenza, a Waldensian during the first seventeen years of his life, then, under Pope Alexander VI., A. D. 1261, turned preaching friar and became one of the ablest Romish advocates of his day, who is as much entitled to be heard as any one and whose testimony, considering so little is to the contrary, should be *conclusive*, wrote of the Waldensians: " Inter omnes has sectas, quae nunc sunt, vel fuerunt, non est perniciosior Ecclesiae quam Leonistarum. Et hoc tribus de causis. Prima est quia est diuturnior. Aliqui enim

[1] Idem, p. 413.
[2] Idem, p. 511.
[3] Idem, p. 510.

dicunt quod duraverit a tempore Sylvestri; aliqua a tempore apostolorum. Secunda quia est generalior. Fere enim nulla est terra in qua haec secta non sit." Translated: Among all the sects which are now or have been, no sect is more pernicious than the church of Leonists. And this for three causes—first, because it is of longer endurance, some, indeed, saying it has endured from the time of Sylvester; others, from the time of the Apostles. Second, because it is more general. There being certainly —enim—almost no country—nulla terra—in which this sect does not exist. On this Dr. Montgomery with Wadington,[1] well remarks: "Reynerus remains a witness that in *his day their claim to antiquity was well known*, which popish writers will now fain represent as a novelty of modern times. *And, moreover, it may be fairly taken for granted that if Reynerus, who wrote a little more than a century after the days of Waldo, had regarded the claim to antiquity as utterly unfounded, he would not have failed to exclaim loudly against those who had the audacity to advance it.* The writers of his time do not err on the side of excessive gentleness. Nor does M. Charvaz himself, notwithstanding his pretensions in that way, when he calls Leger a liar for asserting as on the authority of Polichdorf, the prevalence of an opinion among the Vaudois of his time that they had existed, at least, from the sixth century."[2] Reinerus farther says of them: "Unlike all other sects, which infuse horror by the enormity of their blasphemies against God, these Lyonese retain a great appearance of piety, all the more as they live uprightly before the eyes of men, and believe only that which is good about God, they also believe the entire articles of the symbolica, apostolic creed; only that they abhor the

---

[1] Wadington's Ch. Hist., p. 290.
[2] Israel of the Alps, vol. 2, p. 513.

church of Rome and her priesthood, to accept which the mass of the laity are readily inclined."[1]

Again, St. Bernard, born 1091, one of the ablest Romish advocates, said: "There is a sect which calls itself after no man's name, which pretends to be in direct line of apostolic succession; and which, rustic and unlearned though it is, contends that the church is wrong, and that itself alone is right. It must derive its origin from the devil, since there is no other extraction which we can assign to it."[2]

Of A. D. 1025, says Robinson: "Atto, bishop of Vercelli, had complained of such people *eighty years before* and so had others *before him*, and there is the highest reason to believe that they had *always* been in Italy."[3]

Bernard de Fontcaud, of the twelfth century, in his work, Contra Valdenses et Arianos, says but little of the Waldenses, but in his preface says: "Valdenses dicti sunt nimirum a valle densa"—the Waldenses are called from the dense valley.[4] This is sufficient to show that they were not originally named from Waldo, and strongly implies they ante-dated him. Nowhere in his book does he mention Valdo. Living in Waldo's age and writing against the Waldenses, to have made no mention of their origin or of Waldo *is utterly irreconcilable with the notion that they originated with Waldo.*

In A. D. 1096 Pope Urban issued a bull in which he mentions the French side of the same valleys as infested with heresy.[5]

---

[1] Wadington's Ch. Hist., p. 590, Biblotheca Patrum, apud Lenfants Guerre des Hussites, 54:2, sec. 5.
[2] Wadington's Ch. Hist., p. 290.
[3] Robinson's Eccl. Researches, p. 408, on testimony of Uchelli Ital. Sac. tom, IV Vercellences Epis. ep. xliv.
[4] Israel of the Alps, vol. 2, p. 414.
[5] Idem, p. 484.

A. D. 1119 the Council of Toulouse decrees the Inquisition against heretics dwelling in Italy and partly in France.[1]

A. D. 1192 "Statuta synodalia Odinis Episcopoi Tullensis, de haereticis . . . qui vocantur Vadoys"—synodical laws against those called Vaudois. The *immense numbers* of the Waldenses, calling forth so many curses of Romanism, demonstrate Waldo not their founder, as this is *too early* for them to have attained such strength and influence. Claude Seyssel, Archbishop of Turin, who visited the Waldenses of the Piedmontese valleys in 1517, who was in the valleys before the Reformation, "informs us (vol. v.) that the heretics of the valleys had *all along* been ascribing an antiquity to their sect similar to that which, according to Reiner, was claimed by the Leonists."[2]

I have now shown that Romish expressions, from the sixteenth to the tenth century are overwhelming testimony to the Waldenses existing long before Waldo. Thus, one of the main pillars of Dieckhoff's and Herzog's building is gone. I think I could here safely leave their antiquity as made out. But, as certain professors of church history are dishing out to young ministers Dieckhoff and Herzog, the ancient dialect of the Waldenses, (1.) says Muston: "The patois of the Vaudois valleys has a radical structure far more regular than the Piedmontese idiom. The origin of this patois was *anterior* to the growth of Italian and French—antecedent even to the Romance language. . . . The existence of this patois is, of itself, a *proof* of the high antiquity of the mountaineers, and of their constant preservation from foreign

---

[1] Idem, ibid.
[2] Dr. Gilly, in Todd's Books of the Vaudois, p. 170.

THE WALDENSES OF APOSTOLIC ORIGIN.   271

intermixture and changes. Their popular idiom is a precious monument."[1]

This demonstrates that the Waldenses never came from France, which the theory of their origin with Peter Waldo of Lyons, requires to be true.

(2.) Testimony of Waldensian manuscripts proves their antiquity. Says Dr. Gilly, a specialist on their history, and generally recognized of high authority—pronounced by Muston "one of the most voluminous, learned and interesting of all modern authors who have written on the subject of the Vaudois:"[2] "In the Grenoble MS. the year is denoted by Arabic characters, a mode of notation which was not commonly used in the twelfth and thirteenth centuries; but it was introduced by the Moors and Saracens into the Sub-Alpine and Pyrenæan regions *long before*. . . . There is no difficulty in believing that the Grenoble Codex is a MS. of the thirteenth century, and that the version it contains may have been of a still *older* date."[3]

Metivier, writing to Dr. Gilly—Dr. Gilly places the Noble Lesson in the early part of the twelfth century—says of it: "The irregularity of the metres favors your hypothesis of the *early* date."[4]

Muston observes, of the Noble Lesson: "In the inequality of the measure and the simple assonance of the rhymes these verses bear the marks of *high* authority."[5] Muston further remarks: "Let us suppose the Noble Leyczon to have been composed not in the year 1100, but in the year 1200 and let us see if it could be the work of

---

[1] Israel of the Alps, vol. 2, p. 406.
[2] Idem, p. 428.
[3] Todd's Book of the Vaudois, pp. 192-193.
[4] Idem, p. 156.
[5] Israel of the Alps, vol. 2, p. 470.

the disciples of Valdo. The poem is in the *Romance* language; it was not in the language of *Lyons*. . . . The disciples of Valdo left the city between 1180 and 1190. Would they not require some years to acclimatize them in a new country, and is it to be supposed that in so short a time they could have learned a new language so as to produce in it most *perfect* works (most perfect for that time at least); and that amidst the difficulties of their settlement they could have had *leisure* for the composition of a poem of such length? Could they *immediately* after their arrival in these mountains exhibit the character of *extension* already acquired, of firm *establishment* and *tranquility* and *duration* which this poem ascribes to the Vaudois? It appears to me that any impartial mind will find *much more difficulty in admitting all these things without evidence, as those are obliged to do who maintain that the Vaudois are descended from Valdo—than in admitting that they were anterior to him on the testimony of this work*, dated in the year 1100 and of the *authors of the twelfth century, whom we have quoted*. The difficulty becomes an *impossibility* if we hold to the date of the Nobla Leycon, and there is *nothing to set it aside, or* if we merely admit it was composed before 1180; *for nothing at that period can explain the production of it by the disciples of Valdo*. The latter is not only not *named in it*, but there is not the *least allusion* which can be supposed to refer to him. This . . . is very extraordinary if its composition was owing to his direct influence, and if it was produced by his disciples."[1]

Herzog, Gieseler, Neander, Todd, *et al*, put the Noble Lesson at the end of the twelfth century.[2] But

---

[1] Israel of the Alps, vol. 2, p. 459.
[2] See Todd's Books of the Vaudois, p. 184.

both Dieckhoff and Muston say this " would evince the existence of the Vaudois long before the time of Valdo." [1]

Nor does Dieckhoff agree to the method of dealing with the Noble Lesson, by which Herzog, Neander, Gieseler, Todd and others attempt to get rid of its earliest date. "He cannot believe that the eleven hundred years are to be reckoned from any other period than the beginning of the Christian era; he rejects this as an unnatural interpretation of the line." [2] Dieckhoff's words are: "Rechnung auf diese viel zio kunstlich—the reckoning of this is much too artful. Kunstlich is from kunst which means 'trick.' I, therefore, here submit, first, admitting that the Noble Lesson was not written in or about A. D. 1100—that it was not written as Todd, Neander, Gieseler, M. Schmidt and others claim—but Herzog finally dated that 1400—until about a century later, it demonstrates the existence of the Waldenses before Waldo's history. But, second, Dieckhoff himself being witness that the method of dating the Noble Lesson on the latter part of the twelfth century is but artificial, a trick—*kunstlich*—we have the date of that poem, as once near universally claimed, showing the Waldenses to have existed before Waldo's time. Herzog also, "maintains that the Noble Lesson is certainly of Vaudois origin in opposition to Dieckhoff." [3] Because a copy of the Noble Lesson was found to have the date 1400, the term four being partially erased, Herzog gave up the date of about 1200 and accepted Dieckhoff's position, that no Waldensian literature can be given a date earlier than 1400. [4] But Todd was not convinced that

---

[1] Idem, pp. 530, 459.
[2] Israel of the Alps, vol. 2, p. 530.
[3] Idem, p. 539.
[4] Dr. A. H. Newman, in Bap. Quart. Rev., July 1885, p. 307.

this MS. date of 1400, is correct, but held it as undecided.[1] His forgetting that other copies should have weight, illustrates how such men as Herzog have drawn their conclusions. Just as this conclusion had been formed came Preger, of Munich, another specialist in this department of history, with a genuine Waldensian document of the early part of the thirteenth century. Thus, the destructive critics on Waldensian literature illustrate their brethren on Biblical literature.

Prof. Albert H. Newman, well says: "Dieckhoff doubtless went further than the *facts* in his possession, *warranted* in his rejection of Waldensian testimony and in his respect for that of Roman Catholic inquisitors."[2] Of this same poem, after a thorough examination of both sides of the question, Leger says: "La date l'an 1100 qu'on lit dans ce poema merite toute confiance"—the date 1100 which is given the poem is worthy of all confidence.[3]

Gilly, a more reliable authority than Leger, says: "For my own part, I believe the Noble Lesson to be of more ancient date than the British Magazine and its correspondents are inclined to allow, even of the early part of the twelfth century."[4] Dr. Montgomery well concludes his discussion, after thoroughly considering the discussions of Dieckhoff, Herzog and others: "*The date in the Noble Lesson, not affixed, but embodied in the poem, seems so to resist all attempts made against it; that of itself, it may be held sufficient proof of the existence of the Vaudois under their present name in the beginning of the twelfth century.*"[5]

---

[1] Todd's Books of the Vaudois, Preface, p. 14.
[2] Dr. Newman, in Bap. Quart. Rev., July 1885, p. 305.
[3] Todd's Books of the Vaudois, p. 126.
[4] Todd's Books of the Vaudois, p. 152.
[5] Israel of the Alps, vol. 2, p. 540.

Herzog concludes that instead of their being of Hussite origin numbers of the Waldensian MS. "must be older than the time of the Hussite influence"—from 1298 to 1415 A. D.[1] Owing to the attempt to impute the Waldensian writings to the " Hussite influence," and, thus, get them out of the way as proof of Waldensian antiquity, I call special attention to this concession of Herzog.

In speaking of the Noble Lesson, do not forget that, while not so strong evidence as it is, other Vaudois manuscripts prove the antiquity of the Waldenses. Dieckhoff is forced to concede that " there is *abundant* evidence of the existence of Vaudois books at an *early* date."[2] Dieckhöff's attempting to weaken the force of this concession by proving these manuscripts had become very rare by the end of the sixteenth century, proves only that a drowning man will readily catch at a straw, since there are sufficient copies of them to attest Waldensian antiquity. While, to an extent deserved, frequent characterization of some alleged Waldensian manuscripts and some Waldensian writers as "*falschung*," "*falscher*," " *absichtsvolle Falschung*"—falsifying, forged, full of intentional falsifying — is thus well animadverted on by Dr. Montgomery: "The authority of the dates assigned to the Vaudois documents by Leger, he has of course little difficulty in overthrowing; and when he censures Leger's use of manuscript documents as uncritical, his judgment may be admitted as in all probability as quite just; but when he imputes to the persecuted Vaudois minister the tricks of a literary imposter, it is not easy to repress a feeling of indignation that such a charge should be advanced and sustained as it is by proofs so *ridiculously slender*. . .

[1] Idem, p. 538.
[2] Israel of the Alps, vol. 2, p. 525.

. . So anxious is he to make out a dishonest intention that he forgets the possibility of honest quotation with reference to a particular point, whilst what has no immediate bearing on that point is omitted. . . . The object of all this labor to make out charges of dishonesty is to throw discredit upon *every* quotation made by Vaudois historians from old Vaudois documents, and to create a suspicion of forgery concerning the existing documents themselves."[1]

As but one illustration of Dieckhoff's reckless criticisms, Dr. Gilly says and proves it true of one Vaudois writer whom he attempts to impeach: "I think it right to remark that I have found proof of his credibility in several points where his veracity has been doubted."[2] As another illustration: "And here it may be incidentally noticed as somewhat strange, that with Morels' letter before him, Dieckhoff should have represented the opinion of the existence of the Vaudois as anterior to Valdo as a post-Reformation tradition; for, in *that* letter, their high antiquity is twice asserted." Morels' letter was written to Bucer and Œcolampadius in 1530.[3]

But the antiquity of the Waldenses does not essentially depend—as Herzog, Dieckhoff and some others think—on the question of literary criticism or upon the Waldenses having been *called* Waldenses before Waldo's day. Far from it. We can omit all the argument from literary criticism in the foregoing and concede Dieckhoff's, Herzog's and Todd's criticisms and conclusions on and from Waldensian manuscripts and yet prove the existence of Waldenses long before the time of Waldo

---

[1] Idem, p. 525.
[2] The Books of the Vaudois, by Todd, p. 169.
[3] Idem, p. 524.

(1.) The testimony of Romish writers of and near Waldo's time clearly proves the Waldenses existent long before that.

(2.) The testimony of Waldensian tradition proves that Waldenses existed long before Waldo's day. That they taught long before the Reformation period, they had a continuous existence to or near the time of the Apostles, we have seen. All the Romish attempts to make this out a claim which originated since the Reformation is certainly baseless. As well deny that the traditions of such Biblical events as the flood are of value as testimony to the facts of those events as to deny that traditional testimony to Waldensian antiquity is of great value. While tradition is worthless as to the truth of *doctrine* and *opinion*, yet, as to alleged historical facts its value is incalculably great. In controversy with the Romish church, Protestants have often overlooked the difference between tradition as to opinion and doctrine and tradition as to fact; then rushed as far to one extreme as to the value of tradition as the Romish party has gone to the other. I do not hesitate to say that the testimony of tradition to the antiquity of the Waldenses is far stronger than all the testimony of the so called " higher criticism " and of the few Romish controversialists whom Dieckhoff and company array against Waldensian antiquity. Of course, tradition can be overthrown by undeniably historical facts which contradict it. But no conscientious historian will claim there is as much as *one* such fact unmistakably against the antiquity of the Waldenses.

(3.) On the contrary, the facts are on the side of the antiquity of the Waldenses. When pressed to the wall by Muston, M. Schmidt, rather a specialist as a historian on this point, acknowledged: " I have never maintained that there were no manifestations of anti-catholic spirit before the days of Valdo. . . . Even admitting that the heresy in question was analogous to the Vaudois doctrines, this would prove only that before Valdo there were persons holding something similar to what he afterwards believed."[1] Says Muston: "The reader will observe that M. Schmidt grants almost all I desire, for it is by no means necessary to prove that Valdo was descended from the Vaudois; it is enough if the Vaudois be acknowledged to have existed *before* his time."[1]

Says Muston: "About the middle of the sixth century a part of the bishops of Upper Italy refused to adhere to the decision of the Council of Chalcedon, held in 553; and in 590, nine of them *separated* from the Roman church, or rather they solemnly renewed their *protestation of independence* of it. The bishops being then elected by the people of their diocese, we may presume without doing any violence to history, that the later were imbued with the same doctrines and the same spirit. The truth of this state of things in Upper Italy, is attested in the seventh century by a new bishop of Milan, Mansuetus, A. D. 677. To combat the opinion that the pope is the head of the church he directs attention to the fact that the Councils of Nice, Constantinople and many others had been convoked by the emperors and not by the pope. This bishop himself was not afraid to condemn Pope Honorius as a Monothelite. And this gives us a new proof of the independence then enjoyed by the diocese of Milan, across which the Vaudois named, would have been obliged to pass, in order to reach Rome. The kingdom of Lombardy was itself solicitous for the preservation of this independence. Thus everything contributed to its maintainence; and it may be supposed that satisfied with

---

[1] Idem, p. 3.

the first successes obtained in the towns, Rome thereafter paid less regard to the relics of independence which might still subsist in the mountains. We know, however, that ancient manners and ancient liberties have at all times been less easily eradicated from such situations. However we are not reduced to the necessity of supporting this idea by mere inferences, and the eighth century still presents us examples of resistance to the pretentions of the Papal See in Upper Italy. As these pretentions are more strongly urged we find the resistance becoming all the more vigorous in the following centuries, and we can follow its traces quite on to the twelfth century, when the existence of the Vaudois is no longer doubted by any one.

. . . But the grasping ambition of the church of Rome, overcoming by degrees the resistance made in quarters nearest to its center of action, forced back toward the chain of the Alps, the limits, still becoming narrower, of that independence inherited from past ages, which had at first opposed it over the whole of Upper Italy. This independence was *defended* in the ninth century by Claude of Turin, in whom, at the same time, we behold the most distinguished advocate of evangelical doctrines whom the age produced. Whilst the bishop of Milan contented himself with the deploring condition of the Roman church, by which he had been reduced to subjection, but in whose iniquities he did not take part, the bishop Turin boldly declared against the innovations which she had sought to long introduce into the sphere of his influence and power. The numerous works of this prelate on different books of the Bible, had prepared him for defending it against the attacks of popery; and strong in the might of truth, Claude of Turin owned Jesus Christ as the sole Head of the church, attached no value to pretended meritorious works, rejected human traditions, acknowledged *faith* † *alone* as securing salvation, ascribed no power to prayers made for the dead, maintained the symbolical character of the Eucharist, and, above all, opposed with great energy the worship of images, which he, *like his predecessors*, regarded as absolute idolatry. Thus the doctrines which characterized the primitive church and which still characterize the Vaudois church at the present day have never remained without a witness in the countries inhabited by the Vaudois. . . . Rendered distinct by her isolation their church found her own pale a *separate* one for this reason only, that she herself had never changed. But as they did not form a new church; they could not receive a new name; *because they inhabited the valleys* they were called Vaudois." [1] In his work on the Vaudois, Bert in 1849—a good authority—from pp. 386, 390, throws "light upon the autonomy of the diocese of Milan, to which the Vaudois valleys at an early period belonged," remaining "completely independent of the Romish church so-called." [2]

Wadington: In "the valleys of Piedmont" Waldo "*found* a people of congenial spirits. They were called Vaudois or Waldenses—(men of the valleys); and, as the preaching of Peter may probably have confirmed their opinions and cemented their discipline, he acquired and deserved his surname by residing among them. At the same time their connection with Peter and his real Lionese disciples established a notion of their identity; and the Vaudois, in return for the title which they had bestowed, received the reciprocal appellation of Lyonnese; such, at least, appears the most probable among the many varying accounts. There are some who believe the

---

† The Baptist position.
[1] Israel of the Alps, vol. 1, pp. 7-10.
[2] Idem, vol. 2, p. 406.

Vaudois to have enjoyed the uninterrupted integrity of the faith even from the apostolic ages; others suppose them to have been disciples of Claudius Turin, the evangelical prelate of the ninth century. At least, it may be pronounced with *great certainty* that they had been *long* in existence *before* the visit of the Lionese reformer."[1] Of Claude of Turin, Neander says: "The interest of practical Christianity stands foremost in all his commentaries. Grace, the source of genuine sanctification; the temper and disposition, the main thing to be regarded in the disposition of moral worth; a disposition of love to God, purified from all reference to reward, the essence of the genuine Christian temper, worship of God in the spirit, the characteristic of all true piety. . . . And it is easy to understand, therefore, in what sort of a relation he must have been placed to the reigning sensuous element in the religious tendency of his age. . . . From this ethical point of view, he would necessarily be led to dispute many of the marks by which his contemporaries were accustomed to judge respecting good works. Thus, to the merit of good works, according to monkery, he opposed St. Paul's doctrine of grace. . . . He saw with extreme pain how the essence of Christianity was here placed in making pilgrimages to Rome, in adoring images and relics, in various species of outward works; how men were taught to trust in the intercession of the saints, to the neglect of earnest moral efforts of their own. "He beheld a superstition which bordered closely on paganism, obtaining in the worship of saints, of images, of the cross, and of relics. . . . He disclaimed violently against superstition; he banished from the churches the images and crosses, which seemed to have

[1] Wadington's Ch. Hist., p. 290.

become objects of religious adoration. He says himself on the subject: 'When I was induced to undertake the office of pastor, and came to Italy, I found, contrary to the doctrine, all the churches full of the lumber of consecrated gifts; and because I began alone pulling down what all adored I was calumniated by all, and unless the Lord had helped me, they would, perhaps, have swallowed me up alive.' Pope Paschal expressed displeasure at his conduct. . . . But it is remarkable that though popes countenanced the fanaticism of the multitude this expression of displeasure had no farther injurious effect on Claudius. . . . In general he denied that St. Peter possessed any continuous power to bind and to loose. The 'title to an apostolicus does not belong to him who administers a bishopric founded by an Apostle, but to him who fulfils the apostolic vocation; to those who occupy the place without fulfilling the vocation should be applied the passage in Matthew 23:12.' As may be inferred from the language of one of his opponents, Claudius was cited to appear before an assemblage of bishops; but he did not present himself, as he could easily see that it would be impossible for him to come to any understanding with the bishops of this country; and perhaps in the contempt which he expressed for them, he yielded too much to his indignation against superstition."[1]

Claudius, having been sent to his field by "Lonious the Pious,"[2] and possessing a powerful protector in the Frank emperor,[3] was, with his field independent of popery.

[1] Neander's Ch. Hist., vol. 3, pp. 432, 433, 437, 439; also Schaff-Herzog Ency., vol. 1, p. 491.
[2] Kurtz's Ch. Hist., vol. 1, p. 369.
[3] Neanders' Hist. Chr. Ch., vol. 3, p. 433.

THE WALDENSES OF APOSTOLIC ORIGIN. 283

The first church instead of building up several small churches in one locality, extended its work throughout that territory by missions. In this plan there were many pastors to the same church, so as to secure pastoral care of each mission. But these missions and their pastors continued under the care of the mother church. This gave the pastor of the mother church a *pastoral* care over all the missions and their pastors. This is the case now in quite a number of Baptist churches. Yet, as arbitrary or executive the authority was in the mother *church;* its pastor had only moral authority. Consequently, there was nothing in this resembling any heirarchal or Episcopal government. By the pastor of the mother church, by degrees, stealing the authority of his church, after a few centuries he became what is now known as a diocesan bishop. Of course, this became the case in some localities much sooner than in others. While the Turin churches were not yet popish, when Claude went among them they were certainly rapidly on the road there. This prepares us to see how it was that Claudius when called to account for his Scriptural course, by bishops and pope, treated them all with contempt. It also prepares us to understand that the church government of Turin was not Episcopal diocesian in the sense these terms now imply. Robinson observes of the Turin bishop: "The bishop was little more than a rector. He had no suffragan bishops and no secular power in the valleys."[1]

Thus, there is a strong reason to believe that the Waldenses, in the Turin diocese, had continued from apostolic times, and that the Lord had Claudius sent among them in the time to save them from wandering so far as to lose their apostolic character. Nor does the

[1] Robinson's Eccl. Resh., p. 462.

conclusion follow that they were fully identified with the Turin diocese, even had it been a modern Episcopal diocese. As Episcopal government is unknown in pure Waldensian history, had the Turin government been Episcopal, the conclusion would naturally be that the Waldenses were not, in full, ecclesiastically identified with the bishop of Turin† but that from time immemorial they had made his diocese their *refuge*, because his freedom from popery or non-subjection to it, with his great evangelical feeling, assured them a refuge and home. The point of this argument is not necessarily that the bishop of Turin and his diocese were Waldenses—I think they were—but that genuine Waldenses existed there long before Waldo's day. Nor is it the point that they were called Waldenses long before Waldo, but that they were, in teaching and practice, Waldenses. As we have demonstrated, the names are no conclusive evidence of identity. They, themselves, says Keller, repudiated, " during many centuries the name of Waldenses."

Says Dr. Allix, in Chapter XI of his Remarks on the Churches of Piedmont: " Here, then, we have found a body of men in Italy before the year one thousand and twenty-six who believed contrary to the opinions of the church of Rome and who condemned their errors."[1]

---

† Had the Bishop of Turin and his diocese been Romish, and the Waldenses had their membership in his churches, it would not follow that they were not Baptists; since, in different ages, Baptists, to escape persecution, probably while in secret, maintaining their own organizations, have been, yet, members of the Romish or of some persecuting Protestant church. Even to-day this is the case. Thus, Rev. Edmund F. Merriam, Editorial Secretary of the American Baptist Missionary Union, in The Watchman of Boston, January 4, 1894, of the Baptist in Sweden, under Lutheran persecution, writes: " In accordance with the peculiar laws, they *still* remain as nominal *members of the State church*, but are almost everywhere permitted the free and untrammelled exercise of their own religious worship. In *former* times there was *much* persecution." This may serve as the answer to the objection: " Waldenses and other dissenters could not have been Baptist churches because they were, sometimes, members of the Romish church, even *permitting* their infants to be baptized." Of course, the right or the wrong of it is a wholly different question, to which there are two sides.

[1] In Idem, p. 408.

THE WALDENSES OF APOSTOLIC ORIGIN. 285

Gilly says: "It is certain that when Waldo fled from Lyons, he and his 'poor men of Lyons' took refuge among the mountaineers of Provence and Lombardy, *whom he found* to be, and not whom he caused to be, impugners of Romish errors."[1]

Again, says Gilly: "That this region was infected with what was heresy before Waldo went thither appears first on the evidence of Peter Clugny, who, distinctly speaking of that locality, wrote in the year 1127 and 1143 against heretics . . . secondly, of a passage in Vol. 3 of 'Historiæ Patriæ Monumenta,' which states that the whole of that mountain territory was infected with heresy in 1164."[2]

Armitage, an intemperate opposer of Baptist Church Perpetuity, while generally ready to cast doubt on it, and admitting it only when no way to get out of doing so, claiming the evidences of Waldenses existing before Waldo, is "too scanty and fragmentary to be used with confidence for historical purposes" finds the proof so strong that he feels forced to concede: "There is *ground* for the belief that an *evangelical* people lived in the isolated Cottion Alps before the twelfth century."[3] He adds: "Some Waldensian writers think they can trace their origin back to the days of Constantine and even to the Apostles."[3]

In Limborch's History of the Inquisition, Amsterdam, 1692, there is recorded, from the year 1311, the following confession of a woman, a member of a weaver family, which had for generations belonged to the Waldenses: "The Waldenses belong to the number of those disciples which *descended from the Disciples and Apostles*

---

[1] Todd's Books of the Vaudois, p. 194.
[2] Idem, p. 203.
[3] Armitage's Hist. Bap., p. 294.

of Christ; from those Apostles upon whom Christ transferred the power to bind and to loose; and these Waldenses retain that potency even as Christ gave it to St. Peter and others. The chaplains and monks know the meaning of the Holy Scriptures well enough, and also the divine law, but they do not desire that the people should understand it, in order to establish their own power over the people; for if they with clearness and without concealment would teach the law of God as Christ revealed it then they would not receive that which they require." As Dr. Grimmell remarks on this: "When it is remembered that is a confession of a woman—Jaqueta Textrix de Cumba Rotgir—the suspicion of a *studied invention fails;* but if it be taken into account that a like tradition is repeated throughout the different countries of Europe, wherever Waldenses were found, the pristine *root of the same* will appear unmistakably."[1] Dr. Grimmell farther says: "That Peter Waldo was not the founder of the sect is clear from the records of the synod held at Bergamo, 1218, where the 'Poor men of Italy' claimed a history *independent* of Waldus, who flourished about the year 1170. The 'Italian Brethren' are doubtless identical with the Arnoldists of Lombardy, named after Arnold of Brescia in 1155."

Dr. Newman observes: "We can hardly escape the conviction that the Italian Brethren arose independently of Waldo. They do not recognize his authority and they have no special reverence for his name."[2] Says Dr. Newman: "During the early years of the twelfth century, *sixty years before Waldo* began to teach, Southern France and Northwestern Italy were permeated with a far more

[1] Essay Before the New York Baptist Ministers' Conference.
[2] Bap. Quart. Rev., July, 1885, p. 317.

evangelical teachings of Peter de Bruis and Henry of Lausanne. The views of these teachers are well known to have been *substantially Baptists*. It is not possible that the influence of this teaching should have become completely extinct by Waldo's time. There is *much* evidence of the persistence of evangelical teaching in Italy from the *earliest time*. The Humilati of the twelfth century and the followers of Arnold of Brescia may well have been the proudest of early evangelical influences. They probably were. . . . *Herzog and Dieckhoff attached far more importance to the proof that Waldo was the founder of the Waldenses than it deserved.* To be sure it was worth while to know the facts. But these when arrived at prove *very little* with regard to the great evangelical party of the Middle Ages—commonly known by the name Waldenses. This name was undoubtedly derived from Waldo of Lyons. The immediate followers of Waldo were known by *various* names, ' Waldenses ' and ' Poor men of Lyons' being among the most common. . . . But to say that the whole evangelical movement originated with Waldo, because the term Waldenses is applied to them by Roman Catholic writers, is a very different thing, *and is at variance with the facts of history.* . . . It is Dr. Ludwig Keller's great merit to have traced the history of the old evangelical party through the dark ages of persecution, and to have exhibited, in a masterly manner, the relations of this party to the great religious, industrial, social and scientific movements of the Middle Ages. . . . These results are in the highest degree gratifying to evangelical Christians in general and especially to Baptists. *Keller insists throughout that the old evangelical party was fundamentally Baptist.*"[1]

[1] Bap. Quart. Rev., July, 1885, pp. 321-322.

Dr. Brockett who has made this study a specialty says as we have seen, that the Waldenses, Paulicians, etc., were indentical. The Paulicians "planted the standard of the cross in northern Italy, south of France; and from the good *seed* sown by these faithful souls, who, under the guise of peddlers or traveling merchants, scattered the word of God everywhere, there sprang up congregations of the Albigenses, the Vaudois, the Cathari (an old name of the Paulicians), the Waldenses and the Paulicani, a corruption of the name by which they were best known."[1]

In a letter to the author, Dr. W. W. Everts, Jr., says: "I think the Waldenses, Albigenses, Petrobrussians and Henricians, etc., all stood on the shoulders of the Paulicians."

Muston says: "The Vaudois were 'more probably' holding 'some *connection*' with the Petrobrussians."[2]

The Petrobrussians and the Waldenses were so clearly one that, to get rid of the Waldensian documents to Waldensian antiquity, the great Romish controversionalist, Bishop Bossuet—ascribed them to Peter de Bruis.[3]

Says Muston of 1165, before Waldo's day: "A numerous detachment of Albegeois, leaving the south of France, took refuge in the valleys of Piedmont, whereby they united themselves with the Vaudois both in doctrine and worship."[4]

A. D. 1119, "Council of Toulouse; decrees of the Inquisition against the heretics who existed partly in Italy and partly in France."[5] The Romish opponent,

---

[1] Idem, vol. 4, p. 427.
[2] Israel of the Alps, vol. 2, p. 417.
[3] Idem, p. 443.
[4] Idem, p. 484; Morrison's Hist. Ref., p. 35.
[5] Idem, p. 484, from Gallios' Hist. del Inquis, pp. 81, 83, 84.

THE WALDENSES OF APOSTOLIC ORIGIN. 289

Father Stephen, almost a contemporary of Waldo, says the "Poor men of Lyons"—Waldo's followers—"*joined* with other heretics of Provence and Lombardy whose errors they have adopted and propagated." ("Postea in provinciæ terra et Lombardiæ cum aliis haereticis se admiscentes, et errorem cerrorem bibentes et serentes.")[1]

Muston quotes a personal letter from M. Gieseler: "Indeed it *cannot be doubted* that *before* the days of Waldo Peter de Bruis and Henry condemned the errors of the Catholic church. . . . Nor is it improbable that Peter sowed the *seed* of his doctrine in his native valley and left followers there; and thus we can explain how Pope Urban found the valley full of heretics. And it is also likely enough that of the remaining disciples of Peter and Henry many *joined* the Valdenses, in whom they found the *same* zeal for the doctrine of the Bible; and *thus* it probably came to pass that no trace of the Petrobrussians and Henricians appear at any subsequent period."[2]

Consequently Neander says: "It was not without some foundation of *truth* that the Waldenses of this period asserted the high antiquity of their sect, and maintained that from the time of the secularization of the church—that is, as they believed from the time of Constantines' gift to the Roman bishop Silvester—such an opposition as finally broke forth in them, had been existing *all along*."[3]

Says Wadington of the Waldenses: "Their *origin* is not ascertained by any authentic record; and being immemorial, it may have been coeval with the *introduction* of Christianity. Among their own traditions there is one,

---

[1] Idem, p. 510.
[2] Idem, vol. 1, p. 3.
[3] Neander's Hist. Chr. Ch., vol. 4, p. 605.

which agrees well with their original and favorite tenet, which objects to the possession of property by ecclesiastics. It is this—that their earliest fathers, offended at the liberality of with which Constantine endowed the church of Rome, and at the worldliness with which Pope Sylvester accepted these endowments, seceded into the Alpine solitudes; that they there lay concealed and secure for so many ages through their insignificance and their innocence. *This may have been so—it is not even very improbable that it was so.* . . . If on the other hand we should identify those dissenters (as some have done) with the Cathari, the Gazari, Patereni, Publicani, and others of the same age, who were collateral branches of the Paulician family, and others of the same age, we are not, indeed, any longer at a loss to *trace* their succession to a *very high antiquity.*" [1]

I conclude the discussion of the Waldenses—leaving out much other matter on the subject—with the following summary of facts and conclusions:

(1.) Whether the Waldenses were ecclesiastically one with Claude of Turin is immaterial. If not so, they found shelter under his wing.

(2.) As he was anti-papal, and was not a bishop in the modern sense, the Waldenses may have been ecclesiastically one with him.

(3.) In either case the Waldenses of Turin and vicinity have an antiquity to apostolic times.

(4.) The Waldenses of Turin may have been one wing of the Paulicians *or* they may have been descended from the Apostles by *another line*—perhaps some of them *there* existed from century one.

[1] Wadington's Ch. Hist., pp. 554-555.

(5.) Whether the Turin Waldenses had their continuity through the Paulician line, or by having remained there from the first century *or* by still another line, is immaterial, as in either case, they have apostolic perpetuity.

(6.) While Waldo may have been the founder of a party he *certainly* did not originate the Waldenses.

(7.) If Waldo did found a party it probably was absorbed and assimilated by the previously existing Waldenses and others like them.

(8.) Even if Waldo's party had never been absorbed and corrected by the others, since the Waldenses whence Baptists are descended are the great and *original* body of the Waldenses, which were never a part of the Romish church, the apostolic continuity line is in no way disturbed. As we have seen, Waldo's party — if he founded one — joined the others.

(9.) The Waldenses were but Petrobrussians, Henricians, Arnoldists, Catharists, Albigenses and Paulicians. In doctrine, organization and practice they were essentially the same. Whether they were all of one line of descent from the Apostles is a question of no practical importance; though most of them probably descended through the Paulician line.

(10.) While there is much direct evidence proving the mass of Waldenses were ecclesiastically,† from the very first, in no way a part of the Romish church, the

---

† A favorite and deceptive method of assaulting the apostolic origin of the Waldenses and others is to prove that many of them—including, in many cases, their leaders, as in the cases of Waldo, Arnold, Grebel—came out of the Romish church, and, in some cases, were soon after found with Romish trumpery. But since many thousands, in past ages and the present, thus leave the Romish church for the true church such cases have no bearing on the origin of the party with which they finally identified themselves. As near all the first converts to Christianity, made by the Apostles, were from the Jews this fallacious method could thus be made, prove the church was thus then *originated*.

discussion of this subject in this and the previous chapter, has incidentally furnished other proof of this.

(11.) While Dieckhoff and Herzog have rendered service in examining and sifting Waldensian literature and have shown that unauthorized dates, etc., have been assigned certain documents, yet their adoption of the wildness of the "higher critics" and reliance on a class of bitter and uncandid Romish writers render their *conclusion* unreliable, especially, in view of the overwhelming proof to the contrary.

(12.) The blind apishness and the assumption with which some writers and professors of church history, and some others, have adopted Dieckhoff's and Herzog's conclusions, that Valdo originated the Waldenses, has a parallel in those writers and professors who, because of the "higher criticism" from Germany, have swallowed its conclusion on the Old Testament—much learning; very little common sense and original judgment.

(13.) Admit all of Dieckhoff's and Herzog's positions on the manuscripts of the Waldenses, yet by overwhelming proof, we have evangelical life and Waldenses running back in unbroken line to apostolic times.

(14.) After all discussions and assaults on Waldensian history, the very latest scholarship supplies sufficient material for proof that the Waldensian history, as understood in the days of Gilly, Leger, Allix, etc., is *substantially* correct.

(15.) Thus, "there is no bug under the chip" which any believer in "Baptist succession" needs fear— the evidence supplied by these assailants and their concessions itself being sufficient assurance.

(16.) I have given this especial discussion, under the head of Waldenses, only because that name figures so much in church perpetuity.

CHAPTER XXII.

The Waldenses Perpetuated in the Anabaptists and Baptists.

Inasmuch as Hussites—the evangelicals of Bohemia—figure so much in the period to be now noticed, I here stop a moment to notice them as finally becoming one with the Waldenses. Being prepared by the work of the Waldenses, Albigenses, etc., finally through intercourse with them, they became one with them. Hase says: "The Waldenses were *connected* with the Hussites by fraternal ties, recognized finally in the Reformation, the very objects which their ancestors had been obscurely seeking."[1] Dr. Montgomery calling attention to the "connection" exhibited by Dieckhoff "between the Vaudois literature and that of the Bohemian churches" observes: "That a *connection* subsisted, in times previous to the Reformation, between the Vaudois or Waldenses of the Alps and the Bohemian Christians, (who were often called Waldenses,) has indeed been long known. But this is well deserving of more investigation than it has yet received."[2] Thus we have seen Waldensian influence and Waldensian organization swallow up the Hussites. Mr. H. Haupt, a German specialist, in this line, has recently, with Preger, another recent and like German specialist, found the "Waldenses strongly rooted in Bohemia and Moravia *long before* the outbreak of the Hussite revolution, and Waldensianism of a type that

---

[1] Hase's Chr. Ch., p. 610.
[2] Israel of the Alps, vol. 2, p. 526.

would naturally lead to the peculiar type of Taborism."[1] "Between this Taborite production and that of the Vaudois documents Dieckhoff points out correspondences which unquestionably are not accidental. . . . Several Vaudois works are found to agree very closely in matter, even often in words, with the parts of this Taborite Confession. The Vaudois Treatise on Purgatory contains quotations from the sermons of John Huss."[2]

Dr. A. H. Newman, says: "We have evidence of the great influence and aggressiveness of Waldenses of the most pronounced or anti-Romanist type in Bohemia throughout the entire fourteenth century."[3] Wattenbach in his "Ueber die Inquisition gegen die Waldenser in Pommern und der Mark Brandenburg, Berlin, 1886," shows that "intimate relations," at a very early time, by the Waldenses "had been established with the Taborites, the Bohemian brethren, etc., of Bohemia, and the names of Wickliff and Huss were known and honored."[4] "Matthias Flacius Illyricus, who, in the sixteenth century, surpassed all his contemporaries in scientific historical investigation and who studied the mediæval sects to more purpose than any of his successors until the present century, on the basis of manuscript sources, some of which are lost and some of which are still available, reached the conclussion that the entire evangelical movement in Bohemia, including the work of the well-known precursors of Huss (such as Conrad of Waldhansen, Miltz of Kremsier, Matthias of Janow, etc.,) the Hussite movement, the Taborite movement, the Unitas Fratrum, etc., *was deeply indebted*

---

[1] Recent Researches concerning Mediæval Sects, by Dr. A. H. Newman, p. 208
[2] Idem, p. 527.
[3] Idem, p. 170.
[4] Idem, p. 176.

to the earlier Waldensian movement."[1] "It is interesting to know that the old evangelical party, represented by the Waldenses and the Bohemian brethren, were not only the first to prepare a good German version of the Scriptures, but that they were, after the invention of printing, among the first to utilize this art in the dissemination of evangelical views, through versions of the Scriptures and through religious works of their own composing."[2]

Turning more directly to the subject, that the Anabaptists are the continuation of the Waldenses and of others which were Waldenses under other names, H. Haupt, just referred to, says Dr. A. H. Newman: "Has incidentally shown that the relation between the Romanic and the German Waldenses was more intimate than has been supposed by Herzog, Dieckhoff and Preger, and that they were *practically identical* in faith and practice. . . . Haupt has also demonstrated the fact that all German Bibles printed before the reformation were derived from this *Waldensian version*, three of the editions having been completely Waldensian, and the fourth a Catholic recension of the Waldensian version. Even this Catholic recension, and its successors, had no Episcopal authorization and were probably set forth by those who were under Waldensian influence. To the *Waldenses*, therefore, Germany was indebted for the translation and the circulation of the Scriptures, and so for the great religious movement which the so-called Reformation probably hindered more than it forwarded."[3] "Herzog compares the track of the Waldensian history to that of a mole, emerging now and then from the hidden recesses of the earth into the light, but incapable of being continuously

---

[1] Idem, p. 206.
[2] Idem, p. 220.
[3] Baptist Quart. Rev., Oct., 1885, p. 526.

traced."[1] This Herzog illustration of Baptist history may well be accepted, remembering that the "mole" has made so many upheavals and they so near together that we can readily follow its course. Says Prof. Geo. P. Fisher, D. D.: "There had been opposition to infant baptism in earlier days among the Waldenses and other sects, as well as from individuals like Peter of Bruges, and Henry of Clugny." Peter de Bruis and Henry—"But this one tenet was not the soul characteristic of the Anabaptists in which we find the *continuance or reproduction of former ideas and tendencies.*"[2]

Of the Waldenses, says Kurtz: "They were most numerous in the south of France, in the east of Spain and in the north of Italy; but many of their converts were also found in *Germany, in Switzerland, and in Bohemia.* . . . They gradually retired from France, Spain and Italy into the remote valleys of Piedmont and Savoy."[3] The Anabaptists being consequently, few in Italy and France, these countries did not have the Reformation; while Germany, Switzerland and Bohemia, being the seats of the Anabaptists, were its origin—the Anabaptists the continuance of the Waldenses.

"Universal Knowledge"—Chamber's Encyclopedia —of the Waldenses, says: "They were subject to persecutions in 1332, 1400 and 1478 and driven into *many* parts of Europe, where their industry and integrity were universally remarked. So *widely* had the sect been scattered that it was said *a traveler from Antwerp to Rome could sleep every night in the house of one of their brethren.* In Bohemia *many* of them had settled, and they, without

---

[1] Idem, July 1885, p. 301.
[2] Fisher's Hist. Chr. Ch., pp. 424, 425.
[3] Kurtz's Ch. Hist., vol. 1, p. 459.

forsaking their own community, had *joined* the Hussites, Taborites and Bohemian brethren." [1]

The reader will please read this quotation in connection with the first part of this article, where he will see *how* the Waldensians, the Bohemians, Hussites and the Taborites were thus united.

Again, of the Anabaptists and infant baptism: "Opposition to this doctrine was kept alive in the various so-called heretical sects that went by the general name, Cathari (*i. e.*, purists) such as the *Waldenses, Albigenses, etc.* Shortly after the beginning of the reformation the opposition to infant baptism appeared anew among the Anabaptists." [2]

Lemme, in his review of Keller's "Van Stanpitz," discussing in a judicial way the character of the Waldenses, says: "In calling the pre-reformatory Waldensian churches evangelical Keller necessarily raises the question as to their evangelical standpoint; because in recent times it has been maintained that the Waldenses were essentially mediæval and monkish. . . . The classing of the apostolic life as the Waldenses cherished it with the monkish life ideal is, as a matter of fact, *not a result of scientific investigation, but is dogmatic prepossession.* . . . They are evangelical . . . in making the Scriptures the sole authority, and with respect to the conception of the church, in the rejection of ecclesiastical authority, and the vindication of the universal priesthood. . . . This impulse to set up externally churches of the *saints* could not feel content with Luther's reformation and turned aside into Anabaptism." [3]

[1] Vol. 15, p. 132.
[2] Idem, vol. 1, p. 347.
[3] Recent Researches Concerning Mediæval Sects, p. 204.

Says Vedder: Herberle writes in the Jahrbucher fur Deutsche Theologie (1858, p. 276 seq.) of the Anabaptists: "It is well known that just these principles are found in the *sects of the middle ages*. The supposition is very probable that between these and the rebaptizers of the Reformation there was an *external historical connection*. The possibility of this as respects Switzerland is all the greater, since just here the traces of these sects, especially the Waldenses, can be followed down to the *end* of the fifteenth century. But a positive proof in this connection we have not. . . . In reality the explanation of this agreement NEEDS NO PROOF of a real *historical* union between Anabaptists and their predecessors, for the abstract Biblical standpoint upon which the one as well as the other place themselves is sufficient in itself to *prove* a union of the two in the above-named doctrines."[1]

Notwithstanding Vedder's antipathy to "succession" he concedes, "a *moral certainty* exists of a *connection* between the Swiss Anabaptists and their Waldensian and Petrobrussian predecessors, sustained by *many significant facts*, but not absolutely proved by historical evidences. Those who maintain that the Anabaptists originated with the Reformation have some *difficult* problems to solve, among others, the rapidity with which the new leaven spread and the wide territory that the Anabaptists soon covered. . . . Though the Anabaptist churches appear *suddenly* in the records of the time, contemporaneously with the Zwinglian Reformation, their *roots* are to be sought *farther back*."[2]

Again Vedder says: "It is a curious and instructive fact that these Anabaptists' churches were most numerous

[1] A Short History of Baptists, by Vedder, pp. 73-74.
[2] Idem, pp. 73-75.

precisely where Waldenses of a century or two previous had most flourished, and where their identity as Waldenses had been lost. That there was intimate relation between the two movements *few doubt who have studied this period and its literature*. The torch of truth was *handed on from generation to generation, and though it often smouldered and was even apparently extinguished, it needed but a breath to blaze up again* and give light to all mankind."[1]

Says Dr. William R. Williams: " Amid the sufferers under Alva, when the Netherlands were so drenched with human gore, multitudes were of our faith; and they had their share in that land in early versions of the Scriptures for the general use of the faithful. . . . Indeed, many of the Holland Mennonites hold the Waldenses to have been the first propagandists on Holland soil, of *these* views, in their flight northward from persecution in France and Italy. It has been said by one of the early Mennonite writers that the oldest families of the Mennonites, in certain towns of Holland, had names of *Waldensian origin*, and claimed to be the progeny of such exiled forefathers. Venema, himself a Pedobaptist, living in Holland, a theologian and scholar of such eminence that Adam Clarke said of his . . . Commentary on the Psalms, that it was a Goliath's sword as described by David, ' There is none like it;'—this eminent scholar, beyond the reach of denominational bias, and speaking of the ancient history of his own country, ascribes to the Baptists of Holland an origin *earlier* than the time of the Munster orgies, where too many would cradle them."[2]

Bishop Latimer, . . . speaking of some Anabaptist martyrs from Holland . . . makes the

[1] Idem, p. 71.
[2] William R. Williams' Lect. on Bap. Hist., pp. 127-128.

remark, "that these glad sufferers at the stake were but like those old heretics, the Donatists of early ages."[1]

Venema, above quoted, says: "The immediate origin of the Mennonites is, in my judgment, more justly to be traced to the *Waldensians and to those of the Anabaptists* who wished a renewal of the innocence and purity of the primitive church, and that the reformation of the church should be carried farther than Luther and Calvin had arranged it. The Waldensians, apart from the question as to the origin of Christ's human nature, in the chief articles had, in almost all things, like views with the Mennonites, as is evident from their history as I stated it in the *twelfth century*. . . . To find other beginnings as the source of Mennonism is needless, much less those invidious ones, placing them in fellowship with the men of Munster and other like fanatics. From these they cleared themselves, both in old time, and now through a long space of years have so vindicated and justified themselves, in life and institutions that longer to confound them with that class can be done only by notable injustice and gravest insult."[2]

Again says Dr. Williams: "In 1500, at the opening of the century, when Martin was ignorant as yet of the Bible and soon to enter an Augustinian monastery, the Moravian brethren possessed *two hundred places of worship*. They were the *inheritors of the labors of Huss and Jerome, of British Lollards, of Wickliffe and Waldo and laborers yet earlier than these* and whose rewards are safe with God."[2]

Again: "There were Anabaptists and Anabaptist martyrs in Holland *before* Menno himself had left the

[1] Idem, p. 129.
[2] Idem, pp. 144-145.

Roman communion."¹ Says Armitage: "The great Baptist movement on the Continent originated with *no particular man nor in any one place.* It seems to have sprung up in many places about the *same* time, and its general growth was wonderful, between 1520 and 1526, half a century."² "There was, however, a *remarkable association* between the Waldensians of the Dispersion and the *Baptists* of the sixteenth century, both in *doctrine and practice.*"³

Goebel, in his History of Christian Life in the Rhine Provinces, says that "wherever in Germany, *before* the Reformation, there were large bodies of Waldensians *there* during the Reformation large bodies of *Anabaptists* sprang up."³

Dr. Armitage, with all his antipathy to Church Perpetuity, is thus forced into line, in part, with many church historians: "Indeed in some cases, the *Baptists evidently sprang from the Waldensians.*"³

T. J. Morgan, D. D., when Professor of Church History in the Chicago Baptist Theological Seminary, said: " We further assert our principles, more or less clearly proclaimed, have found advocates in *all ages.* . . . The Donatists in the fifth and sixth centuries resisted the interference of the State in ecclesiastical affairs. The Paulicians and Bogomiles, the Albigenses, the Waldenses, and the much stigmatized Anabaptists preached, protested and suffered in behalf of principles more or less clearly Baptistic."⁴

Bullinger, in his preface to his sermons on the book of Revelations, (1530,) says of the Waldenses: " What

---

1 Idem, p. 146.
2 Armitage's Hist. Bap., p. 329.
3 Idem, p. 304.
4 In *The Standard*, Chicago.

shall we say, that for *four hundred years or more* in France, Italy, Germany, Poland, Bohemia, and other countries throughout the world, the Waldenses have sustained their profession of the gospel of Christ; and in several of their writings as well as by continual preaching, they have accused the pope as the real anti-Christ, foretold by the apostle John, and whom therefore we ought to avoid. . . . Although it has been often attempted by the most powerful kings and princes, instigated by the pope, it has been found impossible to extirpate them, for God hath frustrated their efforts."[1] "Thomas Walden, who wrote against Wickliff, says the doctrine of Peter Waldo was conveyed from France into England, and among others, Wickliff received it. In this opinion he is joined by Alphonsus de Castro who says that Wickliff only brought to life again the errors of the Waldenses. Cardinal Bellarmine also is pleased to say that 'Wickliff could add nothing to the heresy of the Waldenses.' "[2]

The first editor of the complete book of Reinerius was Father Gretzer, in 1613, who in the book said of the Waldenses: "Vera effigies hereticorum nostræ aetatis prasertim Anibaptistarum"—This is a true picture of the heretics of our age ESPECIALLY *of the Anabaptists.*[3]

Dr. Limborch, Professor in the University of Amsterdam, at the Reformation period, said: "To speak candidly what I think, of all the modern sects of Christians the Dutch *Baptists* mostly resemble the Albigenses and the Waldenses."[4] Zwinglius, of the same age:—"The institution of Anabaptism is no novelty, but for thirteen hundred years past has caused great disturbance in the

---

[1] Jones' Ch. Hist., p. 354.
[2] Idem, p. 357.
[3] Idem, p. 358.
[4] Limborch's Hist. Inq., vol. 1, chap. 8; in Jones' Ch. Hist., p. 358; in Armitage's Bap. Hist., p. 304.

church, and has such a strength that the attempt to contend against it in this age appeared for a time futile."

Bullinger further says: "Let others say what they will of the German Anabaptists; I see nothing in them but gravity; I hear nothing but we must not swear, must not do any one injury, etc. The Donatists and the Anabaptists held the *same* opinions. . . . The Baptists display their ignorance when they assert that no constraint should be used in regard to religion or faith, they are similar in every particular to the old Baptists, the Donatists."

In 1522 Luther says: "The Anabaptists have been for a *long time* spreading in Germany."[1] The late E. T. Winkler, D. D., quoting the above, says: "Nay, *Luther* even traced the Anabaptists back to the days of *John Huss*, and apologetically admits that the eminent reformer was *one of them*."

Dr. Ludwig Keller, the Munster archivist, a Lutheran, a specialist on this subject, an expert authority and who has done more to clear up this subject than probably any other writer, in the *Preussische Jahrbucher* for Sept. 1882, says: "There were 'Baptists' *long before* the Munster rebellion, and in all the centuries that have followed, in spite of the severest persecutions there have been parties which as Baptists or 'Mennonites' have secured a permanent position in many lands. . . . A contemporary, who was not a Baptist has this testimony concerning the beginning of the movement: 'The Anabaptist movement was so *rapid* that the presence of Baptist views was speedily *discoverable in all parts of the land*. The Baptists obtained a large number of adherents. Many thousands were baptized, and they attracted to

[1] Michelet's Luther, p. 99

themselves good hearts.' . . . A contemporary chronicler estimates that already, in 1531, the number of executions in the Tyrol and Gortz was nearly a thousand. At Ensisheim, the seat of the father Austrian government Sebastian Franck puts the number at six hundred. In Linz, in six weeks, seventy-three persons were burned, drowned and beheaded. An Anabaptist chronicler, whose statements in general are regarded as very trustworthy, states that in the Palatinate, about the year 1529, 'the Palsgrave Ludwig, in a short time, put to death on account of their faith, between one hundred and fifty and two hundred.' " He goes on, mentioning many similar cases of their great numbers shown in their persecutions. " In Moravia, where the Baptists for a *long time* found protectors, persecution began in 1528. . . . A recent opponent of the Baptists, the Church historian, Carl Hase, expresses his opinion concerning these events in these words: ' The energy, the capacity for suffering, the joy in believing, which characterized the Christians of the first centuries of the church reappeared in the Anabaptists.' Indeed, one can not but be astonished at the steadfastness of these men, who so joyfully went to death, and disdained to purchase life by a word of recantation. *Only once, at the time of Roman persecution of the Christians, does the entire history of the Christian church furnish an example of such slaughter.* . . . Not to speak of the Netherlands, where at the beginning of 1530, according to the words of a contemporary, there was hardly a village or a city in which the danger of revolution on the part of the Baptists did not seem to be imminent. Let us now turn our attention to the German provinces. . . . The more I examine the documents of that time, at my command, the more I am *astonished at the extent* of the diffusion of Anabaptist views, an extent of which no other investigator has any knowledge. In all the cities in the archbishopric, with scarcely one or two exceptions, there were Anabaptists, and even in the country towns and villages. The same was true of the neighboring districts. . . . Many Baptist churches cannot be enumerated for the *reason* that their existence was a profound *secret.* . . . For the details I refer to original documents cited by me in another place, and will here only refer to the fact, that in the evangelical cities, Bremen, Hamburg, Lubec, Wisemar, Rostock, Stralsund, Brunswick, Hanover, Lunebury, etc., it can be proved that there were either fully established churches, or, at least, individual Baptists (and that, too, many among the clergy). It is not to be *doubted*, also, that in the progress of scientific invention still farther traces will be brought to light. . . . Much rather can it be proved that in the lands mentioned *Baptist* churches existed for *many decades* and EVEN CENTURIES."[1]

Dr. A. H. Newman, a high authority on this subject, says: "It may be permitted to the writer to say that he is in thorough sympathy with Keller's general view of the old evangelical party and of the Reformation of the sixteenth century.[2] The reader will please especially not overlook the latter part of Keller's statement, in my last quotation from him, that instead of saying that like other non-Catholic sects, Baptists are the children of the Reformation, he says and has given ample proof of the statement, of their great prevalence when the Reformation began: 'Baptist churches existed for many decades and even *centuries' before the Reformation.*"

---

[1] Translated by Henry S. Burrage, D. D., in Bap. Quart. Rev., vol. 7, pp. 28-33.
[2] Recent Researches concerning Mediæval Sects, p. 171.

Dr. E. T. Winkler says: "It is well known that the Anabaptists of Holland disclaimed any historic connection with the fanatical Anabaptists of Germany, but claimed a descent from the Waldenses."[1]

Dr. Howard Osgood: "In Switzerland and in Germany it has been found *impossible* to decide when the Baptists first *appeared*, or which were the first churches of Baptists in these lands; and it is quite as difficult to decide the question about the Baptists of *England*."[2]

In the same paper, Dr. Osgood says of the Anabaptists of the sixteenth century: "The persecution of *centuries* had taught them concealment," plainly implying their existence centuries before the days of Luther . . . . "When they first appeared in the Netherlands *cannot* be decided. Ypeij and Dermout say Anabaptists were according to the archives of Groningen expelled thence in 1517."

Here, Dr. Osgood quotes from Prof. Van Oesterzee, in Herzog Encyclopedia 9, p. 346 — "They are peculiar to the Netherlands and are *older than the Reformation*, and therefore must by no means be confounded with the Protestantism of the sixteenth centuries, for it can be shown that the origin of the Baptists reaches *much farther back and is more venerable.*"

Dr. Osgood, in the same paper, says: "Long *before* Menno was converted and became a Baptist, Baptists were found in the Netherlands and were united in *churches* from the borders of France to the northern bounds of Friesland and witnessed a good confession."

Dr. G. C. Lorimer in the same paper, of the Baptists and the Reformation, says: "Their existence antedates

---

[1] Dr. Winkler refers to Moehler's Symbolism, p. 4.
[2] In *The Standard*, Chicago.

it by *centuries*. . . . In 1518, six years before Luther appeared before the Diet of Worms, a letter was addressed to Erasmus from Bohemia, describing a people who *never had any affinity with Rome*. Two of these brethren waited on Luther and Erasmus to congratulate them on their secession from Rome, but the same were declined because they were *Anabaptists*. . . . It may be possible to show, as I think it is, that primitive Christianity perpetuated itself in the Novatian communities which, according to Kertz, prevailed 'almost throughout the Roman empire' and which were subsequently known as Donatists, Montanists, bodies of believers who are classed *together* by Alzog, Abrard, Herzog, Jacobi and Frike and with whom the Baptists of our day are in *substantial accord*. . . . All this could be very likely substantiated and an unbroken succession established."

Cardinal Hossius, President of the Council of Trent, which met Dec. 15, 1545, and one of the most learned Romanists of his day, said: " If you behold the cheerfulness in suffering persecutions the *Anabaptists* run before all other heretics. If you will have regard to their number it is like that in multitude. They would swarm above all others if they were not grievously plagued and cut off with the knife of persecution. If you have an eye to outward appearance of godliness, both the Lutherans and Zwinglians must grant that they *far surpass them*. If you will be moved by the boasting of the word of God, those be not less bold than Calvin to preach, and their doctrine must stand above all the glory of the world; must stand invincible above all power, because it is not their word, but the word of the living God. Neither do they cry less boldly than Luther that with their doctrine they shall judge angels, and surely, however, so many have written against this heresy whether they were Catholics or heretics or reformers, they were able to everthrow it, not so much by the testimony of Scripture as by the authority of the church."[1] Hossius farther says: "If the truth of religion were to be judged of by the readiness and cheerfulness which a man of any sect shows in suffering, then the opinion and persuasion of no sect can be truer and surer than that of the Anabaptists, since there have been none, *for these twelve hundred years past*, that have been more generally punished, or that have more steadfastly undergone, and even offered themselves to the most cruel sorts of punishment than these people. . . . The Anabaptists are a pernicious sect, of which *kind the Waldensian brethren seem to have been. Nor is this heresy a modern thing, for it existed in the time of Austin.*"[2] Thus this great Romanish scholar concedes the sameness of the Waldenses and Anabaptists, and that they already existed in 354, the time of Austin.

The Romish Bishop Baltes, of Alton, Ill., indirectly concedes the apostolic descent of the Baptists, when he thus concedes he cannot find any human head for them: "If you go to the dictionaries of religion you will find the name of the founder of every *other* denomination than the Catholic. The only objection I have met with as to this proposition is a *Baptist;* he contended that you could not find any one who founded the Baptist denomination." The Bishop did not so much as venture to deny this statement.[3]

Hase: "The Waldenses were reduced in numbers because they had been burned by their persecutors, but some congregations *still remained* in the south of France

---

[1] Hatchett's Heresies, translated by R. Shacklock, vol. 48, edition of 1565, Underhill, pp. 88-89.
[2] Ree's Reply to Wall, p. 20—in Trilemma, p. 132.
[3] In the *Globe-Democrat* of 1878; see also Chapter VI for other Romish testimony.

and in the secluded valleys of Piedmont. . . . In the commencement of the fifteenth century heretical congregations of almost every kind were scattered and broken up. But it was only in secret that those forms of opposition were maintained or organized *which in the sixteenth century came forward under the name of Anabaptists.*" [1]

As explanatory, says Armitage: "A word here may be necessary as to the proper naming of this interesting people; were they Baptists or Anabaptists? They are commonly characterized as 'Anabaptists' by friends and foes; yet this name was especially offensive to them, as it charged them with *re*-baptizing those whom they regarded as unbaptized and because it was intended as a stigma. By custom their most friendly historians call them 'Anabaptists,' yet many of their candid historians speak of them as 'Baptists.' The Petrobrussians complained that Peter of Clugny 'slandered' them by calling them 'Anabaptists,' so did their Swiss and German brethren after them. The London Confession, 1646, protests that the English Baptists were 'commonly, though unjustly, called Anabaptists.'" [2]

Mosheim: "The true *origin* of that sect which required the denomination of Anabaptists, by their administering anew the rite of baptism to those who came over to their communion . . . is *hid* in the *remote depths of antiquity*, and is, of consequence, extremely difficult to be ascertained. This uncertainty will not appear surprising when it is considered that this sect started up all of a *sudden in several countries at the same point of time*, under leaders of different talents and different intentions, and at the very period when the first contest of the reform-

---

[1] Hase's Hist. Chr. Ch., pp. 342-343.
[2] Armitage's Hist. Bap., p. 327.

310   CHURCH PERPETUITY.

ers with the Roman pontiffs drew the attention of the world. . . . It may be observed . . . that the Mennonites are not entirely mistaken when they boast of their descent from the *Waldenses, Petrobrussians and other sects*, who are usually considered as *witnesses of the truth* in the times of universal darkness and superstition. *Before* the rise of Luther and Calvin there lay concealed in almost all the countries of Europe, particularly in Bohemia, Moravia, Switzerland and Germany, *many* persons who adhered tenaciously to the following doctrine which the Waldenses, Wickliffites and Hussites had maintained, some in a more disguised, and others in a more open and public manner, viz: that the kingdom of Christ or the visible church was an assembly of real *saints* and ought, therefore, to be inaccessible to the wicked and unrighteous, and also exempt from all those institutions which *human* prudence suggests, to oppose the progress of iniquity, or to correct and reform transgressors. *This maxim is the true source* of all the peculiarities that are to be found in the religious doctrine and discipline of the Mennonites; and it is most certain that the greatest part of these peculiarities were approved by many of those, who, *before* the dawn of reformation, entertained the notion already mentioned relating to the visible church of Christ. . . . The drooping spirits of these people who had been dispersed through many countries and persecuted everywhere with the greatest severity, were *revived* when they were informed that Luther, seconded by several persons of eminent piety, had successfully attempted the reformation of the church."[1]

Jones quotes a part of this from perhaps a better rendering. Maclaine, translator of the edition from which

---

[1] Mosheim's Eccl. Hist., cent. 16, sec. 3, chaps. 3, 1-2.

I quote, says he has "sometimes taken considerable liberties with my author," thus: "Before the rise of Luther and Calvin there lay concealed, in almost all the countries of Europe, persons who held tenaciously to the principles of the modern Dutch *Baptists*." [1]

"Religions of the World," by fifteen eminent scholars, whose names are given, all, or near all, being Pedobaptists and Romanists, published by Gay Bros. Co., 14 Barclay street, New York, 1884, says: "Baptists claim a *higher* antiquity than the eventful era of the Reformation. They offer *proof* in that their views of the church and the ordinances may be traced through the Paterines, the Waldenses, the Albigenses, the Vaudoise, the Cathari, and the Poor Men of Lyons, the Paulicians, the Donatists, the Novatians, to the Messahians, the Montanists and the Euchites of the second and closing part of the first century to the Apostles and the churches they founded. . . . *Their claim to this high antiquity it would seem is well founded, for historians, not Baptists, and who could have no motive except fidelity to facts, concede it.*" [2]

Samuel Schmucker says of the Baptists: "As a sect they never existed . . . until the rise of Peter Waldo in the *twelfth century* who established† the sect of the Waldenses among the mountains of Piedmont. One of the most prominent doctrines of him and his followers was the impropriety of the baptism of infants and necessity of immersion to the validity of baptism." [3]

The Athenian Society, of England, over two hundred years ago, and made up wholly of Pedobaptists, a Society pronounced equal to the famous Royal Society of which it

---

† This links the Baptists to the Waldensis. In Chapter XXII we have proved the Waldenses have a continuity from Apostolic times.
1 Jones' Ch. Hist., p. 358.
2 Pages 405-406.
3 Schmuchers' Hist. of All Religions, pp. 36-38.

is said: "All the endeavors of great men, of all nations and ages, from the beginning of learning till this time, have not contributed so much to the increase of learning as the Athenian Society." They commenced previous to 1790 a weekly periodical, called the Anthenian Gazette which name was subsequently changed to the Athenian Oracle. This work was conducted by a committee of twelve of their most competent men, selected from the learned professions. Their volumes are quoted with confidence as authorities by Hannah Adams and other distinguished writers. In 1691 this society was thrown into controversity with the Baptists, respecting the antiquity of their church, and they affirmed that "there never was a separate and distinct congregation of Baptists until about *three hundred years after our Savior*."[1]

Let it not be forgotten that I have proved the Waldenses did not originate with Waldo, and that when Baptist churches are conceded to have existed as early as A. D. 300 and since that, the side of Baptist opponents is virtually surrendered.

The "New Royal Encyclopedia," edited by Wm. Hall, with other learned men of London, begun in 1788 and completed in three volumes, says in its article, "Anabaptists." "It is to be remembered that the Baptists or Mennonites in England and Holland are to be considered in a very different light from the enthusiasts we have been describing; and it appears equally uncandid and invidious to trace their distinguished sentiments, as some of their adversaries have done, to those obnoxious characters and then to stop in order as it were, to associate them with the idea of tubulence and fanaticism, with which it certainly has no natural connection. Their connection with some of those oppressed and infatuated

[1] Supplement to Ath. Ora., vol. 4, p. 161—in Howell on Com., p. 255.

people in denying baptism to infants, is acknowledged by the Baptists, but they disavow the practice which the appelation of Anabaptist implies; and their doctrines seem referable to a *more ancient origin*. They appear to be *supported by history* in considering themselves the descendants of the *Waldenses*, who were so grievously oppressed and persecuted by the despotic heads of the Romish hierarchy." [1]

Sir Isaac Newton: "The modern *Baptists* formerly called Anabaptists are the only people that *never* symbolized with the papacy." [2]

In his debate with Bishop Purcell, Campbell said: "Every sect and individual is *passive* in receiving a name. . . . . The disciples of Christ are the same race, call them Christians, Nazarenes, Gallileans, Novatians, Donatists, Paulicians, Waldenses, Albigenses, Protestants or what you please. *A variety* of designations affects not the fact which we allege; we can find an unbroken series of Protestants—a regular succession of those who protested against the corruptions of the Romish church and endeavored to hold fast the faith once delivered to the saints from the first schism in the year 250, A. D., to the present day; you may apply to them what description or designation you please." [3]

Again: "The Baptist *denomination* † *in all ages and all* countries has been, as a body, the constant asserters of the rights of man and the liberty of conscience. They have often been persecuted by Pedobaptists; but they never politically persecuted, though they have had it in their power." [4]

† Notice that Mr. Campbell is not here speaking of only "principles and practices," but he is speaking of organized churches—"*denomination.*"
[1] In Trilemma, p. 137.
[2] Life of Whiston.
[3] *Quoted*, from p. 77.
[4] *Quoted*, from A. Campbell on Baptism, p. 449, "Copyrighted, 1851."

Mr. Burnett, one of the most ardent Campbellite editors, says: "The *Baptists have connection with the Apostles through their line of succession,* which extends back three hundred and fifty years, where it *connects* with the Waldensian line, and *that reaches to the apostolic day*. This is not a Baptist line but the Baptists have connection with this line, and through it have connection with the Apostles. We were talking about successional connection. Baptists also have connection with the Apostles in what they teach and practice."[1]

Challenging one of his own brethren, Mr. Burnett — on the position that if the Baptists are not from apostolic times—says: " But he should march right up to the difficulty and show us where the church was seventy-five years ago."[2] †

Though these testimonies can easily be multiplied, I deem it amply enough to conclude them with the testimony of Drs. Dermout and Ypeij. Says Dr. William R. Williams: "Ypeij held an ecclesiastical professorship and was a voluminous author on historical themes, and his various works are yet largely cited. Dermout, his associate in the history, was a Reformed church preacher at the Hague . . . the Hague being the city of the royal residence. Sepp, . . . a scholar of reputation, in his essay—which in 1860 obtained the prize of the Teyler Society—on the theologians of Holland from the close of the eighteenth to the middle of the nineteenth century rates Dermout among the most powerful of the

---

† To the Campbellite attempt to evade the force of this, by saying: "But Brother Burnett meant that the Hard Shell Baptists have the succession and the missionaries are a young sprout from them." I leave the chapter in this book on who are the Old Baptists as sufficient reply. If Mr. Burnett or any of the Campbellites are sincere in saying that the Anti-mission Baptists are the successors of the Apostles *why don't they join them?*

[1] Christian Messenger, Dec. 8, 1886.
[2] Christian Messenger, March 9, 1887.

nation's preachers in his own age. . . . C. M. Van Der Kemp," another German scholar, " describes . . . Ypeij as professor of theology in connection with the Reformed Church in a distinguished university in our land," and Dermout, as "by his position the regular teacher in one of our most distinguished churches, court chaplain to His Majesty, and secretary and permanent member of the Supreme Reformed Church Synod." Sepp says: " Borger, one of Holland's most brilliant scholars, ... was accustomed to rate Dermout, as being above even Van der Palm, who as a scholar, writer and preacher, has won a reputation, not only pervading Holland, but reaching Great Britain and our own country also." With the archives of Europe before them, Drs. Ypeij and Dermout wrote: " Gerchied de Nederl, Hervormde Kerk," in which they say: "We have already seen that the Baptists—those who in former times were named Anabaptists, and in later times Mennonites— were *originally Waldenses*, the men who in the history of the church, in time *so far back*, have obtained a well-deserved renown. In consequence, the *Baptists* may be regarded as being from of old the *only* religious denomination that have continued from the *times of the Apostles*, as a Christian society who have *kept* the evangelical faith pure through *all the ages hitherto*.

The constitution, *never* perverted internally or externally, of the society of the Baptists, serves them as a *proof* of that truth, contested by the Romish church, that the reformation of religion, such as was brought about in the sixteenth century, was necessary, was indispensable, and serves, too, as the refutation, at the same time, of the Roman Catholic *delusive fancy*, that their own is the oldest church society."[1] The title of this work in English

[1] In Dr. William R. Williams' Lect. on Bap. Hist., pp. 172-173

is: "History of the Reformed Church of the Netherlands." It was published 1819, at Breda.

If history can demonstrate anything this chapter has demonstrated that the Anabaptists of the sixteenth century are the successors of the Waldenses — are the genuine Waldenses.

We have now seen that through the Montanists, the Novatians, the Donatists, the Paulicians, the Albigenses, the Cathari, the Arnoldists, the Petrobrussians, the Henricians and the Waldenses—all essentially identical—the Anabaptists, or Baptists of the sixteenth century have a Church Perpetuity to the church of the first century.

In the language of Dr. Armitage, as his noble soul arose above his antipathy to Church Perpetuity: "*Let us at least respect our ancestry enough to join the latest and best continental writers in calling them Baptists.*" [1]

In succeeding chapters what little grounds to doubt the Baptists of to-day being the Anabaptists of Reformation times is removed.

---

[1] Armitage's Hist. Bap., p. 328.

CHAPTER XXIII.

BAPTIST CHURCHES IN ENGLAND LONG BEFORE, UP TO AND AT THE TIME OF JOHN SMYTH.

Rev. Francis Thackeray, A. M., formerly of Benbrooke College, Cambridge, from his Researches Into the Ecclesiastical and the Political State of Great Britain, is quoted: "We have reason to believe that Christianity was preached in both countries, Gaul and Britain, before the close of the first century. The result of my investigations on my own mind has been the conviction that about 60, A. D., in the time of St. Paul, a church existed in Britain." There are authorities of great weight who maintain that the gospel was introduced at an earlier period than the one mentioned by Mr. Thackeray. As Christianity was certainly introduced very early into Britain, so far as the perpetuity question is concerned, the exact date is immaterial. Inasmuch as Baptists understand that the first churches were Baptist churches, to stop to prove to them that the first churches in Britain were Baptist churches, is unnecessary. Immersion continued in England, as Dr. Wall informs us, until the Reformation period, except in sickness, and this at a late day exception.

Of A. D. 627, Bede says, describing baptism: "He washed them with the water of absolution *in the river* Glen."[1]

"He baptized *in the river* Swale, which runs by the village cataract; for as yet oratories or fonts could not be

---

[1] Bede's Eccl. Hist., book 2, chap. 14.

made in the early infancy of the church in these parts."[1] "A man of singular veracity informed him that he himself had been baptized at noon day . . . in the presence of King Edwin, with a great number of people, *in the river* Trent."[2]

Bede says: "The Britains preserved the faith which they had received *uncorrupted and entire* in peace and tranquility until the time of the Emperor Diocletian." Diocletian died A. D. 313.[3]

Of this persecution Bede says: "When the storm of persecution ceased the faithful Christians, who, during the time of danger, had hidden themselves in woods and deserts and secret caves, appearing in public, rebuilt the churches which had been leveled to the ground, etc."[4]

There is no record of Baptists having ever become non-existant in England. *The earliest dawn of the Reformation finds Baptists in England.* Of the beginning of the eleventh century in England, Crosby says: "Though the baptism of infants seems now to be pretty well established in this realm, yet the practice of immersion continued many years longer; and there were not persons wanting to oppose *infant baptism*. For in the time of William the Conqueror and his son William Rufus, it appears that the *Waldenses* and their disciples, out of France, Germany and Holland had their frequent recourse and residence, and did *abound in England*. Mr. Danvers cites Bishop Usher, who, he says, tells us, ' that the Berengarian or *Waldensian* heresy, as the chronologer calls it, had about that time, viz., A. D. 1080, *generally* corrupted all France, Italy and England. And further,

---

[1] Bede's Eccl. Hist., book 2, chap. 14.
[2] Idem, chap. 16.
[3] Idem, book 1, chap. 4.
[4] Idem, chap. 8.

the said bishop tells us, out of Guitmond, a popish writer of that time, that not only the meaner sort of the country villages, but the *nobility and gentry* in the chiefest towns and cities were infested therewith; and therefore doth Lanfrank, who was Archbishop of Canterbury, in the time of both these kings, about the year 1087, write a book against them.'

"In the time of Henry I. and King Stephen the said Bishop Usher tells us, out of Popliner's History of France, that the Waldenses of Acquiain did, about the year 1100, spread themselves and their doctrines all Europe over, whereof he mentions England in particular. About the year 1158, there came about thirty persons of the Waldensian sect over into England and endeavored to disseminate their doctrines here: these are supposed to *reject infant baptism;* the two chief of them were Gerburdus and Dulcinus. . . . Mr. Danvers cites Rodger Hovedon, who, in his annals upon the year 1182, saith: 'That Henry the II. was then favorable to the Waldensian sect in England; for, whereas, they burnt them in some places of France, Italy and Flanders by great numbers, he would not in the least suffer any such thing here, he being in his own wives' right possessed of Aquina, Poictou, Guien, Gascoyn, Normandy, etc., the principle places which the Waldenses and Albigenses inhabited, and who, being his subjects in France, had the freer egress into his territories here.' In the time of Richard I. and King John we read of no opposition made against them. . . . In the time of Henry III., about the year 1235, as saith Bishop Usher, out of Matth., Paris, 'the orders of the Friers Minorites came into England to suppress the Waldensian heresy.' In the time of King Edward the II., about the year 1315, Walter Lollard, a German preacher, a man of great renown among the *Waldenses,* came into England. He spread their doctrines very much in these parts, so that afterwards they went by the name of Lollards."[1]

Fuller: "By Lollards, all know the Wickliffites are meant; so that from Walter Lollardus, one of their teachers in Germany . . . and flourishing many years before Wickliffe, and much consenting with him in agreement."[2]

Fuller points[3] out sixty-two differences between Wickliffe's views and Romanism. No less than eighteen of them distinguish Baptists from Methodism, Campbellism and other forms of Arminianism; while several of them distinguish Baptists from Presbyterianism. I have room for only the following: (1.) "Those are heretics who say that Peter had more power than the rest of the Apostles." (9.) "The pope is *'anti-Christ.'*" (12.) "*Bishop's* benedictions, confirmations, consecration of churches, chalices, etc., be but tricks to get money." (14.) "That in the times of the Apostles there were *only two* orders, namely, priests and deacons. That a bishop doth not differ from a priest." (18.) "He defined a church to consist *only of persons predestinated.*" (26.) "That general councils, etc., have no authority." (28.) "That men are not bound by vigils or canonical hours." (30.) "That to bind men to set and prescript forms of prayers doth derogate from that liberty God hath given them." (31.) "That chrism and such other ceremonies are not to be used in baptism." (34.) "That those are *fools* who affirm that infants cannot be saved without baptism; and also that he *denied that all sins are abolished in baptism.* That baptism doth *not confer,*

[1] Crosby's Hist. Eng. Bap., vol. 2, pp. 43-46—of preface.
[2] Fuller's Ch. Hist. Great Britain, cent. 15, book 4, secs. 17-18.
[3] Idem, cent. 14, book 4, sec. 6.

but *only signifies* grace, which *was* given *before.*"
(43) "That religious sects *confound the unity* of Christ's church who instituted *but one order of things.*"
(44.) "That he denied all sacred initiation into orders as leave no character behind them." (56.) "That God loved Peter and David *as dearly* when they grievously sinned as he doth now when they are possessed of glory." (59.) "That all things come to pass by fatal necessity"—*a misrepresentation of the Bible doctrine of election as held by the Wickliffites*, which Arminians now make against Baptists. Looking over these thirteen charges of heresy against Wickliffe we find numbers 9, 12 and 14 are condemnations of every form of episcopacy; that 26 condemns Methodist, Episcopalian, Presbyterian and other ecclesiastically legislative bodies; that 34 condemns infant baptism and water salvation; that 56 affirms the final preservation of saints; that 59 and 18 teach election, etc.; that 18 teaches a church is made of only the professedly regenerate; and that 43 teaches that God is not the originator of different denominations, but that He has *but one* church. No one acquainted with Baptist views needs to be informed that these are *distinctively Baptist principles*.

As to the action of baptism, Wickliffe was certainly a Baptist.

Says Armitage: "He always retains the preposition 'in' and *never with* '*in* water,' '*in* Jordan.'"[1]

Says Armitage: "Froude finds a resemblance between some of Wickliff's views, and others have claimed him as a *Baptist*."[2]

William R. Williams, says: "Rastell, one of the judges of England in the days of Queen Mary, has pre-

[1] Armitage's Hist. Bap., p. 316.
[2] Idem, p. 315.

served in his Entrees *legal documents*, coming down, some of them, from his grand-father, Sir John More, a justice of the King's Bench, and father of the illustrious chancellor, Sir Thomas More. In this volume, Rastell has preserved a Latin writ, sending over to the bishop for judgment, according to the canon law, three several groups of Lollards who *all rejected infant baptism*. . . . One who had personally known Wickliffe and sympathized with early Lollardism in England, but afterwards left that communion, gave as the reason, that among other errors the Lollard followers of the Great Reformer at Lutterworth *rejected the baptism of infants.*"[1] Of early English and other Baptists: "*They were the inheritors* of the labors of Huss and Jerome, of British Lollards, of Wickliffe and Waldo, and laborers yet earlier than these, whose memories and whose rewards are safe with God whom they meekly and faithfully served, and then went down unrecorded by their followers to a forgotten or a dishonored grave."[2]

Whether Wickliffe was a full fledged Baptist may be a little doubtful; but that he inherited the doctrine and the life of previous and contemporaneous Baptists, and gave them a great movement forward is clear, filling England with Baptist views and true Baptists. As Neal remarks: "If Wickliffe himself did not pursue the *consequence* of his own doctrine so far, yet *many of his followers did, and were made Baptists by it.* . . . *All* our historians *agree* in affirming that the doctrine of Wickliffe spread *very extensively* throughout the country; inasmuch that according to Knighton, a contemporary historian, '*more than half the people of England embraced*

---

[1] Lect. on Bap. Hist., by William R. Williams, pp. 126-127
[2] Idem, pp. 145-146.

them and became his followers.' "[1] This is almost the equivalent to saying "more than half the people of England," following Wickliffe's teachings to the consequences, became Baptist churches.

"That the denial of the *rite of infants to baptism* was a principle generally maintained among the Lollards or followers of Wickliffe, is *abundantly confirmed by the historians of those times.* Thomas Walden, who wrote against Wickliffe, terms this reformer 'one of several heads who arose out of the bottomless pit *for denying infant baptism*, that heresies of the Lollards of whom he was the ringleader.' "[2]

Neal shows how Wickliffe received his doctrine by succession from the Baptists before him: "Walsingham, another writer says, 'it was in the year 1381 that the damnable heretic, John Wickliffe, received the cursed opinions of *Berengarius*,' one of which unquestionably was the *denial of infant baptism.*"[2]

Collier says that in 1538: "Some few who were Dutch *Baptists*—three men and a woman—had faggots tied to their backs at Pauls' Cross; and one woman and one man of the same sect were burnt at Smithfield. Cranmer . . . with some others, had a commission from the king to try some Anabaptists; which by comparing the dates of the commission with that of the execution we may conclude the trial passed upon the persons above mentioned."[3] Of this same commission, Collier says: "They had likewise an authority to seize all *Anabaptist* books, to forbid the reading of them, to burn and destroy them as they thought fit."[4]

[1] Neal's Hist. Pur , vol. 2, p. 253.
[2] Idem, p. 354.
[3] Collier's Eccl. Hist. Great Britain, vol. 4, p. 429.
[4] Idem, vol. 9, p. 162.

May, 1575: "On Easter day . . . a conventicle of Dutch Baptists was discovered at a house without the bars at Oldgate. Twenty-seven of them were seized and committed."[1]

Bishop Thomas Vowler Short says, that in 1549 "Complaints had been brought to the council of the prevalence of Anabaptists. . . . To check the progress of these opinions a commission was appointed."[2]

Of the Baptists in England, Cramp says: "Ten were burned by pairs in different places in 1535, and fourteen more in 1536. In 1538, six Dutch Baptists were detected and imprisoned; two of them were burned. Bishop Latimer refers to these circumstances in a sermon preached before Edward the VI., in the year 1549. 'The Anabaptists,' said he, 'that were burnt here in divers towns in England—as I heard of credible men, I saw them not myself—went to their death even intrepid, as you will say, without any fear in the world, cheerfully. Well, let them go.'"[3]

"There is some reason to believe that a Baptist church existed in Cheshire at a much earlier period. If we may credit the traditions of the place, the church at Hill Cliffe is five hundred years old. A tombstone has been lately dug up in that burial ground, belonging to that church, bearing date 1357. The origin of the church is assigned in the '*Baptist Manual*' to the year 1523. This, however, is *certain* that Mr. Warburton, *pastor of the church died there in 1594.* How long the church had *then been in existence*, there are no written records to testify."[4] "Henry the VIII had a keen scent for

---

[1] Collier's Eccl. Hist. Great Britain, vol. 6, p. 543.
[2] Bishop Vowler Short's Hist. Ch. of Eng., p. 92.
[3] Bishop Latimer's Ser., p. 160, in Cramps' Bap. Hist., p. 232.
[4] Cramp's Bap. Hist., p. 232.

heresy." He continued the bitter persecution against the Baptists. "The hatred to Baptists was farther shown in excepting them from the general acts of pardon. Such acts were published in 1538, 1540 and 1550, but those who held that 'infants ought not to be baptized' were excluded from the benefit. Thieves and vagabonds shared the king's favor, but Baptists were not to be tolerated. . . . Among the 'Articles of Visitation' issued by Ridley in his own diocese, in 1550, was the following: 'Whether any of the Anabaptist sect, or other, use notoriously any unlawful or private conventicles, *wherein they use the doctrines of the administration of sacraments*,† separating themselves from the rest of the parish.'" [1]

Quoting from Cardwell's Documentary Annals of the Church of England, vol. 1, p. 91: "A royal commission was issued by Edward the VI, empowering thirty-one persons therein named, Cranmer at the head and Latimer as one of its members, to proceed against all heretics and condemners of the Book of Common Prayer. The 'wicked opinions' of the *Baptists* are specifically mentioned." [2] "But they could not put down the Baptists, who grew and flourished in spite of them. Congregations were discovered in Essex, at Feversham, in Kent, and other places. . . . *They met regularly for worship and instruction; the ordinances of the gospel were attended to*,† contributions were made for the support of the cause, and so great was their zeal that those who lived in Kent were known to go, occasionally, into Essex to meet the brethren there—a journey of four score miles, which in the six-

---

† This shows they were not Baptists in only "sentiment" or "principle," but that they were Baptists organized into Baptist churches.
[1] Cramp's Bap. Hist., pp. 232-234.
[2] Idem, p. 235.

teenth century was no small undertaking. . . . *This, however, is clear, that they were Anabaptists.*" "There were *many Baptists* among the sufferers in Queen Mary's reign. Some endured painful imprisonments, and some passed to heaven through the fire."[1]

Under Queen Elizabeth, "Bishop Jewell . . . . writing to Peter Martyr, under date of November 6, 1560, said: 'We found at the *beginning* of the reign of Elizabeth a *large and auspicious corps* . . . of Anabaptists, . . . which I know not how, but as mushrooms spring up.' *Many* Baptists continued to elude the proclamation, to depart from the country. 'Persons holding these views were *still* in the realm. And they *continued* to seek shelter in England from persecution, but the Queen and her minions were indefatigable in their attempts to ferret them out and drive them away. . . . . . Permitted or not, however, they were *there* and they were neither *idle nor unsuccessful.*' Collier, the ecclesiastical historian, says: 'The Dutch Anabaptists held private conventicles in London, and perverted a great many.' "[2]

In the ancient town of Leicester, England, in the upper part of an old town hall, is a library in which are some very ancient works. Several years ago was discovered a MS. against the Baptists, on the title page of which is: "Imprinted at London, by G. B. Deputie to Christopher Barker, printer to the Queen's most excellent majesty, 1589." It reads: "The Anabaptistical sect were very bold of late. They pressed into her majesty's presence; they complained to her highness of great persecution—how justly your lordship knows—

[1] Cramp's Bap. Hist., p. 242.
[2] Idem, p. 248.

which by the queen's commandment did examine and commit them."—Robert Some.

Says Benedict, quoting Jones: "Towards the middle of the *twelfth* century, a small society of these Puritans, as they were called by some, or *Waldenses*, as they were termed by others, or *Paulicians*, as they are denominated by an old monkish historian—William of Newbury—made their appearance in England. This latter writer speaking of them, says: 'They came originally from Gascoyne, where being as *numerous as the sand of the sea*, they sorely infested all France, Italy, Spain and England.'"[1] On the page whence this quotation is made, Benedict puts these down as "Baptists." In former articles I have demonstrated them Baptists. Ivimey says: "The archbishop farther informs us, on the authority of Matthew Paris, of Westminster, that 'the Berengarian or *Waldensian* heresy had, about the year 1180, *generally* infected all France, Italy and *England*.' Guitmond, a popish writer of that time, also says that, 'not only the weaker sort of the country villages, but the *nobility and gentry* in the chief towns and cities were infected therewith; and therefore Lanfranc, archbishop of Canterbury, who held this seat, both in the reigns of William the Conqueror, and his son, William Rufus, wrote against them in the year 1087.' The archbishop adds from Poplinus' history of France, that 'the *Waldenses* of Aquitain did about the year 1100, during their reign of Henry I, and Stephen, kings of England, spread themselves and their doctrines all over Europe,' and mentions England in *particular*."[2] Says the Schaff-Herzog Encyclopedia: "During the reigns of

---

[1] Benedict's Hist. Bap., p. 305.
[2] Ivimey's Hist. Eng. Bap., vol. 1, p. 55.

Elizabeth and James, a large number of Baptists fled from Holland and Germany, to England."[1]

Says the Penny Encyclopedia: "Little is known of the Baptists in England *before* the sixteenth century. Their name *then appears* among the various sects which were struggling for civil and religious freedom. Their opinions at *this early period* were sufficiently popular to attract the notice of the *national* establishment, as is evident from the fact that at a convocation, held in 1536, they were denounced as detestable heretics, to be utterly condemned. Proclamations allowed to banish the *Baptists* from the kingdom, their books were burnt, and several individuals suffered at the stake. *The last person who was burnt in England was a Baptist.*"[2] Of the times *before* John Smyth, Froude says of the English Baptists: "History has for them no word of praise; yet they were not giving their blood in vain. . . . In their deaths they assisted to pay the purchase money of England's freedom."[3] "On them the laws of the country might take their natural course and no voice was raised to speak for them."[4]

Says Dr. John Clifford: "The Waldenses, some of whom held *Baptist* views, *abounded in England*, in the days of William the Conqueror, and bishop Lanfranc wrote against the heretics, in 1087. It is *likely* that a church formed on Baptist lines existed at Hill Cliffe, a mile and a half from Warrington, as early as 1357, and it is *certain* that John Wickliffe, who was born in 1324 and died in 1384, was not far from the Baptist faith, while it is notorious that *many* of the Lollards held and practiced it

[1] Schaff-Herzog Ency., vol. 1, p. 211.
[2] Vol. 3, pp. 416-417.
[3] Froude's Hist. Eng., vol. 2, p. 359.
[4] Idem, p. 358.

with great daring and burning zeal. . . . A large accession of force actually found living expression in a few *Baptist* societies in the *fourteenth*, fifteenth and sixteenth centuries, as at Hill Cliffe, in Cheshire; Boking, in Essex; Feversham and Eyethorne, in Kent; and Epworth and Crowle, in Axholme. But the times were not favorable to the organizing of these . . . churches into a compact, coherent, and aggressive unity; nor yet to the creation of any means by which they might *report* their existence and doings to subsequent generations. Even in the days of Elizabeth, to be a *Baptist was to be a criminal*. The hour had not yet dawned for the emancipation of the human conscience. But it was coming; and the persecuted Baptist was permitted to take a *momentous* part in ushering in the sublime hour in the history and progress of the human race." [1]

"At Crowle, in Lincolnshire, a few miles from Gainesborough, there was, according to an old church book, a Baptist society as early as 1599. To that rural community, Smyth went in 1604, and 'debated nearly all night with Elders Henry Hiliwise and John Morton, who defended our cause.'" [2] Barclay, in his comprehensive account of the Inner Life of Religious Societies of the Commonwealth, declares (p. 12): "We have strong reasons for believing that on the continent of Europe, small *hidden* societies, who have held many of the opinions of the *Anabaptists, have existed from the time of the Apostles*. In the sense of the direct transmission of divine truth and the true nature of spiritual religion, it seems probable that these churches have a *lineage or succession, more ancient than the Roman church*." [3] Even

---

[1] The Origin and growth of Eng. Bap., by Dr. John Clifford, pp. 6-8.
[2] Idem, pp. 15-16.
[3] Idem, p. 9—of "Notes."

Vedder—a bitterly prejudiced opponent to succession—is driven to concede: "We are entitled to affirm with regard to Baptists in England . . . that *traces* of them appear in *historical* documents *early* in the sixteenth century."[1]

The late C. H. Spurgeon, in Ford's Christian Repository, years ago, said: We care very little for the 'historical church' argument, but if there be anything in it at all, *it ought not to be filched by the clients of Rome*, but should be left to that community, which *all along* held by 'one Lord, one faith and one baptism.' . . . The afflicted Anabaptists, in their past history, have had such fellowship with their suffering Lord, and have borne such pure testimony, both to truth and freedom, that they need in nothing be ashamed. . . . It would not be *impossible* to show that the first Christians who dwelt in the land were of the same faith and order as the churches now called Baptists. . . . The rampant ritualist, W. J. E. Bennett, of Frome, in his book upon 'The Unity of the Church Broken,' says: 'The historian Lingard tells us there was a sect of fanatics who infested the north of Germany, called Puritans; Usher calls them *Waldenses;* Spelman, *Paulicians* (the same as Waldenses). They gained ground and spread over *all England;* they rejected all Romish ceremonies, denied the authority of the pope, and more particularly refused to baptize infants. Thirty of them were put to death for their heretical doctrines near Oxford; but the remainder still held on to their opinions in private until the time of Henry the II., 1550; and the historian, Collier, tells us that wherever the heresy prevailed, the churches were either scandalously neglected or pulled down and infants left unbap-

---

[1] A short Hist. of Bap., p. 108.

tized.' We are obliged to Mr. Bennett for this history, which is in all respects authentic, and we take the liberty to remark upon it, that the reign of Henry the II. is a period far more worthy of being called remote than the reign of Henry the VIII. and if Baptists could trace their pedigree no further, the church of Thomas Cranmer could not afford to sneer at them as a modern sect. . . . *All along* our history from Henry II. to Henry VIII. there are *traces* of the Anabaptists, who are usually mentioned *in connection with the Lollards*, or as coming from *Holland*. . . . *All along* there must have been a *great hive* on the Continent of these 'reformers *before* the Reformation,' for despite their being doomed to die almost as soon as they landed, they continued to invade this country to the annoyance of the priesthood and the hierarchy. . . . During the Reformation, and after it, the poor Anabaptists continued to be the victims. . . . The only stint allowed to persecution in the lower countries was contained in a letter to the Queen, Dowager Mary of Hungary, ' care being only taken that the provinces were not entirely depopulated.' . . . Latimer, who could not speak too badly of the Baptists, nevertheless bears witness to their *numbers* and intrepidity. Here I will tell you what I have heard of late, by the relation of a credible person and a worshipfv man, of a town in this realm of England, that hath *above five hundred heretics of this erroneous opinion in it*. . . . Bishop Burnett says that in the time of Edward the VI. Baptists became *very numerous*, and *openly* preached their doctrines, that ' children are Christ's without water.' . . . Among the 'Articles of Visitation,' issued by Ridley in his own diocese in 1550, was the following: 'Whether any of the Anabaptist sect and others use notoriously •any unlawful or private conventicles wherein they do use doctrines or administration of sacraments, separating themselves from the rest of the parish.' It may be fairly gathered from the 'Articles of Visitation' that there were *many Baptist* CHURCHES *in the kingdom at the time.* This is also clear from the fact that the Duke of Northumberland advised that Mr. John Knox should be invited to England and made a bishop, that he might aid in putting down the Baptists in Kent. "Marsden tells us that in the days of Elizabeth 'the Anabaptists were the most numerous, and, for some time, by far the most formidable opponents of the church. They are said to have existed in England since the days of the Lollards.' In the year 1575 a most severe persecution was raised against the Anabaptists of London, ten of whom were condemned, eight ordered to be banished and two to be executed. . . . Neither from Elizabeth, James or Charles the I. had our brethren any measure of favor. No treatment was thought to be too severe for them; even good men execrated them as heretics for whom the severest measures were too gentle. Had it been possible to destroy this branch of the true vine, assuredly the readiest means were used without hindrance or scruple. Yet it not only lives on, but continues to bear fruit a hundred fold. . . . When Charles the I. was unable any longer to uphold episcopacy, liberty of thought and freedom of speech were somewhat more common than before, and the Baptists increased very rapidly. Many of them were in Cromwell's army. . . . *The time will probably arrive when history will be rewritten.*"

Says Robinson: "I have seen enough to convince me that the present English dissenters, contending for the sufficiency of Scripture, and for primitive Christian liberty to judge of its meaning, may be traced in authentic manuscripts to the Nonconformists, to the Puritans, to the Lollards, to the Vallences, to the Albigenses, and, I suspect, through *the Paulicians and others to the Apostles.*" [1] Thus, an eminent secular historian says that he is convinced of the succession from the apostles of those whom my previous articles have proved were Baptist churches.

Evans: "Dissidents from the popular church in the early ages . . . were found *everywhere*. Men of apostolic life and doctrine contended for the simplicity of the church and the liberty of Christ's flock in the midst of great danger. . . . *The Novatians, the Donatists* and others that followed them are examples. . . . That these early separatists taught doctrines now held by the *Baptists*, might be made to appear from their own works and the statements of their *adversaries*. . . . A *succession* of able and intrepid men taught the same great principles in opposition to a corrupt and affluent State church, and many of these taught those peculiar views of Christian life and doctrine which are *special* to us as Baptists. *Beyond all doubt* such views were inculcated by the *Paulicians, the primitive Waldenses and their brethren*. Over Europe they were scattered and their converts were very numerous *long before* the Reformation." [2]

In 1538, under Henry the VIII., there were so many Baptists as to bring upon themselves the fiercest hatred. [3]

In 1549 "the mild Cranmer, Ridley and others felt as much, nay, more horror struck at an Anabaptist heretic than a dozen papal advocates." "An ecclesiastical com-

[1] Robinson's Claude, vol. 2, p. 53; in Evans' Hist. Early Eng. Bap., vol. 1, p. 1.
[2] Evans' Hist. Early Eng. Bap., vol. 1, pp. 1-2.
[3] Idem, p. 51.

mission in the beginning was issued out for the examination of Anabaptists."[1]

"To stamp the character and principles of these troublers of the commonwealth, the Legislature, closing its session in 1551, exempted the *Baptists* from the pardon which was granted to those who had taken part in the late rebellion."[2] This was in the reign of Edward VI. Not long after this, under the reign of Queen Mary, "Intense as the hatred to the Reformers was, it did not diminish in intensity when it hunted the Anabaptists from their seclusion. Nowhere were they safe. *Spies* everywhere haunted their steps."[3]

Under Queen Elizabeth, in 1557, Bishop Cox wrote that "sectaries are showing themselves mischievous and wicked interpreters. Of this kind are the *Anabaptists*."[4] Dr. Parker in his letter declining the Archbishopric of Canterbury says: "They say that the realm is *full* of *Anabaptists*."[5] This was about 1560. "In the fourth year of her reign a proclamation was issued by the Queen commanding 'the *Anabaptists* and such like heretics which had flocked to the coast towns of England . . . and had *spread* the poison of their sects in England, to depart the realm in twenty days."[6] Of Marsden, Evans says: "One of the latest, and, we are bound to say, one of the calmest and most candid writers on the Puritanic history, says: 'But the *Anabaptists* were the *most numerous*, and for sometime the most formidable opponents of the church. They are said to have existed *in England* since *the days of the Lollards.*'"[4]

[1] Evans' Hist. Early Bap., vol. p. 69.
[2] Idem, p. 79.
[3] Idem, p. 97.
[4] Idem, p. 147.
[5] Idem, p. 148.
[6] Idem, p. 149.

"Dr. Wall . . . seems anxious to persuade his readers that there were no Baptists in England when Henry the VIII. ascended the throne at the commencement of the sixteenth century, A. D. 1511. *But upon that supposition it is not easy to account for the sanguinary statutes which in the early part of this reign were put forth against the Anabaptists.* . . . *If the country did not abound with Baptists at this time why were those severe measures enforced against them?* . . . In 1536 the sect of the Anabaptists is *specified* and condemned. *In fact it is easy to trace the Baptists in England at least a hundred years* prior to the time mentioned by Fuller"— at least to 1438. "In the year 1539 . . . we find certain legal documents promulgated, one of which was" against the "Anabaptists." . . . "From this it appears that the Baptists not only existed in England, but that they were in the habit of availing themselves of the art of printing . . . in the defense of their peculiar and discriminating tenets. . . . Bishop Burnet informs us that at this time," 1547, "there were *many* Baptists in *several parts of England.*" [1]

"It happened on Easter, the third of April, A. D. 1557, that thirty *Anabaptists* of both sexes had assembled together in a house near Alligator . . . for the purpose of mutual exhortation and prayer; but being detected by the neighbors, they were nearly all taken to prison."[2] Quoting an enemy of the Baptists: "For the Dutch Anabaptists held private *conventicles* in London and perverted a great many."[3] Their churches were called "conventicles." "In 1589 the same fact is admitted by Dr. Some in his reply to Barrow, etc. 'He affirms that there were *several* Anabaptist conventicles

[1] Neal's Hist. Pur., vol. 2, pp. 354-355.
[2] Idem, p. 160.
[3] Idem, p. 166.

in London and other places.' They were not Dutchmen, certainly not exclusively so, for he says: 'Some persons of these sentiments have been bred at our universities.' "[1] "A Romish writer charges Elizabeth, in an infamous work, published in 1538, with making the country a place of refuge for . . . *Anabaptists*."[2] Commenting on Dr. Some's words, quoted above, Ivimey says: "It seems then that the Baptists had, at this early period, formed *distinct churches* of persons of their own sentiments, both in London and in different parts of the country."[3] A large ecclesiastical convocation, in 1536, condemns the "Anabaptists."[4] Fuller says of 1538-39: "These Anabaptists, for the main, are but 'Donatists new dipped,' and this year their name first appears in the English chronicles, for I read that four Anabaptists, three men and one woman, all Dutch, bore fagots at Paul's Cross, Nov. 24th, and three days after, a man and a woman of their sect was burned at Smithfield."[5] Of 1575, Fuller says: "Now began the Anabaptists wonderfully to increase in the land. . . . For on Easterday, April 3rd, was disclosed a congregation of Dutch Anabaptists without Aldgate in London."[6] Says Ivimey: "There were some good honest dissenters, who are mentioned as a new sect newly sprung up in Kent, in the year 1552. Of this sect were Joan Boacher, Joan of Kent, who, we are *sure*, was a Baptist. It is highly probable therefore that they were all Baptists of whom Mr. Pierce speaks. If so the churches of Kent can boast of *great antiquity*. . . . It has been already mentioned

---

[1] Neals' Hist. Pur., p. 166.
[2] Idem, p. 167.
[3] Ivimey's Hist. Eng. Bap., vol. 1, p. 108.
[4] Fuller's Ch. Hist. of Britain, cent. 16, book 5, secs. 34-35.
[5] Idem, cent. 16, book 5, sec. 11.
[6] Idem, cent. 16, book 9, secs. 12-13.

that there is traditionary evidence that the general Baptist church of Canterbury has existed 250 years; and that the church of Eyethorn is nearly of as early an origin. In a letter from the present pastor of that church I am informed that 'more than 220 years ago persons of the general Baptist denomination met for the worship of God at Eyethorn.'"[1] As the volume which I quote was written in 1814, this would date the Canterbury church as already existing in 1564 and the Eyethorn church in 1594. Here, existing in Kent, is one church in 1552, the Canterbury in 1564 and the Eyethorn in 1594. How long these three churches existed before we had record of their existence no one can tell. Goadby says: "The church at Eyethorn, Kent, owes its origin to some Dutch Baptists who settled in the country in the time of Henry VIII. . . . According to a long prevalent tradition, ('uninterrupted and uncontradicted, says one authority,') Joan Boucher, or Joan of Kent, was a member of the Baptist church of Eyethorn."[2] "In the Calendar of State Papers, (Domestic Series, 1547-1580,) under date of Oct. 28th, 1552, we have the entry: 'Northumberland, to Sir William Cecil. Wishes the king would appoint Mr. Knox to the Bishopric of Rochester. He would be a whetstone to the archbishop of Canterbury and a confounder of the *Anabaptists* lately sprung up in Kent.' . . . One singular fact, perhaps without a parallel in the history of this ancient General Baptist church at Eyethorn, deserves to be mentioned; the names of the pastors from the close of the sixteenth to the last quarter of the seventeenth century, were John Knott. The first John Knott became the pastor of the Eyethorn church somewhere between *1590* and 1600 and the last

[1] Ivimey's Hist. Eng. Bap. vol. 2, pp. 216-217.
[2] Goadby's Bye Paths to Bap. Hist., p. 23.

John Knott removed to Chatham in 1780."[1] Writing of this, before 1876, Goadby remarks: "It is worthy of record that the church of Christ in this little village continued *more than three hundred years* without a single unfriendly division and with a steadfast adherence to the faith and practice of the Primitive church."[2] This dates it before 1576.

"The Bocking Braintree church-book, still in existence, carries back the authentic records of the church for more than two hundred years, but there is *no question* but the origin of the church itself dates back to the days of Edward VI."—between 1547 and 1648.[3]

Queen Elizabeth reigned from 1558 to 1603. Goadby says: "Tiverton church is said to have existed since the *last years of Queen Elizabeth*."[3]

"We have *reliable* evidence that a Separatist, and probably a Baptist church, has existed for several centuries in a secluded spot of Cheshire, on the borders of Lancashire, about a mile and a half from Warrington. No spot could be better chosen for *concealment* than the site on which this ancient chapel stood. Removed from all public roads, enclosed by a dense wood, affording ready access into two counties, Hill Cliffe was admirably suited for the erection of a 'conventicula illicita,' an illegal conventicle. The ancient chapel built on this spot was so constructed that the surprised worshipers had half a dozen secret ways of escaping from it, and *long* proved a meeting place suited to the varying fortunes of a hated and hunted people. Owing to the many changes inseparable from the eventful history of the church at Hill Cliffe, the earliest records have been lost. But two

[1] Goadby's Bye Paths to Bap. Hist., pp. 24-25.
[2] Idem, p. 26.
[3] Idem, p. 28.

or three facts point to the *very early existence* of the community itself. In 1841 the then old chapel was enlarged and modernized; and in digging for the foundation, a large baptistry of stone, well cemented, was discovered. How long this had been covered up, and at what period it was erected, it is impossible to state; but as some of the tombstones in the graveyard adjoining the chapel were erected in the early part of the sixteenth century, there is some *probability for the tradition* that the chapel itself was built by the Lollards who held *Baptist* opinions. One of the *dates on the tombstones is 1357*, the time when Wickliffe was still a fellow at Merton College, Oxford; but the dates most numerous begin at the period when Europe had just been startled by Luther's valliant onslaught upon the papacy. . . . Many of these tombstones, and especially the oldest, as we can testify from a personal examination, look as clear and as fresh as if they were engraved only a century ago. . . . Hill Cliffe is undoubtedly one of the oldest Baptist churches in England. . . . The *earliest deeds* of the property have been irrecoverably lost, but the extant deeds, which go back considerably over two hundred years, described the property as being 'for the Anabaptists.' "[1]

Of the Hill Cliffe church Rev. D. O. Davis, of Rockdale, England, who attended the Southern Baptist convention in Birmingham, Ala., in 1891, as a representative of the English Baptists, says: "The oldest Baptist church in this country is Hill Cliffe. . . . Tradition declares *that church is 500 years old*. A tombstone was recently discovered in the burial ground of the place bearing date of 1357. In digging the foundation to enlarge the old chapel *a large baptistry* was discovered which was

Goadby's Bye Paths to Bap. Hist., pp. 22-23.

made of stone and well cemented. The baptistry must have belonged to a previous chapel. Oliver Cromwell worshiped in this church. It is one of the *pre-historic* churches, and a *regular Baptist church*."[1]

Of Henry VIII, from 1509–1547, Goadby says: "Bitterly as he hated the Papist party . . . he revealed a still more bitter hatred for all *Baptists*, English and Continental." He gave them ten days to leave England, burnt them and issued a fourth proclamation "appointing Cranmer and eight others to make diligent search for Anabaptist men, books and letters."[2]

Under this, Goadby says: "Like the Israelites in Egypt, 'the more they were afflicted the more they multiplied and grew.'"[3] Under the reign of Edward VI, 1537–1548, Goadby says that in spite of their persecutions "their numbers increased." Strype tells us that "their opinions were believed by honest meaning people;" and another writer affirms that the articles of religion issued just before the king's death "were principally designed to vindicate the English Reformation from the slur and disgrace which the Anabaptists' tenets had brought upon it, *a clear proof that the Baptists were at that period neither few nor unimportant*."[4] Remember this was before John Smyth's baptism.

Of the English Baptists, of the seventeeth century, Goadby says: "All these are scions of this stock of Anabaptism that was transplanted out of Holland in the year *1535*, when two ships laden with Anabaptists fled into England, after they had missed the Enterprise at Amsterdam."[5]

[1] Shackelford's Comp. of Bap. Hist., p. 274.
[2] Goadby's Bye Paths to Bap. Hist., pp. 72-73.
[3] Idem, p. 74.
[4] Idem, p. 75.
[5] Idem, p. 105.

To add many other testimonies to the existence of Baptist churches in England long before and at the time of John Smyth's baptism is an easy task. There is, to this, a most superabundantly overwhelming mass of proof. But I rather owe an explanation for having already produced such an avalanche of proof. That explanation is: Owing to John Smyth being so persistently thrown up to the Baptists as the founder of English Baptist churches, I have given this vast amount of refuting proof to silence forever every honest man who has been throwing John Smyth's baptism up against Baptists. In other words: This mass of testimony is given because so many think the English Baptists, of the early part of the seventeenth century, were the first Baptist churches in England since very early times.

There remain two objections or evasions. The first is: Is there proof that the Baptists who antedated Smyth were organized into churches and that these churches were in existence in England when he was baptized?

Notwithstanding that the foregoing shows this can be answered only in the affirmative, to not leave any possible room for doubt, I add the following:

(1.) Just as the principles of a political party, of any secret society necessarily bring into organization their adherents, so Baptist principles organized their adherents into Baptist churches. (2.) Just as the principles of anything are dependent on organization for their perpetuity operation and dissemination, so the perpetuity and the dissemination of Baptist principles are the demonstration of the existence of Baptist churches. (3.) In all times of which we have the history of Baptists in particular and fully, where there were many Baptists, there have been Baptist churches. (4.) The New Testament provision for the church to preach, administer the ordinances and the discipline of the kingdom, and to preserve the gospel institutions, guarantee the continuity of the church —of the *preserver as much as of the things to be preserved*. These four premises furnish the conclusion that the existence of Baptists in England, previous to and at the time of John Smyth's baptism, are sufficient assurance of the then existence of Baptist churches. (5.) But, their "*conventicles*" are synonymous with "churches."

Says the late E. T. Winkler, D.D., a great scholar, of very extensive research in church history: "Conventicle ordinarily occurred as the synonym of ' a church so called.' It was applied to the assembly, the place and the organization, just as the word church (ecclesia) was among early Christians, or as the word 'meeting' is in New England. To use an impressive term of John Stuart Mill, it connoted a church. The Baptist conventicles were for the most part Baptist churches. . . . The term is from the Latin ' conventiculum,' which signifies a 'little assembly.' It was commonly used by the ancient writers to indicate a *church*. Thus Lactantius (5:11) relates that a certain persecutor in the age of Diocletian, ' burnt a whole people together with their conventiculum (church) where they all met together.' Arnobius (Contra Gent. 4:352) complains: ' Why are our churches, (conventicula) where the supreme God is worshipped, pulled down?' And Ambroisiaster says that ' wherever the church extends local congregations are established (conventicula) and elders and other officers are ordained in these churches'" [1]

Webster defines conventicle: "An assembly or gathering. An assembly for *religious worship*, and, oppro-

---

[1] Dr. Winkler in Ala. Bap. and Relig. Herald, 1875.

biously such an assembly held by nonconformists or dissenters from the established church of England."¹

"Now, as conventicles were the name of disgrace cast on, 'schools' was the term of credit owned by the Wicklivites for their place of meeting."² Thus, we see how even the term "schools" was applied to churches. Universal Knowledge—Chambers' Encyclopedia—says: "Conventicle was first given as an appellation of reproach to the *assemblies* of Wickliffe's followers, and was after applied to the meetings of the English and Scottish nonconformists."³

The laws prohibiting conventicles clearly imply that they were often churches. Thus they read: "That if any person, upwards of sixteen years, shall be present at any *assembly, conventicle* or meeting under colour or pretence of any exercise of religion, in any *other manner than according to the liturgy and practice of the Church of England* . . . the offender shall pay five shillings for the first offence."⁴ Perkins, the leading Puritan writer of the Elizabethan age, says: "The *church* of the Papists, of the . . . Anabaptists . . . are no churches of God."⁵ Thus Perkins says that the conventicles claimed that they were genuine churches. Says Dr. Winkler: "Owen says (Works, vol. 13, p. 184.) 'The Donatists rebaptized those who came to their societies because they professed themselves to believe that all administration of ordinances not in their *assemblies* was null, and that they were to be looked upon as no such thing. Our *Anabaptists do the same thing.*'" Owen

---

[1] Unabridged Dictionary.
[2] Fuller's Ch. Hist. Britain, cent. 15, book 4, secs. 17-18.
[3] Volume 4, p. 568.
[4] Neal's History Puritans, vol. 2, p. 266.
[5] Perkins' Works, vol. 3, p. 286—quoted by Dr. Winkler; also Burrils' Law Dic., vol. 1, p. 281; Hook's Ch. Direc., p. 167, referred to by Dr. Winkler.

having lived from 1616 to 1683, Dr. Winkler adds: "Should any one object to the late date or the pertinency of Owen's testimony, we commend to his consideration the *contemporaneous* description of the conventicles of Essex and Kent, which were prosecuted by the orders of the council in the year 1550. 'These congregations,' says Underhill, 'were supported by the contributions of their members; (Struggles and Triumphs of Religious Liberty, p. 113) mutual instruction was practiced and the *fellowship of the gospel regularly maintained.*'"

(6.) The name "Anabaptist" inevitably implies Baptist church organization. Baptist means one who baptizes. The name "Anabaptists" was given to Baptists because all who joined them from other denominations were received into their *churches* by "rebaptism." The very name Anabaptist, therefore, so clearly and inevitably implies church organization that only the reluctance to admit the existence of Baptist churches, long before and up to Smyth's day, seems sufficient explanation for the resort to the evasion, that while there was a continuity of Baptists long before and up to the time of John Smyth, they were not churches! Baptist persecutors of those bloody times would have been glad had they been Baptist only in name—that they were not *churches*. Thus, in 1550, occurred the visitation in the diocese of Ridley, wherein the officers were to ascertain "whether any of the Anabaptist sect or others use notoriously any unlawful and private conventicles *wherein they do use doctrine or administration of sacraments* separating themselves from the rest of the parish."[1]

(7.) Laying all this aside, I have already proved that the Hill Cliffe and other churches have a *history far back*

[1] Quoted by Dr. Winkler, in Ala. Bap.

of the time of John Smyth; and that two years before Smyth organized his church he spent nearly all night "in debate with elders" of the Crowle *church*, which existed in 1599, how long previous, no one knows.

Thus, I have inconfutably demonstrated that there were Baptist churches, and *many* of them, in England long before and up to Smyth's time. Hence, Dr. Howard Osgood, one of the most eminent authorities on Baptist history, says: "If we would make the first Baptist church to appear under Helwise, in 1614, *then we must deny the historical evidence of the conventicles of Baptists in the previous century.* If we make the church founded in London in 1633 the first Calvinistic Baptist church in England, we *assume* that all the Baptists and Baptist churches of the sixteenth century were Arminian in their views, *which has never been shown, and is contrary to all probability.* Baptists were found in the north and west but principally in the east of England. Under the dreadful persecution of the Tudors, the churches *knew little of each other*, unless they were situated near together.† We *hear* more of the Calvinistic church formed in 1633, *because it was situated in London and performed an important work in the following years.* Joan Bucher, who was a member of the *Baptist church* in Eyethorne, Kent, burned by order of Henry VI, held this doctrine."[1]

If any one set up the claim that persecution had rid England of Baptists before Smyth's time, let him turn back and read the previous part of this chapter, in which he will see that instead of this being true, it was, as with

---

† Here we see why Baptist churches are so hard to trace in history. Being often concealed and unknown to their contemporaries and their books burned, that we have so much evidence of their existence can but be a wonderful providence, for which we ought to be thankful. Baptists, being thus concealed, their very existence was necessarily often unknown to each other. This is why that, though there were Baptist churches in England at the beginning of the seventeenth century, they were unknown by those who sent to Holland to get true baptism.

[1] In *The Standard*, of Chicago, 1875.

the churches of the first three centuries, that "Semen est sanguis Christianorem"— the blood of martyrs is the seed of the church—they lived in spite of persecutions. As Dr. Osgood remarks: "*No persecution was severe enough to extirpate the Baptists from England*, though it caused them to keep their meetings and their views very quiet. † Banishment, whipping, or death at the stake awaited any public exhibition of their 'conventicles.' † *Before* hand was laid to the reformation of the established churches in England, Baptists were *numerous* in the kingdom, and the reigns of Henry VIII, Edward VI, Mary and Elizabeth are blotted with the blood of martyred Baptists."[1]

Universal Knowledge—Chamber's Encyclopedia—says of the Baptists: "This denomination of Christians refuse to acknowledge any great name as the founder of their sect. They *trace* their origin to the primitive church itself, and refer to the Acts of the Apostles and the Epistles, as, in their opinion, affording incontestable evidence that their leading tenents had the sanction of inspiration. When Christianity became corrupted by the rise of anti-Christ, they point to the maintainance of *their Scripture practice among the Cathari and the Albigenses and other sects of the middle ages*, who, in the midst of surrounding darkness, *continued* to hold fast the apostolic testimony. They sprang into *notice* in England under Henry the VIII and Elizabeth. They were persecuted under both reigns."[2]

---

† See note to p. 345.
[1] In *The Standard*, of Chicago, 1875.
[2] Vol. 1, p. 341.

CHAPTER XXIV.

JOHN SMYTH'S BAPTISM AND THE ORIGIN OF ENGLISH BAPTISTS.

Inasmuch as the alleged self-baptism of John Smyth has been used to the discredit of Baptists, it is thought best to devote this chapter to its treatment and to the explanation of its alleged relation to them.

(1.) Instead of that baptism being the origin of English and American Baptists it was not even done in England. This alleged baptism was done in Amsterdam, in Holland, in 1608.[1]

(2.) Smyth never had any connection with the Regular or Particular Baptists, of which denomination are American Baptists.

Though but poorly informed on the differences between the Particular and the General Baptists of England, Mosheim was sufficiently informed to know they were different religious bodies. He says: "The sect in England which rejects the custom of baptizing infants, are not distinguished by the title of Anabaptists, but by that of Baptist. It is probable that they derive their origin from the *German and Dutch Mennonites*. The English Baptists differ in many things. . . . They are divided into two sects. One of which is distinguished by the denomination of General or Arminian Baptists, on account of their opposition to the doctrines of absolute and unconditional decrees; and the other by that of Particular or Calvinistic Baptists, from the striking

---

[1] Armitage's Hist. Bap., pp. 453-454.

resemblance of their system to that of the Presbyterians, who have Calvin for their chief."[1]

Armitage and other historians recognize the difference between these two bodies.[2]

(3.) Admitting Smyth as the founder of English Baptists, the report that he baptized himself is so far from being proved true that the contrary is more probably true. Cramp says: "There has been *much dispute* respecting the manner in which they proceeded, some maintaining that Smyth baptized himself and then baptized others. It is a thing of *small consequence*. . . . The probability is that one of the brethren baptized Mr. Smyth, and that he then baptized the others."[3]

Armitage notices the rumor: "Smyth and his congregation met in a large bakery for a time, but he soon saw his mistake in his *hasty see baptism*, and offered to join the Dutch congregation of *Baptists*. . . . Part of his congregation under the leadership of Helwys would not unite with Smyth in this movement, but excluded him from their fellowship and warned the Dutch church not to receive him."[4] Armitage enters upon an extended discussion of "whether Smyth dipped himself," "whether he was poured," etc.[5] Refuting some slanders against Smyth, Armitage says: "There is not a *particle* of evidence that he *affused* himself, and it is a cheap caricature to imagine that he disrobed himself, walked into a stream, then lifted handfuls of water, pouring them liberally upon his own head, shoulders and chest."[6]

[1] Mosheim's Eccl. Hist., cent. 16, sec. 3, chap. 3, 21.
[2] Armitage's Bap. Hist., pp. 454, 460, comp.
[3] Cramps' Hist. Bap., p. 287.
[4] Armitage's Hist. Bap., p. 454.
[5] Idem, pp. 457-463.
[6] Idem, p. 459.

"Some time before Smyth's death he frankly *retracted his error* in baptizing himself and them."[1] In view of all this, well does Armitage, agreeing with Cramp, say: "*Whether he dipped himself is not clear.*"[2] These accounts, are so far obscure and contradictory that, to use them as conclusively proving that Baptist churches originated in self baptism, comes nearer proving the cause of the one who uses them hard pressed than it comes to proving a discreditable origin of Baptist churches.

(4.) The proof is very strong that the charge of self baptism and of a new baptism among Smyth's followers is a slander. Crosby, than whom there is no higher authority on this period of Baptist history, says: "I do not find *any* Englishman among the first restorers of immersion in this latter age accused of baptizing himself but only the said John Smyth; and there is *ground to question the truth of that also.* Mr. Ainsworth, Mr. Jessop, and some others, do indeed charge him with it; but they write, as has already been observed, with so much *passion and resentment,* that it is not unlikely such men might *take up a report* against him on *slender evidence,* and after *one* had published it, the *others might take it from him without any inquiry into the truth of it.* The defenses which he wrote of himself are not to be met with; and in the large quotations that his adversaries take out of them *I do not find one passage* wherein he acknowledges himself to have done any such thing, or attempts to justify any such practice; which, surely, had there been such, would have *hardly escaped his notice.* . . . Says Mr. Smyth: "A man cannot baptize others into a church, *himself* being *out* of the church, or being no

---
[1] Armitage's Hist. Bap., p. 463.
[2] Idem, p. 457.

member. Here are two *principles* laid down by Mr. Smyth which contradict the account they give of him. That upon the supposition of the true baptism being lost for some time, through the disuse of it, 'tis necessary there should be *two* persons who must unite in the revival of it, in order to begin the administration thereof; and that the first administrator be a *member of some church*, who should call and empower him to administer it to the members thereof. Now it is reasonable to conclude, that his practice was conformable to *this*."[1] Ivimey adopts Crosby's argument.[2] That any reasonable person can see its force, I feel sure.

Dr. Cutting, when professor of history in Rochester University, wrote: "The biographers of Mr. Smyth, and the Baptist historians, Crosby and Ivimey, have been entirely skeptical in regard to this alleged self-baptism. It has been argued that the charge proceeded from *enemies only*, and that if there had been any truth in it, some intimation of the propriety of such an act would have been found somewhere in the writings of Mr. Smyth, or in those of his friends."[3] Noticing the statement, made by Mr. Robinson, that Smyth baptized himself, Prof. Cutting says: "Was Mr. Robinson mistaken? He was *not an eye witness*, he was in Amsterdam for a *brief* time only, and then went to Leyden. He '*heard*' the manner of establishing the new church narrated. Did he *understand correctly what he heard?*" Or, did he misinterpret *instituting baptism among themselves*, by supposing that to mean self-baptism? The controversy seems to be narrowed down to this single question. . . . On the supposition that Mr.

---

[1] Crosby's Hist. Eng. Bap., vol. 1, pp. 97-99.
[2] Ivimey's Hist. Eng. Bap., vol. 1, p. 119.
[3] Cutting's Hist. Vindications, p. 58.

Robinson misinterpreted what he heard, the circumstances of the case render it easy enough to suppose that the statement might pass to history uncontradicted."[1] "Mr. Smyth was already dead, and Mr. Helwisse, if still alive, was in England. It is not certain, however, that Mr. Helwisse was still living."[1] Thus, the story, of which Baptist enemies make so much, rests mainly on the testimony which Mr. Robinson received of Mr. Smyth's *enemies*, which he may have *misunderstood* and which was thus started on foot after Mr. Smyth's death, after Mr. Helwisse was probably dead, but if living, had left the country, and which was *never noticed by Mr. Smyth or any of his friends!*

(5.) The latest, and seemingly the true statement, is by Dr. John Clifford, one of the most scholarly and prominent of living English Baptist ministers. Before me lies a complimentary copy from himself, of his excellent work, entitled: "The Origin and Growth of the English Baptists." From pages 15-16 I copy the following on this point: "At Crowle, in Lincolnshire, a few miles from Gainsborough, there was, *according to an old Church Book*, recently copied, a Baptist society *as early as 1550*. To that rural community Smyth went in the year 1604, and 'debated nearly all night with Elders Henry Helwisse and John Morton, who defended our cause well.' Not yet, however, was he convinced, but after three months' reflection, his mind had advanced beyond the position of the Separatists. He had, says the Church Book, 'consulted the Scriptures and admitted that he was deceived in the way of Pedobaptistry,' and 'so, embraced the faith in a true christian and apostolic baptism,' and on the 24th of March, 1606, at midnight,

[1] Cutting's Hist. Vindications, p. 58.

to avoid the satellites of the persecuting Church, and under the glare of the torchlight, '*he was baptized by Elder John Morton, in the River Don*, and then walked to Epworth, a distance of two miles in his wet clothes.'"

Dr. Clifford says: "The church book from whence this statement is taken about John Symth's baptism, *belonged to the church* at Epworth and Crowle, in Lincolnshire. The Rev. Jabez Stuttered, minister at Epworth and Crowle, heard his deacons speak of the existence of this work; and being interested, found that it was in the possession of Rev. Smith Watson, a minister at Butterwick, hard by. He obtained a sight of it, and discovered that it consisted of a few moth eaten leaves, which had been given to Mr. Smith Watson by an old Baptist family of the district, who met with it in an old chest many years before. Mr. Stuttered thought the pages might be of value, and the opinion of an *expert* a *skilled antiquarian*, of the district, was sought and he reported as follows:

'NOVEMBER 9th, 1866.

'As keeper of the Manor Charts of North Lincolnshire, I have examined the old Baptist Records, and believe them to refer to the last days of Queen Elizabeth and James the First. And recommend the friends connected with the Baptist cause, to quickly copy them or they will surely vanish away.'

'F. CHAPMAN, Antiquarian.'"

The book was guarded with jealous care, but at the request of the deacons, and with their aid, Mr. Stuttered made a number of extracts, and after some time forwarded them to me. I was surprised at their contents, and especially at the statement concerning John Smyth's baptism, and asked to see the original; meanwhile Smith Watson had deceased, and the book could not be found.

Search has been made again and again, but, at present in vain. The following document bears date December the 16th, 1879:

"We, the undersigned deacons of the Baptist church at Butterwick, Epworth, Crowle, *having seen and handled the Old Records* of seven or eight leaves, long before Rev. J. Stuttered came into the country, and at our request and desire, and with our assistance he copied the same moth-eaten records. We, *as a church*, tendered him our sincere thanks and requested him to send them to the editor of the General Baptist Magazine for insertion. When copied they were taken back to Butterwick, and consigned to the care of the late Rev. Smith Watson, and now we cannot, at present, place our hands on the document, or it would have been sent for Mr. Clifford's inspection.

PETER GLOSSOP,   ANDERSON HIND,
BENJAMIN BATTY, JOHN CHAPMAN,
THOMAS SMITH,   GEORGE SINCLAIR,
                 WM. CHAMBERLAIN."[1]

(6.) Were we to admit this slander on John Smyth, and that the error was not corrected it effects but few of the Baptists:

(*a.*) Because there were Baptists in England before the time of Smyth.

(*b.*) Because, at the time of his baptism, there were Baptist churches near him.

Armitage says that the "Dutch Baptists of London rallied around Helwys and John Murton, his successor"—Smyth's successors.[2] By the way, who can believe the Dutch Baptists would have given this help to Smyth's church had it originated as Baptist enemies allege?

---

[1] The Orgin and Growth of the Eng. Bap., by Dr. John Clifford, pp. 10-12.
[2] Armitage's Hist. Bap., p. 454.

Of the origin of what is generally regarded the Particular Baptists of England, Neal's History of the Puritans says: "When, after long search, and many debates, it appeared to them that infant baptism was a mere innovation, and even a profanation of a divine ordinance, they were not brought to lay it aside without many fears and tremblings. . . . They were persuaded that believers were the only proper subjects of baptism, and that immersion or dipping the whole body into water was the appointed rite. But as this was not practiced in England" —a great mistake of Mr. Neal, originating with the little then known of Baptists —"they were at a loss for an administrator to begin with. After often meeting together to pray and confer about this matter, they agreed to send over into Holland Mr. Richard Blount, who understood the Dutch language, to a *Baptist church there;* he was kindly *received* by the society and their pastor and upon his return he baptized Mr. Samuel Blacklock, a minister; these two baptized the rest of the company, to the number of fifty-three. Some few others of this persuasion were among the *original planters of New England.*"[1]

Thus an eminent Pedobaptist historian established the "succession" of English Baptists through the Baptists of Holland who were the original Waldenses and their descendants. Vedder, notwithstanding all his prejudice, admits this account as true, and pronounces the baptism of the English Baptist as *henceforth correct.*[2]

W. W. Everts, Jr., a very high authority on church history, severely criticises Dr. Dexter for giving so little attention to this, which was in order to discredit the Baptists through John Smyth, and says, of one of his false statements: "I cannot account for such a statement

---

[1] Neal's Hist. Pur., vol. 2, p. 361.
[2] Short Hist. Bap., p. 117; also, Cutting's Hist. Vind., p. 36.

except by supposing an *animus in the writer* that *delights* to make early Baptists out a disorderly set."¹ Inasmuch as they would not have sent to Holland unless they believed the Holland Baptists were in the Continuity Line we have, here, incidental evidence of the Holland Baptists then being *well and widely known* as historical successors of the apostolic church.

Crosby thus narrates it: "This agrees with an account given in the matter in an *ancient manuscript*, said to be written by William Kiffin, who lived in those times." Crosby, after giving the account, just quoted from Neal, concludes: "So that those who followed this scheme did not derive their baptism from the aforesaid Mr. Smyth, or his congregation at Amsterdam, it being an ancient congregation of foreign Baptists in the Low Countries to whom they sent." ²

Some have misunderstood the above accounts to be of Smyth's alleged rebaptism and church. But Orchard is correct in saying: "The *Particular* Baptist church in London, at its formation, A. D. 1633, deputed Mr. Blount to visit a church in Holland, and receive from a Waldensian Baptist, scriptural immersion. The Baptists are the only Christians that can prove a scriptural immersion and order descended to them from the days of John the Baptist." ³

Armitage says the "church referred to in the above account was that of which Messrs. Jacob and Lathrop had been pastors." "A number of this society came to reject infant baptism, and were permitted to form a distinct church, Sept. 12th, 1633, with Spilsbury for their pastor. . . . In 1638, William Kiffin, Thomas

---

1 In *The Standard*, Chicago.
2 Crosby's Hist. Eng. Bap., vol. 1, pp 101-103.
3 Orchard's Hist. Bap., vol. 1, p. 261.

Wilson and others, left Lathrop's independent church, then under charge of Mr. Jessey, and united with Spilsbury's church."[1]

Orchard says: "Mr. Spilsbury's name not being mentioned by Kiffin, suggested to previous writers, that his account was of another church, erected about the same time, yet as Mr. Kiffin joined a church at Wapping, it is natural to conclude he gave a statement of the rise of his own community. Mr. Spilsbury might have been selected as a teacher only during their infancy; and Blacklock, or some other minister, might have succeeded him. Edwards, saying this was one of the first, admits of more existing at the same time."[2]

That the reader may not be confused by Spilsbury's church being mentioned in London and Kiffin belonging to it in Wapping, I will here inform him that Wapping, at that time was a pleasant suburb of London." The Wapping and London church is identical.[3]

Orchard's suggestion, that Spilsbury was pastor during only the infancy of the church, is unnecessary since Blacklock having been baptized by Blount and then baptizing the others do not necessarily imply Spilsbury was not pastor at that time. As now, owing to sickness or other causes, pastors have others baptize for them, so Blacklock may have baptized for Spilsbury, after baptizing him. But however this may be — of which the scantiness of the records leaves doubt—it in no way effects the scriptural perpetuity of baptism.

Finally, concluding the John Smyth affair, and the Spilsbury church, *do not forget that this is the account of only two churches and their successors, while I have proved*

---

[1] Armitage's Hist. Bap.
[2] Orchard's Hist. Bap., vol. 2, p. 262.
[3] Goadby's Bye Paths to Bap. Hist., p. 35.

there were at that time many other Baptist churches in England. As Armitage says of the Spilsbury church: "The fact that a part of this congregation did not know that the immersion of believers had been practiced in England *cannot be accepted* as descisive proofs that the *Baptists were strangers* to that practice, still less that it had never been known in England before 1641."[1] Benedict says: "The account of Mr. Spilsbury is said, in the margin, to have been written from the records of that church; but from anything that appears *there is nothing to justify the conclusion* of Mr. Crosby *that this was the first Baptist church*, as the account relates simply to the origin of *that particular church*—to state which, it is probable, was Mr. Kiffin's design, rather than to relate the origin of Baptist churches in *general* and which *he must certainly* have known were in existence *previous* to that period."[2]

Benedict after saying: "It must be admitted that some obscurity hangs over the history of the *oldest* Baptist communities in this kingdom," in a note, says: "From all the fragments of history, I am inclined to believe that Baptist churches, under various circumstances, have existed in England from the time of William the Conqueror, *four or five centuries prior to those of which any definite accounts have come down to us.* . . . Here churches in persecuting times are mere household affairs which must of *necessity* be *hid* from public view. More than three centuries had elapsed before the Baptists in England had any knowledge that a church of their **order** existed in Chesterton in 1457. Mr. Robinson brought

[1] Armitage's Hist. Bap., p. 440.
[2] Benedict's Hist. Bap., p. 337.

the facts to light by examining the manuscript *records* of the old bishop of Ely." [1]

Goadby, of the English Baptists of the seventeenth century says: "All these are *scions* of that stock of Anabaptism *transplanted out of Holland* in the year 1535, when two ships laden with Anabaptists fled into England." [2]

Armitage says: "All these are scions of what was transplanted out of Holland in the year 1535, when two ships laden with Anabaptists fled into England, . . . here it seems *they have remained ever since.*" [3] This is an adopted quotation from a "History of Anabaptists of High and Low Germany," written in 1642, " now among the Kings' Pamphlets." Barclay also reports that in 1536 'Anabaptist societies in England sent a delegation to a *great* gathering of their brethren in Westphalia. It appears, therefore, that the origin of English Baptists, as a *distinct sect*, is to be found among the English Baptist refugees who were driven from the *Netherlands.*" [3]

Here see my previous chapter on English Baptists before and at the time of John Smyth, which proves Baptists in England long before and up to 1535.

Crosby says of Smyth: " If he were guilty of what they charge him with, it is no blemish on the English Baptists, who neither approved of any such method, *nor did they receive their baptism from him.*" [4]

Dr. Smith, editor of *The Standard* at Chicago, formerly Lecturer on Church History to the Chicago Baptist Theological Seminary, says: " As we have said on former occasions, John Smyth is not counted on as one of the *founders* of the Baptist denomination." [5]

---

[1] Benedict's Hist. Bap., p. 337.
[2] Goadby's Bye Paths to Bap. Hist., p. 105.
[3] Armitage's Bap. Hist., pp. 445-446.
[4] Crosby's Hist. Eng. Bap., vol. 1, p. 99.
[5] In *The Standard*, Chicago.

Well did "Hercules Collins, a Baptist minister of Wapping," England, in a work published in 1691, say of the English Baptists having received their baptism from John Smyth: "It is absolutely untrue, it being *well known to some who are yet alive* how false this assertion is; and if J. W. will but give a meeting to any of us, and bring whom he pleases with him, we shall sufficiently show the falsity of what is asserted by him in this matter, and in many other things which he hath unchristianly asserted."[1]

[1] Ivimey's Hist. Eng. Bap., vol. 1, p. 140.

CHAPTER XXV.

THROUGH WELSH BAPTISTS, BAPTISTS HAVE A CONTINUITY FROM APOSTOLIC TIMES TO THE PRESENT.

Armitage quotes from Thomas' History of the Welsh Baptists: "The first Baptist church in Wales, AFTER the Reformation, was found at Ilston, near Swansea, in Glamorganshire, in 1649. . . . It was under the commonwealth that Vavasor Powell, Jenkin Jones and Hugh Evans formed the first Open Communion Baptist churches in Wales, and that John Miles formed the first Strict Communion churches there. The first Welsh Baptist association was organized in 1651."[1] These words, so carelessly chosen, have given an excuse for Baptist opponents to claim that this was the origin of Welsh Baptists. But, in connection with this statement, Armitage says: "Davis, Bishop of Monmouth, finds a wide difference between the christianity of the ancient Britons and that of Austin in 596. The first followed the word of God, the other was mixed with human tradition. Dr. Fulk denied that Austin was the apostle of England, and charged him with corrupting the true christianity which he found in Britain, by Romish admixture. Fabin, himself a Catholic, shows that he imposed sundry things upon the Britons, which were refused as contrary to the doctrine which they had at first received. Bede says that the Culdees followed the Bible only and opposed the superstitions of Rome. Culdee, from Culdu, is a compound Welsh word, cul, thin, du, black; and means a

---

[1] Armitage's Hist. Bap., pp. 599-600.

thin, dark man, as their mountaineers, who were noted for their godliness. The monks got possession of the Culdee colleges by degrees, and continued to preach without forming churches. Some claiming that the Welsh Baptists sprang from the sturdy stock; for individuals are found in Glamorgan, the Black Mountains, Hereford and Brecon counties, who walked apart from Rome *before the Reformation*. Stephens, the late antiquarian of Merthyr, thought that the bards of Chavi of Glamorgan kept up a secret concourse with the *Albigenses*. *This is probable, as some of them were conversant with the Italian poets.*

"'Holy Rhys,' famous in 1390, was learned, and his wife was of the 'new faith,' (Lollard), for his son, Ieuan, was expelled from the Margam Monastary for holding their opinions, or 'on account of his religion.' His grandson also was imprisoned by Sir Cradoe for being of the 'new faith' . . . . The *Lollards swarmed in Wales*, where Old Castle hid for four years after escaping from the Tower. He was a native of the Welsh Cottian Alps, the Black Mountains, having been born at Old Castle about 1360.

"*It is a disputed point as to where and when Baptists first appeared in Wales.* There are *presumptive* evidences that individuals held their views from the opening of the seventeenth century, and some have thought that the first Baptist church was formed at Olchon, 1633. Joshua Thomas, of Leominster, perhaps the most reliable authority on the subject, doubts this. He leans to the belief that there were Baptists then at that date,"—and here comes in the quotation made in the beginning of this chapter.[1]

[1] Armitage's Hist. Bap., p. 509.

The reader will see that instead of Armitage dating the origin of Welsh Baptists in the seventeenth century, he says the "first *after* the Reformation" meaning the first of which we have a *clear* account of its origin, while he gives strong evidence of Welsh Baptists existing many centuries previous to the seventeenth century, leaving it a "*disputed* point as to when and where Baptists first appeared in Wales." Considering that Dr. Armitage is so ready to slur "Succession," this is no insignificant concession in favor of Church Perpetuity.

Considering that the Romish church has always opposed rendering the Scriptures into the language of the people and that she has done so only when forced by increasing light to do so; and, further, that such versions are exclusively the trophy of Baptists, the following, from Dr. Armitage, is presumptive evidence for Welsh Baptists having continued in Wales throughout the dark ages: "Portions of the Scriptures were translated into manuscript before the Reformation, but some of them were lost. Taliesin, a bard of note, in the sixth century, gave paraphrase in verse of a few passages, and it is said that there was a manuscript translation of the gospels in the thirteenth century in the library of St. Asaph's cathedral. In the thirteenth century it was already looked upon as old, and the Archbishop of Canterbury allowed the priests to exhibit it as a sacred thing . . . . . Dafydd Ddu, another bard, wrote a poetical paraphrase in the fourteenth century on a part of the Psalms, the song of Zecharias, the angels' greeting to Mary, and the song of Simeon, found in Luke's Gospel. Some other fragments of Scripture were given by others."[1]

[1] Armitage's Hist. Bap., p. 598.

The statement that there was no Bible in Wales at the time of the Reformation, except in cathedrals, in view of the foregoing and of the undoubted existence of evangelical Christians there and of their history being known only by *occasional glimpses*, should be taken with *much allowance*.

Including Wales, Bede says the Britains were converted to Christianity in the second century and that they "preserved the faith, which they had received uncorrupted and entire, in peace and tranquility, until the time of Diocletian, A. D. 286."[1]

In the year 603, Augustine, called also Austin, was sent to convert the Welsh Baptists to the Romish church. Bede records that they met him, charging him with pride, contradicted all he said, and that he proposed to them: "*You act in many particulars contrary to our custom*, or rather the custom of the universal church, and yet, if you will comply with me in these three points, viz.: to keep Easter at the due time; to administer baptism, by which we are again born to God, according to the custom of the *Roman* Apostolic Church; and jointly with us preach the Word of God to the English nation, we will readily *tolerate* all the other things you do, *though contrary to our custom*."[2]

Bede says: To this "they answered, they would do *none* of these things, nor receive him as their archbishop; for they alleged among themselves that 'if he would not rise up to us, how much more will he condemn us, as of no worth, if we shall begin to be under his subjection?' To whom the man of God, Augustine, is said in a threatening manner, to have foretold, that in case they would not join in unity with their brethern, they should be

---

[1] Bede's Eccl. Hist., Book 1, Chap. 4.
[2] Idem, book 2, chap. 2.

warred upon by their enemies; and if they would not preach the way of life to the English nation, they should at their hands, undergo the vengeance of death. All which, through the dispensation of divine judgment, fell out exactly as he had predicted."[1] But Bede states that fifty of their ministers "escaped by flight" from the slaughter of "twelve hundred" of their ministerial brethren.[1] These were amply sufficient to propagate the true gospel; thus, preserving the perpetuity line to the Reformation.

Fabian, who died in the year 1512, states that Augustine's proposition to those Welsh Baptists was: "That ye give Christendom to children." Thus read the editions of 1516, 1533, 1542. The last edition, which is not so correct an edition, made in 1811, reads: "That ye administer baptism . . . as to the manner of the church of Rome," as evidently meaning, as Danvers, Davye, Ivimey and "several Cambro Americans maintain" the same as to baptize infants.[2]

Of Augustine's time, Goadby says: "A large and flourishing body of British Christians were now living in Wales, whither they had sought refuge from the cruelties of the Saxons. Undisturbed in their liberties and their worship in the fastnesses of Wales, they had waxed stronger and stronger. At Caerleon, in the south, and at Bangor Is-y-Coed, in the north, large and flourishing monasteries, or, more properly speaking, missionary stations, were established. Bangor alone could number, in association with it, *over two thousand* 'brethren.' These societies had *little in common* with Romanish monasteries. The greater part of the 'brethren' were *married laymen*, who followed their

---

[1] Bede's Eccl. Hist., book 1, chap. 4.
[2] Evan's Hist. Early Eng. Bap., vol. 1, pp. 5-6.

worldly callings, and those among them who showed aptitude for study and missionary work were permitted to give themselves to the reading of the Scriptures and holy services. All were maintained out of a common fund, and yet a large surplus was distributed in the shape of food and clothing."[1]

Here Goadby follows with an account, substantially that of Bede and Evans, quoted in the foregoing.

Crosby says: "It was in the year 469 that the Saxons invaded England. They made a complete conquest, overthrew Christianity and set up the heathen idolatry. But those Christians which escaped fled into Cornwall and Wales, where they secured themselves and *maintained the true Christian faith and worship.* Jeffrey, of Monmouth, in his book, De Brittanorum Gestis, Lib. IV, cap. 4, as cited by Mr. Danvers, tells us that in the country of the Britains Christianity flourished, which *never decayed*, even from the Apostles' time. Amongst whom, he says, was the preaching of the gospel, sincere doctrine and living faith, and such form of worship *as* was delivered to the churches by the Apostles themselves; and that they, even to death itself, *withstood the Romish rites and ceremonies.*"[2] Crosby strengthens this statement with the testimony of other authorities, too numerous and lengthy to here cite. Crosby, here, also repeats the foregoing account of Austin's attempt to convert the Welsh Baptists, of his bringing on them persecution, because they continued in the faith and of fifty of their ministers escaping from the massacre to continue the pure gospel.

Benedict says: "The Welsh Baptists have the fullest confidence that their sentiments *always* have lived in the

---

[1] Goadby's Bye Paths to Bap. Hist., pp. 3-4.
[2] Crosby's Hist. Eng. Bap., vol. 2, pp. 14-15 of preface.

mountainous retreats, from the apostolic age to the present time, although the people were not always congregated in churches. Their country, in their estimation, was another Piedmont, where the *witnesses* for the truth found *shelter and concealment* in times of universal darkness and superstition. . . . My impressions are *very strong* in favor of a *high antiquity of the Baptist order in Wales*. With the *first* dawn of returning light, *long before* the ecclesiastical changes on the continent, or England, we see the Welsh Baptists among the *first reformers;* and they did not appear to be *novices* in the business, but entered into the defence of their sentiments, and the carrying out of the usual operations of the denomination, as to churches and associations, like those who had been familiar with their principles."[1] In this connection Benedict mentions the churches which are so mentioned by Armitage as to be used by Baptist opponents to prove they were the first Baptist churches in Wales, he having mentioned them as "the oldest in Wales of whose origin any DISTINCT *information* has come down to us."[2]

Speaking of Wales as a refuge of ancient Welsh Baptists, Armitage says: "The vale of Olchon is difficult of access, and there the first Welsh dissidents found the most ready converts, who sheltered themselves in the rocks and dens. The Darren Ddu, or Black Rock, is a terribly steep and rough place, in which the Baptists took refuge, rich and poor, young and old, huddled together."[3]

Davis' History of Welsh Baptists is an abridged translation of Thomas' History of Welsh Baptists, of which Mr. Davis says: "We have collected all we deem necessary from every other author on the subject" and

[1] Benedict's Hist. Bap., pp. 344-345.
[2] Idem. p. 345.
[3] Armitage's Hist. Bap., p. 600.

added it to it; and Armitage says: "Thomas is, perhaps, the most reliable authority on the subject."[1]

Davis says: "About fifty years before the birth of our Savior the Romans invaded the British Isle, in the reign of the Welsh king, Cassibellan; but having failed, in consequence of other and more important wars, to conquer the Welsh nation, made peace and dwelt among them many years. During that period many of the Welsh soldiers joined the Roman army and many families from Wales visited Rome, among whom there was a certain woman named Claudia, who was married to a man named Pudence. At the same time Paul was sent a prisoner to Rome and preached there in his own hired house for the space of two years, about the year of our Lord 63. Pudence and Claudia, his wife, who belonged to Cæsar's household, under the blessing of God on Paul's preaching, were brought to the knowledge of the truth as it is in Jesus, and made a profession of the christian religion. Acts 28:30; II. Timothy 4:21. These, together with other Welshmen, among the Roman soldiers, who had tasted that the Lord was gracious, exhorted them in behalf of their countrymen in Wales, who were at that time vile idolators. . . . The Welsh lady Claudia, and others, who were converted under Paul's ministry in Rome, carried the precious seed with them, and scattered it on the hills and valleys of Wales; and since that time, many thousands have reaped a glorious harvest. . . . We have nothing of importance to communicate respecting the Welsh Baptists from this period to the year 180 when two ministers by the name of Faganus, and Damicanus, who were born in Wales, but were born again in Rome, and

---

[1] Armitage's Bap. Hist., p. 599.

became eminent ministers of the gospel, were sent from Rome to assist their brethren in Wales. In the same year, Lucius, the Welsh king, and the first king in the world who embraced the christian religion, was baptized. . . . About the year 300, the Welsh Baptists suffered most terrible and bloody persecution, which was the tenth persecution under the reign of Dioclesian. . . . Here, as well as in many other places, the blood of martyrs proved to be the seed of the church."[1]

Of A. D. 600, Davis says: "Infant baptism was in vogue long before this time in many parts of the world, but not in Brittain. The ordinances of the gospel were then exclusively administered there according to the *primitive* mode. Baptism by *immersion*, administered to those who professed repentance [†] toward God and faith in our Lord Jesus Christ, the Welsh people considered the *only* baptism of the New Testament. That was their *unanimous* sentiment as a nation, from the time that the christian religion was embraced by them in the year 63, until a considerable time after the year 600. . . . They had no national religion; they had not connected church and State together; for they believed that the kingdom of Christ is not in this world."[2] Here Davis gives the account quoted in the foregoing, of Augustine's attempt to convert them to *infant* baptism and to the Romish church and of the persecution ensuing from his failure to do so. From this persecution Davis says: "The majority of the Welsh people submitted to popery; at that time more out of fear than love. Those good people that did not submit, were *almost* buried in its

---

[†] They were not Campbellites; but they followed the New Testament in putting repentance before faith.
[1] Davis' Hist. Welsh Bap., pp. 6-9.
[2] Idem, p. 14.

smoke; so that one knew but *little* of them from that time to the Reformation."

"Since the above was written we find that Theopholis Evans, in his Drych y prif œsoedd, or Looking Glass of the Ancient Ages, could *see the remnant of the Welsh Baptists through the darkness of* popery, to the year 1,000. And Peter Williams, a *Methodist* preacher, who wrote an exposition of the Old and New Testaments in Welsh, has followed them through thick clouds till they were buried out of sight in the thick smoke, in the year of our Lord, 1115. However, *it is a fact that cannot be controverted, that from this time to the Reformation there were many individuals in Wales whose knees had never bowed to Baal of Rome.*"[1]

"The vale of Carleon is situated between England and the mountains of Wales, just at the foot of the mountains. It is our valley of Piedmont, the mountains of Merthyn Tydfyl, our Alps; and the crevices of the rocks, the hiding places of the lambs of the sheep of Christ, *where the ordinances of the gospel to this day have been administered in the Primitive mode, without being adulterated by the corrupt church of Rome*. It would be no wonder that Penry, Wroth and Erbury, commonly called the first reformers of the Baptist denomination in Wales, should have so many *followers at once*, when we consider the field of their labors was the vale of Carleon and its vicinity. Had they, like many of their countrymen, never bowed the knee to the great Baal of Rome, nor any of the horns of the beast in Britain, it is probable that we should not have heard of their names; but as they were great and learned men, belonging to that religion, (or rather irreligion) established by law, and particularly as

---

[1] Davis' Hist. Welsh Bap., p. 15.

they *left that establishment and joined the poor Baptists*, their names are handed down to posterity, not only by their friends, but also by their foes, because more notice was taken of them than those scattered Baptists in the mountains of the Principality. As this denomination has *always existed in this country* from the year 63, and had been so often and severely persecuted, it was by this time an *old* thing. . . . The vale of Olchon, also, is situated between mountains almost inaccessible. How many hundred years it had been inhabited by Baptists before William Erbury ever visited this place, we cannot tell. . . . *It is a fact that cannot be controverted that there were Baptists here at the* COMMENCEMENT *of the Reformation;* and *no man on earth can tell where the church was formed, and who began to baptize in this little Piedmont. Whence came these Baptists?* It is *universally believed* that it is the oldest church, *but how old none can tell*. We know that at the Reformation . . . they had a minister named Howell Vaughn, quite a *different sort of a Baptist* from Erbury, Wroth, Vavasor Powell and others, who were the great reformers, but had not reformed so far as they should have done, in the opinion of the Olchon Baptists. And that was not to be wondered at; for they had dissented from the church of England, and probably brought some of her corruptions with them, but the *mountain Baptists were not dissenters from that establishment*. We know that the reformers were for mixed communion, but the Olchon Baptists received no such practices. In short, these were plain, strict apostolical Baptists. They would have order and no confusion—the word of God their only rule. The reformers, or reformed Baptists, who had been brought up in the established church, were for laying on of hands on the baptized, but these Baptists whom they *found* on the mountains of Wales were no advocates of it. . . . The Olchon Baptists . . . must have been a *separate people, maintaining the order of the New Testament in every generation from the year 63 to the present time.*"[1] "But a Baptist has not the least trouble about what is called a lineal or apostolical succession. His line of succession is in faithful men, and it is a matter of indifference with them, when or where they lived, by what name they were called, or by whom they were baptized or ordained."[2]

[1] Davis' Hist. Welsh Bap., pp. 19-20.
[2] Idem, p. 171.

CHAPTER XXVI.

AMERICAN BAPTIST CHURCHES ORIGINATED INDEPENDENTLY OF ROGER WILLIAMS. ROGER WILLIAMS A BAPTIST ONLY IN PART, AND NEVER A MEMBER OF ANY BAPTIST CHURCH. TWO BAPTIST CHURCHES ORGANIZED IN AMERICA BEFORE WILLIAMS' SO-CALLED BAPTIST CHURCH WAS IN EXISTENCE.

The claim that Roger Williams originated the first Baptist church in America has no historical foundation. Isaac Backus, whom Neander highly regarded as a historian, of the records of the first church of Providence, which are the foundation of this claim, says: "The diversity of sentiments mentioned in this volume . . . brought such darkness over their affairs that no regular *records* before 1770 are now found therein."[1] This leaves the first church of Providence, *during the first one hundred and twenty years of its claimed existence, with no "regular records."* " *No records of their society or church remain. Mr. Benedict gave twelve names, and his error has been widely copied without questioning.*"[2] "The church at Providence never has had any creed or any covenant; till the year 1700 it had no meeting house, but in fine weather worshipped in a grove and, when inclement, in private houses; *nor till the year 1775 had it any regular records.*"[3] No wonder at Benedict saying: "The more I study on this subject, the more I am unsettled and confused."[4] Of the

---

[1] Backus' Hist. Bap., vol. 2, p. 285.
[2] Bap. Quart., vol. 10, p. 199.
[3] Adlams' "First Bap. Ch. in Am.," p. 24.
[4] Benedict's Hist. Bap., p. 443.

uncertainty as to the early state of things in Providence, Backus says: "It was difficult for one to give an exact account of their religious affairs in that colony that did not live among them. It is certain that" Mr. Hubbard "and the Governor were both mistaken in calling those of Providence 'all Anabaptists.'"[1] In view of so grave a mistake as to who were Baptists at the time when it is claimed Roger Williams founded the first Baptist church in America, pray tell us how we can be certain Williams ever organized any Baptist church, and, if so, how we can know *when? Consequently*, those who say Roger Williams organized the first Baptist church in America *concede* they know *nothing* as to the truth or falsity of their statement. Says Cramp: "A church was immediately formed, of which Mr. Williams became pastor. But he soon vacated the office; some think after the lapse of only a few months, while others are of the opinion that he resigned when he embarked for England to procure a charter for the colony, and that it was on that occasion that Mr. Chad Brown was chosen his successor."[2] Says Vedder: "Whether the first church of Providence is the the lineal successor of this church founded by Roger Williams is a *difficult* historical question, about which a positive opinion should be expressed without *diffidence*. Tradition maintains that the line of succession has been unbroken, but the records to prove this are *lacking*."[3] Armitage says: "It is difficult to know how far the so-called[4] 'records' of the Providence church may be relied upon." Armitage concedes that from the time when Williams lost faith in the legality of his so-called

---

[1] Backus' Hist. Bap., vol. 1, p. 87.
[2] Cramp's Hist. Bap., p. 461.
[3] Vedder's Short Hist. Bap., p. 55.
[4] Armitage's Bap. Hist., p. 663.

church, "The early history of the church becomes a perplexing confusion; *if any minutes were kept they cannot be found.* In fact, during the so-called King Philip's war, in 1676, most if not all the houses in Providence were destroyed by the Indians, and the records, if there were any, of course, perished in the flames. About a century ago Rev. John Stanford preached for a year to the first Baptist church in Providence, and made an honest attempt to collect the most reliable information that he could command and formulated a Book of Records. . . . It was *impossible* for him to construct a *reliable* history without authentic material. All that he had was tradition, and a few fragments, and he thus complains of his scanty supply: '*No* attention to this necessary article has been paid;' and he farther says that he attempted this collection 'under almost *every* discouraging circumstance.' After doing the best he could, his *supposed* facts are so fragmentary as to leave gaps unfilled, with their value so impaired that few careful writers feel at liberty to follow them entirely. They contain so many *contradictions* which the Doctor was unable to explain, and which perplex *all calm* investigators; for example, they state that Williams was pastor of the church four years instead of four months; that it is not known when Thomas Olney was baptized or ordained, and that he came to Providence in 1654; whereas, in another place they state that he was in the canoe with Williams when the Indians saluted him with 'what cheer.' . . . Prof. Knowles complains of these errors; also Dr. Caldwell, a most candid and careful writer, says in his history of this church, that this record 'contains many errors, which have been repeated by later writers, and sometimes as if they had the authority of the original records.' Of the above contradictions he remarks: 'Mr. Stanford, in the records, confounding Mr.

Olney with his son, makes the following statement, which is an almost unaccountable mixture of errors.' Where such serious defects abound in records it is clear that little firm reliance can be placed upon their testimony, and this without reflection on the compiler, who stated only what he found and attempted no manufacture of facts to complete his story. We are obliged to consult sidelights and outside testimony, therefore, and take it for what it is worth, according to the means of information enjoyed by contemporaneous and immediately succeeding witnesses. These are *not numerous* in this case, nor are they very *satisfactory*, because their testimony does not always *agree*, nor had they equal means of knowing whereof they spoke. Hence, several *different theories* have been put forth on the subject." [1]

In view of the foregoing, I will conclude the point, as to the records, in the language of the *Journal and Messenger*, of Cincinnati: "It will be seen from such accounts that it is very difficult to establish *anything* of this history, *beyond a peradventure* and that it is taking a *good deal for granted* to admit the claims of a church which *kept no records for over one hundred years*. In order that the First Baptist church of Providence may be regarded as the first in America, we have to proceed upon the *Catholic* system of fixing dates, etc., and argue that there must have been a first church, and since we cannot certainly fix upon any other as that one, then this was the best, and the indisputable claim. But we are not quite ready to adopt this method of settling historical claims." The claim of the Williams church to have been the first Baptist church in America, is a *late claim*. Says Prof. J. C. C. Clarke, of Shurtleff College, in a

---

[1] Armitage's Bap. Hist., p. 662.

most masterly review of the subject, after a thorough examination of the *original* records of these times: "A Mr. Lechford, having visited Providence about 1640, wrote: 'At Providence lives Master Williams and his company of divers opinions; most are Anabaptists. They hold there is no true, visible church in the Bay, nor in the world, nor any true ministry.' A hundred years later, the *oldest residents* of Providence were ignorant of any tradition that Roger Williams was the *founder or a member* of the Baptist church there."[1] Thus we see that even the tradition upon which the claim of the Providence church rests is perfectly worthless, in that *it* originated over a century after the time in which it is claimed Williams originated that church, and that the claim of that church originated a century later than the disputed dates of origin for the Providence and Newport churches. Mr. Adlam, one of the highest authorities on this subject, says: "The *general* opinion of Roger Williams being the founder and pastor of the first Baptist church, is a *modern theory; the farther you go back, the less generally it is believed; till coming to the most ancient times, to the men who knew Williams, they are such entire strangers to it, that they never heard that he formed the Baptist church there.* The first, and the second and the third, and almost the fourth generation must pass away before men can believe that any others than Wickenden, Brown, etc., were the founders of that church."[2]

Facts as to Roger Williams and his so-called church. *First.* Williams, while a Baptist in some points, was not a Baptist in so many others, that he never was a Baptist in an ecclesiastical sense. Instead of any *orderly* Baptist

---

[1] Bap. Quart. Rev., vol. 10, p. 200.
[2] Adlams' "First Bap. Ch. in Am.," p. 14.

church recognizing any one as a Baptist, who had let an unbaptized man who was a member of no church, baptize him, and then, he in turn, had baptized his baptizer, and, *thus* originated a church, it would *unhesitatingly* refuse him any church fellowship, and *disown his acts*. Yet this is the history of Roger Williams' baptism and so-called church. If possible, Williams' course is still more inexcusable in view of the fact that Baptist administrators could more easily have been procured from England than the charter he assisted John Clarke to get from there. Why did he not, if he was a Baptist, do like Spilsbury's church of London, or Oncken, of Germany—send off and get the true baptism? Yea, worse and worse, why did he not get John Clarke or Hansard Knollys to baptize him, as they were on the ground? Cramp says: "Hansard Knollys was *then* preaching at Dover . . . and was one of the 'godly Anabaptists' mentioned by Cotton Mather."[1] Knollys was a graduate of the University of Cambridge. As a Baptist minister of London, after returning there, often preaching to an audience of one thousand hearers. Of Knollys' coming to America, Backus says: "Persecuted in England he fled to America. Forbidden at once to remain in Massachusetts he went to Piscataqua, soon afterwards called Dover. Here he met with immediate opposition, but according to Winthrop (vol. 1, p. 326) 'he gathered some of the best minded into a church body and became their pastor.' "[2]

Rev. C. E. Barrows says: "We are informed that there were Baptists among the *first* settlers of Massachusetts Bay."[3] This statement is made on the authority of Cotton Mather.

[1] Cramp's Bap. Hist., p. 461.
[2] Backus' Hist. Bap., vol. 1, p. 82.
[3] Semi-Centennial Discourse of R. I., in 1875.

As we have seen, in the case of Williams, Clarke and Knollys, Baptists, to escape persecution for their opposition to infant baptism, fled to Rhode Island, where they had liberty. Settling in Newport, Clarke would find Baptist *material* which his faithfulness as a preacher must have immediately organized into a Baptist church."[1] "Mr. Hansard Knollys was minister there from the spring of 1638 to the fall of 1641."[2] "The church was traduced from without and was rent with dissension within, and its pastor returned to England."[3]

Cramp, after confirming the above, adds: "It is observable that Mr. Knollys' arrival was in the spring of 1638. Roger Williams' baptism did not take place till the winter of that year."[4] He "was a Particular or Calvinistic Baptist." Prof. A. C. Lewis, D. D., of the McCormick Theological Seminary, of Chicago, says: "There were Baptists in New England *before* Roger Williams. Of this Cotton Mather informs us distinctly. . . . Numbers of them *came with the early colonists*. . . . *Hansard Knollys was one of their number*."[*] Coming from one who asserts that Williams organized the first American Baptist church, this statement is the more valuable in refuting Baptist opponents.

Prof. Paine, Professor of Church History in Bangor Theological Seminary, says: "There were Baptists in America before Roger Williams."[*] While the future of Knollys church after its first three years history, is uncertain, yet its three years' existence, before he

---

[*] Recent Letter to the Author.
[1] Semi-Centennial Discourse of R. I , in 1875, p. 36.
[2] Backus' Hist. Bap., vol. 1, p. 83; Crosby's Hist. Bap., vol. 1, p. 120: Cramp's, p. 436.
[3] Ibidem.
[4] Cramp's Bap. Hist., p. 436.

returned to England, was amply sufficient for it to have given valid baptism or the "succession" to others.

At the same time John Clark, another Baptist minister, was on the ground. Prof. J. C. C. Clarke says: "That Clarke *brought with him* the doctrine of the English 'Particular Baptist church,' is probable from *many* indications. He was a preacher in Rhode Island in 1638, but was *never a preacher except according to the early Baptist practice of eldership. No change of his views is known to have occurred.* His doctrinal writings preserved were very clear, and are in accord with the Baptist confessions of faith. The church which he established on Rhode Island was *early in correspondence with Mr. Spilsbury's church in London.* Governor Winthrop records that Mr. Clarke was a *preacher* on the Island in 1638. . . . In another reference he calls him *their minister.*"[1]

Confirmatory of John Clarke having come to this country a Baptist minister, Rev. C. E. Barrows says: "Clarke was certainly never a member of John Cotton's church in Boston."[2] Had he not come over here a Baptist he would have probably joined Cotton's church on his arrival in America.

Second. William's history, after he organized his so-called Baptist church, is irreconcilable with his Baptist claim. Speaking of Williams organizing his society, Vedder says: "Soon after arriving at the conclusion that his baptism by one who had not himself been baptized in an orderly manner, was not valid baptism, he withdrew himself from the church, and for the rest of his life was

[1] Baptist Quart. Rev., vol. 10, pp. 187-188-194, compared.
[2] Semi-Centennial Discourse of R. I., 1875, p. 37, note.

unconnected with any religious body, calling himself a 'seeker.'"[1]

Armitage says: "In view of the fact that Williams remained with the Baptists but *three or four months*, some have seriously doubted whether he formed a church there after that order at all."[2]

Prof. J. C. C. Clarke says: "If Mr. Williams formed a Baptist church, no clear evidence of such act remains."[3]

Dr. Dexter, a historical critic, who was a Congregationalist, says: "But the denomination of Christians, known as Baptists, having canonized him, although *never such a Baptist as they are*, and for but a very short period of time a Baptist at all, have manifested great reluctance to give due consideration to a large portion of the evidence bearing upon the case, etc."[4]

Notice that only such a Baptist as is essentially the Baptist denomination is a Baptist, and, that Dr. Dexter says that Williams was not *that kind*. No wonder that Benedict says: "*Many* of the accounts of him would make him more of a Quaker than anything else"—even though he wrote against the Quakers and was never recognized as one of them.[5]

S. Adlam, than whom no man has given this subject more investigation, says: "I can see *no* evidence that Roger Williams, in the ordinary acceptation of the term, established a *Baptist* church in Providence."[6]

Prof. J. C. C. Clarke says: "Early in 1639 occurred Roger Williams *brief and irregular assumption* of the Baptist name."[7]

---

[1] Vedder's Short Hist. Bap., p. 155.
[2] Armitage's Hist. Bap., p. 662.
[3] Baptist Quart. Rev., vol. 10, p. 200.
[4] Quoted from Roger Williams, by Dexter, p. 1.
[5] Benedict's Hist. Bap., p. 444.
[6] Adlams' "First Bap. Ch. in Am.", p. 32.
[7] Baptist Quart. Rev., vol. 10, p. 199.

Mr. Williams' organization, soon after its origin, came to nothing. Cotton Mather, who was *Williams' contemporary*, says: "He turned Seeker and Familist, and the *church came to nothing*."[1]

Armitage concedes: "What became of Williams' 'society' after he left is not very clear."

Cotton Mather says: "Whereupon his *church dissolved themselves;*" and Neal that "His church hereupon crumbled to pieces."[2]

Armitage concedes that the authority for the belief that Williams' church did not dissolve when he left it is the *fabulous* Church Records and a *doubtful* expression of Mr. Scott, who was one of them.

Adlam: "That the church which Williams began to collect fell to pieces soon after he left them is what we should *expect*, and is, as far as I can learn, the *uniform* declaration of the writers of *that day*."[3]

Backus, who hesitates which position to take says: "*Many* New England historians . . . represent that the church soon broke up, because Mr. Williams did not long walk with it."[4]

Mr. Adlam says: "There is one writer whose testimony is of the highest value on this subject; I allude to Thomas Lechford, who was in New England from 1637, until about August 1641, and among other places, he visited Providence, somewhere I judge about the close of 1640, or the beginning of 1641. He inquired with *great diligence* into the ecclesiastical affairs of the country, and gave a faithful account. Against the Baptists he had no special prejudices, more than against the Congregational-

---

[1] Mathers' Eccl. Hist. New Eng. in Backus' Hist. Bap., vol. 1, p. 90.
[2] Armitage's Hist. Bap., p. 663.
[3] Adlam's First Bap. Ch. in Am., p. 32.
[4] Backus' Hist. Bap., vol. 1, p. 88.

ists, for he was an Episcopalian. But whatever were his own convictions, I have gained, in many respects, a more exact view of New England during these four years from him, than from any other person. When speaking of Providence he says: 'At Providence, which is twenty miles from the said island, (Rhode Island, which he had visited), lives Master Williams and his company of divers opinions; most are Anabaptists; they hold there is no true visible church in the Bay, nor in the world, nor any true ministry.' . . . Lechford, then, a purely unexceptional witness, confirms what others have said—that Roger Williams' church, after he left them, crumbled to pieces. We have seen from Callendar, that in his day, the *oldest men*, those *who knew him, and were unacquainted with many of the most ancient inhabitants, never heard that Roger Williams was the founder of the Baptist church there!* So soon and so completely was that church dissolved."[1]

So Drs. W. E. Paxton, J. R. Graves, S. H. Ford, Prof. J. C. C. Clarke and a host of other authorities. Historians are generally agreed that Williams soon left his so-called Baptist church. How anyone could expect it to not dissolve when Williams left it, remembering the boundless influence he had over it, is more than I can conjecture.† Give Roger Williams whatever is due him

---

[1] Adlam's First Bap. Ch. in Am., pp. 35-36; Crosby's Hist. Eng. Bap., vol. 1, p. 117.

† In view of (1,) that Williams' society, because of *essential* defects, could not now be recognized by any true Baptist church as Baptists; (2,) Mr. Letchford's testimony, after a personal investigation in Rhode Island, that Williams' society had dissolved; (3,) of the most ancient inhabitants of Providence never having heard there was any Baptist church in Providence originated by Williams—see p. 384 of this book; (4,) of Brown University being built on the present site " because it was the home of Chad Brown, the first minister of the Baptist church;" (5,) of the tablet of its bell not even mentioning Williams as the founder of the Baptist church; (6,) of the most ancient inhabitants of Providence understanding that Brown, Wickenden, Olney, Tillinghurst, originated the first Baptist church of Providence; (7,) of the Congregationalists *passing* Providence to go the *greater distance* to Newport, in 1650, to join a Baptist church which they would not have done had there been a Baptist church in

for advocating the great Baptist position of Liberty of Conscience; but in the name of all principle, all order, ecclesiastical precedent, of the Bible and of history, *cease calling him a Baptist*, or his little disorderly and four-months-old society a Baptist church!

No church or minister ever originated with the Roger Williams' so-called Baptist church. This is evident from the *immediate disbanding* of the Williams society. Thomas Olney, whose name is on the list of the society,

Providence; (8,) of, as Backus said of the *early* New England historians,—"*many* New England historians represent that the (Williams) church soon broke up;" (9,) of Cotton Mather's statement—he was Williams' contemporary—that "his church soon dissolved;" (10,) of the improbability of its surviving the great influence of its unscriptural formation and the example of Williams leaving it; (11,) of Prof. Whitsitt's concession, that late investigators hold that Williams' society dissolved soon after he left it; (12,) of Dr. Dexters, statement—he is one of Prof. Whitsitt's highest authorities—that Williams never was such a Baptist as Baptists of America are—in view of these twelve points against Williams' society not having dissolved soon after he left it, Prof. Whitsitt's attempt to revive the fabulous concern of Williams and to palm it off as a Baptist church, and one continuing for eighty years, is to say the very least, exceedingly weak and as bold in *making* history as it is weak. Prof. Whitsitt starts out to prove the Williams claim by the utterly groundless assertion, that: "Evidences of the existence of the church founded by Roger Williams for about eighty years are numerous!" Indeed! How strange that Backus, Adlam, Callender, Cotton Mather, Prof. J. C. C. Clarke, Prof. David Weston, Dexter, Armitage, Ford, Graves, etc., etc., and the oldest inhabitants of Rhode Island, never found out the "numerous" evidences! Yea, how strange that Prof. Whitsitt himself, after this assertion, falls back, *mainly*, on the bitter, hasty and inconsiderate letter of Mr. Scott, which says *nothing* more on the disputed point than that Williams left the society. *It says nothing as to how long it continued after he left it.* With all Armitage's antipathy to Church Perpetuity and sympathy for the Williams claim, this Scott letter has so *little bearing* on the subject that he concedes it utterly uncertain as to "what became of his society after he left it"—Armitage's Bap. Hist., p. 663. Prof. Whitsitt's statement, that "there were two distinct Baptist churches in Providence for many years after 1652," has no bearing on the subject." No one denies this. It is about as good proof (?) for Prof. Whitsitt's position as the existence of more than two now in Providence is for it. Prof. Whitsitt's attempt to evade the force of Cotton Mather's positive testimony, by saying that Mather's grandfather knew nothing of the existence of Clarke's church, is against him, since Cotton Mather's not recording any non-existence of Clarke's church while he did the non-existence of Williams' proves he investigated the facts instead of blindly following his grandfather. Prof. Whitsitt virtually surrenders the question when he says, "Roger Williams was never a Baptist. . . . I do not think he was very much of a Baptist a day in his life." "I do not suppose that Williams was very much of a Baptist. He founded a Baptist church simply because there was no other sort to be found, there was nothing else for them to do. He had never had anything to do with Baptists any time in his life. He formed a church now simply because he was in that particular situation. He had no particular leading that way; he never was a Baptist at heart. I do not reckon there was any body in that colony who was a Baptist. I have a notion they formed a Baptist church simply because they had nothing else to do."—Lect. to his class. Now, Prof. Whitsitt, or any one else, is welcome to all Baptist claims he can get out of any such a thing of any such origin as he concedes to the Williams affair. See pp. 381, 382, 384, 385, 386 of this book.

organized by Williams, on its reorganization, became its pastor. Owing to absence of records no one knows *when or how* that church was reorganized; but it was not probably reorganized before 1650. We can only infer its reorganization from its having been dissolved and from its being in existence in 1652. Commenting on facts, accepted by all, Adlam says: "These statements prove that in 1652, '53 or '54, two distinct Baptist churches existed in Providence . . . the six principle was under the care of Wickenden, Brown and Dexter, while the five principle church was under the charge of Thomas Olney. They also prove that Olney's was the original, and Wickenden's, Brown's and Dexter's six principle, the seceding church. *First*. Every writer, including the records, mentions Brown, Wickenden and Dexter as former pastor of that church. *Second*. The present church from 1652 to 1770, was known only as a six principle, while Olney's was the five principle church. From this it follows that the existing church in Providence was not founded in 1639, *but in 1652; it was not the first in the State*, for it came out of an older church." [1]

Callender, in 1738, says: "*The most ancient* inhabitants *now alive*, some of them above *eighty years old, who personally knew Mr. Williams, and were well acquainted with many of the original settlers never heard that Mr. Williams formed the Baptist church there, but always understood that Brown, Wickenden, Dexter, Olney, Tillinghurst, etc., were the first founders of that church.*" [2]

Adlam says: "Two other things deserve passing notice. (1.) The college in 1770 was built on the present site, 'because it was the home of Chad Brown, the first minister of the Baptist church.' (2.) On the bell

[1] Adlam's First Bap. Ch. in Am., pp. 10-11.
[2] Adlam's First Bap. Ch. in Am. p. 13.

and on the tablet, Roger Williams is not mentioned as the *founder* of the Baptist church."[1] Instead of the Olney church swarming, Backus says: "The diversity of sentiments mentioned in this volume, p. 1-4, brought such darkness over their affairs, that no regular records before 1770 are now found therein."[2]

Adlam says: "A melancholy interest invests the last notice we have of this ancient church. It continued till early in the last century when it became extinct, *leaving no records*, and but few events in its history behind. The fullest information I have found is in a note by Callender, on the 115 page of his discourse. Speaking of this church he adds below: 'This last continued till about twenty years ago, when becoming destitute of an elder, the members were united with other churches. . . . This was written in 1738. The church had then been extinct about twenty years; that is it lost its visibility about 1718. . . . And thus passed away the *original* church, and the waves of time have almost obliterated its remembrance from the minds of men.'"[3]

Adlam says: "When Olney's church was formed I cannot tell; but as Comer, dating the Newport church no farther back than 1644, says it was the first of the Baptist denomination in America, Olney's church could not have been formed until *after* that period. I think it could not have been formed until about the year 1650. My reasons are, I find *no trace* of a Baptist church in Providence, after the failure of Roger Williams, *till after that year*. The first intimation of a church there, I find in the fall of 1651, when Holmes, after being scourged in Boston, returning home says: 'The brethren of our town (Reho-

---

[1] Adlam's First Bap. Ch. in Am. p. 14.
[2] Backus' Hist. Bap., vol. 2, pp. 285, 290-291.
[3] Adlam's First Bap. Ch. in Am., pp. 16-17.

beth,) and Providence, having taken pains to meet me four miles in the woods, we rejoiced together. This occurred in September, 1651. That it was as late as I have fixed appears also from another circumstance. I have not been able to find a single individual, out of Providence, who united with that church *until 1652;* but every Baptist up to that time, known to belong to a church, live where he may, belonged to the church at *Newport.* We know that in the year 1651, the Newport church had members in Lynn, and in Rehobeth, in Mass., and that persons came from Connecticut to unite with it. The case of the brethren in Rehobeth is peculiarly in point. In 1650 they left the Congregationalists and became Baptists. *If at that time a church had existed in Providence, a neighboring town, how naturally they should unite with it, so near and easy of access, and not go all the way down to Newport to unite with the church there.* The only way to account for this is that there was no church in Providence, and no administrator there to whom they could apply. . . . If before 1644 a church did exist in Providence, how is it, that neither *friend nor foe*" (meaning of ancient times) "has noticed her, that every Baptist passed *by* her, even her nearest neighbors, and hurried down to Newport." [1]

The following, from an able writer, gives the matter in a nutshell: (1.) "The church which Williams formed came to nothing or was dissolved soon after he left. (2.) It was reorganized, or another was formed under Thomas Olney as its pastor, who was one of the eleven baptized by Roger Williams. Olney continued to be pastor of this church until his death in 1682, somewhat over thirty years. (3.) In 1653, or 1654, which

---

[1] Adlam's First Bap. Ch. in Am., pp. 36-39.

was a few years after the formation of Olney's church, there was a division in that church on the question of laying on of hands . . . and a separate church was formed . . . under the pastorate of Chad Brown, Wickenden and Dexter. . . . *This church is now the First Baptist church of Providence.* (4.) The parent church, under Olney, gradually dwindled away, and became extinct about the year 1718, some seventy years from its origin. (5.) *No church was formed from Olney's after the division already mentioned, and no ministers are known to have gone out from it.* Olney's baptism, whether valid or invalid, was not propagated. (6.) Nearly a *century* passed before the church formed from Olney's began to colonize, in 1730. (7.) None of its ministers, or the ministers of the churches formed from it, received their baptism from *Williams*, or from any one whose baptism descended from his. (8.) The Baptist churches of America could *not* have descended from Roger Williams, or from the temporary society which he formed."

By relying on what I have shown all concede to be unreliable—the records of the first church of Providence—Benedict attributes to the old Williams and Olney organizations what is true of only the church established by Wickenden, Brown and Dexter, viz., the honor of being the "prolific mother of many Baptist communities."

As J. R. Graves wrote: "It cannot be shown that any Baptist church sprang from the Williams affair. Nor can it be proved that the baptism of any Baptist minister came from Willliams' hand."[1]

Reuben A. Guild, LL. D., Librarian of Brown University, and one of the most reliable historians of Baptist

---

[1] Trilemma, p. 13.

affairs in Rhode Island, says: "In regard to whether churches have gone out from the First Church of Providence by letters of dismission, I cannot say. In the early days everything was primitive. For near seventy years the church had no meeting house . . . kept no records, etc., etc." Dr. Guild being an ardent advocate of the First Church claims this is a virtual concession that no one can show that any church or preacher ever originated with Roger Williams and his society.[1]

In April, 1889, Dr. Caldwell, pastor of the First Church of Providence said: "We celebrate, after all, an *unknown day;* there is no *record* of the exact date of our beginning." Adlam says: "Comer, the first and for the *earliest* history of our denomination, the *most reliable* of writers, ascribes distinctly and repeatedly this priority to the Newport church. He had formed the design, more than a hundred and twenty years ago, of writing the history of American Baptists; and in that work, which he only lived to commence, but which embraces an account of his church, he says in one place: 'That it is the first of the Baptist denomination,' and, closing his history of it, says: 'Thus I have briefly given some account of the settlement and progress of the first Baptist church on Rhode Island, in New England, and the first in America.'"[2] Adlam adds: "This was written in 1730; and to those acquainted with Comer, nothing need be said of the value of his testimony. For others, I will add from Benedict a brief notice of his character: 'He began his education in Cambridge, and finished it in New Haven. He bid fair to be one of the most eminent ministers of his day; his character was unspotted, and his talents respectable and popular; he had conceived the design of writing

---

[1] Letter to Author of this book, dated Apr. 25, 1893.
[2] Adlam's First Bap. Ch. in America, p. 19.

the history of the American Baptists, and for the purpose of forwarding it, traveled as far as Philadelphia, (a great undertaking at that day), opened a correspondence with persons in the different colonies, and also in England, Ireland, etc.' This excellent man, who took *unwearied pains* to procure for his history the *most correct information*, was especially distinguished for the *extreme accuracy* of his dates, was, when he wrote the above, himself a six principle Baptist; was intimately acquainted with the church at Providence and had advantages for knowing its early history *that no other historian has since possessed*. From the way in which he asserts it, the priority of the Newport church must have been a *universally conceded fact*. . . . Besides his carefulness, he was, when he wrote the above, on the most favorable terms with the church in Providence, while a difficulty had occurred between him and the Newport church which caused him the most painful feelings. . . . Now, it was while suffering from the above cause, when, if ever, he was under temptation to suppress the truth, that he most *unhesitatingly* affirms the Newport church to be the first of the Baptists in America."[1]

Armitage says: "Comer's testimony carried great weight with these authors, and *justly*, for he was a *most* painstaking man, possessing a *clear* and *strong mind* under *high culture*, ranking with the *first men of his day*. . . . Morgan Edwards says of him: 'He was curious in making minutes of *every* remarkable event, which swelled at last into two volumes. . . . He gathered many facts from Samuel Hubbard and Edward Smith, both *contemporary* with the events which they related to him.'"[2]

[1] Adlam's First Bap. Ch. in Am., pp. 19-21; Backus' Hist. Bap., vol. 1, p. 497.
[2] Armitage's Hist. Bap., p. 665.

On Comer's testimony, taken in connection with the foregoing facts of this chapter, the priority of the Newport church ought to be considered as settled.

But I am not done. Backus says of the Newport church: "The first certain date in their church records is taken from a manuscript of Mr. Samuel Hubbard in 1648, which says the church was formed about the year 1644, and by what I have quoted from Winthrop and Hubbard, it appears as likely to be *earlier* as later than that time. The entry of the first Baptist church in Newport, here referred to, was made by John Comer as late as 1725, and is as follows: 'Having found a private record of Mr. Samuel Hubbard, who was a member of the church, by which I find that the church was in being as far back as October 16, 1648, (but how long before justly I can't find by any manuscript, but by private information it was constituted in 1644.)"[1]

Prof. Weston, the editor of this edition of Backus' History, in a note, says of Callender having given 1644 as the date for the origin of the Newport church: "There is probably no evidence that Callender or any subsequent writer who has given the above date, had any authority for it beyond the tradition preserved by Comer. Backus represents that an earlier date is possible. *Many* regard the weight of evidence in its favor. Some have placed it as far back as 1638, supposing that the church was founded by Clarke and his company on their arrival in Rhode Island. . . . They reason from the improbability that the inhabitants of Rhode Island would remain *four years without an organized church*, and from the testimony of Winthrop in 1641, that 'divers of them turned professed Anabaptists,' and that there arose a contention and schism

---

[1] Backus' Hist. Bap,, vol. 1, p. 125.

among them. *These indications are not without force.*" [1]

A note to the minutes of the Philadelphia Association, p. 455, reads: " When the first church of Newport, Rhode Island, was one hundred years old, in 1738." This dates the beginning of the Newport church 1638.

Both the Newport and the Providence churches were members of the Warren Association. Prof. Weston informs us, on the authority of its minutes of 1840, that that *Association* regarded 1638 as the origin of the Newport church."[2]

The inscription on John Clarke's tombstone reads that: " He, with his associates, came to this Island from Massachusetts, in March, 1638, and on the 24th of the same month obtained a deed thereof from the Indians. He *shortly after* gathered the church aforesaid and became its pastor." [3]

The statement of this stone accords with that of Governor Winthrop of that time, who says that " Mr. Clarke was a preacher on the Island in 1638, but does not call him pastor, although in another reference he calls him *their minister*. Governor Winthrop also says that a church was formed at Newport in 1639 in a disorderly way." [4] †

J. R. Graves, after an extended investigation of this subject, concludes: " After all the investigations I have made, I have come to the conclusion that the date of the Newport church is 1638, and any other date is altogether arbitrary." [5]

The *Canadian Baptist*, of August, 1885, says: " The church in Newport is probably the oldest Baptist church

† This "disorderly" way, evidently, is what he calls the Baptist way.
[1] Backus' Hist. Bap., vol. 1, p. 125.
[2] Idem, vol. 1, p. 125.
[3] Adlam's " First Bap. Ch. in America," p. 36.
[4] Bap. Quart. Rev., vol. 10, p. 194—Prof. J. C. C. Clarke.
[5] Adlam's " First Bap. Ch. in America," p. 45.

in the United States. It is now known that a church was in existence there in 1638, of which John Clarke was pastor."

The Newport *Daily News* says:— "The first positive date we have in the history of the first Baptist church of Newport is 1648, with a reference to the fact that certain persons were members of the church in 1644. There is no reason to suppose that if this was the date of the organization of the church it would not have been mentioned in this connection. There is no record of the demise of Dr. Clarke's church or of the formation of any other in these years. There is every reason to believe that the present church is the one founded by Dr. Clarke in 1639, or, perhaps, 1638. The first meeting house was built very soon after the organization of the church at the place now known as the 'Green End.'"

The *Central Baptist*, of St. Louis: "It now appears from the histories of the first Baptist church, Newport, Rhode Island, and the First Baptist church, Providence, the one prepared by Rev. C. E. Barrows, pastor of the Newport church, and the other by Dr. Caswell, that the former church was founded in 1638. . . . These histories are the *most authentic yet prepared*, and seem to demonstrate that Roger Williams was not the founder of the first Baptist church in America."

I will now notice only a few of the many fountains of American Baptist streams, which were independent of Roger Williams. Morgan Edwards thus gives the origin of Delaware Baptists: "To come to the history of this modern church we must cross the Atlantic and land in Wales, where it had its beginning in the following manner: In the spring of the year 1701, several Baptists, in the communities of Pembroke and Cærmarthen, resolved to go to America; and as one of the company, Thomas

Griffith, was a minister, they were advised to be constituted into a church; they took the advice; the instrument of their confederation was in being in 1770, . . . the names of their confederates follow: Thomas Griffith, Griffith Nicholas, Evan Richmond, John Edwards, Elisha Thomas, Enoch Morgan, Richard David, James David, Elizabeth Griffith, Lewis Edmond, Mary John, Mary Thomas, Tennet David, Margaret Mathias and Tennet Morris. These fifteen people may be styled a *church emigrant.*"[1] Thus, Delaware Baptists originated from an emigrant Baptist church from Wales.

Massachusetts Baptist churches thus began in Boston: "Some Baptist friends from England" had a "meeting" called, "the church was formed, consisting of"—and here follow the names.[2] Only two of these names are mentioned by Benedict as not being Baptists up to the formation of this church. Speaking of a number of those who went into this church Backus says: " Goodall came recommended from Mr. Kiffin's church in London; Turner and Lambert from Mr. Stead's church in Dartmouth, having been regular walkers in the Baptist order *before* they came to this country."[3]

The first Baptist church in Virginia, and, "in some sense, the mother of all the rest," was constituted under the pastoral care of Rev. Dutton Lane, and by Rev. "Daniel Marshall," who got his baptism in regular order from a regular Baptist church in the Philadelphia association.[4]

The first Baptist church in Pennsylvania thus originated: "In 1684 Thomas Dungan removed from Rhode Island. . . . This Baptist preacher and

[1] Benedict's Hist. Bap., p. 626.
[2] Idem, p. 383.
[3] Backus' Hist. Bap., vol. 1, p. 288.
[4] Semple's Hist. Va. Bap., pp. 5, 370, comp.

pioneer was probably accompanied with associates of his own faith. Here he founded a church of his own order, which in the end was shortly absorbed by the next company I shall name."[1] The next company, absorbing the church first named, was "Welsh emigrants, who settled in Pennepeck, or Lower Dublin, 1686." This church was made up of regular Baptist members.[2] The first Baptist church in Philadelphia was organized in 1698, of English Baptists, some of whom were of Hansard Knollys' church "in London."[3]

Maryland Baptist churches were begun in 1742, by "Henry Sator, a layman. . . . Soon after his settlement in this colony he invited Baptist ministers to preach in his house, by which means a few, from time to time, were proselyted to his sentiments, and after many years a church was gathered in his neighborhood." †[4]

In North Carolina the first Baptist "church which ever existed was gathered by one Paul Palmer, about the year 1727. . . . Mr. Palmer is said to be a native of Maryland, was baptized at Welsh Tract, in Delaware, by Owen Thomas, the pastor of the church in that place."[4]

South Carolina Baptist churches began thus: "Of the early settlers of South Carolina, a considerable portion *were Baptists.* They came in separate colonies about the year 1683, partly from the west of *England* . . . and partly from *Piscataqua*, in the district of Maine. Of the former some settled at Ashley and Cooper Rivers,

---

† Thus it has often been the case that one Baptist has been the instrument in God's hand in originating a Baptist church. One of the best churches of which the author was ever pastor originated in a similar effort, from a Bro. Stewart. Baptist reader, if there is no Baptist church in your community, "go thou and do likewise;" and the Lord will be with you. No well-informed and true Baptist will put his or her membership into a non-Baptist church.

1 Benedict's Hist. Bap., p. 595.
2 Idem, p. 596.
3 Idem, p. 601.
4 Idem, p. 681.

others about the mouth of the Edisto River. The latter settled at a place called Summerton, situated on Cooper River, and a short distance from Charleston. Here they were formed into a church under the care of Rev. William Screven. Among the settlers from England, the wife of Mr. Blake . . . and her mother, Lady Axtell, were members of the Baptist church. Those who came from Piscataqua in Maine were led hither by Rev. William Screven, who, with a considerable number of his brethren, fled from the intolerant laws of the Pedobaptists of New England. Charleston church, founded in 1683. This ancient community was formed by the united labors of these two classes of settlers, under the supervision of the distinguished man who presided over it, to the end of his long and useful life. . . . Rev. William Screven, the founder of this church, became its first pastor." [1]

We have seen that Massachusetts Baptists began according to the Baptist way of beginning. In the following appears the origin of Maine Baptists, in which we see where Mr. Screven, who originated the first church of South Carolina Baptists, began his work in America. " Kittery, the oldest town in the province, incorporated 1647, was selected as the first place to raise a Baptist standard. . . . It was soon known that in Kittery were several persons professing to be *Baptists*. From whence they came, is now unknown. In the course of events, an opportunity offered to them the privilege of church communion, agreeable to their own theological views. The nearest Baptist church was at Boston, Mass., over which Rev. Isaac Hull then presided. At the advice of Mr. Hull, these Baptists of Kittery united with his church. William Screven, an early emigrant from *England*, was

---

[1] Benedict's Hist. Bap., pp. 701-702.

one of their number. Being a man of more than common talents, and devoutly pious, he officiated as leader in their worship. The brethren at Kittery and in Boston were satisfied that the great Head of the Church had designed and called him to preach the gospel of Christ. He was accordingly licensed by the church in Boston to 'exercise his gifts in Kittery, or elsewhere, as the providence of God may cast him.' The Baptists in Kittery, being now blessed with a minister and situated at so great a distance from Boston, deemed it expedient for their own spiritual advantage, and for the cause of Christ in new settlements, to unite in a separate church."[1] Backus says: "A Baptist church was also formed this year from that of Boston, at Newbury."[2]

The first Baptist church in New York, of which we have any certain knowledge, was organized by Rev. Valentine Wightman "about 1712."[3] Mr. Wightman was from the North Kingston church in Maine, thus: "From North Kingston" he "went and settled at Groton," and from Groton he went to New York.[4] The North Kingston church originated in a revival in 1710, held by Elder Baker, from Newport.[5] Thus, New York Baptist churches originated from Newport Baptists, in the regular succession line.

Georgia Baptists thus began, in the regular succession from South Carolina Baptists: "In the year 1751, Mr. Nicholas Bedgegood . . . embraced the distinguishing sentiments of the Baptists; this gentleman *went over to Charleston, S. C., about the year 1757, and*

---

[1] Benedict's Hist. Bap., p. 506, and Backus' Hist. Bap., vol. 1, p. 400.
[2] Backus' Hist. Bap., vol. 1, p. 405.
[3] Benedict's Hist. Bap., p. 541.
[4] Backus' Hist. Bap., vol. 1, p. 466; vol. 2, p. 516; Benedict's Hist. Bap., p. 541, comp.
[5] Backus' Hist. Bap., vol. 2, p. 505.

was baptized and united to the Baptist church in that city, then under the pastoral care of the Rev. Mr. Hart. He soon discovered talents for usefulness, and was licensed to preach; his ordination to the gospel ministry took place in the year 1759. And it appears his labors were not in vain in the Lord; for in 1763, he had the happiness to baptize several persons . . . to whom, with a few other Baptists, (probably a branch of the Charleston Baptist church,) he administered the Lord's Supper. This was the first semblance of a Baptist church—this the first Baptist communion ever held in the State." [1]

I have now shown that in the States which were the great fountains of the many Baptist streams, running out into the new States, Baptists, instead of beginning with Roger Williams, began in the regular continuity line.

Take even Rhode Island. Were we to admit that the present Providence church is the Roger Williams church, yet we would have Rhode Island Baptists, to a very great extent, originating from other churches. Of John Clarke's church in Newport, Backus says; "Mr. Richard Dingley," its second pastor "in 1694, left them and went to South Carolina." [2] Thus, through Dingley, South Carolina inherited baptisms from the John Clarke church. John Comer, another of Clarke's successors to the Newport pastorate, removed and gathered the first Baptist Church in Rehobeth." [2] John Clarke's church, about 1729, "increased to a hundred and forty-two members, being the *largest church then in the colony*." [3]

Of the John Clarke church, and others, Backus says: "On June 21st, 1729, they had the *largest* association of

---

[1] History Georgia Bap. Ass., p. 1, by Jesse Mercer; Benedict's Hist. Bap., p. 722.
[2] Backus' Hist. Bap., vol. 2, p. 498.
[3] Idem, p. 499.

Baptist ministers and churches that had *ever been seen in America.*"¹

"The first Baptist church in Connecticut was formed in Groton about 1705. Elder Valentine Wightman came from North Kingston, and settled in Groton, and was the first pastor of this church."² Having shown the Kingston church a daughter of John Clarke's church, thus, we see Connecticut Baptists originated from it.

Why do not Baptist opponents call attention to the swarms of Baptists from the Newport church? Why do they not call attention to other churches, also, being the fountain head of American Baptist churches? Simply because they could not close the people's eyes against Baptist church claims; or, in many cases, because of ignorance and thoughtlessness.

Of the first Baptist church in Swansea, Massachusetts, Davis says: "In 1663, John Miles came over from Wales, and began the church which has continued to this day."³

Samuel Jones, a Baptist minister of Wales, came to America about 1686, settling in Pennsylvania. John Phillips, a Welsh Baptist minister came to America about 1692. Thomas Griffiths, a Baptist minister of Wales, emigrated to America "in the year 1701, and fifteen of the members of the church in the same vessel."⁴ Morgan Edwards, a Baptist minister of more than usual learning "from Wales" "arrived here May 23rd, 1761, and shortly after became pastor of a Baptist church."⁵

---

[1] Backus' Hist. Bap., p. 499.
[2] Idem, p. 516.
[3] Davis' Hist. Welsh Bap., pp. 39-40.
[4] Idem, pp. 67-71-72.
[5] Idem, pp. 77-78.

John Thomas, a Baptist minister, came from Wales to America in 1703.[1] David Evans, a Welsh Baptist minister, arrived in America in 1739.[2] Several of the members of the Rehobeth church in Wales "went to America, and formed themselves into a church at a place called Montgomery, Pennsylvania, early in the eighteenth century."[3] Benjamin Griffiths, a Baptist minister of Wales, became their pastor. Nathaniel Jenkens, also, was a member and pastor of this church.[3] Thomas Davis, a Welsh Baptist minister, left Wales for Long Island, about 1713. Cape May church had its foundation "laid in 1675, when a company of emigrants, from England, arrived in Delaware."[4] Abel Morgan, a Baptist minister, came from Wales early in the eighteenth century.[5] In 1737, *thirty members of a Baptist* church in Wales *with " their minister*, came to Pennsylvania and organized the Welsh Tract church."[6]

"Richard Jones, a native of Wales, arrived in America, and became pastor of the church at Burley, Virginia, in 1727."[7] Caleb Evans, a Baptist minister of finished education, of Wales, "went to America and settled in Charleston, South Carolina, in 1768."[8]

Here, then, are fourteen Welsh ministers and some churches, in the regular succession line from Europe. From these, of course, have come hundreds of American Baptist churches, and thousands of Baptists, and many Baptist ministers. Yet these are but a few examples of American Baptist churches and ministers in the Baptist Perpetuity line from Europe. Davis says: " *Wales has been a nursery of Baptists*. . . . Many of the American churches were founded, either wholly or in part, by

---

[1] Davis' Hist. Welsh Bap., p. 88.
[2] Idem, p. 98.
[3] Idem, p. 114.
[4] Idem, p. 115.
[5] Idem, p. 68.
[6] Idem, p. 125.
[7] Idem, p. 134.
[8] Idem, p. 138.

Welsh Baptists. There are several Welsh churches in America. Wales has supplied the American churches with many useful ministers. . . . Indeed, most of the Baptists in the State of Pennsylvania, for a great number of years from the beginning . . . were either emigrants from Wales or their descendants."[1]

The late and lamented E. T. Winkler, D. D., of Alabama, said: "The Baptist church (if that be the name for it) did not commence with Roger Williams, but with a more illustrious personage, in the beginning of the Christian era. . . . He had little ecclesiastical prominence. He was pastor of the newly formed church in Providence only a few months. And there were *other* Baptists scattered among the various colonies, who had no historical connection with him. Indeed, it is affirmed with confidence that *no Baptist church in our country traces its descent from Roger Williams.* Thus, for example, the Baptist church at Swansea, in Massachusetts, came from Swansea in Wales, and brought their *records* with them across the Atlantic.[2] In Great Britain we have had churches from the *immemorial antiquity.*"

The *Journal and Messenger*, Cincinnati, says: "He ought to know that no one professes or believes, except it be some one *ignorant* of all the important facts, that Roger Williams was the founder of the Baptist church. The *most* that has ever been claimed for Roger Williams is that he founded *a* Baptist church, *but it cannot be proven that the church he founded was at all what a Baptist church is to-day, or that the church that he founded continued to exist more than four months to a year*, without an essential change of character, or that from *it ever sprang any other church*, which has, in turn, propagated

---

[1] Davis' Hist. Welsh Bap., pp. 157-158.
[2] Backus' Hist. of New Eng., p. 117.

its kind, or that Roger Williams ever baptized any one, who in turn became a baptizer, unless we except Ezekiel Holliman, whose only subject was Williams himself, so that *nothing can be more absurd* than that Roger Williams founded the Baptist church." In another issue the same paper says: "The position of American Baptists is not effected by the answer to the question as to Roger Williams. The *more intelligent* Baptists of this country do not look upon Williams as the founder of their denomination. . . . *It is quite certain that Williams never was a Baptist in the present acceptation of the term. Moreover it is quite as certain that he never baptised any one who transmitted his baptism.* His baptism, whatever it was, began and ended with *himself and his few companions.* . . . Very few Baptists in this country trace their ecclesiastical organization to *Rhode Island* and none to *Roger Williams.*" Another editorial in the same paper, of May 2, 1877, says: "In our judgment the facts are these: Roger Williams was the founder of a church *resembling* in *some* respects, a Baptist church. . . . But in four months he became dissatisfied with his own baptism, and renounced it as invalid, because it was not administered by one who had been baptized himself. *For a time,* consequently, there does not appear to have been any *organized church in Providence,* and inasmuch as no records were kept by that which is now the first Baptist church in Providence, for *more than one hundred years* it is quite difficult to fix upon the time of its organization. . . . It is quite certain that the Baptists of this country did not *originate with Roger Williams;* for many of them were Baptists when they came from England. . . . And these formed churches, a second in Newport, in 1656; in Swansea, Mass., in 1653; in Boston, in 1665; in Middleton, N. J., in 1686;

in Lower Dublin, Pa., in 1689; in Philadelphia, in 1698; and in several others previous to the year 1700. And no one of these traces its origin to Roger Williams, to the church that he founded, or to any of those baptized by him. It is an error, therefore, to speak of Roger Williams as the father of American Baptists."

The *Standard*, of Chicago, says of the history of the Williams church: "It is the most complicated and difficult tissue of facts and conclusions and inferences and probabilities that was *ever* woven probably in American ecclesiastical annals."

In 1877, when pressed, Prof. John Clarke Ridpath, a Methodist historian, wrote to the *American Baptist Flag:* "There is a vast difference between the statement that Roger Williams was the founder of the first Baptist church in America, and the statement that he was the founder of the Baptist denomination. The latter statement I have never made." The Roman Catholic bishop of New Orleans, speaking of the statement that the Baptist churches of America originated with Roger Williams, says: "This is saying too much; he was prominent among them."[1] H. W. D., President of the Campbellite College at Bethany, Va., says: "Cannot say that the American Baptist church originated with Roger Williams."[1] As admitting all any one claims for the Roger Williams' affair, as being the first Baptist church in America, would effect but few Baptists of America, Benedict, in derision exclaims: "I have lately seen an intimation, in a tract put forth by an opposer of Baptists that all the denomination of America sprang from this old Roger Williams' church, which commenced its operations with lay bap-

---

[1] Recent Letter to the Author.

tism; and of course, no soul of the denomination has been regularly baptized, or has any claim to apostolic succession."[1] †

Concluding this chapter: I have shown that there were Baptists among the first immigrants into New England; that both the Dover and Newport Baptist churches were existing when Roger Williams organized his society; that Williams proved himself not a Baptist by preferring baptism from an unbaptized man to getting either of these or Baptists in England to baptize him; that he showed himself not a Baptist by living and dying out of a Baptist church; that the society he organized soon dissolved; that it never perpetuated or propagated itself in any way; that the first church of Providence is not the Williams church, but was organized, probably, about 1652; that

---

[1] Benedict's Hist. Bap., p. 459—note.

† As an illustration of the cloud of conjectures which imagination and opposition to Baptists have gathered over the Williams affair and over Clarke's church, swallowing Dr. Dexter's—Dexter was a scholar but a most bitterly prejudiced Baptist opponent—statement, that Baptists, in 1638 and 1639, did not practice exclusive immersion—a baseless fabrication which I have exposed in a previous chapter, Dr. Whitsitt says that Williams never was immersed and that "there is no reason to suppose that the baptism administered by Mr. Clarke at Newport was any different from the one administered at Providence; and, possibly, Williams went there and sprinkled them over again. I do not know. If the Baptists at Newport adopted the same mode of baptism that was practiced at Providence, it must have been sprinkling. I am inclined to think that they sprinkled in each case." The reader will see that this is *purely guess* work, dished out to young ministers as *historical* instruction! And all on the *baseless guess* work of the *bitter Baptist opponent*—Dr. Dexter! It would look like such guessers should easily guess out a "Baptist succession," even were there no history proving it. But, strange to say, *the guessing seems to be all done against Baptist history!* Now, as to the facts: (1.) As to Williams' case. Prof. Reuben A. Guild, LL. D., Librarian of Brown University, with the original documents before him, wrote me, April 25, 1893: "Winthrop, under date of March 16, 1639, says that Williams 'was rebaptized by one Holliman. Then Mr. Williams rebaptized him and ten more.' Governor Winthrop was a dear friend and correspondent of Williams and knew what he was writing about. . . . Perhaps Prof. Whitsitt makes the point that rebaptism was not immersion. *It has always been so regarded in these parts from the beginning.* Williams himself has placed himself on record as a believer in *dipping*. In the Winthrop papers (Mass. Hist. Collections, fourth series, vol. 6), under date of 1649, more than ten years after his 'rebaptism,' he speaks of John Clarke as *dipping* believers at Seekonk, and adds: 'I believe this practice comes nearer the practice of our Great Founder, Jesus Christ, than other practices of religion do.'" Prof. Albert H. Newman, D. D., L. L. D., a specialist in Baptist history, wrote me, December 13, 1892: "It seems *highly probable* that Roger Williams was immersed, though I once was of the contrary opinion. Coddington, who seems to have *witnessed* the ceremony, described it sometime afterward as *immersion*."

(2.) As to John Clarke, I have shown by Prof. J. C. C. Clarke, who has given

the John Clarke and Dover churches were the first Baptist churches ever organized in America; that no one, or scarcely any one, claimed that the first church of Providence was the first Baptist church in America until near a century after Williams' time; that early history shows the Newport and Dover churches organized before Williams' church; that the advocates of the first church of Providence being the oldest in America *concede* their case exceedingly doubtful; that the John Clarke church swarmed with numerous churches and ministers; that, inasmuch as Baptist churches of America originated generally from European immigration we could admit the first church of Providence to be the Williams and the oldest American Baptist church, without implying it is the mother of American Baptist churches to any notice-

the *original* records of Rhode Island the *most thorough investigation*, that he came to America *a Baptist preacher*. Prof. Reuben A. Guild, LL. D., after proving that Williams was immersed—in the letter from which this note quotes —adds: " As to John Clarke, I have already answered your question. He was pastor of the First Baptist church of Newport, and he '*dipped*' believers at Seekonk. Would he administer this rite to others and be a Baptist pastor and preacher when he had not been dipped or immersed himself? I think not He was a scholarly and common sense man. The tradition and belief is that he was *baptized in England*." Prof. Albert Newman, in the letter quoted in the foregoing, says: " It is *certain* from Mr. Williams' own account of Clarke's church that Clarke *practiced immersion*, and we may infer from this that he was himself immersed."

Prof. Whitsitt attempts to prove John Clarke was a Congregationalist, by assuming that he was made a freeman in Massachusetts and that no man could there, at that time, be a freeman without, at the same time, being a Congregationalist. But the Professor is wrong again. The John Clarke, of whom he speaks as having been made a freeman, is not the John Clarke who organized the Newport church. Prof. David Weston editor of Backus' Church History and the lamented critical Professor of Church History in Hamilton Theological Seminary, says: " The John Clarke who was admitted a freeman in Boston, May, 1635, must have been a different person from the founder of the Rhode Island plantation. The latter writes in the ' Narrative '—' In the year '37 I left my native land, and in the ninth month of the same I (through mercy) arrived in Boston. I was no sooner on shore than there appeared to me differences among them concerning the covenants.' . . . Mass. Historical Collections, fourth series, vol. 2, p. 72. The date thus given in the ' Narrative ' is verified by the fact that the difficulty on the question of covenants, which Clarke found in the colony as soon as he was on shore, does not seem to have arisen till 1836."—Note to Backus' Hist. Bap., vol. 1, pp. 70-71. To this must be added, since the John Clarke who organized the Newport church did not arrive in America till 1637, he could not possibly have been the John Clarke who " was admitted a freeman " in 1635! Prof. Whitsitt is a good brother and valuable historian, but, in attempting to follow Dexter and to maintain the exploded Williams claim, he has but involved himself in inextricable confusion, absurdities and contradictions.

able extent. The "*Christian Messenger,*" a most bitter Campbellite paper, concedes: "*We have never considered that Roger Williams' baptism had any material effect upon Baptist succession. The Baptist churches of America did not originate with the Roger Williams church, nor receive their baptism from it, at least the great mass of them did not.*"

CHAPTER XXVII.

THE REGULAR BAPTISTS, OFTEN CALLED MISSIONARY BAPTISTS, ARE THE "OLD" OR PRIMITIVE BAPTISTS.

Unable to meet the overwhelming testimony for Baptist Church Perpetuity, Baptist opponents attempt to "darken counsel" by asking: " But who are the 'old Baptists?' " Some of them, when meeting the Regular Baptists, affirm "the Anti-missionary Baptists are the oldest;" when meeting the Anti-missionary Baptists, they affirm the " Regular Baptists are the oldest ! ! "

Inasmuch as Baptist history demonstrates that in every age, in non-essential matters, Baptists have differed from Baptists of other ages, by such matters we are not to identify Baptist churches of the present with those of the past. Thus, speaking of 1691, Crosby says: " If I am not mistaken this was the first church of the Baptists that practiced the holy ordinance" of singing in public worship.[1] In the early history of American Baptists whenever a preacher changed his field he was reordained. When a preacher "got out of his parish he was nobody."[2] In the latter half of the last century protracted meetings were unknown among Baptists.[2] In 1840, Baptists protracted meetings often continued a year.[2] † Church houses, singing books, associations, and many other things to which Baptists hold, are not

---

† Why does not some opponent of Church Perpetuity attempt to prove, by these different customs, that Baptists of the nineteenth century are not the successors of Baptists of the eighteenth !

[1] Crosby's Hist. Eng. Bap., vol. 1, p. 299.
[2] Prof. Whitsitt's Lect. to his Classes.

mentioned in the Bible and have been unknown to ages of Baptist history. While the constitution and the organization of the churches is, in the New Testament, in particulars, prescribed and described their methods of work and most of the forms of their worship are left to be decided by the *spirit* of the gospel and sanctified common sense. Missionary boards, like associations, hymn books, etc., are of comparatively modern origin. Like associations, etc., missionary boards, are mere Baptist *expediencies*, not being essential to the existence of Baptist churches. Anti-missionary Baptists had as well—because they have associations, hymn books, and many other customs which ancient Baptists did not have—deny that they themselves are the "Old Baptists" as to deny that the Regular Baptists are the "Old Baptists," because they have missionary boards. Since the Anti-mission Baptists have neither missions, pastors' support, nor educational enterprises, the question, dividing the two, IS REALLY NOT PLANS OF MISSIONS, OF EDUCATION, BUT IT IS MISSIONS OR NO MISSIONS, AND EDUCATION OR NO EDUCATION, AND MINISTERIAL OR NO MINISTERIAL SUPPORT. *It is whether the churches shall do any missionary and educational work and support their ministers.*

Regular Baptists do all this. Anti-missionary Baptists *not only do not this, but they bitterly oppose it*—so bitterly that they *would exclude from their fellowship any who should do these obligations.*† That the churches, *when able to do so*, should so support their ministers as to leave them free from all worldly care, is, from the following Scriptures as clear as that Christ is the Son of God: "The laborer is worthy of his *hire.*"—Luke 10:7. "Let

---

† They sometimes make little gifts to their preachers. But they would so starve them out that I have never known one of them whom the church, by supporting, freed from the entanglements of the world.

the elders that rule well be counted worthy of *double* honor, especially those who *labor* in word and doctrine. For the Scripture saith: 'Thou shalt not muzzle the ox that treadeth out the corn. And the laborer is worthy of his *reward*.' "—I. Tim. 5:17-18. " Who goeth a warfare at his *own charges?* * Who planteth a vineyard and *eateth not of the fruit thereof?* * Or who feedeth a flock and eateth not of the milk thereof? * Say I these things as a man, or saith not the law the same also? † For it is written in the law of Moses: 'Thou shalt not muzzle the mouth of the ox that treadeth out the corn.' Doth God take care for *oxen?* Or saith he it altogether for *our sakes? For our sakes*, no doubt this is written. . . . If we have sown to you in spiritual things is it a great thing if we should *reap your carnal things?* . . . *Even so* HATH THE LORD ORDAINED THAT THEY WHO PREACH THE GOSPEL SHOULD LIVE OF THE GOSPEL."— I. Cor. 9:7-11-14. Paul, in order that he should not prejudice the heathen, in *planting* the Corinthian church, charged nothing for his services, but says: "I robbed other churches, taking WAGES from them to do you service."—II. Cor. 11:8.‡ Therefore, Paul says it is as unlawful for a preacher to make his living as for a soldier to do so—"no man that warreth, *entangleth*, himself with the affairs of this life, that he may please him who chose him to be a soldier. And if a man strive for masteries, yet is he not crowned except he strive lawfully. The

---

* The Anti-missionary Baptist preachers do.

† Thus, we see that Paul teaches that gospel ministers are to be as well supported as were the Jewish.

‡ Οψώνιον, here rendered "wages," Thayer's Lex., defines: "A soldier's pay, allowance that part of a soldier's pay given to soldiers in place of pay, [*i. e.*, rations] and the money in which he is paid." Here is express authority for "*salaried* preachers." But it is no authority for the wickedness of making money the *object* and *motive* of preaching.

husbandman that laboreth must first be *partaker of the fruits.*"—II. Tim. 2:4-6.

Turning to history, we find that during ages persecution prevented Baptists from building educational institutions and conducting missions on as extensive a scale as to-day, or supporting their pastors as well as to-day. But, such opportunities as they had for this work were often improved. The Waldenses, etc., were pre-eminently a missionary church, their missionaries so widely scattering the gospel seed as to revolutionize Europe, produce the Reformation, and, consequently, the liberty and the Christianity of our own times. Whittier has put into verse the story of a secret possessor of a precious Biblical manuscript, a traveling Waldensian merchant, who guardedly unfolds his treasure to a noble lady, to whom he had been exhibiting his costly silks:

"Oh lady fair, I have yet a gem, which purer lustre flings
Than the diamond flash of the jewelled crown on the lofty brow of kings;
A wonderful pearl of exceeding price, whose virtue shall not decay,
Whose light shall be as a spell to thee and a blessing on thy way?
The cloud went off from the Pilgrim's brow as a small meagre book,
Unchased with gold or gem of cost, from his flowing robe he took.
Here, lady fair, is the pearl of price, may it prove as much to thee.
Nay, keep thy gold, I ask it not, for the Word of God is free."

The reader here turn to and read pages 189-190 of this book—the statements of Professors Osgood and **Everts** as to the ancient Baptists being missionary Baptists.

But, the split between the Regular Baptists and the Anti-missionary Baptists having occurred in the early part of the nineteenth century I will come to a later and more historical period.

The London Confession, "put faith by the elders and brethren of many congregations of Christians (baptized upon a profession of their faith) in London and the country," A. D. 1689, which both sides recognized and both used as their main confession before the split, reads: "The work of pastors being constantly to attend the service of Christ, in his churches, in the ministry of the word and prayer, with watching for their souls as those who must give an account to him; it is incumbent on the churches to whom they minister, not only to give them all due respect, but also to communicate to them in *all good things*, according to their ability, so that they may have a *comfortable* supply; *without being themselves entangled in secular affairs;* and may also be capable of exercising hospitality towards others; and this is *required* by the law of nature, and by the express order of our Lord Jesus Christ, who hath ordained that they that *preach the gospel should live of the gospel.*"[1]

The General Association of "Particular" or "Calvinistic" Baptists of England and Wales—the one which adopted the Confession, just quoted, which was first[2] published in 1677—which met "to consult of proper means to advance the glory of God and the well being of their churches," raised a fund of money: (1.) "To communicate thereof to those churches that are not able to maintain their own ministry; and that their ministers be encouraged *wholly* to devote themselves to the great work of preaching the gospel. (2.) To *send* ministers that are

---

[1] London Confession of 1689, chap. 26. sec. 10; in Cutting's Hist. Vindication. p. 168; Crosby's Hist. Baptists, vol. 3, p. 102; Goadby's Bye Paths to Baptist History, p. 228.
[2] Crosby's Hist. Baptists, vol. 3, p. 258.

ordained, or at least, solemnly called to preach the gospel in both country and city where the gospel hath or hath not yet been preached, and to visit churches. (3.) *To assist* those members that shall be found in any of the aforesaid churches, that are *disposed to study*, have an inviting gift, and are found in fundamentals, in attaining to the *knowledge and understanding of the languages, Latin, Greek and Hebrew.*"[1]

The ministers and messengers of thirteen churches, "in and about London, in assembly, in 1704, recommended;" "That it would be *highly useful*, that a fund of money be settled and maintained, either by subscriptions or collections, as each church shall think most expedient, for the *education of pious young men* . . . for the better fitting of them for the work of the ministry; and also, for the furnishing of others, who have not time to attain the knowledge of tongues and some other parts of useful learning, with such English books as may be thought most proper, for their assistance and improvement. And that this be recommended to each particular church."[2]

Of ministers supporting themselves : "In some places this was occasioned through the *necessity*, the people being poor, and few in number, and exposed to many hardships by persecution, for that they were *obliged* to it for the support of themselves and families; and when it is thus no one can justly blame either the minister or the people.* . . . Upon the glorious Revolution in 1688, whereby not only the nation in general was delivered from popery and slavery, but the Protestant Dissenters

---

* The position of "Missionary Baptists."

[1] Crosby's Hist. Baptists, vol. 3, pp. 251-252; Ivimey's Hist. Eng. Baptists, vol. 1, pp. 491-493; Goadby's Bye Paths to Bap. Hist., p. 205.

[2] Crosby's Hist. Eng. Bap., vol. 4, p. 7; Goadby's Bye Paths to Bap. Hist., p. 216.

from their hardships which they had long suffered from the established church, they endeavored to effect a *reformation in this matter;*† and having now their liberty secured them by law, they hoped to maintain a more regular ministry, and *provide better for their maintenance.* And the first thing they proposed in order to this, was to publish a treatise in vindication of this rite, and therefore fixed on Mr. Keach as the most proper person to do it. Accordingly a small treatise was prepared, in which Mr. Keach effectually proves it to be the duty of every congregation, if capable of it, to *maintain* their minister. . . . And that this treatise might come forth with the more authority, and tend the better to answer the good design of its being published, it is recommended to all the congregations of baptized believers in England and Wales by several of the ministers, thus: ' Beloved Brethren, we having read and considered this ensuing treatise, and do conclude it may be of great profit to the churches of Jesus Christ. " We fearing some congregations have not so duly weighed and considered the matter of their *indispensable duty* to the ministry, in respect of providing such a *maintenance* for those who labor amongst them, and are over them in the Lord, as they *ought to do,* by which means it may be feared that many of them may be *hindered or obstructed* in attending to their work, in serving Christ and his people, as the nature of their sacred employment and office *requires;* and the present day especially calls for, and as *the Lord himself hath ordained.* Therefore our earnest desires are, that our brethren, both ministers and members, would be pleased to get this little book, and both read and well weigh what is said therein." [1] This was in July, 1688.

† A Reformation many of our churches are suffering for.
[1] Crosby's Hist. Eng. Baptists, vol. 4, pp. 293-295.

An act of a General Assembly of these same Baptists, held in London, from May the 3d to May the 24th, 1692, reads: "That *all churches make quarterly collections*, in what method they think best for the *encouragement of the ministry, by helping those ministers that are poor, and to educate brethren that may be approved, to learn the knowledge of those tongues, wherein the Scriptures are written.*" [1]

Says Ivimey of the English Baptist church of this period: "Their example, too, is worthy of imitation, as they strove to promote General Association of the churches who were agreed in doctrine and discipline; *in providing the advantages of literature for young ministers;* and in catechising the children of the congregation. The *weekly money subscription* . . . was adopted and recommended by a general assembly of the ministers and messengers of more than one hundred churches in London in 1689." [2]

In the beginning of the last century Thomas Hollis, a London merchant, and whom Crosby calls "a Baptist by profession" and who wrote of himself, "who profess myself a Baptist," [3] in the Harvard College founded two professorships, one for *divinity*, the other for mathematics and material and experimental philosophy. Out of the incomes as interest of his donations, he ordered four score pounds per annum in our money to each of the professors, and ten pounds apiece per annum to ten poor scholars of laudable character, *designed for the work of the gospel ministry*, as a help to defray the charge of their education." [4] *

* Crosby's last volume of History was published A. D. 1740; Ivimey's in 1830. Crosby's was published long before the split; Ivimey's when it was occurring. About 1792—long before the "split" was thought of or an Antimission Baptist existed—the "Particular Baptist Society for Propagating the Gospel Among the Heathen" was organized.
[1] Crosby's Hist. Eng. Baptists, vol. 3, p. 265; Goadby's Bye Paths to Bap. Hist., p. 209.
[2] Ivimey's Hist. Eng. Bap., vol. 2, p. 10; of its introduction.
[3] Crosby's Hist. Eng. Bap., vol. 4, p. 206; Backus' Hist. Bap., vol. 1, p. 510.
[4] Crosby's Hist. Eng. Bap., vol. 4, p. 229; Backus' Hist. Bap., vol. 1, pp. 495-512.

The Somerset Association, in England, at its meeting in 1655, recommended that the churches "follow after *largeness of heart* . . . in the *maintainance of those who dispense the word unto you, that* such dispensers may give themselves *wholly* unto the work."[1]

The Midland Association, in England, at its meeting in 1655, made a similar recommendation, and that, by money, the churches enter into " a joint carrying on of any part of the work of the Lord."[2]

On Mr. Hardcastle, accepting the call of the Broadmead church, 1671, we read: "They subscribed *every one* according to their *ability* . . . to be delivered twenty pounds† each quarter to the said pastor. And that it might be paid, it was ordered that every person bring in their quarterage a month before every usual quarter of the year. And so they all that could give came one after another into the said room, and told what they were of themselves free to pay, and then straightway returned out of the room into the meeting again. . . . It pleased the Lord to stir up their hearts to raise the said sum of eighty pounds per annum; for some servants subscribed ten shillings * per year, others six shillings; other members mean in the world, but rich in grace, gave ten shillings, others twenty, some thirty shillings, some others forty shillings, some fifty shillings, some three pounds, some four pounds per annum, one five pounds, and another six pounds per annum. Of those who subscribed to the pastor's maintenance there is to be observed the grace of God in some. One aged brother, named Henry

---

† This was $397.26 per year—a much better support than pastors now generally receive.

* About $2.40. Think of this as the life of the genuine "Old Baptist," when we have men in our churches owning fine farms who do not give this much!

1 Goadby's Bye Paths to Bap. Hist., p. 184.
2 Idem, p. 187; Andrew Fuller's Works, vol. 1, p. 52.

Pierce, a very mean poor man to appearance, in person and habit, and by profession or trade but a journeyman or shoemaker, that *lived up in a cock-loft,* yet his heart was so enlarged for and by the Lord that he would subscribe, and did pay, *not less than twenty shillings per annum.* And one other member, a sister named Margaret Webb, that had *two children to maintain,* that lived very near, and took great care to carry the world about, to live therein honestly toward all and labored very hard so to do, yet she would subscribe towards the carrying on of the gospel, and did *pay forty shillings per year.* Which example did provoke, if not shame, * others."[1] Eight years after this, this good sister died, and the records of this church read: "Sister Webb, one of the deaconesses, was interred after the meeting was done at Walbarrows. She was about sixty-four years of age. . . . She left a good savour behind her; did much good with her little. She labored hard in her way of distilling waters, and gave constantly while she lived *forty shillings* a year for the pastor and left fifty pounds for the use of the congregation."[2]

Goadby says of English Baptists of the early part of the seventeenth century: "It was a *standing rule in most of their churches that all absent* members should send their weekly contribution to the church's treasury.† . . . There are not many indications in the middle of the seventeenth century that the Baptists had any great need to spur the flagging generosity of their members. It is

---

* Let this have the same effect on the illiberal soul who reads this. This amount was about $10.60.

† This rule all our churches *ought* to adopt and enforce. By it "absent" members would not only continue to help, but would, in many cases, be prevented from carelessness and backsliding.

[1] Broadmead Records, pp. 162-163; Goadby's Bye Paths to Baptist History, p. 229.

[2] Idem, p. 404; Goadby's Bye Paths to Baptist History, p. 240.

toward the close of that century that we first meet with symptoms of the decline of their fervor and benevolence. . . . By and by we begin to find minutes about 'the increase of covetousness.' "[1]

Turning more to the history of the Welsh Baptists of the seventeenth century, we read: "In the Association held at Abergavenny, this church proposed to revive the *old plan of supporting ministers* in weak and destitute churches. . . . William Thomas was appointed home missionary for six months and received from Swansea *five pounds;* Llantrisaint, *two pounds and ten shillings;* Carmarthen, *two pounds and ten shillings.* . . . Our Welsh brethren were great advocates for the ancient order of things. They adopted the old plan of supporting *missionaries.* The gospel through the channel of *missions* has made its way to many parts of the world."[2]

August, 1711, the Blænaugwent church resolved "Never to grieve their ministers, who should labor among them in word and doctrine, but *cheerfully to assist them in temporal things.*"[3] The churches of the Welsh Association "*doubled*" their contributions to missions.[4] "In the year 1654 there were several young men in this church—Llanwenarth church—who were exercising their gifts as public speakers . . . and as the church had increased considerably they *contributed thirty pounds for the support of their minister* that year."[5] "The Welsh ministers received *money* from the London fund."[5] In the Llanwenarth church "James Edwards commenced

[1] Goadby's Bye Paths to Baptist History, p. 308.
[2] Davis' History Welsh Baptists, p. 31.
[3] Idem, p. 69.
[4] Idem, p. 85.
[5] Idem, p. 98.

the work of the ministry in 1750. He also went to the same *college*. . . . Morgan Harris . . . went to Bristol *College* in 1776."[1] "John Phillips was baptized in 1720. Having exercised his gifts for some time he went to Bristol *College*. . . . He returned to Wales and preached at Usk for some time."[2] Speaking of the Welsh Baptists at the time when the "split" occurred,[†] Davis says: "The traveling preachers received a *stated sum*, so that a man of a strong constitution, who can preach twice every day, as Christmas Evans, John Elias and others do, would receive a *considerable sum* for his services. For this purpose the churches have a *fund* or treasury."[3] *

---

* The following from the *London Freeman*, of 1892, corrects a report which is almost received as history: "The assertion which has appeared in print several times recently that the Rev. John Ryland, Sr., M. A., father of Dr. Ryland, said to Dr. (then Mr.) Carey, when the latter suggested at a meeting of ministers at Northampton, in 1785 or 1786, the duty of sending the gospel to the heathen: 'Young man, sit down; when God wishes to convert the heathen he will do it without your help or mine,' is *not true*. Dr. Ryland in his Life of Andrew Fuller, says in a foot note on page 112, sec. ed., that his father had left Northampton before the minister's meeting of 1876, and that he (Dr. Ryland) well remembered both of the discussions which took place at the minister's meeting in 1785 in which '*no room was left for that ill natured anecdote.*' Dr. Ryland also says: 'I never heard of it until I saw it in print and *I cannot credit it*. No man prayed and preached about the latter day glory more than my father, nor did I *ever* hear such sentiments proceed from his lips as are here attributed to him. It is true he admitted the idea of a personal reign of Christ upon the earth between the first and second resurrection, and supposed that this period is properly to be styled the millennium; but he also expected that long before this the gospel would be spread all over the world, and I never remember his expressing an expectation of miraculous gifts being granted for that end.' Mr. Ryland, Sr., died July 24, 1792. Dr. Rippon preached his funeral sermon, in which he says among the last things Mr. Ryland read, 'and with which he was *much pleased*' was his son's circular letter to the Northampton Association of that year. The subject of the letter was 'Godly Zeal,' and in it Mr. Ryland, Jr., specially recommends to serious attention 'the sketch which Bro. Carey has lately given of the state of the heathen world, and proceeds in moving terms to invoke compassion, prayer and a tion. In the face of this testimony to the *baselessness* of the anecdote ought the memory of a devoted and energetic servant of God to be blackened by an imputation so *utterly out of keeping with the writings he has left behind and with all family traditions of his sayings?*"

A LINEAL DESCENDANT OF JOHN RYLAND.

† There has been no split outside of the United States. The "Missionary Baptists" being yet in line with their brethren of Europe is presumptive proof that they are the "Old Baptists."

1 Davis' Hist. Welsh Bap., p. 100.
2 Idem, p. 111.
3 Idem, p. 202.

418   CHURCH PERPETUITY.

The missionary and the educational work of European Baptists was, by Baptist immigrants, and otherwise, carried into the United States of America. The Philadelphia Baptist Association, was organized in 1707, the Charleston, in 1751, and the Warren, in 1767. These three associations figure more in the early history of American Baptists than do any others. The Philadelphia association is the oldest of American Baptist associations. In the first century and a quarter of its history it did probably more in giving type to the Baptists of America than all other associations within that time did.

In 1764, the Philadelphia association "agreed to inform the churches to which we respectfully belong, that inasmuch as a charter is obtained in Rhode Island government, toward erecting a Baptist *college, the churches should be liberal in contributing* towards carrying the same into execution."[1] At its meeting in 1766, it "agreed to recommend *warmly* to our churches the interests of the college, for which *subscription* is opened *all over the continent.* This college hath been set on foot upwards of a year, and has now in it three promising youths under president Manning."[2] At its meeting in 1767 it "agreed that the churches should be *requested to forward the subscription* for Rhode Island *college.*"[3] In the minutes of 1769, we read: " We receive pleasing accounts from Rhode Island *college. . . .* The colony has raised 1,200 pounds towards the building, which will begin early in the spring. About 1,000 pounds lawful currency of New England, have been sent us from home towards making up a *salary* for the president; and *all* †

---

† Not an Anti-missionary Baptist preacher in this mother of American Baptist associations.
[1] Minutes Philadelphia Association, p. 91.
[2] Idem, p. 99.
[3] Idem, p. 101.

the ministers of the association have explicitly engaged to exert themselves in endeavoring to raise money for the same purpose. . . . Voted that fourteen pounds Jersey currency be given Mr. Thomas Eustick, towards *defraying* * *his expenses at college.*" [1]

In its minutes of 1774, we read: "The minutes and letters from Charleston association, South Carolina, were read. The plan adopted by them respecting Rhode Island *college* recommended to us. Agreed to *recommend the same to the churches* we stand respectively related unto; and whoever shall see good to *contribute to the money* so gathered, agreeable to the plan to be remitted . . . or brought unto next association." [2] At its meeting of 1774, it says: "The *money* raised for increasing the fund of Rhode Island college is as follows," etc. : [3]

Prof. Whitsitt says: "Why didn't they found the college at Philadelphia? I suppose the motive that sent them to Rhode Island was the desire to do a work for the Baptists in that part of the world. And I presume this was the best way of capturing Rhode Island." [4] Thus BROWN UNIVERSITY STANDS AS MOST CONCLUSIVE PROOF THAT THE REGULAR BAPTISTS—often called Missionary Baptists—ARE THE "OLD BAPTISTS."

We have seen that the Philadelphia association at its meeting in 1769, raised money to educate Thomas Eustick for the ministry. At its meeting in 1790, it says: "As it appears expedient that Mr. Silas Walton should continue another year under the tuition of Dr. Jones, and as Mr. Carter, of Virginia, has generously

---

* What so-called "Old Baptist" association ever raised a dollar to educate a young man for the ministry.
[1] Minutes Philadelphia Association, p. 109-110.
[2] Idem, p. 135.
[3] Idem, p. 142.
[4] Prof. Whitsitt's Lect. to his Classes.

given five pounds towards his assistance, it is agreed that we will be accountable for *twenty pounds* in addition thereto."¹ In the minutes of 1791, we read: "Voted that the *money* raised last year, remaining in the treasury's hands, be allowed on the *usual* terms, to brother David Stout, who is a candidate for the ministry."² In its minutes of 1792: "Elders Patten, Chugan and Vaughn, agree to travel for three months in the ensuing year . . . to preach the gospel to the destitute; and this association recommend that a sufficient sum be *subscribed by* the churches, and paid immediately into the hands of Col. Samuel Miles, *to bear their expenses*."³ In its minutes of 1722 we read: "It was proposed for the churches to make inquiry among themselves, if they have any young persons hopeful for the ministry, and inclinable for *learning*, and if they have to give notice of it to Mr. Able Morgan . . . that he might recommend such to the *academy* on Mr. Hollis' account."⁴ In its minutes of 1800 we read: "It is recommended to our churches that a sermon be *annually* preached among them, and after it a *collection* be made, the amount to be forwarded to the association at their subsequent meeting, in order to augment the *fund for the education* of such pious young men as appear promising for usefulness in the *ministry* of the gospel."⁵

At its meeting in 1794 it said: "In consequence of information communicated to this association by brother William Rogers, it is desired that all *donations* for the propagation of the gospel among the Hindoos, in the East Indies, be forwarded to him."⁶ In the minutes of 1795 we read: "Agreed that the church be advised to make

---
1 Minutes Philadelphia Association, p. 254.
2 Idem, p. 271.   4 Idem, p. 27.   6 Idem, p. 298.
3 Idem, p. 283.   5 Idem, p. 350.

collections for the *missionaries to the East Indies.*"[1] At its meeting in 1800 it "Resolved, that it be particularly urged on our churches, that, as stewards of God, and influenced by a strong desire to spread the cause of our blessed Redeemer, they endeavor to raise, as early as possible, and to maintain a *fund* for the assistance of such ministers as may be called to supply destitute churches, or otherwise publish the gospel in their connection. . . . The church of Philadelphia having presented a query on the propriety of forming a plan for establishing a *missionary* society: This association, taking the matter into consideration, think it would be most advisable to invite the general committee of Virginia and different associations on the continent to unite with us in laying a plan for forming a *missionary* society, and *establishing a fund for its support, and for employing missionaries among the natives of our continent.*"[2] In its minutes of 1803 we read: "The plan of a *missionary society* was read, and with some alteration approved and recommended. It also recommended that sermons be preached for the *education* and *mission* funds."[3]

Silas Hart, 1795, died and left to the Philadelphia association, by will, "property sufficient to yield an annuity of fifty pounds, to be kept in the hands of trustees and applied to the *education of young preachers.*"[4] Living at that time, Semple says: "This is certainly an important case to the Baptists of Virginia."[4]

Roanoke association of Virginia, at its meeting in May, 1809, had before it "the erection of Baptist *seminaries of learning*" as among the subjects "of the

---

[1] Minutes Philadelphia Association, p. 307.
[2] Idem, p. 350.
[3] Idem, p. 381.
[4] Semple's History Virginia Baptists, pp. 192-193.

greatest importance to which it attended."¹ At its meeting in 1807, "considerable agitation of mind was excited . . . in consequence of a query introduced from the church at Charlotte: Whether it was a maxim established among the Baptists, that 'human learning is of no use.' This query arose out of an illiberal assertion, contained in a letter to Mr. Rice, a Presbyterian preacher, of Charlotte, to the chairman of the *committee* of *missions*, and which was published in the assembly's Missionary Magazine,† of May, 1807; in which Mr. Rice declares, that, among Baptists of this neighborhood, it is a maxim very firmly established, that human learning is of no use. The association took up the business and appointed a committee of certain brethren to answer and explain the subject. The answer which was strong and energetic, composed by Mr. Kerr, was printed. No reply * or attempt to establish the assertion has been made by Mr. Rice as yet." ²

At the "general meeting of correspondence," in 1808, representing " Dover, Goshen, Albemarle, Appomattox, Roanoke and Meherrin associations," of Virginia, we read: " It also appeared from several publications that the Baptists of Virginia had been *misrepresented*, as to their sentiments respecting human learning. It was determined at this meeting to rebut this † calumny, by publishing a few remarks on the subject in the form of a circular letter, which was accordingly done." ³ This body, at its next meeting—next year—favorably considered

---

† The reader will here see that this association not only had a "Committee of Missions," but that it published a magazine in their interests.
* Had these been Anti-missionary Baptists, Mr. Rice could but have received their thanks instead of the "strong and energetic" silencing reply.
1 Semple's History Virginia Baptists, p. 234.
2 Idem, p. 245.
3 Idem, p. 88.

"the establishment of some seminary or public school, to admit *young* preachers to acquire literary knowledge."[1]

The Dover association of Virginia, at its meeting in 1790, "answered in the *negative*" the question: "Is a minister in duty bound to serve a church who do not † support him?"[2]

The New River association of Virginia, at its meeting in 1804, answering the question: "Are the *poor* bound by the gospel to give to the *rich* for preaching the gospel?" Answered: "The Lord *loveth the cheerful giver*, according to what he hath, and not according to what he hath not."[3] Commeting on this, Semple well says: "All things considered, a better answer could not probably have been given."[3]

In its circular letter, the Middle District association, in 1791, said: "We fear *covetousness* and want of reasonable support of the ministry, is one great reason why we are so languish in religion.* When our ministers ought to be out and working in God's vineyard, behold they are forced to leave the flock, hungering for the bread of life, while they are struggling to provide necessaries for their families."[4] Commenting on this, Semple says: "When we consider the *many publications* upon this subject, as well as the clear and obvious manner in which it is laid down in the Scriptures, it is somewhat astonishing that this duty is still so little attended to. What is man at his best estate?"[4]

The Ketocton association of Virginia, at its meeting in 1791, had before it the question "as to the propriety

---

† An Anti-Mission Baptist preacher taking this position would be disfellowshipped by all *so-called* "Old Baptists."

* Here is the explanation of the languishing condition of many of our present churches.

[1] Semple's Hist. Virginia Bap., p. 89. [3] Idem, p. 271.
[2] Idem, p. 94. [4] Idem, p. 196.

of a church's *requiring* of *each* of her members to contribute to the expenses of the church according to their property," in answer to which "the association determined that a regulation of that kind in a church was *lawful*, and that persons that would not submit to it deserved *exclusion* from the privileges of the church . . . *the correctness of which cannot be doubted upon right principles*." [1]

"The Georgia association was organized in 1784. In 1801 a letter was addressed to this body on the 'propriety and expediency of forming a *Missionary Society* in this State for the purpose of sending the gospel amongst the Indians, bordering on our frontiers, which was *unanimously and cordially approbated*,' on which Jesse Mercer remarks: 'The ministers of those times had too much of the spirit of the Apostles in them to be *afraid of missions*.' " [2]

Of its meeting in 1814 its minutes say: "According to a suggestion in the letter from the Whateley's Mill church, Brother Mercer presented and read the circular letter and constitution of the 'Savannah Baptist Society for *Foreign Missions* and then moved for the approbation of the association, which was given most *willingly and unanimously* — whereupon it was thought proper to recommend the subject *for its evident importance*, to the consideration of the churches. . . . The glorious effort *to evangelize the poor heathen in idolatrous lands*." [3] In its minutes of 1815 we read: "Received from the Baptist Board of *Foreign Missions* for the United States, through its agent, Rev. Luther Rice, the report of the Board, accompanied by letters desiring the aid of this

---
[1] Semple's History of Virginia Baptists, p. 303.
[2] Mercer's History of Georgia Baptists, p. 40.
[3] Idem, p. 55.

body in their *laudable exertions, to spread the gospel of Christ among the heathen in idolatrous lands.* The association † *unanimously* agreeing to co-operate in the grand design . . . resolved itself into a body for *missionary* purposes." Jesse Mercer says, at that time, "*No complaint was ever heard*† of" these missionary resolutions and acts.¹ At its meeting in 1808, answering the question, "Should a brother be continued in fellowship, who, though able, will not assist in supporting the gospel?" it answered: "We are of the opinion where the ability is obvious on the one hand, and the unwillingness positive on the other, and the brother cannot be brought to his duty by proper means, *he ought to be excluded.*" ²

Writing, about 1838, Jesse Mercer says: "It will be seen by a reference to these reports, etc., that the *missionary* operations of those times *greatly* interested the feelings of those who have entered into their rest before us. It will be seen, too, with how much truth and justice the missionary enterprise is now assailed as something new under the sun. *Then* prejudices, now powerful, were *unknown.* Then strife and opposition, now rampant, *showed not their deformed heads.*" ³

Turning now to the associations which the Antimission Baptists claim we find that *they* were originally Missionary Associations. The Kehukee association, of North Carolina, was organized in 1765. The churches composing it "adopted the Baptist confession of faith, published in London, in 1689 . . . upon which the Philadelphia and Charleston associations were founded." ⁴

---

† Baptists, at this time, wholly Missionary Baptists.
¹ Mercer's Hist. of Georgia Bap., p. 56.
² Idem, p. 132.
³ Introduction to Mercer's Hist. Georgia Bapt., p. 7.
⁴ Burkitt's and Read's Hist. Kehukee Association, p. 33.

In this chapter we have seen that the English Baptists who first adopted this Confession were strictly Missionary Baptists and that "in educational and missionary work" the Philadelphia and Charleston associations were in closest fellowship. The churches of this association, before they were organized into it, by *missionary work of* Mr. Gano, as *missionary* of the Philadelphia association, were reclaimed from Arminianism, and from a languishing condition.[1]

The churches of the Kehukee association covenanted " to be ready to communicate to the *defraying* of the churches expenses, and for the *support of the ministry*."[2]

At this association in 1787 the question was asked: "What measures shall a deacon take who sees the necessity of the ministers support and his conscience bids him do his duty, in consequence of which he frequently excites the brethren to their duty; yet, after all, to his daily grief, he finds they neglect their duty?" To this question the association answered: "It is our opinion that it is the members *duty* voluntarily to contribute to their minister's support, and if the deacon discovers any remiss in their duty, that he shall *cite him to the church;* and if the church find him negligent in his duty, we give it as our advice, that the church should *deal†with him for covetousness.*"[3]

At its meeting in 1788 this association (1.) "Do recommend to the consideration of the different churches for their approbation or disapprobation," the "raising a *fund* in the first place by their own *contribution*. (2.) By

---

† Think of a "Hard Side" Baptist church or Association giving this answer!

[1] Benedict's Hist. of Baptists, p. 682; Burkitt's and Read's Hist. Kehukee Association, pp. 32-33.

[2] Burkitt's and Read's Hist. Kehukee Association, p. 35.

[3] Burkitt's and Read's Hist. Kehukee Association, p. 94.

public contributions from the inhabitants, twice in the year at least. Which money so collected and deposited in the hands of some person, and subject to the orders of the church, to be appropriated to the aid of any traveling preacher, whom they shall judge to be sent of God to preach."[1]

In the circular letter to this association, in 1791, we read: "We proceed, in our circular letter, at this time, to make a few observations on the necessary *support* of gospel ministers; although we are sorry that there should be the least occasion to write or speak on that subject. . . . *Ministers have a divine right to maintenance from the people.*"[2]

T. H. Pritchard, D.D., one of our most scholarly and critical writers, says:

"I shall now prove from unquestionable historical facts that the associations which are now anti-missionary were in favor of foreign missions up to the year 1826, '27 and '30, and hence have no claim to the title of the Old School Baptists.

"I will begin with the Baltimore association, perhaps the most famous body of this modern sect in the United States. Their minutes for 1814 contain the following record: 'Received a corresponding letter from Bro. Rice, one of *our missionary brethren*, on the subject of encouraging missionary societies.' This Bro. Rice was Luther Rice, who was then just from Burmah, where he had gone as a missionary with Adoniram Judson.

"In 1816 these minutes in their circular letter say: 'The many revivals of religion which are witnessed in various parts of the country—the multiplication of Bible

---

[1] Burkitt's and Read's Hist. Kehukee Association, pp. 95-96.
[2] Idem, pp. 161-162.

societies, missionary societies and Sunday schools, both in our own and foreign countries, are viewed by us as showing indications of the near approach of that day when the knowledge of the Lord shall cover the earth.' The minutes of the same year state that 'the standing clerk was instructed to supply the corresponding secretary of the Foreign Mission Board with a copy of our minutes annually.' In 1817 ' Bro. Luther Rice presented himself as the messenger of the Baptist Board of Foreign Missions and was cordially received.'

"Elder James Osborne was a member of this body, which cordially received a foreign missionary and at this very session was appointed a home *missionary*. This man Osborne, who *was a leader in the anti-mission secession*, both in Maryland and North Carolina, I remember to have seen in Charlotte when I was a small boy. He was a handsome, dressy man, full of conceit, and very fond of talking of himself and of selling his own books.

"From the same authentic source, the minutes of the Baltimore association, we learn that in 1828 they called themselves ' Regular Baptists,' just as we do now; the same year they express their *joy at the intelligence of the conversion of the heathen*, and as late as 1827 the association expressed, by *formal resolutions*, their sorrow at the death of Mrs. Ann H. Judson and their *great interest in the mission* with which she was connected, and it was not till 1836, when the association met with the Black Rock church, and then by a vote of sixteen to nine, that fellowship was withdrawn from churches favoring foreign missions, Sunday schools, etc."

To come back now to North Carolina, I can prove that the Kehukee and Country Line Associations, two of the most influential of the *anti-mission* party, were *once missionary bodies*. In Burkitt and Read's History of the

Kehukee Association it is stated on page 139, that in 1794, a special day was appointed to pray God for a *revival of religion*, and on page 145 that it was the *custom* of ministers of that date to *invite penitents to come forward and kneel down to be prayed for*, just as we do in our revival meetings now.

In Bigg's History of the Kehukee Association, page 162, it appears that this association appointed delegates to meet at Cashie Church, Bertie County, in June, 1805, with delegates from the Virginia, Portsmouth and Neuse associations, and at this meeting arrangements were made to *collect money for missionary* purposes. That it appears that the Kehukee was not only in *fellowship* with the Portsmouth and other *missionary* Baptist associations, but *that the very first missionary society ever organized in the State, was in the bounds of this body.*

In 1812 this association sent $3, in 1813 $5, and in 1814 $5, to the general meeting of correspondence of North Carolina, which was an organization of the *Missionary* Baptists.

The same history of the association shows that in 1817 it was in correspondence with the General Convention of the Baptists which met that year in *Philadelphia* and *which was supporting Judson and other foreign missionaries, and it was not till 1827 that this association took a decided anti-missionary ground.*

The evidence to show that the Country Line Association was a missionary body up to the year 1832 *is perfectly overwhelming*. Its minutes show that in 1816, '17 and '18 that body sent delegates to the general meeting of correspondence, and in 1816 Elder George Roberts, one of the ministers of this association, was the *Moderator of the general meeting* of correspondence of which Robert T. Daniel was the *agent*, and which developed into the

North Carolina Baptist State Convention. In 1818 this association sent $32.45 to the North Carolina *Missionary Society* by the hands of Bro. John Campbell.

And what is still more remarkable, there was a very prosperous *Woman's Mission Society in this Association*, the minutes of which, kept by John Campbell, show that the "*Hyco Female Cent Society*" was formed at Tynch's Creek meeting house, in County Caswell, in October, 1816; in March, 1817, it met at Bush Arbor meeting house; in March, 1818, it met at the same place; in 1819 at Grave's meeting house, and the fifth annual meeting was held in September, 1820, at Arbor; all of these churches are now anti-mission, but *were then missionary* bodies, and the persons who preached the *annual sermons*, R. Dishong, J. Landus, Barzillar Graves, Abner W. Clopton and S. Chandler, *were all Missionary Baptist ministers*.

In 1832 the County Line Association was in regular correspondence with the Flat River and Sandy Creek associations, both of which were *then* and *still are* missionary bodies.

In 1832 James Osborne, of Baltimore, visited this association, and under his presence it was induced to withdraw fellowship from the Missionary Baptists.

Now, from this brief statement of unvarnished facts we see that the Missionary Baptists *are just where the Apostles were and where all of the name were till 1827-8* when *a new set arose*, calling themselves, according to Elder Bennett's Review, page 8, at first, *The Reformed Baptists* in North Carolina, and then the Old Baptists, the Old Sort of Baptists, Baptists of the Old Stamp, and finally adopted the name of the Primitive Baptists.

There are many things about these brethren which I like, and I would not needlessly call them by an offensive name, but I cannot style them either Old School or Primitive Baptists, for in so doing I *should falsify the facts of history*, and acknowledge that I and my brethren have departed from the faith of the Apostles and Baptist fathers. In no invidious sense, therefore, but from necessity, I am obliged to call them *New School or Antimissionary Baptists*. [1]

After years of pretty thorough and careful reading I have been unable to read the name of even one church, association or writer that ever opposed missions or education before about 1810.

As there is no difference in doctrine between what are called Missionary Baptists and what are called Antimission Baptists, I notice only that which really divides them—missions, education, support of pastors and other religious enterprises. To be sure, the Antimission Baptists have often run the doctrine of Divine Sovereignty and Election into fanaticism and other errors. But the Regular Baptists, by the Arminians among them, have equalled their errors. So neither can well throw up errors of doctrine to the other.

I conclude this part of the chapter in the language of David Benedict, "a leading Baptist historian": " Old School and Primitive Baptists are appellations so entirely out of place that I cannot, as a matter of courtesy, use them without adding, *so-called*, or some such expression. I have seen so much of the missionary spirit among the old Anabaptists, Waldenses and other ancient sects—so vigorous and perpetual were the efforts of those Christians, whom we claim as Baptists, in the early, middle and late ages, to spread the gospel in all parts of the world, among all nations and languages where they could gain access,

---

[1] In *Biblical Recorder*.

that it is plain that those who merely preach up predestination, and *do nothing*, *have no claim to be called by their name.*"¹ * †

Turning to the Freewill "Baptists," in the foregoing chapters we have seen that Baptists of past ages have been what are denominated "Calvinistic" Baptists. ‡

The "Communion Question" being one fundamental difference between the Freewill "Baptists" and the Regular Baptists, I will briefly notice it. The Baptist Confession, of 1643, "printed in London, Anno 1646" reads that, disciples "ought to be baptized, and *after* to partake of the Lord's Supper."²

---

* To add to the foregoing testimony would be easy. Thus, in the eleventh century, "the Albigenses had congregations and *schools* of their own."—Schaff-Herzog Encyclopedia, vol. 1, p. 47. Long before the Reformation the Baptists of Bohemia kept a *school* for young ladies, and their mode of *education* and the purity of their manners were in such high repute that the daughters of a very great part of the nobility of Bohemia were sent thither to be educated."—Robinson's Ecclesiastical Researches, p. 532. Dr. Ray quotes from Perrin's History Waldenses, p. 117: "In the year 1229 the Waldenses had already spread themselves in great numbers throughout all Italy. They had *schools* in Valcamonica alone, and they sent *money* from *all parts of their abode* in Lombardy for the maintenance and support of said schools."—Baptist Succession, p. 40. "Bristol College, England, was founded in 1710 for the education of Baptist ministers. This was more than a century before the origin of the Anti-mission Baptists. Before their origin it had educated many preachers."—Cramp's History of the Baptists, p. 491.

† Benedict says of the Anti-mission Baptists: "A large amount of their documents are before me which contain the resolutions and decrees of their churches and associations. . . . From these it appears that if any of their members shall unite with any society for the promotion of the cause of benevolence or moral reform, they shall, *ipso facto*, be expelled from their fellowship and communion; the missionary, Bible, tract and Sunday school and temperance societies are especially named; and generally a sweeping clause is added, embracing the 'so-called' benevolent institutions of the day! These prohibitions extend not only to actual membership in these bodies, but to any contributions of their own personal funds for their support! No collection for any of these objects can be made in any of the churches where they have the control, nor are their members allowed to cast in their mites when the box goes around in any neighboring congregation in which they may be present. This, I believe, is a picture of what are called the non-fellowshipping resolutions of the anti-mission party. This is a yoke we may well suppose could not set easy on the necks of independent Baptists; many for peace sake may submit to it for awhile, but it will not be long endured by any but those who have thoroughly imbibed, *esprit du corps*, the spirit of the party."—Benedict's History of the Baptists, p. 936.

‡ These views are the Bible teaching. Calvin held some extreme views on this line which Baptists have never believed or professed. But as "Calvinism" has come to be the term by which the views of Baptists on divine sovereignty, atonement and election are commonly known, I use the term.

1 Benedict's History of the Baptists, pp. 935-936.
2 Article 39—in Cutting's Historical Vindication, p. 122.

The Confession of 1689 reads: "Baptism and the Lord's Supper are ordinances of positive and sovereign institution, appointed by the Lord Jesus, the only law giver, to be continued *in his church* to the end of the world . . . *to be administered by those who are qualified* and thereunto called according to the *commission of Christ*." [1]

Replying to an open communionist, an anonymous critical historian,[2] in the *Examiner*, near twenty years ago, said: "They cannot bring a *single Confession of Faith from all Baptist history before the rise of the Freewill Baptists*, about one hundred years ago," to prove that Baptists were formerly open communionists. "They can bring only one in all that history which *appears* to prove it, and that one *excluded Arminians from communion*, hence would exclude the authors or the main author of these assertions. *All* the Continental Baptist bodies from 1521 onwards . . . practiced *strict communion*. English General Baptists, from the beginning of their history in 1610, were strict. Their Confessions published in 1611, 1660, 1663 and 1678 plainly require baptism before communion. *Their churches would not even allow attendance upon other worship*. They said, 'The whole Scripture is against such Balaamitic and wavering actions.' They were *never open communion until* in the last century they became *Socinians*. The Confessions of Faith of the Particular Baptists in England are *emphatic* for strict communion. . . . The same is true of *all* the Confessions that can be found in Baptist history until 1688. Then the Century Confession of London which is always pleaded for open communion appeared. . . . This confession itself makes communion a church ordinance,

---

[1] Chapter 28—in Cutting's Hist. Vindication, p. 171.
[2] I think, Dr. Buckland.

and puts it after immersion; but as these brethren avoweu their aim to show how little Baptists differed from Presbyterians and Congregationalists they granted an appendix that while most of the churches adhered to strict communion some few did not; and they recognized this fact and would not impose conditions upon these."

Rev. Dr. Underwood,[1] of Chilwell College, Nottinghamshire, in a paper, read before the English Baptist Union, at Birmingham, Oct., 1864, said: "In the matter of communion our churches are far from being uniform. *Until within a very few years* nearly all our churches were *close and strict.*"

In the language of Rev. Porter S. Burbank, one of the most representative Freewill Baptist defenders: "The Freewill Baptist connection in North America commenced A. D. 1780, *in which year its first church was organized.*"[2]. From history and its own confession the Freewill Baptist sect is certainly of modern origin.

The Six Principle "Baptists" are of the seventeenth century—Rev. A. D. Williams, their representative, being witness.[3] They being Arminian in showing Baptists have ever been Calvinists, the foregoing chapters, have demonstrated them not in the line of Church Perpetuity.

The so-called "German Baptists" or Tunkers thus originated in Germany, in 1708: "The first constituents were Alexander Mack and wife, John Kipin and wife, George Grevy, Andreas Bhony, Lucas Fetter and Joanna Nethigum. They agreed to read the Bible together, and edify one another in the way they had been brought up, for as yet they did not know there were any Baptists in the world. However, believers' baptism and a Congrega-

---

[1] Goadby's Bye Paths to Baptist History, p. 52.
[2] Religious Denominations of the United States, p. 74.
[3] Idem, p. 88.

tional church soon gained on them, insomuch that they were determined to obey the gospel in these matters. They desired Alexander Mack to baptize them, but he deemed himself in reality unbaptized, refused, upon which they cast lots to find who should be the administrator; on whom the lot fell hath been carefully concealed. However, baptized they were in the river Eder, by Schwartzenau, and then formed themselves into a church, choosing Alexander Mack as their minister."[1] So, without looking into their other errors, we can safely set aside the so-called "German Baptists" as Tunkers from all claim to Church Perpetuity.

The German Seventh Day Baptists were originated in Germany, in 1728, by Conrad Beissel, one of the Tunkers. It is, therefore, a split off the Tunker sect.[2]

The origin of the Seventh Day English Baptists as a *church* is thus given by Rev. G. B. Utter, one of the most eminent representatives of that sect: "The Seventh Day Baptists in America date from about the same period that their brethren in England *began to organize churches.*" Then he dates its American rise in 1671.[3] Prof. W. W. Everts, Jr., writes me that the ancient Baptists observed the *first* day of the week as the day of rest and worship. Save among Judaizers, who practiced *circumcision and other such errors* there were no scattered advocates of the seventh day, nor any permanent organization in its interest, until the rise of these so-called Seventh Day Baptists. Seventh Day "Baptists" certainly are a modern sect.

'Religious Denominations in the United States and Great Britain," published by "Charles Desilver," is

---
[1] Religious Denominations, p. 92.
[2] Idem, p. 109.
[3] Benedict's Hist. of Baptists, p. 921.

probably the best book in its line. I have now examined all the different "Baptists" which it mentions—six beside the Regular Baptists—and have found that not one of them has any true claim to be the New Testament Baptists in the Church Perpetuity line.

LET IT BE EMPHASIZED, THAT: ALL THIS TALK ABOUT THERE BEING TWENTY-SEVEN DIFFERENT KINDS OF BAPTISTS, AND THAT WE CAN'T KNOW WHICH OF THEM IS THE OLD BAPTIST CHURCH, ORIGINATES IN IGNORANCE, OR IN PURE HATRED TO THE BAPTIST CHURCH AND DISREGARD FOR VERACITY AND IS "DARKENING OF COUNSEL."

Like the fable of the dog on the hay, bitter and unscrupulous Baptist assailants, knowing their own churches are but *modern* sects, and that they cannot appropriate Church Perpetuity are determined to leave "unturned no stone" to make the people belive that "Baptists are in as bad a fix as we are." † Owing to this attempt to mislead honest men and women I have given the question, Who are the Old Baptists? much more space than it deserves.

† In their avowing, in one breath, that, "it is not necessary that any church should have been perpetuated from apostolic times; that a modern origin is no discredit to any church;" then, in the next, trying to overthrow Baptist claims on the people, by denying their claim to Church Perpetuity, these controversalists clearly demonstrate themselves insincere!

CHAPTER XXVIII.†

BAPTIST CHURCH PERPETUITY TESTED BY THE FRUITS OF BAPTIST CHURCHES.

Christ says: "By their fruits ye shall know them." Matt. 7:20.

In fruit-bearing Baptist churches of to-day need dread no comparison with Baptist churches of the apostolic age

1. The life and the influence of Baptist churches for a spiritual church.

Rejecting all inherited church membership, rejecting bringing people into the church in infancy, rejecting bringing them in on motives of policy and rejecting bringing them in anyway or for any reason before they are born of God, and contending for *exclusion* of all known unregenerate persons from church fellowship; among the great denominations Baptists to-day, as in all the past, stand alone. Thus, they stand alone for a church of only spiritual persons. On other churches Baptists have exerted an inestimable influence for good. In 1863 the adherents of the Heidleberg Catechism celebrated its three hundredth year and published of it a handsome tercentenary edition, edited by prominent divines and with an elaborate historical introduction. These learned writers say: This Catechism assumes that "the baptized children of the church are *sealed and set over to the service of God by the sanctifying and separating act of baptism itself*, and

---

† The reader read this chapter in connection with the Introduction to this book.

that they belong to the congregation and the people of Christ. . . . In this respect, however, it was only in keeping . . . with the *general* thinking and practice of the church in the *age of the Reformation;* and it is not difficult to see that the *entire catechetical system in particular of the sixteenth century*, owed its *whole* interest and vigor and success to the same theory of christianity and *no* other. It is *not intelligible on any other ground;* and with the giving away accordingly of the old belief in BAPTISMAL GRACE and educational religion we find that it has in a *large measure* lost its hold upon the practice of our modern churches, in *large measure altogether.*"[1]

Listen to these writers tell what has, in such a great measure rooted out the Romish doctrine of infant church membership and baptismal grace, on which the writers say the sixteenth century Reformers built modern churches: "The BAPTIST PRINCIPLE, as it may be called, has entered *widely* into their *theology and church life*, bringing them to make *large concessions* practically; so that they find it hard to bear up against its assumptions and pretensions, and are more and more in danger of being swept away by it from their ancient moorings, and driven forth into the open sea of spiritual fanaticism and unbelief. This unquestionably is the great reason why in certain quarters within these communions such small stress has come to be laid on infant baptism. . . . .
We are surrounded now, as we have just seen, with a wholly different practice which is the fruit and evidence of a wholly different faith. What that faith is, or rather what it is not, has been mentioned already in general terms. It is the absence of a belief in that side of christianity which is represented to us in the idea of the church being in any

[1] Tercentenary Edition of the Heidleberg Catechism, pp. 112-113.

way the *organ* and *medium of grace* for the children of men. In this respect our modern sects are generally of one mind. . . . *They are all of them thus constitutionally Baptistic;* having no power to see in the church membership of infants and young children anything more than an *empty* form, and never daring to make any *practical* earnest with the thought of their *sanctification to God. Such has come to be the reigning habit of thought, it is but too plain with our American christianity in general at the present time.*"[1] Thus, these great Pedobaptist scholars lamentably concede that *Baptist principles* have almost wholly converted the Pedobaptist world from infant baptism, from baptismal grace and from a consequent unspiritual church—they concede that Baptist influence has led them to abandon the infant baptism part of the old catechism, which was "at once cordially welcomed by all but Romanists and extreme Lutherans," and which "was speedily translated into many different languages," and which "is, virtually, the platform occupied at the present day by the largest portion of the Protestant church, especially in regard to its moderate Calvanistic and sacramental doctrines."[2]*

Before the British Congregational Union, Dr. Bonner, the Moderator, in 1858, said: "The pre-eminence given by the Baptists to the *personality*† of the christian character and profession becomes a valuable force arrayed on the side of scriptural evangelism against human traditions, sacredotal and ecclesiastical pretensions. It is the

---

* The *Christian Register* (Unitarian) says: "We believe that no branch of the christian church has done more to uproot a superstitious belief in the pernicious doctrine of baptismal regeneration than the Baptists. It is just here that a sharp line has divided them from the Romanists, Lutherans and the old-time Episcopalians."

† This is the principle that rejects *inherited* christianity and infant baptism.

[1] Tercentenary Edition of the Heidleberg Catechism, pp. 118-119.
[2] Kurtz's Church History, vol. 2, p. 152.

direct *antidote* and *antagonist* to the official virtue and authority upon which the church of Rome has based the grand apostacy. . . . On *this principle*, perhaps, we may account for a new reformation in Germany, being *apparently* identified with the diffusion of *Baptist* sentiments in so many States, and for the virulence with which those who teach them and those who adopt them are so persecuted and oppressed by governments inspired by ecclesiastical jealousies and alarm."

Froude, an eminent English historian, not a Baptist, in his Life of Bunyan, says: "The Baptists, the *most thoroughgoing and consistent of all Protestant* sects. If the sacrament of baptism is not a *magical* form but is a *personal* act, in which the baptized person devotes himself to Christ's service, then to baptize children at an age when they cannot *understand* what they have done *may well seem irrational* if not *impious*."

Joseph Cook, Congregationalist: "I remember where I am speaking; I know what prejudices I am crossing; but I know that in this assembly, assuredly nobody will have objection to my advocacy, even at a *little expense of consistency with my own* supposed principles, of the necessity of a spiritual church membership, if I say that" the Baptists have "been of *foremost* service in bringing into the world, among *all* the Protestant denominations an adequate idea of the importance of a *spiritual* church membership. I know that no *generous heart or searching intellect* will object to this statement." Again, says Mr. Cook: "I thank the Baptists for having *compelled other denominations* to recognize the *necessity* of a *converted* membership." †

---

† That "other denominations," especially Methodists, to a deplorable degree, yet retain the doctrine of an unconverted church membership must not be overlooked. Southern Methodists are more Romish than are Northern Methodists.

(2.) In Baptists remaining faithful to the great evangelical trusts we have their scriptural fruit.

A mispronunciation of a word led to the slaughter of the gallant six hundred in the charge of Bal-a-kla-va. A slight error in information left Napoleon ignorant of the sunken road at Waterloo, which lost him the battle upon which his destiny depended. The great Romish apostacy began and reached its full development by underestimating the importance of contending for the great principles and the *particulars* of church ordinances and church constitution. This is but the logical and inevitably final result of calling *anything* which is in God's word " non-essential."† Thus, giving his reasons for leaving the Baptist for a Pedobaptist church, a prominent New England minister said: " I no longer regard the Scriptures as final authority in any such *precise and formal* matters as I have heretofore done. I believe them to be divine, but divine in the sense of revealing *principles* of action rather than *precise* examples. I have come to regard christianity as a growth almost as much as a revelation, and that very nearly as much attention is to be paid to its *development* as to its *establishment*. Arising from *this* view of the Scriptures, I have felt a growing *indifference* to theological *distinctions*. *Forms* of doctrines and *modes*, both as they relate to the organization and the ordinances, appear to me of less moment. Baptism itself is of less consequence to me, and, as I now think, a *change* might occur in the form when in the judgment of good *men* it might be wise and necessary."

On the same line Mr. Daugherty, formerly pastor of the Stoughton Street Baptist church of Boston, on leaving the Baptists, said: " I was born and brought up a

---

† The reader please distinguish between essentials for *salvation* and essentials for the *preservation* of the gospel and *full* obedience to Christ.

Baptist and in due time entered Andover Theological Seminary and commenced my ministry a conscientious Baptist. But have come gradually to feel the narrowness of my faith, or, at least, the intense *literalness* of the interpretation of that faith. . . . While I have *no doubt that, philologically and historically, baptism by immersion was the primitive mode*, I consider it to-day among the non-essential things of the Christian church. . . . I cannot be conscientiously any longer tied to the intense literalness of the sect. So I join the Congregationalists."[1]

This reminds us of John Calvin's words, when he was originating the Presbyterian church and substituting the change of " men " for God's plain word : " Whether the person who is to be baptized be wholly immersed, and whether thrice or once, or whether water be only poured or sprinkled upon him is of *no importance;* churches ought to be left at liberty in this respect, to act according to the difference of countries. The very word *baptize, however, signifies to immerse; and it is* CERTAIN *that immersion was the practice of the ancient church.*"[2]

A writer well says: "A Pedobaptist minister, the other day, asked the writer why Baptists were so orthodox on the question of eternal punishment, and other questions now agitating the churches, while Congregationalists and others were becoming so loose and unsound. The question is a *suggestive* one. The only Baptist minister in in this vicinity, so far as we know, who has favored Universalism and other errors is an *open communion* Baptist. The answer is not a difficult one. We believe in the *Word of God* as the supreme authority. We dare not put our wish in the place of *God's* word. We dare not talk of essentials and non-essentials. We bow before every com-

---
[1] *The Standard*, of Chicago.
[2] Calvin's Institute of Christian Religion, book 4, chapter 15, section 19.

mand of the Lord Jesus. *If men make light of one command, why not of another?* If in *any* particular we place our authority above Christ's *why not in every particular?* If a man will say, ' Yes, Christ commands baptism on a profession of faith, but I think something else will do, then the *foundation of all authority* is taken away. *Our only hope is unquestioning loyalty to the divine word.*"

At the faithfulness of Baptists to the truth, without being constrained by ecclesiastical authority over the churches, Baptist opponents stand in admiration and wonder—not seeing that this is the logical result of the *Baptist starting point*, faithfulness to God's word. Dr. Charles Hodge once said to a Baptist preacher: " It has always appeared to me a remarkable fact in providence that, although your church organization allows such *freedom* to the several congregations, your ministers and people have ever been so distinguished for adherence to *sound doctrine*. The experience of Congregationalists in New England is very different from yours."

Before the Congregational Union, Henry Ward Beecher said: " Among all the churches whose flag, red with the blood of Calvary, has *never* lowered or trailed in the dust of defection, who while the Congregational church suffered eclipse, while the Presbyterians in England suffered eclipse, *stood firm*, testifying to the truth as it is in Jesus, none deserve more love and more gratitude than the Baptist churches of America. In *that church the faith of our fathers has never received a shock*, nor been moved. Faithful in the field, *enterprising*, and for the last quarter of a century, with growing enterprise towards education, and now affording some of the ripest scholars in Biblical literature, which the world knows, and thousands of ministers that are second to none in zeal and success."

J. L. Winthrow, D. D., of Chicago, one of the most prominent of American Presbyterians: "I suppose there is *not a denomination*—I speak in no fulsome praise but literally—I think there is not a denomination of Evangelical christians that is *thoroughly as sound* theologically as the *Baptist* denomination. *I believe it.* After *carefully considering it I believe I speak the truth.* Sound as my own denomination is, sound as some others are, and I do not cast unfriendly reflections upon any particular denomination, I do say, in my humble judgment, there is not an Evangelical denomination in America to-day that is as *true to the simple, plain gospel of God, as it is recorded in the Word of God, as the Baptist denomination.*"

John Hall, D. D., who is perhaps the most prominent Presbyterian preacher in America, not long ago, said: "There is a tendency to heap censure on the Baptists of this country, because of their views, generally held and acted upon regarding the Lord's Supper. 'Close Communion' is being assailed by many in the interests of Catholicity. It is a *doubtful Catholicity* to raise a popular cry against a most valuable body of people, who honestly and *consistently* go through what they deem an important *principle.* Our love for our brethren should surely include the *Baptist* brethren. And it is doubtful considering the lengths to which liberal ideas in this country have been carried, *if there be not some gain to the community as a whole* from a large denomination making a *stand* at a particular point, and *reminding* their brethren that there are *church* matters which we are not bound, and *not even at liberty*, to settle according to *popular demand*, as we would settle the *route of a railroad.*" Baptists by taking their "stand" where, in crying "non-essential," the enemy makes his opening assaults on the faith, have thus guarded the precious gospel and been of inestimable blessing to all churches, and to the whole world. *Thus Baptist influence on other denominations is more than ample justification for their existence.*

3. As to *freedom*, Baptist fruit has ever been only good.

Starting from their *great principles*, that religion is a *personal* matter between the soul and God *only*, and that every Christian is a priest to God, Baptists have always and *inevitably*, opposed parent, church or State, making the spiritual choice for any souls. Hence they, as does the New Testament, have always left every believer as a free man or woman in Christ Jesus. This constitutes every believer a ruler in God's kingdom and every citizen a ruler in the State. In a former chapter we have seen that Baptists have given the world religious freedom.

In a recent volume, entitled "The Puritan in Holland, England and America," Douglas Campbell, A. M. LL. B., member of the Historical Association, says: "No words of praise can be too strong for the service which the English Baptists have rendered the cause of religious *liberty*. . . . They have never lost their influence as a *leaven* in the land. In purity of life and in substantial Christian work, they have been surpassed by the members of no other religious body. Having been the *first* British denomination of Christians to proclaim the principles of *religious liberty*, they were also the *first* to send out missionaries to the heathen. . . . In fact, taking their whole history together, if the Anabaptists of Holland had done nothing more for the world than to beget such offspring *they would have repaid a thousand fold* all the care shown for their *liberties.*"

The *Nonconformist and Independent*, of London, the ablest Pedobaptist paper in the world, is thus quoted by

The Standard, of Chicago: "To the *Baptists* must be credited the proud *distinction* first of doctrinal relationship to the earliest christians in Great Britain; and secondly, their *priority* in asserting the principle of liberty of conscience. Their *essential* doctrine was held firmly by the Christian communions which St. Augustine found in England when he arrived on his missionary enterprise, and no efforts of his could convert the Baptists to the ecclesiastical polity of the church of Rome. Coming to a more historical period, 'it is,' says Mr. Skeats, in his 'History of Free Churches,' 'the *singular* and *distinguished* honor of the Baptists to have *repudiated* from their *earliest* history all *coercive* power over the conscience, and the actions of men with reference to religion. . . . They were the *proto*-evangelists of the voluntary principle. . . . From the remote period referred to above, the principles of the *Baptists* have more or less *permeated* and *leavened* the religious life of England. The Lollards are said to have held their views. And Wickliffe is claimed as one of the early adherents of their theory of Christ's teaching. . . . They have had to endure imprisonment, pain and death, for their rejection of the supremacy of the crown, and their assertion of a doctrine which cut at the very *root of priestism*.' "

The New York *Tribune* recently said: "The Baptists have solved the great problem. They combine the most resolute conviction, the most stubborn belief in their own special doctrines with the *most admirable tolerance* of the faith of other Christians." †

---

† Recently, Romanists and their *apes*, in the face of Rome having *only a red* garment, of her *principles* being persecution, and of Romish priests and bishops being set to persecute "heretics," are presenting Maryland as proof that Rome is entitled to the credit of giving religious liberty to the world. Acting under a Protestant sovereign Lord Baltimore could not persecute other

George Washington wrote to the Baptists: "I recollect with satisfaction that the religious society of which you are members, have been throughout America, uniformly and almost unanimously the firm friends of civil liberty, and the persevering promoters of our glorious revolution."[1]

Everywhere Baptists have opposed any union of church and State. Founding Rhode Island, they welcomed all to find refuge under their banner of freedom. Judge Story says of the Baptist founding of Rhode Island: "In the code of laws established by them we read for the first time since Christianity ascended the throne of the Cæsars, that conscience must be free."[2] Bancroft says Rhode Island "is the witness that naturally the paths of the Baptists are the paths of pleasantness and peace."[3] The article on religious liberty in the American Constitution, "was introduced into it by the united efforts of the Baptists in 1789."[4]

Early in this century, the king of Holland proffered the Baptists State financial aid. This, of course, they refused. In Virginia, in 1784, when Baptists, in their struggle for the separation of church and State had well nigh conquered, Pedobaptists proposed the compromise of taxing the people to support all denominations. This compromise they vehemently rejected.*

---

religionists. But listen what law he did pass: "Whosoever shall blaspheme God, or shall deny that the Holy Trinity, or any of the persons thereof, shall be punished with DEATH."—Bancroft's Hist. U. S., vol. 1, p. 256. Death to Unitarians, Jews and Infidels. If Rome is in favor of freedom *why* did she, at that time, *everywhere else* persecute; and why does she persecute to-day, wherever she has the power to do so; and why does she frequently mob opposition speakers in "*free America!*"

* See Curry on Religious Liberty and the Baptists, p. 45; also, Taylor on the same subject, pp. 23-24; Bitting on the same subject, p. 52.

[1] Washington's Life, vol. 12, p. 155.
[2] Taylor on Religious Liberty, p. 23.
[3] Bancroft's History United States, vol. 2, p. 459—old edition.
[4] New American Encyclopedia.

Through the influence of Episcopalians in Georgia, in 1785, a law was passed to establish churches—union of church and State. It gave all denominations equal privileges. But the year it was passed Baptists sent messengers to the legislature and finally procured its repeal.

Thus, that the United States would have been a union of church and State, had it not been for Baptists—for Baptist principles nipping it in the bud—is clear.

In various parts of Europe, England, Scotland, Sweden, Germany, etc., Episcopalians, Methodists, Presbyterians and Lutherans, are united with the State. In the United States, near all the leading Protestant denominations, with the Romish church, receive government aid for their Indian missions. The *Protestant Standard* says: "During three years, the Methodists have received from the government, for Indian missions, $33,345; in six years, the Presbyterians, $286,000; the Congregationalists, $183,000; the Friends, $140,000; the Episcopalians, $102,000; and the Romish church the modest sum of one million, nine hundred and eighty-nine thousand dollars." Not knowing Baptist principles this paper says: "We are surprised to learn that the *Baptists* have not received anything from the government for the work among the Indians."

President Eliott, of Harvard University, is quoted by Dr. Lorimer, as saying: "The chief gain of *three centuries* has been *freedom* of thought;" and Bancroft says that "freedom of conscience, unlimited freedom of mind, was from the first the trophy of the Baptists."

The German philosopher, Gervinus, in his "Introduction to the History of the Nineteenth Century," says of the Baptist of Rhode Island: "Here in a little State the *fundamental principle* of political and ecclesiastical liberty prevailed before they were even taught in Europe. . . .

But not only have these ideas and these forms of government maintained themselves here, but *precisely from this little State have they extended themselves throughout the United States.* They have confused the aristocratic tendencies in Carolina, New York, the high church in Virginia, the theocracy in Massachusetts, and the monarchy in all America. *They have given laws to a continent* and through their moral influence *they are at the bottom of all democratic movements now shaking the nations of Europe."* [1] †

Thus with their motto, freedom for all, and their spirit:

> "They are *slaves* who fear to speak
> For the fallen and the weak;
> They are slaves who will not choose
> Hatred, scoffing and abuse,
> *Rather* than in silence shrink
> For the truth they needs must think;
> They are slaves who dare not be
> In the *right* with *two or three.*"

With this motto and spirit, by the cost of their liberty, of slander, of their blood and their lives, *Baptists have bequeathed the world its religious and civil liberty.*

4. Baptist fruits are gloriously manifest in giving the Bible to the people in their own language.

The first Bible Society for the world was originated in 1807, by a Baptist — Joseph Hughes. The Romish church has always opposed giving the Bible to the people in their own tongues. Only when the light of Christianity made it necessary to give the people the Bible in their own tongues, *to save them to their church,* did the Romish rulers ever consent to do so. Then they must not

---

† See substantially the same statement from Dr. Philip Schaff, on p. 195 of this book.

[1] See a little work by the author of this book, entitled "Liberty of Conscience and the Baptists," published by the "National Baptist Publishing Co.," St. Louis.

interpret it for themselves. Under that condition reading the Bible is so much disencouraged by the Romish rulers that comparatively few Romanists, speaking the English language, own a Bible. Excepting into the Latin and English languages the Romish church has made but few if any versions of the Bible. Among "Protestants" the only Bible society that has ever existed to render the Bible into the English language according to the meaning of *all* the original words, was a Baptist Bible Society—the American Bible Union. Its rules required every translator, according to the world's unsectarian scholarship, to render every word of the originals into the English. *Under these rules* the American Bible Union employed translators of different denominations. It assigned to Pedobaptist scholars parts of the New Testament in which *baptizo* occurs.

In answer to my question: "Does any Greek Lexicon which is a *standard* authority with scholars define *baptizo* by sprinkle, pour, or any word meaning affusion?" I have the following letters: Prof. Thayer, author of Thayer's New Testament, Lexicon—a Lexicon which is of all Lexicons in English, pre-eminently the standard authority on New Testament Greek—wrote me: "See Thayer's N. T. Lex." Turning to Thayer's Lexicon, under *baptizo*, I read: "BAPTIZO—I. (1.) To dip repeatedly, to immerge, submerge. (2.) To cleanse *by dipping or submerging*, to wash, to make clean with water; in the mid. and the I aor. pass. to wash one's self, bathe; so Mark 7:4; Luke 11:38; II. Kings 5:14. (3.) Metaph. to overwhelm, and alone, to inflict great and abounding calamities on one; to be overwhelmed with calamities of those who must bear them. II. In the New Testament it is used particularly of the rite of sacred ablution, first instituted by John the Baptist, afterwards by

Christ's command received by Christians and adjusted to the contents and nature of their religion, viz.: an *immersion in water*, performed as a *sign* of the removal of sin. . . . With prepositions; *eis*, to mark the element *into* which the *immersion* is made, to mark the end, to indicate the effect; *en* with dat. of the thing in which one is immersed."

Having quoted the standard New Testament Lexicon on *baptizo*, I will also stop to quote the standard Classical Lexicon on it—Liddell's and Scott's. I will quote from the English edition which Prof. Fowler, of the Texas State University, says is the best. To him I am indebted for this quotation:

"BAPTIZO. *To dip in or under water*, of ships, to sink or disable them; to draw wine *by dipping* the cup into the bowl; to baptize."

In defining *baptizo* the American edition does not differ essentially from the English.

Prof. M. L. Dooges, Professor of Greek in Michigan State University, answers the question: "Does any Greek Lexicon, which is a standard with scholars, define *baptizo* by sprinkle, pour, or any word meaning affusion?" "None."

Prof. Ezra Abbott, Professor of New Testament interpretation in Harvard University—recently deceased—who was a Bible translator and Biblical scholar of international reputation, answers: "I know of no standard Greek Lexicon which defines baptizo by the words to sprinkle, pour or bedew."

Prof. Van Name, Librarian of Harvard University, answers: "None; so far as I am aware."

Prof. W. W. Goodwin, senior Professor of Greek in Yale University, author of several Greek text books for our colleges and universities, answers: "I have never seen any such definitions as those to which you refer."

Prof. Lewis L. Paine, of Bangor Theological Seminary, Maine, answers: "Originally immersion was the practice of the first churches."

Prof. A. H. Buck, Professor of Greek in the great Methodist University of Boston, Mass.: "I can find no trace of any such lexicon and I have *no reason to believe that any such exists*. I suppose that such meanings as those you have noted in your question are confined to commentaries and DENOMINATIONAL *works and would not be recognized as having any authority* OUTSIDE."

In answer to my question: "Does the world's unsectarian scholarship sustain you in your answer?" Prof. Louis L. Paine says: "Yes." In answer to my question: "Do you, as a Greek scholar, agree with the Professors of Greek in Yale, Harvard, Michigan and Boston Universities, etc., in saying: I know of no standard Greek Lexicon which defines *baptizo* by some word meaning affusion?" Prof. Fowler, Professor of Greek in the Texas State University says: "Yes."

These are all, I believe, Pedobaptist scholars. Yale, Harvard, Boston Universities and Bangor Theological Seminary are leading Pedobaptist institutions. To add pile on pile of such Pedobaptist testimonies, representing both European and American Pedobaptist scholars, is easy. But, surely, these are sufficient to satisfy any unprejudiced person. In the testimony just quoted, without long study, research and much expense, the reader has before him the decision of the *world's unsectarian scholarship* as to the meaning of *baptizo*. In it, that only immersion is the act which Christ commanded for baptism, is as clear and certain as that Jesus Christ is the Son of God. To render *baptizo* into the English would destroy all churches which practice affusion for baptism. Consequently, as does the Romish church, all denominations that practice affusion dare not give the people a full translation of the Bible. They transfer instead of translate *baptizo* into the English. Into some heathen languages, where they are not so much exposed to the criticisms of scholars as they are in English-speaking countries, they translate it into ambiguous terms which they can easily pervert into the interest of sectarianism. They have ever *opposed* with all vehemence, strategy and bitterness, the true rendering of *baptizo*. To say this about professed christians gives me great pain at heart. But the people should know the facts. That I do not misrepresent the facts let the following editorial of *The Independent*, of New York,—the leading American Pedobaptist paper—witness:

"In the early years of the American Bible Society the Baptists, as well as others, contributed their *money* † to its support. In 1835 a by-law was passed by the society discriminating against certain versions made, by Baptist missionaries, and the Baptists, all but a very few, considering themselves unjustly excluded from common rights in the society, withdrew from its support. We remember how earnestly Dr. Leavitt and others, not Baptists, opposed this action of the society. Four years ago, in a revision of the rules, this by-law was omitted. This action was regarded by many as an abandonment by the society of its previous position, and a circular was issued by certain prominent Baptists declaring that, in their view, no reason existed why Baptists should not resume their former position in support of the society; but to test the matter, an application was made for aid to circulate the Burmese translation of the Bible by Dr. Judson. After some delay, this application has been

---

† I have not the figures at hand. But as well as I remember, the Baptists had before this put a large amount of money into this society.

directly refused, the society adhering to the principle of the by-law of 1835. The anticipated re-union is, therefore broken off, Dr. Howard Osgood, the Baptist member of the society's Committee on Versions, resigns his position; and the alienation of the Baptists from co-operation with the society may now be considered permanent. We are glad to say that again a strong and able minority was opposed to the decision.

"The Burmese version of Dr. Judson, who was a man of scholarship as well as Christian zeal, is admitted by the English bishop of Rangoon to be '*a model of idiomatic rendering and of faithful and painstaking labor.*' The society condemns it merely on the ground that it translates the Greek word for *baptize* by a Burmese word meaning *immerse*.

"*That this is a mistranslation the society does not declare. That it is not a legitimate rendering no true seholar would assert.* When the late Dean Stanley declared that 'on philological ground it is quite correct to translate John the Baptist by John the Immerser,' he gave the opinion of the *real scholars of all sects*. The latest standard lexicons—as Cremer's, Wilk's and that of Sophocles—define baptism as immersion *and they all give it no other meaning*.

"The officials of the society do not charge that Dr. Judson's translation is unscholarly, they condemn it SIMPLY BECAUSE IT IS A TRANSLATION. They declare that the Greek word *shall not be rendered into the vernacular* but must be transferred from the one language to the other, simply transliterated into the Burmese sentence. They do not say that there is no word in the Burmese to express the act of Naaman and of John, an act so common that one can hardly conceive a language so meagre as not to have a word of its own therefor; they do not say that some other Burmese word would present the Greek idea better than the word Dr. Judson has chosen; *they say that the Greek word must not be rendered into Burmese at all*, but simply transferred so that its original meaning *may not be expressed.* To be consistent, they should forbid anything to be made known of John's place of baptizing at Ænon, near to Salim, except that 'there was hudata polla there,' and of Philip and the Eunuch it should be reticently divulged merely that 'they katebased eis the water' and 'anebased ek the water.' If it be wrong to give the exact meaning of the words denoting a certain act, *we ought to becloud the mention of the attending circumstances, lest they disclose the nature of the act.*

"No translator like Judson claims, and no scholar stands forth to deny, that the Greek word is adequately rendered by a certain Burmese word; for the society say that the vernacular term shall not be used, but that the Greek word, which of course, to the native will be utterly *meaningless*, must be transferred to the Burmese page, is to say that the *New Testament shall not be placed before the Burman as clearly as it is before the eyes of the Greek peasant.*† The society is guilty of the *most outrageous* obscurantism. It binds its vast powers to the work of *suppressing a complete knowledge of the meaning of Holy Writ.* IT PLANTS ITSELF SQUARELY ON THE POSITION OF THE CHURCH OF ROME—THE POSITION THAT THE COMMON PEOPLE SHALL NOT BE *allowed every word of the Scripture's page, to read it with their own eyes and draw from it what conclusions they think reasonable;* BUT THAT A PORTION, AT LEAST, OF THE SACRED ORACLES SHALL MERELY BE DOLED OUT TO THEM BY THEIR SPIRITUAL GUIDES. *The Society*

---

† This is exactly the way the English speaking and other peoples are treated in *baptizo* not being rendered into their languages.

says that the meaning of this Greek word shall not be given the Burman through an equivalent word of the vernacular. It must be imparted to him only through the explanations of the missionary. This is not the Protestant but only the ROMAN CATHOLIC SYSTEM OF *Bible translation.** There may be weighty reasons in the case of this Greek word for transferring it to the Burmese, as there may be for preferring the transferred *denarius* and *presbyter* to *fifteen cents* and *elder;* but none are evident except *sectarian* ones and our objection is that the society should stringently forbid a legitimate translation and require a transfer.

"The officials of the Bible society are guilty of *real sectarianism.* It is vain to deny that the only objection they have to Judson's translation is that it may have a certain effect in certain controversies. But what has the Bible society to do with sectarian controversies? If a certain translation is incorrect, let them condemn it. *But what have they to do with the question how will it effect this or that dispute.*† If a certain translation seems to be scholarly, they should publish it, no matter what effect it may have on ecclesiastical conflicts. The officials of the society *abandon the majestic neutrality of scholarship and the love of truth* which asks merely whether a given version is correct. They stoop to inquire how it will affect the interests of contending sects. Gentlemen of the big brick house, it is not a *right* thing to do. The

---

* In this the *Independent* is correct only in part. Protestant Pedobaptist Bible socities and boards of Bible translators, without exception, notwithstanding the demands of scholarship, of loyalty to God or of the needs of the people, have never done otherwise than refuse to let the people have *baptizo* in their own language!

† In this the *Independent* concedes that Pedobaptist scholars know the very *life and existence* of Pedobaptists sects depend on keeping the people from knowing God's command. To save their sects, like Rome, they all decided the people shall not have God's word in their own language—save where it does not destroy their sects. Having come out from Rome they are the Reformation incomplete. Hence their Romish course.

only question you have a right to ask is whether the translation of Dr. Judson is faithful to the Greek. If it is not, condemn it; if it is, then publish it, no matter what parties of controversialists be helped or hindered thereby. You were not appointed, gentlemen, to watch the interests of contending *sects;* but to circulate *correct translations of the Scriptures;* and for you to refuse to circulate a given version, NOT BECAUSE IT IS INCORRECT; but because it may have a certain effect on certain *controversies* is a violation of the solemn trusts committed to your charge."

Baptizo, in all the Chinese versions published by Baptist missionaries, is translated by *Tsiny*, to immerse, to dip, to put into water. This term gives no uncertain sound. Says M. T. Yates, "When I had completed the translation of two of the gospels into the Shanghai vernacular, I asked the agent of the American Bible Society in China for means to publish them. He replied: 'I will publish all your translations if you will not *translate baptizo.*' I asked by what authority he could demand of me to *have any portion of God's word untranslated?* He replied: 'Such are my instructions.' But the answer of the American Bible Society's agent will seem very extraordinary when it is known that no word can be transferred into the Chinese, and all words must be translated, and that *baptizo* is actually translated by the word *see-lee*, the washing ceremony, in all the versions in Chinese, which have been published by the American Bible Society, and the British and Foreign Society. As the term *see-lee* never means to sprinkle or pour—other and entirely different words being used to express these ideas —it conveys no definite idea to a Chinese mind. A Chinee wishing baptism once with only this word to guide him, and seeing that Christ was baptized in a river, went into a river and gave the region around his heart a *good scrubbing;* and not being satisfied with this and supposing that perhaps he ought to receive the washing from heaven, stood out in a heavy rain till washed from head to foot. These great Bible societies are determined, if possible, *to hide the true reading of God's word, in regard to this ordinance,* from the heathen."

M. T. Yates and A. B. Cabaniss are authority for these statements.*

"As a member of the Madras Revision Committee, Dr. Jewett had up till 1872 been engaged on the Old Testament only. In that year he was asked to unite in the revision of the New Testament, as it was most needed. He declined at first, but consented, on condition that when the version was published, if not satisfactory to Baptists, our mission would have the right to revise it and publish its own version at its own expense. In 1880 the Madras version was published. It was found to be a version Baptists could not circulate. The word for baptism was *snanamu*. Respecting this word Mr. Loughridge says: 'It is a very unfair statement of the case to say that *snanamu* means merely ablution or bath. True, missionaries speak of making their *snanamu* daily for bodily cleanliness, but ordinary Telugus do not so use the word.' I hope this does not imply that missionaries do not know the meaning of the word, or that they use a word that 'ordinary Telugus' would not use in the same connection. But I have never heard any one say that *snanamu* meant ' *merely* ' ' ablution or bath.' It does mean that, but it may mean *more*. It may mean and sometimes does mean immersion, but not, as Mr. Loughridge affirms, ' *nine cases out of ten* ' when used

---

* Yates is yet a foreign missionary in China, and Cabaniss was formerly one.

as a religious rite. A Telugu pundit, whom Dr. Jewett declares to be the best he has ever known, told me that Hindus make *snanamu*, every day, but they immerse the whole body but once a week; so that *snanamu* instead of being immersion 'nine cases out of every ten,' is *not* immersion six cases out of every seven. When the question of a word for baptism was put to the vote of the mission, *nine-tenths* of the brethren repudiated *snanamu* and adopted a word which means *immersion, and never means ablution, bath, sprinkling or pouring*. But it is a mistake to suppose that *snanamu* was the only objection to the Madras version. A far greater objection was the fact that it REVERSED *the order* of Christ's great commission, making it plainly teach that baptism *preceded discipleship*. Beside these there were numerous errors of translation which we felt bound to correct."[1]

"Here is another fact of great significance. The British and Foreign Bible Society, which ever since 1832 has refused to aid in the circulation of our foreign Baptist version, has directed its missionaries to insert the word '*immerse*' *in the margin of their translations*, and this important action of that society has received the approval of the distinguished prelate just referred to, the Archbishop of Canterbury. In his address at the anniversary of the British and Foreign Biblical Society he took occasion to say with reference to this action of the society: '*I thank them very much for having put the word 'immerse' in the margin of their translations*. I must say I think they were justified in taking this step; and *do not doubt that this conclusion, based upon the real root meaning of the word, will have its effect*.' According, then, to the testimony of this distinguished scholar, the 'real root meaning' of the word baptize is *immerse*, and

[1] A missionary in *The Watchman*, Boston.

the English missionaries 'were justified in putting it in the margin.'"[1]

Quoting from the *Herald of Truth:* "In view of the refusal of the American Bible Society to aid in circulating the Burmese version of the Bible translated by Dr. Judson, a refusal which more than all others necessitated the action of Baptists at Saratoga, in May last, the *Christian Union*, a leading Pedobaptist paper, says: 'In the actual posture of things the American Bible Society is in *the wrong*. That wrong should be corrected.'"[2]

In Baptist growth is great encouragement. The following table on Baptist growth in the United States, is worth preserving and consulting:

A. D.		
1770.	Churches	77
1774.	Churches	421
	Ministers	424
	Members	38,101
1792.	Churches	891
	Ministers	1,156
	Members	65,345
1812.	Churches	2,164
	Ministers	1,605
	Members	172,692
1832.	Churches	5,320
	Ministers	3,618
	Members	384,926
1840.	Churches	7,771
	Ministers	5,288
	Members	571,291
1851.	Churches	9,552
	Ministers	7,393
	Members	770,839

[1] The *Watchman*, Boston.
[2] Texas *Baptist and Herald*.

A. D.		
1860.	Churches	12,279
	Ministers	7,773
	Members	1,016,134
1875.	Churches	21,255
	Ministers	13,170
	Members	1,845,300
1894.	Churches	38,122
	Ministers	25,354
	Members	3,496,988

In 1893 there were 176,077 persons in the United States baptized into Baptist churches. As showing that Christ is a blessing to our physical bodies the death rate of Baptists is far below that of the population of the United States. Baptist net gain in the United States for 1893 was 113,828—being a net gain in one year of more Baptists than there were in the United States ninety-three years ago. There is, in the United States, an average daily increase of 310 Baptists. The Baptist increase in the United States is 160 per cent., while that of its population is 73. A careful estimate shows that for the last decade Congregationalists have increased at the rate of 42 per cent.; Presbyterians at 55 per cent.; Methodist Episcopal church at the rate of 82 per cent.; Baptists at the rate of 99 per cent.; Campbellites at a less per cent. than any of them, while in a number of States they have rather lost.

In the United States Baptists have 54 charitable institutions; 7 theological seminaries; 35 colleges and universities; 32 female seminaries; 47 academies for both sexes. In the theological seminaries there are 54 teachers and 776 pupils, all but four of whom are preparing for the ministry. In the universities and the colleges are 701 teachers and 9,088 pupils. In the female seminaries are 388 teachers and 3,675 pupils. In the academies are 369 teachers and 5,250 pupils. The property of the theological seminaries is valued at $3,401,618; of the universities and the colleges at $19,171,045; of the female seminaries at $4,211,906; of the academies at $3,787,793; of the charitable institutions at $1,360,021.

There are in the United States also 31 Baptist institutions for the education of negroes and Indians, with 176 teachers, 5,177 pupils and property estimated at $1,380,540.

Under the head of education the grand total is: One hundred and fifty-two institutions, 1,791 teachers, 23,966 pupils and property worth $31,866,902. The entire number of pupils preparing for the ministry in the different kinds of schools is 2,223.

The value of Baptist church property in the United States is $78,605,759. In the United States the aggregate reported of Baptist contributions for salaries of pastors, education, mission and miscellaneous objects in 1893 is $12,560,713.95.

In the United States are, in 1893, 20,838 Baptist Sunday schools, with 143,765 officers and teachers and 1,430,933 pupils.

Advocating all these interests are one hundred and twenty-five periodicals.

Being the originators of foreign missions Baptists therein are in the lead.

The Missionary Review, a Pedobaptist periodical, some time ago gave the following figures for foreign missions:

CONGREGATIONALISTS.

Missionaries	416
Native preachers	567
Missionary membership	17,165
Expenditures	$627,861.98

PRESBYTERIAN.

Missionaries	334
Native preachers	220
Missionary membership	12,607
Expenditures	$420,427.00

METHODIST.

Missionaries	191
Native preachers	666
Missionary membership	26,702
Expenditures	$299,174.00

BAPTIST.

Missionaries	162
Native preachers	1,052
Missionary membership	85,308
Expenditures	$274,961.91

Thus, Presbyterians, Methodists and Congregationalists spend annually on foreign fields $1,347,462.98, while Baptists annually spend but $274,961.91. Thus, for less than one-fourth of the missionary money that these leading Pedobaptist churches expend, Baptists have near twice the number of converts on foreign fields that they have. When we consider that *every one of these Baptist converts has professed regeneration*, while a large proportion of theirs came into their churches *without that profession*, these figures make the number of souls saved by Baptist missions *far more than double that of theirs!* †

In Great Britain, for thirty years, the Baptist increase has been 122 per cent., the Methodist 114, Independent 43.

The following from the Baptist Year Book of 1894 is

---

† I have Methodist authority that Methodists, in some foreign work, where there is no Baptist opposition, like the Romish church, have taken the heathen in *by whole villages at a time!!*

A BIRD'S-EYE VIEW OF THE BAPTISTS THROUGHOUT THE WORLD.

	Churches	Ordained Ministers.	Reported Baptisms.	Reported Membership.
NORTH AMERICA.				
Canada: Ontario, Quebec, Manitoba and N. W. Territory	428	279	2,685	36,860
New Brunswick, Nova Scotia and Prince Edward Island	396	259	2,085	43,782
Mexico	45	29	164	1,813
United States	38,122	25,354	176,077	3,496,988
West Indies: Cuba	6	23	169	2,299
Hayti	7	3		202
Jamaica	177	64	2,220	35,269
Other Islands and Central America	12	11	370	6,865
	39,193	26,022	183,720	3,624,078
SOUTH AMERICA.				
Argentine Republic	1	1	5	90
Brazil	12	11	96	453
Patagonia	1			24
	14	12	101	567
EUROPE.				
Austria-Hungary	6	5	566	2,675
Denmark	25	15	190	3,015
Finland	21	15	140	1,329
France	45	35	337	1,979
Germany	139	277	2,596	27,332
Great Britain: England	1,611	1,198	10,568	208,728
Ireland	26	23	273	2,200
Scotland	104	96	1,300	13,208
Wales and Monmouthshire	749	471	5,859	98,122
Channel Islands	5	20	6	249
Non-reporting churches	330	90		20,000
Holland	20	11	105	1,316
Italy	33	31	175	1,151
Norway	27	26		1,950
Roumania and Bulgaria	4	5	4	325
Russia and Poland	67	59	1,337	16,443
Spain	5	4	5	100
Sweden	539	618	2,097	36,585
Switzerland	4	4	21	439
	3,760	3,003	26,579	437,146
ASIA.				
Assam	28	22	866	2,971
Burmah	580	203	2,187	31,672
Ceylon	9	5	45	1,088
China	51	48	444	4,675
India, including Telugus	138	187	6,075	58,432
Japan	16	25	218	1,364
Orissa	20	9		1,436
Palestine	3	1		156
	845	500	9,835	101,794
AFRICA.				
Central (Congo)	22	57	292	982
South	23	23		2,450
West	4	5	20	144
St. Helena and Cape Verdes	2	2		125
	51	87	312	3,701
AUSTRALASIA.				
New South Wales	31	25	167	2,016
New Zealand	29	17	204	2,915
Queensland	24	20		2,035
South Australia	57	31	298	4,128
Tasmania	12	8	84	559
Victoria	53	46	424	5,568
	206	147	1,177	17,221
Grand total, 1893	44,069	29,871	221,724	4,184,507
Total, 1892	42,617	28,820	211,346	4,049,984
Increase	1,452	1,051	10,378	134,523

To summarize some Baptist fruits:

1. Baptists have been truer to the great truths of Christianity than has any other church.

2. Baptists principles have kept and keep the *monument* of the death and the resurrection of Christ—burial in baptism—before the world, ever since Christ walked this earth.

3. Of all the leading denominations, Baptists are the *only* church which has kept and keeps before the world the *blood before the water*, Christ in possession before Christ in profession; and are the only church which has, consequently, ever been and are the great bulwark against baptismal regeneration.

4. Of all the leading denominations, Baptists are the only church which has never believed and does not believe that baptism is any part or any condition of salvation to either the infant or the adult. Consequently, they have never been even tinged by the doctrine of infant damnation, which has colored infant baptism throughout its history. As Dr. Philip Schaff, the leading American church historian, and he a Presbyterian, says: "The Baptist and Quakers were the first Christian communities which detached salvation from ecclesiastical ordinances and *taught the salvation of unbaptized infants and unbaptized but believing adults.*"[1]

5. Of all the great religious bodies, Baptists are the *only* church which has always taught and teaches there can be no *proxy* Christianity, by infant baptism, etc., but, that salvation, its conditions and requirements are a strictly *personal* matter, between only God and the individual soul.

6. Among all great denominations, Baptists are, consequently, the only church which has always stood

---

[1] "The Teaching of the Twelve Apostles," p. 56, by Dr. Schaff.

and stands for *only* a professedly regenerate or spiritual church.

7. Among all great denominations, Baptists are the only churches which contend and have ever contended for excluding from their church fellowship all *known* non-spiritual persons.

8. So far as *only* a spiritual church is the doctrine and the practice of the leading denominations it is due to the standing Baptist testimony, and the persistent Baptist uncompromising war on an inherited and unregenerate church membership.

9. Of all leading denominations which have not been originated within the present century, Baptists are the only churches which have never been united with the State, and which have never persecuted.

10. Baptist churches are the only churches which have, during the Christian era, and until the *present century*, contended for separation of church and State and for absolute liberty of conscience.

11. By their *principles* of liberality, of freedom of conscience and of *every* Christian being a priest to God and Christian ruler, Baptists have given the United States their religious freedom. This they have done at the cost of their property, their good name, their liberty and their lives. This, too, in the face of not only Romish but of Protestant Pedobaptist union of church and State, and of persecution. As Hallam, a secular historian, of Protestant Pedobaptists, well says: "Persecution is the deadly original sin of the reformed churches; that which cools every honest man's zeal for their cause, in proportion as his reading becomes extensive."[1]

---

[1] Hallam's Const. Hist. of England, p. 63, also Wilson's Outlines of Hist., p. 769; May's Const. Hist. of England, vol. 2, p. 293.

Dr. Leonard Bacon, a Pedobaptist, in "Genesis of the New England Churches," remarks of the Baptists: "It has been claimed for these churches, that from the Reformation they have been always foremost and always consistent in maintaining the doctrine of religious liberty. *Let me not be understood as calling in question their right to so great an honor.*"

12. As Guizot, in his "History of Civilization," shows that the despotical and oppressive civil governments of Europe originated from the government of the Romish church, so Gervinus, Philip Schaff and other historians have shown that the free church government principles of Baptists have "extended themselves throughout the United States," "*have given laws to a continent*" and are "*at the bottom of all democratic movements now shaking the nations of Europe.*"

13. Rhode Island, the first absolutely free government of the Christian era, was a Baptist government.

14. A Baptist originated the marginal references to our English Bible—John Canne, in 1673. Baptist loyalty to the Bible, Baptist study of it and comparison of Scripture with Scripture, naturally led to the meeting of the necessity of these references.

15. The first public free school from which has originated the excellent free school system of the United States, was conceived and originated by Dr. John Clarke—a Baptist preacher—in Rhode Island, in 1675.

16. While the Romish, the Episcopal and the Methodist—the Methodist was not then separated from the Episcopal, but was a party to it—churches were almost solidly with Great Britain against the American colonists, in their struggle for independence, Baptists were the foremost promoters of the glorious Revolution, and the name of but one Baptist is given who was a Tory.

17. Bible Societies were originated by a Baptist—Joseph Hughes—being the prime mover of the British and Foreign Bible Society. This is the natural result of the Baptist *pre-eminent* love to *all* the teaching of the Bible and loyalty to *all* its commands.

18. The first church which was organized in what was then called the "Northwestern Territory," was at Columbia, now a part of Cincinnati, which was a Baptist church. This was in 1790.

19. The originator of what is called "Modern Missions," was William Carey—a Baptist. This was in 1792. The General Assembly of the Presbyterian church of Scotland, by a large majority, put on record, in 1796, the following resolution—says *Zions Advocate*: "That to spread the knowledge of the gospel among barbarous and heathen nations, seems highly preposterous, in so far as it anticipates, nay, even reverses the order of nature." As we have seen in a previous chapter, no Baptist church or general Baptist meeting ever tarnished its fair name by such a resolution.

20. The Baptists have *near* twice more converts to Christ in heathen lands than have all the other leading denominations; that, too, when the others have taken many of them into their churches, as only *nominal* Christians.

23. Baptist foreign missions cost *less than one fourth* the money that those of leading Protestant Pedobaptists cost.

24. The International Uniform Sunday School Lesson Service was originated by a Baptist—B. F. Jacobs. This is the natural result of the pre-eminent Baptist love of Bible study and Bible obedience.

25. The world's greatest preacher since the Reformation was a Baptist—C. H. Spurgeon. The purer the gospel, the greater its preacher.

26. The first organized society for the much needed revision of King James' version of the Bible was the American Bible Union—a Baptist society. This was the natural result of Baptist love and loyalty to the Bible.

27. Out of the American Bible Union agitation and work originated the Episcopal organization, resulting in the Revised Version of 1881, on which was employed European and American representative scholars. The revisions of the American Bible Union and its successors are of incalculable value to the world.

28. The only Bible Society which has ever existed for the translation of "*every word*" of the Bible into the English, according to the *world's unsectarian* scholarship, was the American Bible Union—a Baptist Bible Society. In this it is measurably succeeded by the American Baptist Publication Society.

29. By their Bible translation enterprises Baptists have proved themselves the only leading denomination that has thoroughly rejected the *Romish doctrine of keeping the Bible out of the language of the people;* and in rendering every doctrinal or practical word, they have, wherever and whenever they have made a *translation* of the Bible, not "shunned to declare all the counsel of God."

30. In the language of the *New York Tribune:* "The Baptists have solved the great problem. They combine the most resolute conviction, the most stubborn belief in their own special doctrines, with the *most admirable tolerance of the faith of other Christians.*"

Before the Evangelical Alliance, of Chicago, but a little while before his death, Dr. Schaff, the great Presbyterian church historian, said: "The Baptist is a glorious church; for she bore, and still bears testimony to the *primitive* mode of baptism, to the *purity* of the congregation, to the separation of church and State, and the liberty of conscience, and has given the world the 'Pilgrim's Progress' of Bunyan, such preachers as Robert Hall and Charles H. Spurgeon and such missionaries as Judson."

The lines:

> "For *modes* of faith let graceless bigots fight,
> His must be right whose life is in the right."

are very misleading. From the foregoing that life is the fruit of loyalty to *all things Christ has commanded* is the inevitable conclusion. Not that Baptist human nature has made Baptists *better than others* but their many *peculiar* scriptural principles, doctrines and practices have done so.

Looking over Baptist fruits we see that Baptists, standing ALONE for most important practical principles and doctrines *their abandonment or compromise* of these principles and this doctrine *can but work disaster to the world, to Christians of other churches, to themselves and great dishonor to our precious Christ*. Thus Baptist fruits attest Baptists as the only true successors of Christ, of His Apostles and of their being the true witnesses from the apostolic to the present age.

Now, that the liberty of the age presents an open field for Baptists to *push* the great New Testament "fight of faith" to the *final victory*, as Prof. G. D. B. Pepper, D.D., has so well said, for them to not do so would be to prove themselves unworthy of the great trust committed to them, recreant to their duty, dishonoring to the *blood* of Baptist martyrs which has *bequeathed this opportunity to them* and disloyal to God.

With Christian love to all blood-washed souls—*whatever their creed*—with a joyful recognition of the broken and mixed fragments of truth held by others and the good fruits they bear, let us work and pray for the blessed time when all others will have planted themselves on the whole truth and nothing but the truth as it is plainly in the New Testament.

To this end let us cultivate more vital piety, more liberality of heart and fervency of prayer for true pastors and all other faithful preachers, for home and foreign missions, for educational and charitable institutions, less conformity to the world, stricter discipline in our churches, less compromise with the false liberality of an infidel and immoral age, more consecration and faithfulness of the ministry, and a more eager and loving hastening and "LOOKING FOR THAT BLESSED HOPE, AND THE GLORIOUS APPEARING OF THE GREAT GOD AND OUR SAVIOR JESUS CHRIST."

472   CHURCH PERPETUITY.

CHAPTER XXIX.

St. Patrick a Baptist.

The following summarizes the facts as to St. Patrick, and proves he was a Baptist:†

The year of St. Patrick's birth is variously assigned to the years 377 and 387, the latter being the more probable date. His original name is said to have been Succat Patricus, being the Roman appelative by which he was known. The exact place of his birth is uncertain. It was somewhere in Britain. In the sixteenth year of his age, while on his father's farm, with a number of others, he was seized and carried by a band of pirates into Ireland, and there sold to a petty chief. In his service he remained six years. At the expiration of this time he succeeded in escaping. He was "brought up in a Christian family in Britain, and the truth which saved him when a youthful slave in pagan Ireland was taught him in the godly home of Deacon Calpurnius, his father, and in the church of which he was a member and officer." On his escape from Ireland he was twenty-one years of age. Being a stronger Christian the Lord soon called him back to Ireland as the missionary for that blinded country. About this time, or before it, a missionary named Coleman, established a church in Ireland. Some think that "in the south of Ireland, from some very

---

† The recent volume, "The Ancient British and Irish churches, including the Life and Labors of St. Patrick," by William Catchcart, D. D., so ably and fully treats this subject that I give it but a brief notice. Any one wanting more on it s nd to the American Baptist Publication Society, $1.50 for Dr. Catchcart's work.

remote period," "christian congregations had existed." Usher puts Patrick's death at A. D. 493—making his life a long and useful life, and his age, at the time of his death, over one hundred years. The Bellandists make his death earlier—A. D. 460. Dr. Todd inclines to Usher's date. According to accounts of his Irish biographers, he, with his own hands, baptized 12,000 persons and founded 365 churches.

Within the last few years antiquarian scholars have succeeded in stripping his history of much of the Romish fables. The more this has been done, the more he stands out as a Baptist.

Among others I mention the following points of history:

1. At the time of St. Patrick the Romish church was only *en embryo*.

2. In St. Patrick's time the authority of the bishop of Rome was not generally recognized.

3. There is no history to sustain the Romish claim that Patrick was sent to Ireland by "Pope Celistine." (1.) Bede never mentions it. (2.) Patrick never mentions it. (3.) Facts are against the claim. (4.) Throughout his life Patrick acted wholly independent of Rome.†

4. Patrick was a Baptist.

---

† Neander says: "If Patrick came to Ireland as a deputy from Rome, it might naturally be expected that in the Irish church a certain sense of dependence would always have been preserved towards the mother church. But we find, on the contrary, in the Irish church a spirit of church freedom, similar to that in Britain, which struggled against the yoke of Roman ordinances. We find subsequently among the Irish a much greater agreement with the ancient British than with Roman ecclesiastical usages. This goes to prove that the origin of the church was independent of Rome, and must be traced solely to the people of Britain. . . . Again, no indication of his connection with the Romish church is to be found in his confession; rather everything seems to favor the supposition that he was ordained bishop in Britain itself."—Neander's History Christian Church, vol 2, p. 123. An anonymous Irish scholar says: "Leo II, was bishop of Rome from 440 to 461, A. D. and upwards of one hundred and forty of his letters to correspondents in all parts of Christendom still remain, and *yet he never mentions* Patrick or his work, or in any way intimates that he knew of the great work being done there. The Council of Chalons-sur Saone, held A. D. 813, resolved not to admit the presbyters and deacons admitted by the Irish church to the

(1.) He baptized only professed believers. (2.) He baptized by only immersion. In a former chapter has been proved that the ancient Britons were Baptists. Dr. Catchcart says: "There is absolutely no evidence that any baptism but that of immersion of adult believers existed among the ancient Britons, in the first half of the fifth century, nor for a long time afterwards."[1] In St. Patrick's "letter to Crocius" he describes some of the persons whom he immersed as "baptized captives," baptized handmaidens of Christ, "baptized women distributed as rewards" and then as "baptized believers."[2] "Patrick baptized Enda, and he offered his son, Cormac, [to Patrick] who was born the night before, together with the ninth ridge of the land."[3] If Patrick had been a Pedobaptist he surely would have baptized this infant. As well claim the *"ridge"* was here offered for baptism as to claim the child was offered for it. (3.) In church government St. Patrick was a Baptist. Though this appears in the note to this page, I will add proof to it.

---

ministry. The Council of Coleyth, held in England in 816, A. D., adopted a still more sweeping resolution. The Anglician fathers decreed that none should receive even baptism or the eucharist from Irish clergymen, because, said they, we cannot tell by whom they have been ordained, or whether they have been ordained at all. We know that it is enjoined in the canons, that no bishop or presbyter should attempt to enter another parish without the consent of its own bishop. So much the more is it to be condemned to accept the ministrations of religion from those of other nations who *have no order of metropolitans and who have no regard for such functionaries*. When the pope sent Palladius to Ireland to establish there a hierarchy, *Patrick refused to recognize him*, and in the Laebhar Braec (published in Dublin, 1874-5,) the best and oldest Irish manuscript relating to the ecclesiastical history of the island, it is recorded that Paladius was sent by Pope Celestine with a gospel for Patrick to preach to the Irish. 'It suggests that the representative of the pope was seeking to enter into another man's labors, and to reap the fruits of a field which a more skillful workman had already cultivated. Christianity had ere this taken root in the island, and Celestine sent Palladius to found a hierarchy devoted to the papal interests. The stranger sought to conciliate the Irish missionary. . . . But the attempt proved a signal failure and Palladius, after a short residence, was obliged to take his departure. Overwhelmed with disappointment, he embarked to North Britain, where not long afterwards, he died with a fever.' " See also "Ancient British and Irish Churches," pp. 176-177.

[1] Ancient British and Irish churches, p. 50.
[2] Idem, p. 152.
[3] Idem, p. 153.

"Patrick founded 365 churches and consecrated the *same number of bishops*, and ordained 3,000 presbyters."[1] "Stillingfleet refers to an account of a great council of Brevy, Wales, taken from the manuscript of Urecht which represents *one hundred and eighteen bishops* at its deliberations."[2] Considering that this great number of bishops of this little island greatly exceeds the number of bishops of *any* Episcopal organization outside of the Romish or the Greek church, has throughout the world if St. Patrick's church was not Baptist, but Romish his church must *have come near going to seed—in bishops.* No wonder that Bishop Stillingfleet attempts to throw doubt at the number of bishops at the Council of Brevy, "though he admits that Colgan defends the large representation of bishops."[3] Dr. Catchcart, says: "If we take the testimony of Nennius, St. Patrick placed a bishop in *every church* which he founded; and several presbyters after the example of the New Testament churches. Nor was the great number of bishops peculiar to St. Patrick's time; in the twelfth century St. Bernard tells us that in Ireland 'bishops are multiplied and changed . . . *almost every church had a bishop.*' . . . Prof. George T. Stokes declares that prior to the synod of Rathbresail, in A. D. 1112, 'Episcopacy had been the rule of the Irish church; but *dioceses and diocesan episcopacy had no existence at all.*' 'Scotland,' as Collier relates, 'in the ninth century was not divided into dioceses, but all the Scottish bishops had their jurisdiction as it were at large and exercised their function wherever they came. And this continued to the reign of Malcom III,' who was

---

[1] Ancient British and Irish churches, p. 282; Universal Knowledge, vol. 2, p. 28.
[2] Ancient British and Irish churches, p. 281.
[3] Ancient British and Irish Churches, p. 282; Smith's Dictionary of Christian Antiquities, vol. 2, p. 1270.

crowned in A. D. 1057. When Collier speaks of jurisdiction, we must remember they had no jurisdiction in the proper sense; the early Scottish bishops were like their brethren in Ireland, without dioceses and without jurisdiction. Eminent writers like Dr. Todd, of Trinity College, Dublin, freely assert this." [1]

Dr. Carew, of Maynooth, in his ecclesiastical history of Ireland—perhaps unwittingly—admits that a bishop was simply the *pastor of one congregation:* "In effect the system which the Irish church adopted with regard to Episcopal Sees, was entirely similar to that which was followed in these churches which were founded *immediately after the times of the Apostles.* According to this system *every town where the converts were numbered, was honored by the appointment of a bishop,* who resided *permanently* here and devoted his pastoral solicitude *exclusively* to the care of the inhabitants. This ancient usage the fathers of the Council of Sardicia thought it necessary to *modify.* To maintain the respectability of the Episcopal elder, the Council ordered that, for the time to come, bishops should take up their residence in the most important towns." [2] (4.) In independence of creeds, councils, popes and bishops Patrick was a Baptist. "Patrick recognized no authority in creeds, however venerable, nor in councils, though composed of several hundred of the highest ecclesiastics, and many of the most saintly men alive. *He never quotes any canons and he never took part in making any*, notwithstanding the pretended canons of forgers." [3] (5.) In doctrine Patrick was a Baptist. He says Christ who "gave his life for thee is He who speaks

[1] Ancient British and Irish Churches; 282; Smith's Dictionary of Christian Antiquities, vol 2, p. 1270.
[2] Quoted by "An American Irish Baptist."
[3] Ancient British and Irish Churches, p. 159.

to thee." He has poured out upon us abundantly the Holy Spirit, the gift and assurance of immortality, who CAUSES men to believe and become obedient that they might be the sons of God and joint heirs with Christ."[1]

Comgall, of Bangor, Ireland, in the sixth century writes: "Religion does not consist in *bodily* * efforts, but in humility of heart." It is stated by Muirchu that when Patrick appeared before his distinguished assembly Dubthac, the chief poet, alone among the Gentiles arose in his honor; and "first on that day † *believed* in God and *it* was imputed to him for righteousness."[2] (6.) The Supper was taken, as among all Protestants, in *both* kinds. "Lœghaire, king of Ireland in Patrick's time, had two daughters converted under his instructions. When they asked Patrick 'to see Christ's face,' (as they had previously seen their idols) he said to them: 'Ye cannot see Christ unless you first taste of death, or unless you receive Christ's body *and* his blood'"—both elements.[3] (7.) Instead of Patrick believing in transubstantiation, Dr. Catchcart says: "In all the descriptions of the Eucharist quoted there is no evidence that it is the God of glory in every particle of its consecrated bread and wine."[4] (8.) In the later or Romish meaning of the term, there is no indication of Monastacism in Patrick's writing or in the history of the first Irish church. "Monastacism, in the proper sense of the word, cannot be traced beyond the fourth century."[5] Catchcart: "It is difficult to fix the date when the first monastery was

---

* This excludes all kinds of penances.
† This excludes baptism, and all others works as saving.
[1] Ancient British and Irish Churches, pp. 315-316.
[2] Idem, p. 318.
[3] Idem, p. 322.
[4] The Ancient British and Irish Churches, p. 322.
[5] Smith's Dictionary Christian Antiquities, vol. 2, p. 1219.

established in Ireland. *It is certain that Patrick was long in his grave before it took place.* . . . Bangor, in Ireland, was founded by Comgall. Bingham states that it was about A. D. 520, and this date is apparently the true one. He informs us that it was the most ancient monastery in Ireland, as the famous monastery of Bangor was the oldest in Britain.[1] "The monks are frequently termed 'the philosophers' and the monastery their 'school of thought.'"[2] "The monastery was often a nursery or training college for the clergy. . . . The illiterate clergy looks naturally to the nearest monastery for help in the composition of sermons."[3] Neander says: "The Irish monasteries were still the seats of science and art, whence, for a long time afterwards . . . teachers in the sciences and useful arts scattered themselves in all directions. . . . In the Irish monasteries not only the Latin but also the free spirited Greek fathers, the writings of an Origin were studied; so it naturally came about that from that school issued a more original and free development of theology than *was elsewhere to be found*, and was thence propagated to other lands."[4]

Catchcart says: "*Marriage* probably existed, not in, but in connection with, most of the British and Irish monasteries. We see no reason to doubt the statement of Michelet, that 'the Culdees of Ireland and Scotland permitted themselves *marriage*, and were independent, even when living under the rule of their order.' But the mania that celibacy possessed soon spread over the world, and many of St. Patrick's religious, Bible-loving descend-

---

[1] The Ancient British and Irish Churches, p. 292.
[2] Smith's Dictionary of Christian Antiquities, vol. 1219.
[3] Idem, p. 1225.
[4] Neander's History Christian Church, vol. 3, pp. 460–461.
[5] The Ancient British and Irish Churches, p. 311.

ants were caught in its delusive snare."⁵ Guericke: "From the Irish cloisters missionaries went out into various regions and particularly to the Picts in Scotland."¹

Thus, first, Irish monasteries were *originated after Patrick's death;* second, even then exclusive celibacy in them was not their first rule; third, in their earliest history these monasteries differed but little from our educational institutions.

Thus, in only believer's baptism; in only immersion; in church government; in salvation by only the blood; in justification by faith *only;* in rejecting penance; in knowing nothing of transubstantiation; in giving both the bread and the wine to the laity; in being independent of Rome, St. Patrick was a Baptist and the first Irish churches were Baptist churches. To this may be added: St. Patrick and the first Irish churches knew nothing of priestly confession and priestly forgiveness; of extreme unction; of worship of images; of worship of Mary; of the intercession of Mary or of any departed saint; of purgatory; of persecution of opposers of the church—nothing of any of the Romish distinguishing peculiarities.

Were Patrick not turned to dust, and were the body able to hear and turn, he *would turn over in his coffin at the disgrace on his memory from the Romish church claiming him as a Roman Catholic.*

---

¹ Guericke's Church History, p. 262; Kurtz's Church History, vol. 1, p. 298; Lecky's History European Morals, vol. 2, p. 261; Smith's Dictionary Christian Antiquities, vol. 2, p. 1270.

EXPLANATION OF THE ROMISH CHURCH TREE.

This tree begins with a small trunk and increases in size as the beginning and the growth of the Romish Church. The sign board on it, on which is "Romish Church, A. D. 606," shows where we must date the *real* first Romish Church, because there is the first *real* universal bishop or pope. "Baptismal regeneration," "affusion," "infant baptism," etc., as they appear on the tree are recorded in history. Higher up the tree is seen the growth of modern sects out of the Romish, together with their branches and their fruits as corresponding to the nature of the Romish tree out of which they have grown. Historians of different creeds (as seen in the chapter of this book on the Fruits of Baptist Churches,) prove the leading modern churches but the Romish Church *partly* reformed—the Reformation incomplete.

On baptism saving, Dr. Charles Hodge, Presbyterian, says: "Baptism is not only a sign and a *seal*, it is a *means* of grace." Of infant baptism, he says: "It *assures* them of salvation if they do not renounce their covenants."[1] See my book on Campbellism, pp. 5-20, where the Presbyterian faith in baptism as saving is abundantly shown.

As to Methodism teaching water salvation, John Wesley, its originator, says: "By baptism, we, who are 'by nature the children of wrath' are made the children of God."[2] Substantially the same statement is read in recent Methodist theological works, the Discipline and the Church hymn books. All this—see Chapter XXVIII of this book on Fruits of Baptist Churches—results in an unregenerate and worldly church.

Campbellism having been originated by the Campbells and Stone, who were Presbyterian preachers, it is of Presbyterian growth. See my book on Campbellism.

[1] Hodge's Syst. Theolo., vol. 3, pp. 589, 590.
[2] Wesley's Doc. Tracts, p. 249.

Rev. 20:2.

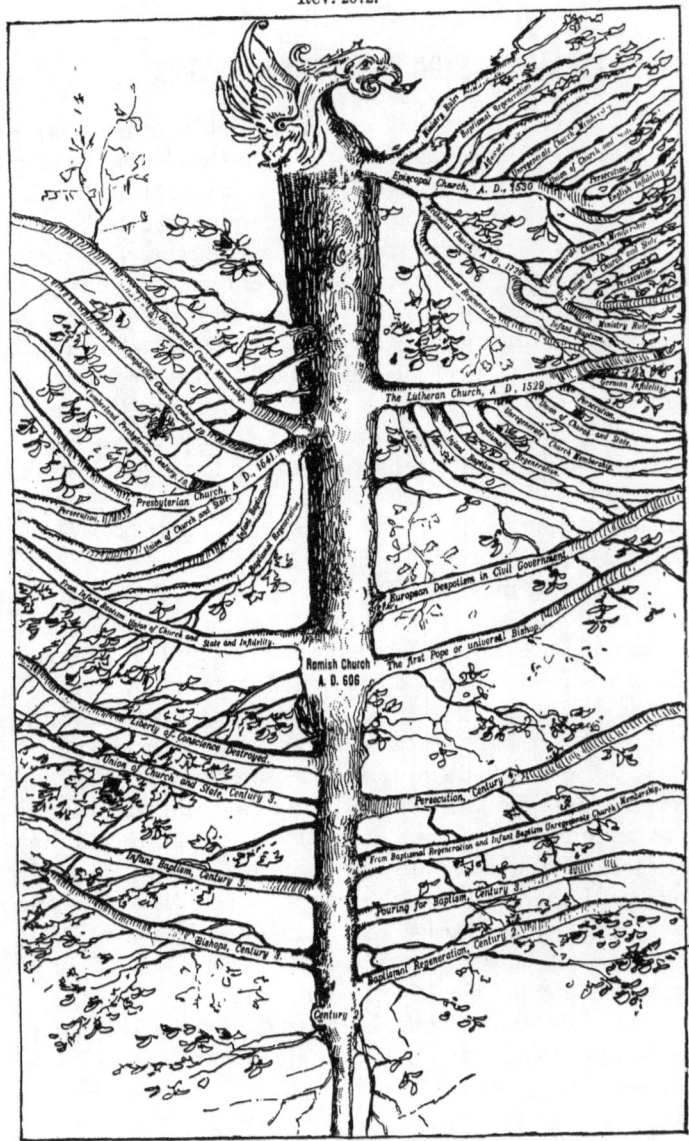

ROMISH CHURCH TREE.

See explanation on other side of this sheet on which this tree is. Also study carefully the chapter in this book on the Fruits of Baptist Churches.

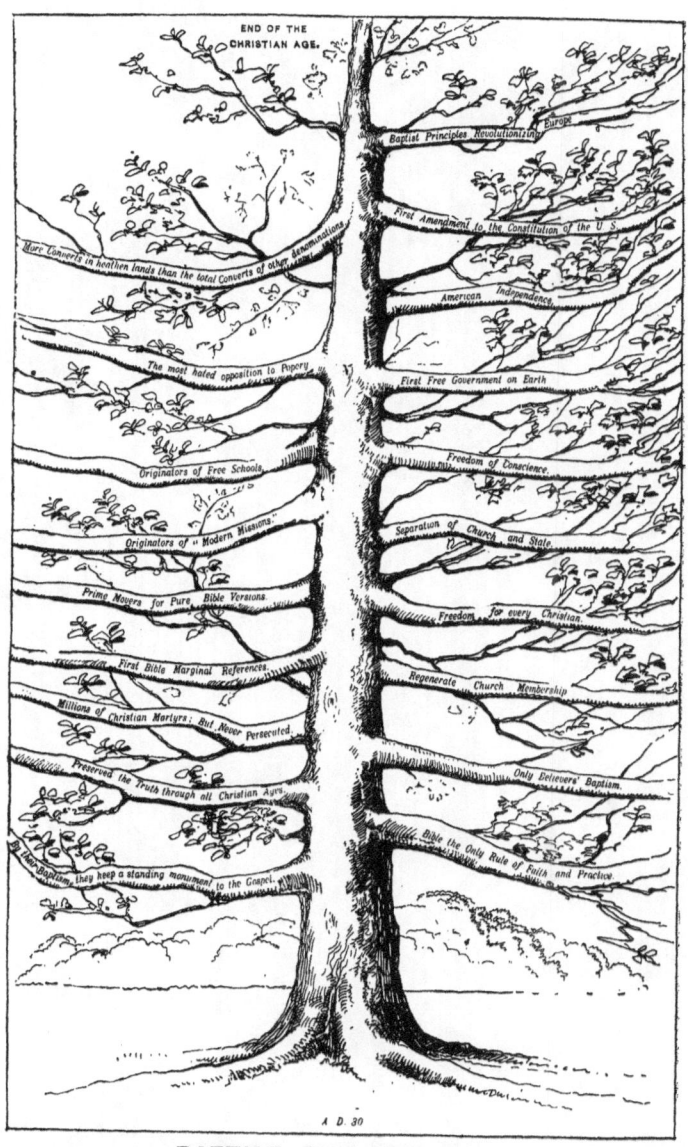

BAPTIST CHURCH TREE.

For explanation see Chapter XXVIII of this book on the Fruits of Baptist Churches.

THE BAPTIST STANDARD BEARER, INC.
A non-profit, tax-exempt corporation
committed to the Publication & Preservation
of The Baptist Heritage.

SAMPLE TITLES FOR PUBLICATIONS AVAILABLE IN OUR VARIOUS SERIES:

THE BAPTIST *COMMENTARY* SERIES
Sample of authors/works in or near republication:
John Gill - *Exposition of the Old & New Testaments (9 & 18 Vol. Sets)*
   (Volumes from the 18 vol. set can be purchased individually)

THE BAPTIST *FAITH* SERIES:
Sample of authors/works in or near republication:
Abraham Booth - *The Reign of Grace*
Abraham Booth - *Paedobaptism Examined (3 Vols.)*
John Gill - *A Complete Body of Doctrinal Divinity*

THE BAPTIST *HISTORY* SERIES:
Sample of authors/works in or near republication:
Thomas Armitage - *A History of the Baptists (2 Vols.)*
Isaac Backus - *History of the New England Baptists (2 Vols.)*
William Cathcart - *The Baptist Encyclopaedia (3 Vols.)*
J. M. Cramp - *Baptist History*

THE BAPTIST *DISTINCTIVES* SERIES:
Sample of authors/works in or near republication:
Alexander Carson - *Ecclesiastical Polity of the New Testament Churches*
E.C. Dargan - *Ecclesiology: A Study of the Churches*
J. M. Frost - *Paedobaptism: Is It From Heaven?*
R. B. C. Howell - *The Evils of Infant Baptism*

THE *DISSENT & NONCONFORMITY* SERIES:
Sample of authors/works in or near republication:
Champlin Burrage - *The Early English Dissenters (2 Vols.)*
Franklin H. Littell - *The Anabaptist View of the Church*
Albert H. Newman - *History of Anti-Paedobaptism*
Walter Wilson - *History & Antiquities of the Dissenting Churches (4 Vols.)*

For a complete list of current authors/titles, visit our internet site at
www.standardbearer.com or write us at:

he Baptist Standard Bearer, Inc.
No. 1 Iron Oaks Drive • Paris, Arkansas 72855

Telephone: (501) 963-3831   Fax: (501) 963-8083
E-mail: baptist@arkansas.net
Internet: http://www.standardbearer.com

Specialists in Baptist Reprints and Rare Books
Thou hast given a *standard* to them that fear thee; that it may be displayed because of the truth. -- Psalm 60:4

www.ingramcontent.com/pod-product-compliance
Lightning Source LLC
Chambersburg PA
CBHW031957220426
43664CB00005B/56